Rural Society in the U.S.: Issues for the 1980s

Also of Interest

Alaska's Rural Development, edited by Peter G. Cornwall and Gerald McBeath

† *Rural Education: In Search of a Better Way,* edited by Paul M. Nachtigal

† *Poverty in Rural America: A Case Study,* Janet M. Fitchen

† *What Happened to Fairbanks? The Effects of the Trans-Alaska Oil Pipeline on the Community of Fairbanks, Alaska,* Mim Dixon

The Family in Rural Society, edited by Raymond T. Coward and William M. Smith, Jr.

The Myth of the Family Farm: Agribusiness Dominance of U.S. Agriculture, Ingolf Vogeler

† *Politics in the Rural States: People, Parties, and Processes,* Frank M. Bryan

† *Education in Rural America: A Reassessment of Conventional Wisdom,* edited by Jonathan P. Sher

Rural Education in Urbanized Nations: Issues and Innovations, edited by Jonathan P. Sher

Women and the Social Costs of Economic Development: Two Colorado Case Studies, Elizabeth Moen, Elise Boulding, Jane Lillydahl, and Risa Palm

The Family in Post-Industrial America: Some Fundamental Perceptions for Public Policy Development, edited by David P. Snyder

† Available in hardcover and paperback.

Rural Studies Series

Rural Society in the U.S.: Issues for the 1980s
edited by Don A. Dillman and Daryl J. Hobbs

Must rural Americans pay the price of urban progress and modern lifestyles? How will the increased pressures of the 1980s affect those who live and work in rural communities? In addressing these overriding questions the authors of this book take a serious look at such issues as who will operate our farms and how those farms will meet rising demands for food, how higher energy costs will change life in rural areas, the current and future needs of rural families and their communities, who in fact lives in these communities, and what can be done about escalating rural crime and recent social changes that have disrupted the traditional patterns of rural society.

Because the United States is an interdependent system of rural and urban, of providers and consumers, these issues are vitally important to all—scholars, policy makers, and citizens alike. The contributors bring us up to date on the contemporary rural scene and offer suggestions for research essential to intelligent decision making about the challenges and problems the 1980s hold in store for rural America.

Don A. Dillman is a professor in the Department of Sociology and Extension and Research Sociologist in the Department of Rural Sociology at Washington State University. He is author of the book *Mail and Telephone Surveys: The Total Design Method* and many other publications on survey methods and rural quality of life. **Daryl J. Hobbs** is director of rural development and professor of sociology, rural sociology, and family and community medicine at the University of Missouri, Columbia. He is a past president of the Rural Sociological Society and is the author of numerous publications on rural development issues.

Rural Society in the U.S.: Issues for the 1980s

edited by Don A. Dillman and Daryl J. Hobbs

Routledge
Taylor & Francis Group
LONDON AND NEW YORK

First published 1982 by Westview Press

Published 2019 by Routledge
52 Vanderbilt Avenue, New York, NY 10017
2 Park Square, Milton Park, Abingdon, Oxon OX14 4RN

Routledge is an imprint of the Taylor & Francis Group, an informa business

Library of Congress Cataloging in Publication Data
Main entry under title:
Rural society in the U.S.
(Rural studies series of the Rural Sociological Society)
Includes index.
1. United States–Rural conditions–Addresses, essays, lectures. 2. Sociology, Rural–United States–Addresses, essays, lectures. I. Dillman, Don A., 1941- . II. Hobbs, Daryl J. III. Series.
HN59.2.R87 307.7'2'0973 81-19858
ISBN 0-86531-100-5 AACR2

ISBN 13: 978-0-367-28640-8 (hbk)

ISBN 13: 978-0-367-30186-6 (pbk)

Contents

Foreword

ALVIN L. BERTRAND

The Rural Sociological Society, sponsor of this volume, is nearing its fiftieth birthday–an appropriate moment to take stock and plan for the years ahead. This volume represents the best thinking of members of the society regarding the future of rural society in the United States. It has been put together by experienced and knowledgeable editors and authors carefully chosen to accomplish what was obviously a challenging assignment. The caliber of the completed work provides unmistakable evidence that a relatively young profession is concerned not only about research but also about the public consequences of it.

This volume will have greater meaning for the reader who has some awareness of the history and development of rural sociology in the United States. As an independent discipline and profession, rural sociology has the distinction of being a truly American invention. Its origin can be traced to the early years of this century when rural problems reached alarming levels. The plight of ruralites was highlighted in a report prepared by members of the Commission on Country Life (appointed by President Theodore Roosevelt in 1908) after a nationwide study. A significant subsequent development was that several individuals with university training in sociology became aware of and interested in rural social problems. These early pioneers, whose names appear in the various histories of the discipline, called themselves rural sociologists and defined their professional effort as the development and application of concepts and theoretical models for the express purpose of improving the life and well-being of rural people. In their applied emphasis, they broke away from the social-philosophical approach

Alvin L. Bertrand is Boyd Professor Emeritus in the Department of Sociology and Rural Sociology, Louisiana State University, Baton Rouge, Louisiana. A past president of the Rural Sociological Society, he has authored eleven books and nearly two hundred other publications.

that had dominated sociology up to that time. A pragmatic approach has continued to be the hallmark of rural sociology research and practice.

Interest in rural sociology continued to grow through the 1920s and early 1930s, eventually culminating in the organization of a professional association, the Rural Sociological Society, in 1937. Today, there are rural sociological associations in all the major regions of the world, plus many smaller national and subnational groups, all backed by the International Rural Sociological Association.

The specific attention and interests of rural sociological researchers in the United States have changed over the years. These changes clearly reflect a sensitivity to major national issues and concerns at various periods of time. To illustrate, the earliest studies, i.e., those done before 1930, were characterized by general surveys of rural communities designed to uncover problems related to education, levels of living, the church, and social welfare. The Great Depression era that followed served to shift the focus of rural sociological research toward problems of rural relief, farm tenancy, farm labor, and population composition and distribution studies. During and shortly after World War II, many rural sociologists contributed to the defense and recovery effort by doing manpower and labor studies and by expanding their population research. From the late 1940s to the late 1960s, research turned toward a more general emphasis on improving the well-being of farmers and rural dwellers. This was in keeping with the nationally sponsored rural development efforts of this time. Studies of the adoption and diffusion of agricultural technology became popular, as did studies of health, social participation, and the aged. As farmers adopted new technology, research concern over the impact of agricultural mechanization became evident. In the past few years, research emphases have again changed in keeping with the times. Studies have tended to reflect national preoccupation with problems related to natural resources and the environment. There has also been a revival of interest in the structure and functioning of agricultural production units and agricultural organizations. Studies of minorities, youth, and crime have also gained prominence, as have investigations of the benefits and burdens of rural industrialization.

All in all, a review of rural sociological research through the years will verify an attempt to provide information and knowledge relevant to the issues and problems of national and rural concern. The productivity of rural sociologists has been enormous in relation to their numbers. Based on a study done by myself and others in 1972, the list of articles, monographs, bulletins, and books published by rural sociologists number in excess of ten thousand items. The specific content of these materials was classified under nineteen major headings and approximately eighty minor headings.

The major reason for the prolificness of rural sociologists has been the support they have received from land grant colleges and universities, principally through agricultural experiment stations and cooperative extension services. With the passage of the Purnell Act in 1925, directors of agricultural experiment stations were given explicit authority to approve research in economics and sociology. At the present time, almost all states sponsor rural sociological research with both state and federal funds – several states have annual budget commitments of close to or over $200,000. In a very real sense, the impact of the Purnell Act was to provide the support needed to launch rural sociology as a viable independent discipline.

Today, the Rural Sociological Society includes approximately 1,000 members. These members can be found in forty of the land grant universities of the nation, throughout liberal arts and state colleges, in a number of key government agencies, and in some private organizations. Wherever rural sociologists happen to be as professionals, they are dedicated to the study and improvement of life conditions for rural people. This book is in keeping with the mission that has been accepted as a professional charge and challenge. The topics selected for discussion represent the issues considered most critical to the future development and well-being of the rural segment of American society, with the strength and viability of the total national society as an ultimate goal. The intent of the book is to alert policy makers and program planners at all levels, as well as rural social scientists, to the research that must be done if the information needed for wise decision making on problem issues is to become available.

In a concluding observation, it is compelling to note that this volume includes an implicit expression of thanks to all of those who have supported rural sociologists and their work. The implied hope of the members of the Rural Sociological Society is that their sponsors and potential sponsors will perceive rural sociologists' profound concern with the major rural social problems that have to be faced in planning for the future. The book also intends to convey that rural sociologists are committed to contributing, to the limit of their capabilities and resources, to the understanding and solution of these problems.

Preface

The purpose of this book is to identify needed social research that will help define and clarify problems facing rural areas of the United States in the 1980s. Each of the chapters was written by an active researcher and has benefited from critiques by several other researchers. The book was commissioned in August 1979 by the governing council of the Rural Sociological Society. The council did so with the intent of identifying cogent public issues and developing a research agenda for social and behavioral scientists who have rural interests.

Since the society's founding in 1937, the rural landscape has changed from being dominated by small farms and farmers to becoming a mosaic of competing interests and concerns. But rural sociology has also changed. The interests and capabilities of rural sociologists of the 1980s are no less heterogeneous than are the current inhabitants of rural America. The specialties of those who identify themselves as rural sociologists range from crime and delinquency to nutritional sociology and from the sociology of natural resources to the structure of agricultural production.

In deciding to sponsor this book, the Rural Sociological Society's council was also giving explicit consideration to a dual heritage that has persisted throughout the society's history. One part of that heritage is the development of a discipline in search of principles governing the social behavior of rural people, with an emphasis on the development of theories and methods needed for testing those theories. Without theoretical concepts and paradigms, there would be no unique contribution for a discipline to make and, perhaps, no reason for its existence. Thus, a major concern of rural sociologists has been to fill a niche deemed important to the understanding of rural people and organizations but left unattended by other disciplines.

The second aspect of this heritage is the commitment to the application of sociological knowledge to solving practical problems. This concern undoubtedly stems from rural sociology being a product of the land grant system and its agricultural colleges. Early in this century, administrators of these colleges saw as their mandate not only improvement of technology for producing food and fiber but also improvement of rural people's well-being. Throughout this century, the major impetus for the growth and development of rural sociology has come from within the land grant system. Previous books sponsored by the Rural Sociological Society have tended to emphasize the former aspect of our heritage rather than its problem-solving aspect, although the two major books – *Our Changing Rural Society* in 1964 and *Rural U.S.A.: Persistence and Change* in 1978 – have contained both aspects. In this book, our emphasis is placed squarely on the latter. It is an explicit attempt to anticipate policy issues that will face rural United States in the 1980s and to identify research needed to facilitate development of that policy.

Another reason for the decision to develop this book was the recognition that the 1970s was a transitional decade for rural United States. Two major changes occurring during the 1970s produced unprecedented confusion about the future of rural America. One is now an established fact, the other is an uncertainty. The fact is that, for the first time since long before the founding of the Rural Sociological Society, rural America is *not* experiencing a population decline. Virtually all rural regions (although certainly not all individual communities) are growing. The uncertainty produced by the 1970s is the change in energy cost and availability. In the past, reliable supplies of inexpensive energy provided the means of overcoming the isolation imposed by long distances. But it remains far from clear what the energy supply situation will be in the 1980s and what changes it will bring to rural America. The population turnaround and energy uncertainty have produced great puzzlement over what community services are needed and where and how they will be provided, the persistence of traditionally rural values, and a host of other issues that permeate all aspects of rural life. The emergence of these two issues undoubtedly make this book much different from one that might have been produced at the beginning of the 1970s.

Finally, the Rural Sociological Society's council was keenly aware of the emergence of many new interest groups and organizations that are concerned with what is happening in rural America. The interests of rural people are no longer expressed simply through major farm organizations and commodity groups, as seemed to be the case in previous decades. Many groups, from Rural America to the National Rural Center, are bringing rural issues onto the public agenda. To put it simply, this book is a response to heterogeneity – the heterogeneity of an emerging rural America, the heterogeneity of the rural sociology profession, the heterogeneity of groups seeking to place rural issues on the public agenda, and the heterogeneity of specific concerns that now influence rural people and their way of life.

We are indebted to many groups and individuals who contributed enormously to turning an idea of what a book on this topic might be like into a finished product. We are indebted to the Advisory Committee, whose names appear on a separate page. They identified more than one hundred chapter topics that they felt the book should cover, they evaluated many of the proposed chapters, and helped whittle the list to the forty-one chapters the book now contains. In addition, we are grateful to the many reviewers, whose names also appear on a separate page, for providing critical reviews of the various chapters. Although the chapter authors and editors are solely responsible for the final volume, without critical reviews on early drafts of the chapters (the lengths of which occasionally exceeded the lengths of the chapters), this book would be a quite different product.

Financial support for editing the book was received from several sources, and we wish to express our sincere appreciation to each of them: U.S. Department of Agriculture–Economics and Statistics Service, the North Central Rural Development Center, the Northeastern Regional Center for Rural Development, the Southern Rural Development Center, the Western Rural Development Center, and the Farm Foundation. Appreciation is also extended to the W. K. Kellogg Foundation; released time for editorial work on the book was provided to Don Dillman under the National Kellogg Fellowship Program. The assistance of the Department of Rural Sociology, University of Missouri, and the Department of Rural Sociology, Washington State University, are also gratefully acknowledged.

Finally, we wish to thank Lynne Lafer, Doris Cottam, and Lela Odell for the office management and clerical assistance that made the timely completion of this book possible.

Don A. Dillman
Pullman, Washington

Daryl J. Hobbs
Columbia, Missouri

Part 1
INTRODUCTION

1
Research for the Rural United States

DARYL J. HOBBS
DON A. DILLMAN

IMAGES OF RURAL PEOPLE AND PLACES

When rural America is mentioned in conversation, it often conjures up a singular image. Some think of farms and farmers; others envision a land of second homes and weekend recreationists. Some see rural America as a place of great wealth; others think of it as people in poverty with little hope of improving their condition. For some, it is idyllic, a place to get away; for others, it is a place to get away from.

The towns and villages of the rural United States also have disparate images. To some these communities are places where everyone is friendly and it would be unthinkable not to speak to passers-by on Main Street. Others see these same communities as places where a new resident can remain a stranger for years. A windshield survey of community activity might lead us to think of dying vestiges from the past or conversely of enduring vitality. Many note that rural community services are conspicuously absent and community leaders unresponsive; others smile with satisfaction in the belief that rural America is where one can successfully fight city—or, more accurately, "town"—hall. Doctors, particularly the highly trained specialists who are the backbone of modern medicine, are often pictured as being miles away from where they are desperately needed, but for many there is the satisfaction of having family doctors who as members of their communities provide care over the course of people's entire lives. Rural communities are sometimes viewed as harbingers of safety against crime or at least as places where people can protect themselves from criminal acts.

All of these views of rural America, its people, and its communities are, to some degree, correct. They are also incorrect. The contrasts to be found within rural America are no less than the differences in colors and shadows displayed by a Grand Canyon sunset.

The word "rural" lacks precision in everyday use because it is so comprehensive yet so imprecise. It refers not only to open spaces and small places but also to what is done there and by whom. It is unlikely that ski vacationers in Aspen, Vail, or Sun Valley would think of themselves as being in, or even temporarily a part of, rural America. Indeed, the services found there and in hundreds of other resort areas match or surpass the most urbane styles, tastes, amusements, and comforts although they are wrapped in rustic exteriors to provide a packaged "rural" experience to the visitors.

In popular culture, the concept of "rural" mixes sizable portions of myth and nostalgia with reality. Perpetuation of the perceived virtues as well as the shortcomings of rural life seem largely attributable to those who write the television advertisements and promote rural chic in songs, clothing, and style. The "rural" of popular culture is the bosom of virtue, honesty, hard work, loyalty, and friendliness. It is Marlboro men who do not drink city beer and grandmas who fry chicken. But popular images also include negative generalizations: rural schools are poor schools, rural health care is poor health care, and rural people are simple in lifestyle and thought.

Beyond the popular images there is an objective rural America whose people are diverse and whose productivity and resources are essential to the overall national economy. In a sense, rural America is the nation's bank account, containing the water, the soil, and the natural resources that provide the basics of existence for the entire society. These resources and the rural people who produce from them have, at various times, suffered from benign neglect or been largely taken for granted, but as we enter the 1980s resource scarcities have become a more prominent concern and food has become a major instrument of national domestic and foreign policy. If rural people have not risen to a higher level of national concern, certainly rural resources have.

It is much easier to speak of rural America than to define it. In general, rural America in this book refers to the people and communities in the nation's nonmetropolitan counties–counties that have no cities with as many as fifty thousand people. But our definition is flexible and, in places, the authors of this book will describe as rural those people who, by virtue of lifestyle, residential location, or occupation, think of themselves as part of rural America in spite of living within the confines (although generally on the fringes) of metropolitan counties.

A HERITAGE OF REGIONAL DIVERSITY

Rural America has always exhibited regional diversity. In an earlier day, the rural regions of the country were largely defined by dominant crops and the forms of culture that were associated with the way they were produced. The South was the Cotton Belt, the Midwest was the Corn Belt, and the Plains States were the Wheat Belt. Similarly, the rural areas of other states became known by major crops, such as timber in the Pacific Northwest; vegetables and citrus fruit in California, Texas, and Florida; and tobacco in North Carolina. Identifying regions with crops was not only a reasonably accurate description of regional variations in agriculture but was also strongly suggestive of regional variations in lifestyle and culture. Most migratory workers have traditionally been associated with fruit and vegetable production; rural Blacks had an equally strong association with cotton production. Later European immigrants largely populated the rural areas of the Corn and Wheat Belts.

Until World War II, these designations of regions by crops provided appropriate agronomic descriptions and were also reasonably valid sociocultural descriptions. The major regions were relatively homogeneous. But following World War II, technological, economic, agricultural, and social forces converged to further diversify rural America and blur the validity of culture by crop designations. Soybeans emerged as a major crop grown nearly everywhere; livestock and poultry production became highly concentrated; labor-intensive industry began to decentralize to rural areas; resort/recreation complexes emerged; major water projects were undertaken; and railroads declined as trucks began carrying freight on interstate highways. As a result of these and numerous other changes, the agricultural population declined as a proportion of rural population, and rural America underwent dramatic diversification. The former variation between regions was replaced by much finer variations even between adjacent communities. Thus, as we move into the 1980s, appropriate rural policy and rural research is heavily influenced by the mixture that is now rural America.

There are also some commonalities that suggest major rural concerns for the 1980s. All rural regions of the country have a portion of the "people left behind"; the South has more than its share. Large-scale agricultural technology in all areas continues to diminish the number of viable farms and is making the socially desired family farm an ever diminishing institution. All rural areas are confronted with rising costs of overcoming the friction of space – it costs more in time and cash for rural people to go to school, go to the doctor, and obtain needed goods and services; these costs are rising faster than incomes. Rural areas are the site of most of the natural resources necessary to national economic growth and well-being. But conflicts are beginning to emerge concerning the threat to rural life by large-scale energy projects, dumping of industrial wastes, and repopulation of rural America.

The diversity of rural America provides the fundamental challenge of identifying the social research needed to address emerging rural problems in the 1980s. The agenda of rural issues and problems for the 1980s is a full one. But the issues and problems are not exclusively rural; the society is much too interdependent for such boundaries to be established.

DO WE KNOW ENOUGH TO ASK THE RIGHT QUESTIONS?

Much conventional wisdom of earlier years has either become false or left unanswered questions. Among those statements that no longer apply are the following: most rural people are farmers; older rural people are mostly poor; rural areas have low crime rates; rural recreation consists of small rustic resorts and tourism by car; agricultural policy is shaped mostly by the major interests of farmers and the organizations that represent them; nonfarm rural people commute farther to work than residents of metro areas; inflation and rising energy costs have made it impossible for people to afford to disperse from cities; society cannot afford rural nonfarm growth because land is necessarily taken away from agricultural production. These and many other descriptions of rural America often taken for granted are questioned in this book.

There is a widely held presumption that knowledge is good and useful because the collective well-being will be advanced by more informed decisions at all levels. Current events continue to challenge the validity of much of our conventional wisdom about both problems and solutions. New terms like "stagflation" are devised to describe previously unencountered circumstances. But, with new events and circumstances, additional information may reconfirm existing conventional wisdom or it may contribute new insights. Thus, as we face the task set out for this book, we intend to be guided by the observation of a former president of the Rural Sociological Society who commented about the problem of identifying research issues: "The problem is not one of knowing how to do research. Neither is it one of whether we will do research. Our dilemma is, do we know enough to ask the right questions?"

But what constitutes the "right" questions? There are basically two sources of research questions. One source is the theory and research traditions of academic disciplines. This is the source of research questions for most academic research—the so-called basic or pure research. But there is also research undertaken with the intention of contributing to the solution of a problem, e.g., reduction of rural poverty, excessive exploitation of natural resources, reduction of crime rates, and preservation of family farms. This so-called applied research depends on the concepts and methods of academic disciplines, but it is intended to be used by other than academic colleagues. The intent of this book is to raise questions and issues pertaining to problems and inequities faced by some rural people and communities. Thus, to the authors of the following chapters, the "right" questions are those addressed to present and prospective rural problems—problems that, if solved, would contribute to improving the quality of life of rural people.

The persistence of some rural problems, however, suggests either that the problems are insoluble or that research and policy have been addressed to the wrong questions. It may even be that policy has ignored research or that policy is an inappropriate or ineffective means of resolving the problems.

The first clue to the difficulty of asking the "right" research questions is to consider the process by which research questions typically get formulated. They come from a variety of sources. Sometimes they arise from past research, which may provide enough new information about an issue that it becomes apparent that additional questions need answers. For example, a research project aimed at determining whether the "quality of life" was higher or lower among rural people than urban people revealed substantial differences among rural people and gave rise to a subsequent project on how occupational aspirations of young people influenced their life in rural areas. The nature of the research process is such that projects sometimes, perhaps typically, raise more additional questions than they in fact were originally designed to answer.

Research questions sometimes result from government policy actions that literally demand that certain answers be found before a program can be implemented. A financial incentive program aimed at attracting more physicians and nurses to rural communities may require research to determine what sizes of incentives are needed under what kinds of payback agreements to make the program work. Sometimes research is required as a precursor to implementation; other times it is required to evaluate and recommend program revisions. As we enter the 1980s, research may be required to find solutions to problems created by the elimination of long-standing governmental programs.

Research issues are sometimes posed by citizens who question conventional wisdom of researchers and unwittingly are responsible for a new line of inquiry. We recall a luncheon meeting some ten years ago with an official of a farm organization who vigorously questioned the researcher's belief that people were migrating to cities because that is where they wanted to live. The official vigorously argued that people were being forced to move to cities and suburbs against their will and, if given their druthers, would live in more rural settings. Although the visitor was unaware of it, his questioning led to the initiation of a new research program that has lasted nearly a decade and provided valuable insight into reasons for the population turnaround of the 1970s, much of which is summarized in Chapter 24 of this volume.

Research also is initiated by a researcher's growing uneasiness over a situation, or a simple hunch that something different is happening; it may be from noticing that many rural addresses are appearing in newspaper crime reports, and trying to reconcile that with the accepted belief that rural areas do not have much crime. Or it may be the realization that a new rural hospital judged to be desperately needed a few years earlier is hardly being used, and hearing from a friend that a similar situation exists in a distant rural community. As a result, the researcher begins to ponder whether the rural medical problem is a matter of physicians, medical care facilities, a change in willingness to seek care in distant cities, or some other cause.

Sometimes research questions arise from nothing more formal than a drive along a familiar road where somehow things seem different from a few months or years before, e.g., new houses on small pieces of land, which raises questions about the rate at which agricultural land is being turned to other uses and the reasons for it. It may be that several new businesses have started construction, suggesting that, for some reason, the climate for economic activity may be changing. It may be nothing more noticeable than the presence of fruit and vegetable stands where none previously existed, which raises questions about changes in crops and/or marketing methods and queries about the reasons for the change.

Another problem of research identification is anticipating the unanticipated. Exactly ten years ago, few people considered the resurgence of growth in rural United States as likely to happen. Concern over the environment obscured thought about energy issues. It takes only a short tour through history to produce the sober realization that the unexpected has always been a major factor in setting the agenda for needed research. Will the age of the microprocessor and interactive technology arrive in full force and dramatically change the basis upon which rural economies can be organized? Will a worldwide food crisis lead to all-out agricultural production and unprecedented wealth among those who produce it? These possibilities seem no less outlandish than did the possibility of a pervasive population turnaround some ten years ago.

Very often, research issues are stated in a way so as to produce generalizable results, i.e., to find the rule that applies to all problems of service delivery. The question asked by some policy makers is not what rule more or less applies, but what specific solution will work for me. The result is often a creative tension.

THE CHALLENGE

The challenge presented to the nearly seventy authors—each a specialist in the topic area of his or her chapter—in this book is whether they can deliberately and systematically do what often happens in an unplanned, even haphazard, way and be sure that they have asked important researchable questions.

Producing a research agenda for the 1980s is partly a matter of imagination, partly a realization of the limits of science, partly a recognition of the limitations of the skills of rural sociologists, and partly a matter of luck. It is little wonder that one is given pause to ponder, "Do we know enough to ask the right questions?"

It is one thing to ask a question and quite another to ask a researchable question. There are literally thousands of interesting questions that could be asked about rural America, but there is little likelihood that definite answers can be provided by any deliberate research program. For example, it is of keen interest to virtually everyone concerned with rural United States to know if and when the population turnaround will end. We doubt that researchers can produce an answer. However, rural sociologists can determine the types of people that are moving to rural places and provide considerable insight into the causes of their migration. They can also build models to help predict the conditions under which the turnaround seems likely to terminate. But to ask when (or if) the turnaround will end requires knowledge of future government policy actions, future energy costs and availability, and a host of other conditions at which we can only guess.

A second factor that limits what is a researchable question is the skills of rural sociologists. Like all scientists, we have certain theoretical and methodological skills but not others. It seems unlikely that we can predict whether the United States will soon experience an acute water shortage, but a program of rural sociological research can provide insight into the conditions under which water conservation programs will be effective. At the same time, our methodologies, e.g., survey research, enable us to find the distribution of a wide range of characteristics of current rural water supplies, from purity to periodicity of shortages, and the factors that influence those characteristics.

Still another limiting factor in the identification of researchable questions is the nature of problems themselves. The essence of this concern is characterized by the frequently heard lament that people have problems but universities have departments. Very few problems lend themselves to solutions by a single discipline. Providing adequate housing for rural people is only partly a social problem having to do with norms and aspirations. Housing is also an economic problem (cost and finance issues), a political science problem (e.g., zoning regulations), and an agricultural production problem (e.g., competition for land and juxtaposing of incompatible uses). Formulation of many research issues means speculating about research problems, the dynamics of which are likely to emerge only through the give-and-take of multidisciplinary teams, where the task of getting the specialized parts to add up to a meaningful whole is sometimes enormous.

This is a presumptuous book. It identifies hundreds of questions – not all of which are earth-shaking but most of which are important. The agenda outlined here goes well beyond the collective capability of the nation's rural sociologists during the decade of the 1980s. But we do not feel that the capacity to address the questions should constrain the issues that are raised. Such a constraint would likely produce relatively provincial approaches to relatively trivial problems. Thus, our concern for the severity and magnitude of the issues raised carries with it an anticipation of research effort more effectively focused on those issues.

One frequently hears the call for more action and less research. In the eyes of many, research is viewed as an esoteric enterprise that can probably be supported as long as there is plenty of money around. Indeed, there is much research that has contributed little other than employment to the researcher. Other research has made contributions to well-being far beyond the original investment. Research is a probabilistic and uncertain process: If significant outcomes could be known in advance, then only research producing such results would be funded. But no research administrator possesses that clairvoyance.

Rural-oriented social science research is not "breakthrough" research – cures for dread diseases will not likely be discovered. Rural social science research does not usually provide quick answers to major policy issues, but it usually helps formulate the options for decisions or helps clarify the issue about which a decision is to be made.

Unless we think ahead to what research is needed, we will likely end up doing more of the same. Thus, the target audience of this book is not just policy makers but also researchers and administrators who are setting the agenda for research in the 1980s and beyond.

2 The Policy Context for Rural-Oriented Research

RONALD C. POWERS
EDWARD O. MOE

Policies designed to affect the people and organizations of rural America are difficult to specify. They must take into account an incredibly wide range of geography, climate, history, population, culture, ethnicity and race, institutions, occupations, and degrees of ruralness. This diversity has produced a vast array of legitimate competing interests. The need to balance the gains and losses among those affected by a particular policy requires careful, insightful policy analysis. The social science research community is interested in and capable of making significant substantive contributions to the analysis of policy and contributing to a better understanding of the institutional framework within which policy is formulated and implemented.

THE RURAL POLICY CONTEXT

Until the late 1930s, a major share of American public policy was oriented toward rural areas and, more specifically, toward agriculture. Landmark legislation from the Civil War through the Great Depression was impressive and had much to do with the development of rural

Ronald C. Powers is director of the North Central Regional Center for Rural Development and a professor in the Department of Sociology and Anthropology at Iowa State University in Ames. A past vice-president of the American Home Economics Association, he is the coauthor of *Social Action and Interaction in Program Planning* and has written many articles on rural development. **Edward O. Moe** was formerly principal sociologist with the

research. The establishment in 1862 of the U.S. Department of Agriculture, the Morrill Act, the Homestead Act, and the Railroad Act opened up additional rural areas to settlement and created institutions to solve problems of agriculture and rural life. The Hatch Act of 1887 (which created the experiment stations), the Smith-Lever Act of 1914 (which created the Cooperative Extension Service), the Purnell Act of 1925 (which funded social science research), and the Resettlement Administration Act of 1933 (which became the Farm Security Administration and later the Farmers Home Administration) all provided institutional mechanisms for assisting in the further development of rural areas.

Although we are concerned about contemporary rural policy and the context for it, a major part of the contemporary rural policy context involves emerging national goals. These national goals are being articulated in legislation directed toward the major conditions of life—jobs, health, education, community services, industry, agriculture, transportation, the environment, and the conditions affecting particular groups, such as minorities, the poor, and the elderly. Most of these national goals and the policies for their achievement are intended to meet needs of all Americans regardless of where they live. We have serious doubts about separate goals for rural and urban areas and the people who reside there. If there are separate goals for rural and urban, the rural goals should be a subset of national goals.

It is the function of policy and program administration to make possible the achievement of national goals with equity under widely varying rural and urban conditions. The case for an urban policy, or a rural policy, rests on devising appropriate means for achieving similar objectives in different contexts.

Our use of the term *rural policy* refers to national policy, and includes national goals as expressed in legislation and the way these goals affect rural areas and institutions; national goals and policies that specifically relate to rural areas, such as the Rural Development Act of 1972; and administrative policies and regulations of the White House and federal agencies that are based on legislative authority and the exercise of discretion in the implementation of programs. Although state and local policies are highly significant, we place major emphasis on national rural policy because it attempts to reflect local and regional interests and is a

---

Science and Education Administration, U.S. Department of Agriculture, Washington, D.C. A past president of the Rural Sociological Society, he is the author of numerous articles and books on rural issues.

part of the context within which local policy and action is developed under our federal system.

The rural policy context at the beginning of this decade is characterized by a number of important features enumerated below. They provide a basis for defining a new role for social science research in assessing current policy and in defining policy alternatives for the future.

Increased Recognition of the Rural Sector

There is growing recognition that most of the nation's natural resources, including its food and fiber, its energy supplies, and 80 percent of its land mass, are in rural areas. Over 30 percent of the people live in the countryside and in small towns and cities under 50,000 population. However, the significance of the rural sector transcends these factors. The myths and realities of rural life have been, and are now, a major factor in shaping American institutions and the American character. As indicated in Chapter 24, Americans generally perceive certain quality-of-life benefits associated with rural life. As described in Chapter 3, many Americans, motivated by those perceptions, have been moving to rural areas.

Resurgence of the Rural Sector

Differential growth in the rural population and in the economy of the late 1960s and the 1970s has created new conditions, new problems, and new opportunities in rural areas. Many small towns and counties have serious problems coping with growth, while other rural areas continue to decline.

Small Scale, Sparsity, and Distance

Rural places are characterized by small size and scale, including small communities, small governments, and small institutions such as schools and health care units. Many small municipalities, towns, and counties are served by part-time officials. Smallness is rooted in the sparsity of population. Extensive travel is often necessary to aggregate the population and resources that are needed to support essential services. Limited resources are a major restraint. There is a growing recognition that institutions and methods of organization that have been efficient for large schools, hospitals, and units of government are neither efficient nor appropriate for small communities and sparsely settled areas.

Diversity

As noted in Chapter 1, the rural sector of our society is characterized by great and frequently unrecognized diversity in its population, institutions, governments, resources, economy, cultures, and lifestyles. Failure to recognize the diversity within the rural sector and between rural and urban areas has resulted in national growth and development policies insensitive to the spatial distribution of their effects. The President's Annual Report to the Congress on Governmental Services to Rural America, entitled *Rural Development* (April 1972), documents the inequitable distribution of benefits. While this condition has moderated somewhat, inequitable distribution of benefits continues, with rural areas continuing to come up short.

Confusion of *Rural* with *Agriculture*

Agriculture is and will remain an important part of the rural sector. It is in the national interest to achieve greater integration of agricultural and nonagricultural interests in the rural economy (see Chapter 33). At the same time, the fact that only one in nine rural residents is directly involved in agricultural production needs to be taken into account.

Weakness of the Rural Constituency

The great diversity of rural areas and interests has frustrated attempts to build a rural constituency that effectively represents all rural people. Existing constituencies represent special interests such as cattle producers, wheat growers, soybean growers, rural housing interests, and rural school interests. Small gains in building a rural constituency have been made through the creation of Rural America, the National Rural Center, and other rural public interest groups. The emergence of these groups indicates the failure of long-established institutions to meet the current needs of rural areas and the failure to recognize that agricultural and rural interests are not synonymous.

The Assumption that National Policy Formulated in an Urban Context Fits Rural Areas

National policy formulated in a highly urbanized context results in a built-in bias. Such policy fails to take into account small units and the accompanying problems of scale, sparsity of population, distance, and other unique social, political, and cultural patterns of rural areas. The bias may be unintended, but it is real and has adverse consequences for rural people.

Growing Complexity of the Rural Policy Context

History and recent events, particularly the movement of many people and interests into the rural sector, complicate the formation of rural policy. Interests that were always diverse are now more diverse. This new complexity affects a wide range of people and their interests. This complexity also affects the intricate process of devising equitable policy.

Prior to the mid-1960s, general farm organizations played a major role in getting rural mail, telephone, and electrical service. Since the late 1960s, which produced the multifaceted environmental movement, farm and commodity organizations have largely turned inward to farm production problems, leaving the establishment of the agenda for rural America to urban-based agrarians. This agenda is characterized by diversity of purpose and means and by urban leadership.

Inadequacies of the Data Base in Rural Areas

The data base for rural areas is inadequate for determining policy and programs. For example, abundant data on schools are not reported separately for rural areas. Most often, rural data have been reported for the category "nonmetropolitan county," which is much too broad to be of value except at the highest level of aggregation. This inadequacy hampers efforts to specify rural problems that need policy attention.

Lack of a Rural Development Policy

Despite numerous national goals expressed through various policies, our country's domestic policy lacks coherence and its elements are often contradictory. What has emerged in various pieces of legislation are some highly abstract goals. There is, for example, the commitment of Congress in Section 901(a) of the Agriculture Act of 1970: "The Congress commits itself to a sound balance between rural and urban America. The Congress considers this balance so essential to the peace, prosperity, and welfare of all our citizens that the highest priority must be given to the revitalization and development of rural areas." This act helped to set the stage for the passage of the Rural Development Act of 1972, the overall purpose of which, as stated in the 1975 Revised Guide to the act, was "to provide for improving the economy and living conditions in rural America." Title V, Section 501, of this act further states that "The purpose of this title is to encourage and foster a balanced national development that provides opportunities for increased numbers of Americans to work and enjoy a high quality of life dispersed throughout our Nation by providing essential knowledge necessary for successful programs of rural development." The Carter Administration's 1979 *Small Community and Rural Development Policy* provided a step forward, but it fell far short of the need. Despite the inadequacies of this policy, it provides a basis on which to build. Among its strengths is a statement of why a rural policy is needed and a statement of some needed organizational and procedural changes. An action agenda is proposed that cites actions already taken and actions to be taken. Little is said about resources, either the redirection of existing resources or the provision of additional resources.

Lack of Integrating Mechanisms for Rural Development

Near the end of the Carter Administration, the federal government had some twenty-five departments or agencies operating in about fifteen program areas and administering over four hundred different programs for rural development. These programs provide a variety of resources for improving rural conditions, including indexed loans, loan guarantees, grants, technical assistance, planning assistance, research, and education. For the most part, the provisions of these programs are applied singly and in isolation from each other rather than in some coordinated, integrated way. Integrative mechanisms to combine the pieces in a comprehensive improvement effort are weak. Those authorized in Title VI of the Rural Development Act were never used. As one step toward integration, strengthening the research, educational, and technical assistance components of loan and grant programs could make an important difference.

The Rural Development Policy Act of 1980 (P.L. 96-355) established a position of Under Secretary of Agriculture for Small Community and Rural Development. The act also specifies certain rural policy development requirements and processes. The impact of this legislation on greater integration of programs is likely to be modest.

The Roles of the U.S. Department of Agriculture and the Land Grant System

The roles of the U.S. Department of Agriculture (USDA) and the land grant system are considered together because they are parts of a common system that has existed in one form or another since 1862. Major disagreements and tension have characterized the system since its inception, but the mutual advantages of the partnership have kept it together. Whether it will continue in recognizable form is an important question.

The USDA has had a unique partnership with rural people. Very early, it gained and maintained their respect and confidence. It served farming and farmers directly and, through them, other rural people and rural interests. Its high credibility with farmers led to requests for assistance with rural schools, health care, and other problems. The USDA's partnership with the land grant universities in the states made possible an effective response to such requests. People were frequently unaware whether the help was from the USDA or the university. It is significant that, out of this partnership, county and state extension workers became, in part at least, federal employees and the educational arm of the USDA.

The emphasis was clearly on agriculture and agricultural research and education, but in the rural agricultural society this relationship spilled over into almost every aspect of life. The county extension worker was seen as a local person subject to local control, which, indeed, he or she was. The situation began to change in the 1930s with the creation of a number of new agencies, e.g., the Soil Conservation Service, the Farm Security Administration (now the Farmers Home Administration), and the Agricultural Adjustment Administration (now the Agricultural Stabilization and Conservation Service). In the great transformations that occurred in agriculture and rural areas over the past half century, the USDA has faced some difficult choices. Is it an "agriculture department," serving agriculture and agribusiness only, or is it a department serving all the people of the nation as consumers and serving the interests of all rural people?

As might be expected, the USDA has been inconsistent. On the one hand, it accepts designation as the lead agency for rural development as stated in Title VI of the Rural Development Act of 1972, strengthened by the *Small Community and Rural Development Policy* and the Rural Development Policy Act of 1980. The USDA declares that most of its resources, principally loans of various types, are allocated for rural development. Perceptions of the USDA's staff and people of other departments and agencies working in rural development, however, are that the commitment to agriculture is primary and that rural development is and will continue to be in a subordinate position. This view is shared by public interest groups and members of Congress concerned about rural development.

In a more basic sense, the problem arises from the USDA having rather exclusive responsibility for agriculture while sharing responsibility with other departments for the range of activities encompassed in rural development, such as economic development (which is shared with the U.S. Department of Commerce) and housing (which is shared with the U.S. Department of Housing and Urban Development). Support for activities that are shared tends to be given lower priority. The combination of shared responsibility and lack of political support for rural development seem to account for the USDA's indecision.

The land grant universities have been equivocal also, and for similar reasons. The agricultural constituency is strong, both at state and national levels; agricultural teaching, research, and extension are more or less exclusive missions of land grant universities. Rural development is a shared responsibility with uncertain support.

Neither the USDA nor the land grant universities have provided the leadership needed to develop national policy pertinent to rural areas, or to help put in place programs of the scale and scope needed to help rural people solve their problems. One theme has been repeated continually since the mid-1800s: The impetus for much of the legislation, policy, and programs that have major effects (positive and negative) on rural areas has originated with urban agrarians. Some of the urban agrarians have come from rural areas, others have not, but the commonality they share is an urban political base and a great diversity in motivations for "helping" rural areas–not all of which turn out to be helpful from the perspective of those in rural areas.

Growing Emphasis on Local Public and Private Institutions

The experience of the last two decades places great emphasis on the critical roles and responsibilities for development of local government, local public and private agencies, and local leadership within the framework of the federal system. In the early months of the Reagan administration, there has been a strong ideological reassertion that local government and private agencies are best able to identify and solve local problems. This has led to a reconsideration of the questions of scale and has placed an emphasis on decentralization.

Built-In Problems of the American Federal System

Some basic and persistent problems affecting both rural and urban areas thwart efforts to achieve development in the American federal system. A National Academy of Science/National Academy of Engineering report (1974) lists these issues: (1) lack of congruence between locally perceived needs and national priorities and programs; (2) failure to match statements of priority with resources, personnel, and funds; (3) tendency for problems to be greater or smaller than the jurisdiction of the relevant unit of government; (4) failure in planning and development to encompass the full social, economic, and political dimensions of problems; (5) failure to integrate planning and development with political processes of decision making and allocation of resources; and (6) inadequacy of research and evaluation tools (both the state of the arts and the use of what is available) to assess processes and ascertain impact of programs.

CHALLENGE OF THE 1980s

This book provides an overview of rural society at the beginning of the decade. It identifies and describes the major issues confronting American society in its rural areas. A major question is how the nation will respond to the issues it confronts, including the differential effects of these issues in rural and urban places. A framework for devising an effective response to these issues is outlined below. Implicit in the major points is a recognition of the urgent need for innovation in the way we assess, formulate, and reformulate policy.

Continuing Clarification of National Goals and Policies

National goals and policies should pertain to all people of the nation wherever they may live. We have serious reservations about separating rural goals and urban goals at the national level. National goals need to be articulated through legislation directed toward the major conditions of life, such as jobs, income, and the environment. It should be a major concern of policy-making and program administration to assure that policies and programs are adapted to urban and rural conditions. Despite an appeal for nationally oriented policy and program administration, some special monitoring is required to make certain that policies and implementing strategies fit rural conditions of smallness, i.e., small communities, small governments, and small institutions with limited staffs and resources.

Monitoring of Policy and Program Impact

The strides that have been made in monitoring policy and program impact are not adequate to meet current needs. Conditions of fiscal restraint make it more necessary than ever to increase the effectiveness of programs. Policies and programs that prove ineffective in meeting their objectives need to be identified and modified. If modifications fail to increase effectiveness, they should be discarded.

This book represents an attempt on the part of social science researchers and their professional society to relate their work to the present and emerging issues in rural society. More possible now than at any time in the past is a new relationship between researchers, policy makers, and program administrators. The growing competence of the research community makes it possible to do policy and program assessment. Testing of policy alternatives is urgently needed. Researchers appear ready to join policy makers and program administrators in further defining issues and in devising policy and development research that meets their needs. Presumptuous as they may seem, it could enhance the use of knowledge and reason in meeting important national goals.

Building Capacity at Local, State, and National Levels

Development programs in both rural and urban areas are increasingly defined as capacity building. Efforts to build capacity are occurring at two levels: (1) at the local level to solve community problems and make continuing adjustments to the larger environment; and (2) on the part of federal and state agencies and programs to provide appropriate assistance and resources needed by local people and institutions to help make their efforts effective. It follows that creation of new capacity at these two levels requires, both within each level and between levels, new procedures and new relationships. Changes will be required.

The achievement of new capacity at the local level will provide the basis for enhanced productivity of people, agencies, and governments. Capacity and enhanced productivity will, in turn, make the development program something more than a collection of direct and disguised transfer payments. Transfer payments and other forms of assistance certainly will be needed—but as means for creating enhanced capacity and increased productivity. The genius of capacity-building efforts, whether rural or urban, is that they build on what exists and devise innovations in process and structure to create new strength.

SETTING A RESEARCH AGENDA

Recent events suggest a disturbing view of the prospects for important needs of social science research during the 1980s. The creation of the Joint Council for Food and Agriculture and the National Research and Extension Users Advisory Group in the 1977 Farm Act and the Reagan administration's recent budget messages all emphasize production-oriented research, including that portion related to energy and natural resource protection and conservation. A major gap still exists between the rhetoric about rural development and the actual support.

All need not be gloom and doom, however. Research aimed at energy solutions, best management tillage practices, and improved community facilities and services have much need for social science input. In many cases, this will require participation in multidisciplinary research teams where social scientists do not represent the lead discipline. The increased sophistication in research theory and methodology that sociologists have gained in recent years should augur well for this approach.

The research agenda will be very untidy because of the number of special policy interests, including groups with varying degrees of animosity toward the USDA and the land grant institutions. These interests make conflicting and competing demands on resources and institutions and on a national economy increasingly forced to back away from being all things to all people.

Among the issues that characterize this situation is the disagreement over the likelihood that the land grant universities will address nonagricultural problems. Many groups have been institutionalized to the point of being competitors for public funding, and are now focusing on their own maintenance as much as on the original task. There has been considerable empire building by groups who want to be involved in action and advocacy and in the research and education function rather than establish linkages with universities. At the same time, there has been a reluctance by universities to address rural institutional problems. There also exists conflict over funding and operation of programs to meet federal policy objectives versus meeting locality-determined needs. This conflict surfaces as a dispute between competitive research support by the federal government and support for a basic system (e.g., the USDA/land grant universities partnership, which is capable of addressing problems as they occur).

The basic policy context for rural-oriented research is characterized by major social and economic changes that impact heavily on rural areas. There are diverse political objectives among those speaking for and acting on behalf of rural areas, with the result that policy consensus, and thus the base for concerted action, is nearly impossible to achieve. We have gone through periodic cycles of rhetoric and legislation addressed to rural problems but with only modest changes in actual resources available for rural-oriented research.

Social scientists themselves have contributed to the present context by emphasizing the development of the discipline more than relevance of the problems. They have often selected "safe" areas of research and engaged in social critiques of the system rather than changing the system. In addition, they have often done a great deal of pedestrian research.

The opportunity and the need for policy-relevant research is substantial. Social scientists interested in rural areas can make an important contribution if they are willing to invest the time and energy necessary to understand and work with other disciplines relevant to the major problems. They must also be willing to take on areas of research that are going to be controversial but operate in a credible manner so the opposing interests will agree that the issues are clarified by the research. There needs to be a shift in the emphasis within the professional reward structure that encourages and supports higher-risk research and direct communication with policy actors. Finally, there is a need to develop national and regional research programs and collectively secure the research support in a manner analogous to agricultural production research. Herein lie the challenges for rural social research in the 1980s.

REFERENCES

Carter Administration. 1979. *Small Community and Rural Development Policy*. Washington, D.C.: The White House.

Part 2

INTRUSIONS FROM THE 1970s

A friend once objected to characterizing a significant event as something that "touches" people's lives; rather, she felt it more appropriate to describe a significant event as a hand that grasps someone by the shoulder and turns that person in a different direction. By her definition, the population reversal that has replaced decline with growth in most rural areas of the United States and the so-called energy crisis are significant events! These are issues for which the trend lines of previous decades have been broken and for which effects are likely to be far-reaching during and beyond the 1980s.

Throughout this book, we will be discussing what is different about rural America in the early 1980s, but none of the topics will show greater discontinuities with the past than the ones covered in this section. Further, the renewal of rural population growth and changes in energy costs and availability have had and will have effects that permeate the statement of issues in all of the following chapters.

Had this book been written a decade ago, a chapter similar to the population reversal chapter by Wardwell would not have appeared. In its place would have been a review of the great exodus out of rural areas during preceding decades and a forecast of continuing population loss through the 1970s. Yet, only a decade later, rural sociologists and demographers spoke easily and confidently of the reversal in migration that has brought renewed vitality and, in some cases, new problems to rural communities. The research issues that face rural sociologists as the result of this reversal are described in Chapter 3 by Wardwell.

Also a short ten years ago we would have been tempted to expectantly label the 1970s as the decade of the environment. Earth Day in May 1970 focused the nation's attention squarely on the "environmental crisis." Energy was at best a "related" factor submerged from view by cheap petroleum energy. But, as the 1980s begin, we have dramatically more expensive energy and a concern for the environment that includes its potential to produce energy. In Chapter 4, Clemente and Krannich explore what this new energy equation may mean for rural America, and they suggest research needed to understand better and plan for the implications. Their chapter previews many issues that reappear in more detail under specific topics of later chapters.

"Big is better" prevailed as a sentiment in 1970 as cities continued to drain population from the countryside and energy seemed cheap enough to fuel any expansion. The desirability of large scale was pervasive throughout people's lives, including their automobiles, homes, airplanes, and other technology that surrounded them. Although the term "appropriate technology" had a literal definition in 1970, the term carried no specific meaning to most people and was seldom heard in conversation. Although still not in the lexicon of most citizens, appropriate technology has a specific meaning to people well-informed on energy issues. Advocates of appropriate technology ask whether big is better most or even sometimes. Chapter 5, by Lodwick and Morrison, describes appropriate technology and identifies research issues that that perspective raises about resources and technology and their relationship to the people who use them. Whereas the other two chapters of this section deal with changes that have already come to rural America, Chapter 5 deals with an unresolved set of issues. Answers to the research questions raised in this chapter should help determine a future compatible relationship between technology and the people who use it.

3
The Reversal of Nonmetropolitan Migration Loss

JOHN M. WARDWELL

Between 1960 and 1970, nonmetropolitan counties lost nearly four million people. But since 1970 these counties have gained approximately three million people. This reversal is the result of an increase in movement out of metropolitan counties *and* a decrease in movement away from nonmetro counties. This migration turnaround has great importance because of all the changes associated with it that are affecting working and living conditions in both urban and rural places. The fact that no one in the late 1960s anticipated these changes means that our models of migration and population distribution contain serious flaws that must be identified and corrected in order to provide more accurate short-term forecasts in the future.

CAUSES OF THE MIGRATION TURNAROUND

There is no single answer as to why the turnaround has taken place in the United States or in any of the more than a dozen other countries that

---

John M. Wardwell is an associate professor in the Department of Sociology and an associate rural sociologist in the Department of Rural Sociology at Washington State University in Pullman, Washington. He is the coeditor of *New Directions in Urban-Rural Migration* and has written numerous articles on rural population growth.

This is Scientific Paper Number 5891, Project 0354, Agricultural Research Center,

witnessed similar changes at about the same time. One of the most important reasons for the change has been growth of employment opportunities in nonmetro counties (Frisbie and Poston, 1978; Hansen, 1973). Almost all types of industries grew more in nonmetro than in metro areas throughout the 1970s (Beale, 1978). This meant that people residing in rural areas had more opportunities to find adequate employment where they lived. It also meant that people who wanted to move to these areas could more easily do so. Approximately 75 percent of new metro-to-nonmetro migrants remain actively engaged in the labor force (Bowles, 1978). These people would not have been able to move if there had not been new jobs to employ them.

Growth of real income through the second half of the 1960s and the first half of the 1970s brought with it a change in consumer expenditures. Often this change benefited nonmetro areas more than it did the large urban areas (Wardwell, 1980). People increasingly were able to live where they preferred and, if necessary, to commute longer distances to work. They acquired the ability to spend more time and money on commuting and on other uses of long-distance transportation. The resulting boom in outdoor recreation is particularly significant because this industry requires sparsely populated open space for leisure activities in mountain, water, desert, and other areas. But the importance of commuting to metro employment should not be overstated. Recent findings reported by Bowles and Beale (1980) indicate that the vast majority of new migrants do not commute to old employment locations in metro centers; rather, they sever employment ties to their former locations.

Energy was cheap during most of the decade, relative to other costs of households and firms. Cheap energy, combined with continued development of the interstate and other highway systems, meant that people could spend a long, leisurely weekend driving to a distant recreation site more economically than they could spend a comparable weekend in a large city. But the development of improved transportation and communication meant more than increased ease of travel for employment and recreation. It meant that the isolation that had historically characterized remote rural areas was greatly lessened. These areas were opened to commercial and industrial development and had the modern telecommunications necessary to integrate more fully their activities with

---

Washington State University, a contributing project to Western Region Project W-118R. The author wishes to thank Edwin Carpenter for his thorough critique and revision of an earlier draft and Lloyd Bender, David Brown, Gordon DeJong, Glenn Fuguitt, Nan Johnson, Kevin McCarthy, and Peter Morrison for their helpful suggestions.

the mainstream of modern urban living.

Another change that contributed to growth of rural areas during the decade was the increased mobility of retirement-aged people. Historically, these people have been among the least mobile segments of the population. It has long been thought that this was due primarily to their comparative lack of financial resources to support residential relocation. During the 1970s, two trends came together to substantially confirm this belief. The number of people in their fifties and sixties increased sharply as a result of the high birth rates in the 1910s and 1920s, and their financial status improved dramatically as a result of the social security and other pension programs introduced in the 1930s and 1940s and improved since then. Once they acquired the ability to move, a large number of older urban residents implemented their residential preferences and moved to more sparsely settled areas and to areas that offered such physical amenities as milder climates and greater recreational opportunities. Thus, it is often the case that recreation and retirement growth go hand-in-hand in nonmetro counties (Dailey and Campbell, 1980).

In many nonmetro counties, a rapid expansion of governmental activities at all levels also contributed to population and economic growth. State and local government grew dramatically, as did enrollments in four-year colleges and universities. In the early years of the decade, defense-related installations and industries also witnessed rapid expansion (McCarthy and Morrison, 1979).

Two themes recur throughout these diverse reasons for change in rural society. The first is that residential preferences of people living in large cities increasingly changed in favor of smaller cities and open rural territory (Zelinsky, 1978; Zuiches and Rieger, 1978). The second is that the nature of urban and rural places changed to make it easier for people to put these preferences into practice. As the desirable aspects of large urban living increasingly became available in smaller places, it was easier for some people to leave the unpleasant and sometimes unsafe conditions of urban living without giving up so many of the attractive features that had drawn them to large cities in the first place. The traditional economic and other gains associated with rural-to-urban migration have diminished, as have the costs associated with urban-to-rural movement. Left with the question, "Why do we have to live in a large city?" millions of Americans have been unable to find a satisfactory answer.

PREVIOUS RESEARCH

All of these changes had been gathering strength throughout the 1960s, and such nonmetro areas as the Ozarks, the Texas hill country, and the

Upper Great Lakes had begun to show a reversal of population loss in the mid- to late 1960s, while many other areas showed a slowing in the rate of population loss (Beale and Fuguitt, 1978). But the 1970 census did not show that these new trends were becoming pervasive across the United States. The first indication of that came in 1973 when Calvin Beale reported that hundreds of previously declining rural counties were suddenly showing population and net migration gains (Beale, 1975). The 1975 current population survey quickly confirmed that, for the first time, more people had moved from metro to nonmetro counties than had made the traditionally larger opposite move (Tucker, 1976). Shortly thereafter, Vining and Kontuly (1978) reported their striking finding that similar reversals of net metro gain had appeared in approximately twelve other societies of northern and western Europe and in Japan. The preliminary findings for the United States were further verified by local population data generated from revenue-sharing estimates (Long, 1980) and by studies of change in counties of employment of workers active in the labor force (Wardwell and Gilchrist, 1980). Continued monitoring of county net migration data on a year-by-year basis showed that the new trends were holding up through the decade (Beale, 1978) with enough reliability to assure that the 1980 census would show the growth patterns that had not been visible in 1970.

Beale's initial findings were greeted with skepticism. As this skepticism gave way to acceptance, rural sociologists, demographers, and economists began to gather the primary data necessary to understand why the turnaround had taken place and why it had occurred when it did. The near-simultaneity of its appearance in several different societies made this question of timing all the more important. In the 1980s, many issues remain to be answered; four of them are described below.

RESEARCH ISSUES

Migration Models

The ability to determine why past models failed to anticipate the turnaround and to implement the necessary modifications of these models to improve forecasting is the single most pressing research issue posed by the migration reversal. The dominant models of population distribution in the 1960s and early 1970s were unanimous in forecasting continuing concentration of the national population into metro areas of increasing size. Metropolitanization and suburbanization were thought to be the certain future of the United States and other highly urban-industrial nations. Without exception, these models failed to anticipate the shift of population from large metro areas to smaller metro centers and rural areas.

Some valuable insights have already been gained in the few years since Calvin Beale first brought irrefutable evidence of the turnaround to light. Earlier models gave insufficient attention to the ways in which migration decisions were influenced by other changes known to be taking place in American society. For example, nonmetro counties experienced employment and income growth that brought them closer to the levels of metro areas. Economic differentials between places have historically been among the most reliable predictors of migration. As the economic gap narrows, other considerations related to the quality of living could become an influential factor in where an individual or household would decide to live and work. Similarly, once incomes reach a certain level, additional income gains frequently become less important. Faced with a choice between an income gain with continued residence in a large city and a smaller gain or no gain at all with residence in a smaller place, many migrants could afford to make the latter choice. Thus, the net direction of population movement could even run counter to the net direction of economic benefits. Considerations of environmental quality, recreational opportunities, or a quiet, countrified lifestyle could compensate for income sacrificed (Stevens, 1980; Zelinsky, 1978).

We need to know more about how these individual and family decision-making processes operate and how best to integrate them with the structural models that have traditionally dominated migration theory. The predictive and explanatory utility of models based on documentary data sources has diminished. These sources include the census, current population surveys, annual county net migration estimates, and surveys of business and employee income and location. Primary data collection efforts by scientists have increased as the limitations of these traditional data sources have been recognized. Surveys of migrants and nonmigrants that allow for a wider range of factors in choosing destinations have been and continue to be conducted (see, for example, Carpenter, 1977; Dailey and Campbell, 1980; DeJong and Keppel, 1979; Ploch, 1980; Stinner and Toney, 1980; and Voss and Fuguitt, 1979).

In order to integrate results of these surveys with traditional models of migration, it is necessary to identify conditions under which noneconomic considerations can complement economic determinants of migration. Analyses of migration patterns by income levels, age and family composition, career stage, and prior residence can contribute to this identification, as can residential preference questions that include specified preference-income tradeoffs. Carpenter (1977) has made a start in refining the question. It is also necessary, as Zuiches discusses in Chapter 24, to identify conditions under which preferences are reliable predictors of later migration behavior.

Monitoring Local Population Change

Better monitoring of population movements can be achieved by developing a catalog of data sources that identifies what information is available at various levels and what questions can be addressed with the contents of these data sources. The speed of societal change and the lag in detecting it have been vividly demonstrated in rural areas that experienced the unexpected growth of the 1970s. As the geographic area of interest becomes smaller, less information is available on an annual basis. The census provides a snapshot of the demographic and socioeconomic conditions in all areas only every ten years. Incorporated localities conduct intermediate censuses to estimate population and per capita income for revenue-sharing purposes. Counties receive annual estimates of population change from births and deaths and estimated net migration; counties also are provided annual employment and income data. Larger units–states, regions, and the nation–enjoy a greater wealth of information between censuses through current population surveys and other administrative and statistical information-gathering programs. But in local communities it remains very difficult to obtain the information needed to reach timely and accurate diagnoses of shifts in migration patterns and in the mix of population that accompanies these shifts.

Migration is affected by changes in a wider variety of conditions associated with local areas. It thus becomes difficult to forecast even short-term changes for small geographic areas. At the same time, the variety and detail of data collected in local areas by state and federal agencies have increased throughout the 1970s. With new federal mandates against initiation of additional statistical information-gathering programs, these administrative data sets must be made available for statistical analysis. As the 1980 census becomes dated and therefore less reflective of the contemporary populations in small places, these administrative data sets can be used to complement information from the census.

Before these sources of information can be used, however, they must be identified and their availability brought to the attention of the people who can make use of them. Some sort of catalog of information should be developed, specifying the level of aggregation (i.e., community, county, state, or nation), population coverage, time series available, and any peculiar problems of definition. Means should be devised to get these information sources out of the programmatic channels within which they have been developed so that they may also be used by researchers, policy makers, and others. The recent decision to withhold funds for the development of a census survey every five years makes this need all the more pressing. Our society is changing too rapidly to permit us to stumble along with comprehensive and reliable information only once every ten years.

Community Impacts

A typology of the consequences of migration-caused community changes must be developed to organize research on local impacts of unanticipated growth. The question of impact is vastly more complex than one of population growth rate. Community adaptation to changes in population composition is frequently more difficult than adaptation to rate, or even direction, of growth. The level and mix of demands placed on the community by newly arriving households is quite different from the demands posed by population growth through high fertility. Yet very nearly the only community growth experience in recent decades has been the growth brought about by the high birth rates of the baby-boom years. While small children present special needs for health care, food, and education, these needs can to some extent be anticipated. Migrants, on the other hand, participate to varying degrees in all sectors of social, economic, and political life. They create demands for jobs, transportation, health services, entertainment, and political representation. Their children impact enrollment trends at all grade levels, and all these changes usually occur without any of the demographic advance warning that is provided by growth through high fertility.

An inventory of consequences can be developed through constructing a matrix of causes and effects cross-classified by migrant motivations and characteristics of places. Such a tool could help to systematize present knowledge and to identify research gaps. Ploch (1980) has studied the impacts of migration to rural areas in Maine on the structure of social relationships in small towns and villages. Voss and Fuguitt (1979) have analyzed migration to the Upper Great Lakes region, while Sofranko and Williams (1980) have done similar research on rural migration to the Midwest. Stinner and Toney (1980) have examined how migrant satisfaction with and assimilation into new small communities is conditioned by Mormon/non-Mormon conflict. DeJong and Keppel (1979) have also studied new residents' satisfaction with nonmetro communities in Pennsylvania. A compendium of these community studies would help to find universals in the response of local areas to migration growth.

Attention has shifted somewhat from documentation of the trends and identification of their causes toward the exploration of these community impacts. Release of data from the 1980 census will give new impetus to defining the dimensions of changes in migration patterns. However, need for intensive local area studies can only grow with this new data development, for it is at the local level that impacts must be explored. Only through the process of aggregating a number of similarly oriented local studies can the task of evaluating the meaning of the turnaround for rural areas be achieved.

The question of impact is incomplete without attention to the consequences for the large metro areas that are now experiencing loss of population and economic activity. A very slight net shift out of large urban centers produces a proportionally greater in-migration rate to the very small place that receives that movement. But both origin and destination must find institutional adaptation to sudden and unanticipated change. Large cities suffer a loss of federal revenues and political representation in addition to the constriction of the employment base. Research is needed to determine if the adjustments to population stability and decline adopted by smaller communities in the past few decades are applicable to the problems of the large metro centers that are now undergoing similar losses.

Influence of Energy

Research is needed to assess the energy dependence of current population and economic dispersal trends. The migration turnaround took place in a period when the costs of energy were low, relative to other costs. If there had been no change in energy cost and supply in the past two decades, it would be safe to forecast a continuation and even an acceleration of the nonmetro growth patterns of the 1970s. But the energy context of national population mobility changed radically at the end of that decade, and there seems little reason to believe that this change has peaked: Costs continue to rise relative to other consumption and production costs, and supply uncertainties are growing rather than declining.

The ways in which our society adapts to newly perceived energy scarcities will involve equity issues that demand a higher priority than the question of impacts on patterns of population settlement. Some of these equity issues are discussed by Clemente and Krannich in Chapter 4. But the influence of those adaptations on settlement patterns cannot be ignored if mobility is the focal point of a research or policy program. Far too little is known of energy impacts beyond the observation that they are pervasive throughout the day-to-day functioning of our society.

It is easy to identify specific types of nonmetro growth that may be halted or changed in form by increased transportation costs—long-distance recreation and some long-distance commuting, for example. It is much more difficult to systematically evaluate metro and nonmetro impacts across the spectrum of activities to determine if, for example, the trend toward convergence between the two would be affected. It is not known whether the net impact will disproportionately affect metro or nonmetro areas or even if this dichotomy is an appropriate or useful tool with which to study energy impact.

It can be argued that almost all of the reasons for the migration turnaround are significantly dependent upon cheap energy and low-cost transportation; the effects of increasing costs would then imply forces toward reconcentration at all levels of population settlement. This would slow the growth of open country and perhaps the smallest villages, and would give new growth impetus to city centers in small metro and nonmetro places and perhaps to suburbs closer to the center of large metro complexes. The center-oriented radial patterns of mass transit systems may experience renewed growth as households seek locations that provide them with alternatives to the private automobile.

On the other hand, it can be argued that the several forces that produced new population and economic dispersal are substantially stronger than increased transportation costs. Under this assumption, households and businesses would absorb the increased transportation costs by making reduced expenditures in areas that are less dependent upon energy inputs, by substituting shorter-distance travel for recreation, by arranging activities so as to make fewer trips, by developing social arrangements for car pooling for shopping, employment, and other activities, and by shifting toward greater fuel efficiency in all aspects of life.

A third view could take advantage of the smaller scale inherent in alternative energy sources and develop community-based and even neighborhood-level means of meeting energy requirements (see Chapter 5). The optimum residential densities associated with alternative, or so-called "soft," energy technologies are not the same as those associated with our dominant centralized grid systems. Residence in smaller communities can become a positive advantage under energy assumptions different from those that have guided the evolution of our current system for bringing energy sources to their end uses.

The future of nonmetro places almost certainly will develop from a mixture of these several forms of adaptation. The quality of rural living is bound to be affected by the mixture that is adopted because of one significant consideration in evaluating the impacts of increasing energy prices. The economic and personal costs of residential relocation will usually outweigh any savings that might be gained through reduced energy expenditures. It is consequently unlikely that a significant degree of relocation will take place because of energy considerations alone. Households that are residentially stable in nonmetro areas are unlikely to adopt migration as a primary response to energy costs or uncertainties. The effect on population mobility will fall disproportionately upon households that are in the process of moving or considering a move *for other reasons.* Thus, if energy changes exert a reconcentrating influence on our national population, this effect is more likely to come about through a decline in the rate of metro out-migration than through any increase in the rate of nonmetro out-migration. Migrants leaving large metro areas are more likely to take alternative transportation opportunities into account than are households that are otherwise residentially stable in either metro or nonmetro locations.

Consequently, the impacts of energy changes on the conditions of rural living are likely to be more important than the impacts of rural migration. Very little is known of the tradeoffs rural residents will implement to minimize the impact of increasing energy costs on their preferred lifestyles. The relative strengths of the values operative in energy-related consumption expenditures are not known. Regional and settlement size variations in these values and behaviors are not known. The degree of dependence of rural economies on the kinds of goods and services that rural residents will give up is not known. About all that can be said with confidence is that rural people are now in the process of adapting to these changes, and we must hurry to catch up with them and begin to understand what they are doing.

REFERENCES

Beale, Calvin L. 1975. *The Revival of Population Growth in Nonmetropolitan America.* Washington, D.C.: Economics, Statistics, and Cooperatives Service, U.S. Department of Agriculture, ERS-605.

______. 1978. "Making a living in rural and small-town America." *Rural Development Perspectives* 1 (November):1–5.

Beale, Calvin L., and Glenn V. Fuguitt. 1978. "The new pattern of nonmetropolitan population change." In Karl E. Taeuber, Larry L. Bumpass, and James A. Sweet (editors), *Social Demography.* New York: Academic Press.

Bowles, Gladys K. 1978. "Contributions of recent metro-nonmetro migrants in the nonmetro population and labor force." *Agricultural Economics Research* 30(October):15–22.

Bowles, Gladys K., and Calvin L. Beale. 1980. "Commuting and migration status in nonmetro areas." *Agricultural Economics Research* 32(July):8–20.

Carpenter, Edwin H. 1977. "The potential for population dispersal: A closer look at residential preferences." *Rural Sociology* 42(Fall):352–370.

Dailey, George H., Jr., and Rex R. Campbell. 1980. "The Ozark-Ouachita Uplands: Growth and consequences." In David L. Brown and John M. Wardwell (editors), *New Directions in Urban-Rural Migration.* New York: Academic Press.

DeJong, Gordon F., and Kenneth G. Keppel. 1979. *Urban Migrants to the Countryside.* University Park, Pennsylvania: Agricultural Experiment Station, Pennsylvania State University, Bulletin 825.

Frisbie, W. Parker, and Dudley L. Poston, Jr. 1978. *Sustenance Organization and Migration in Nonmetropolitan America.* Iowa City, Iowa: University of Iowa Press.

Hansen, Niles M. 1973. *The Future of Nonmetropolitan America: Studies in the Reversal of Rural and Small Town Population Decline.* Lexington, Massachusetts: D. C. Heath and Co.

Long, John F. 1980. *Population Deconcentration in the United States.* Washington, D.C.:

Bureau of the Census, U.S. Department of Commerce.
McCarthy, Kevin F., and Peter A. Morrison. 1979. *The Changing Demographic and Economic Structure of Nonmetropolitan Areas in the United States.* Santa Monica, California: Rand Corp., R-2399-EDA.
Ploch, Louis A. 1980. "Effects of turnaround migration on community structure in Maine." In David L. Brown and John M. Wardwell (editors), *New Directions in Urban-Rural Migration.* New York: Academic Press.
Sofranko, Andrew J., and James D. Williams (editors). 1980. *Rebirth of Rural America: Rural Migration in the Midwest.* Ames, Iowa: North Central Regional Center for Rural Development, Iowa State University.
Stevens, Joe B. 1980. "The demand for public goods as a factor in the nonmetropolitan migration turnaround." In David L. Brown and John M. Wardwell (editors), *New Directions in Urban-Rural Migration.* New York: Academic Press.
Stinner, William F., and Michael B. Toney. 1980. "Migrant/native differences in social background and community satisfaction in nonmetropolitan Utah communities." In David L. Brown and John M. Wardwell (editors), *New Directions in Urban-Rural Migration.* New York: Academic Press.
Tucker, C. Jack. 1976. "Changing patterns of migration between metropolitan and nonmetropolitan areas in the United States." *Demography* 13(November):435–443.
Vining, Daniel R., Jr., and Thomas Kontuly. 1978. "Population dispersal from major metropolitan regions: An international comparison." *International Regional Science Review* 3(1):49–73.
Voss, Paul R., and Glenn V. Fuguitt. 1979. *Turnaround Migration in the Upper Great Lakes Region.* Madison, Wisconsin: Cooperative Extension Service, University of Wisconsin, Population Series 70-12.
Wardwell, John M. 1980. "Toward a theory of urban-rural migration in the developed world." In David L. Brown and John M. Wardwell (editors), *New Directions in Urban-Rural Migration.* New York: Academic Press.
Wardwell, John M., and C. Jack Gilchrist. 1980. "Employment deconcentration in the metropolitan migration turnaround." *Demography* 17(May):145–158.
Zelinsky, Wilbur. 1978. "Is nonmetropolitan America being repopulated?" *Demography* 15(February):12–39.
Zuiches, James J., and Jon H. Rieger. 1978. "Size-of-place preferences and life cycle migration: A cohort comparison." *Rural Sociology* 43(Winter):618–633.

4
Energy

FRANK A. CLEMENTE
RICHARD S. KRANNICH

During the 1970s, no issue commanded as much public attention as the "energy crisis." From the oil embargo in 1973 to the Three Mile Island incident in 1979, policy discussions over energy issues straddled the decade. And if the 1970s witnessed the emergence of energy as a full-fledged international policy problem, the 1980s will witness the necessity for even more difficult public and private decisions regarding the interface between energy and society.

Much of the rural economy and most rural services are predicated on the assumption of relatively cheap and available energy. Until recently, both social scientists and policy makers concerned with future trends in rural society have assumed that people, goods, and services will continue to be highly mobile throughout rural areas. Yet, as the supply of energy is constrained and costs rapidly increase, reverberations are felt throughout rural life. People are forced to change their lifestyles, consider moving to other areas, and forego certain modes of social and familial interaction. Educators, health officials, and other policy makers are faced with an infrastructure which has become increasingly centralized and vulnerable to energy problems. Industrial planners are forced to reconsider rural plant locations as the cost and reliability of transportation become increasingly problematic.

Frank A. Clemente is a professor in the Department of Sociology at Pennsylvania State University, University Park, Pennsylvania. He has written widely on energy and development and was editor for "The New Rural America," an issue of the *Annals of the American Academy of Political and Social Science.* **Richard S. Krannich** is an assistant professor in the Department of Sociology, Utah State University, Logan, Utah. He has published several

In essence, rural policy analysts and decision makers are now witnessing a confrontation between the promises of the 1970s and the realities of the 1980s. During the 1970s the promise of "rural development" appeared finally to be reaching a certain level of attainment. Population turnaround had begun and rural industrial development was becoming significantly more widespread. However, this promise of the 1970s has been seriously jeopardized by the harsh energy realities of the 1980s. The specter of inadequate supplies of energy casts a cloud of uncertainty over the socioeconomic future of many rural communities. Policy makers concerned with this future will be forced to reach a compromise between their image of what rural society should look like and what locally uncontrollable energy problems will allow it to be.

Although energy prices and supplies affect everyone, rural communities especially have become highly dependent upon the availability of relatively low-cost energy, a fact reflected in the economies and living styles of modern Western societies (Anderson, 1976). While rural areas share with all of society a vulnerability to energy constraints that may impose limits on long-term growth and expansion, they also are confronted by conditions that may make them especially vulnerable to declining energy supplies. Distance, once the major limiting factor in the development of rural America, has been bridged in this century as a result of advances in energy-using transportation technology. Encouraged by continuing improvements in transportation, many rural services have been consolidated to the point that travel is not discretionary. It has become essential for working, shopping, going to school, and seeing a doctor. The transportation system is overwhelmingly the individual private automobile.

Two important policy questions relating to energy in rural society will prevail in the 1980s. The first question is the *availability* of adequate energy supplies. How much and what type of energy will be available? How can supplies be fairly allocated? What types of energy development can be most effectively pursued at the least social cost? These are the kinds of questions policy makers for rural areas must be prepared to address if a stable socioeconomic condition is to be maintained in rural areas.

Second, the *cost* of available energy is almost certain to become a major constraint upon many policy decisions in rural areas. The cost of energy

---

journal articles on energy and development.

Research for this chapter was funded in part by the Rockefeller Foundation, through Grant Number RF-TPSU-JB-76049-83. Marvin Olsen and three unidentified reviewers made many helpful comments on an earlier version.

will constrict the range of choices for many–in transportation, housing, industrial locations, and public services.

CURRENT KNOWLEDGE

Energy has not received broad attention in rural sociology–or in any other social science for that matter. Until the 1970s, energy was increasingly available at a reasonable cost and was therefore a generally neglected research and policy issue.

In the 1970s, however, the energy crisis began attracting the attention of rural sociologists and a fugitive literature developed from foundation studies, university reports, and presented papers. Thus, the state of knowledge expanded as energy problems and their implications for rural life became more apparent. More recently, articles dealing with energy issues have begun to appear with some regularity in *Rural Sociology* and other social science journals. It is important to note, however, that with few exceptions (e.g., Buttel and Larson, 1979), this literature has focused on social and demographic consequences of large-scale rural industrialization in the form of energy development projects (e.g., Murdock and Schriner, 1978; Cortese and Jones, 1977; Freudenburg, 1976). Thus, despite the rapid expansion of energy-related research, the current state of knowledge pertaining to the consequences of energy restrictions, developments, and policy alternatives for rural society remains extremely limited.

RESEARCH ISSUES

Nearly two-thirds of the chapters in this book explicitly discuss energy-related research needs. Therefore, we have endeavored to bring into specific focus in this chapter general research issues, some elements of which are developed in considerable detail from the vantage point of another topic in a chapter that follows.

Demographic Trends

In Chapter 3, Wardwell discussed the energy dependence of the revival of population growth in nonmetropolitan America. This topic is also discussed from a rural employment perspective by Tweeten in Chapter 17. Another aspect of this topic stems from a consideration of the manner in which cheap energy has reduced the friction of space, a condition that may now be reversed.

In our view, the 1980s may well be characterized by a second turnaround, with a resumption of migration flows out of rural areas toward metropolitan and urban areas. Even within nonmetro areas, these same forces may contribute to concentrations of dispersed population into small urban places and rural trade centers. The role of small towns and cities in nonmetro America would be significantly altered under such conditions. Smaller-scale, localized "hinterlands" may emerge around the more accessible rural area trade and service centers. Patterns of dominance of distant and increasingly inaccessible metro centers may be reduced with a greater emphasis on local rather than regional or national linkages and markets.

In essence, such potential trends suggest a pattern of population concentration consistent with the objectives of "growth center" components. Under energy shortage conditions, it may well be that many small, dispersed communities will give way to a more limited number of larger, more viable centers providing centralized organization and services for the surrounding rural area. In the 1980s, *researchers need to investigate the socioeconomic viability and desirability of less dispersed rural settlement patterns.*

Industrial Location

The development of industry and other commercial activities in rural areas, considered by Summers in Chapter 16, has long been a policy goal of numerous federal, state, and local programs, including the Rural Development Act of 1972 and the Carter administration's *Small Community and Rural Development Policy* (Carter Administration, 1979). Over fifteen thousand development organizations throughout the United States, including many in rural areas, are actively attempting to encourage local industrial and business expansion.

During the 1970s, nonmetro employment in manufacturing and other industries grew at a rate far exceeding that of metro America, suggesting that the "industrial invasion" of nonmetro America was continuing unabated (Summers, et al., 1976). Whether due to local promotional efforts or to other determinants of industrial and business location, such trends are consistent with policy that focuses on enhanced economic opportunities and development in rural communities. However, the declining availability and rising costs of conventional energy may restrict the movement of industry and other commercial enterprise into rural areas. Increased transportation costs may make decentralized locations prohibitive for some industries. Also, a more restricted commuting field and possible trends toward population concentration may force some businesses to seek more central locations in order to assure an adequate labor supply and a sufficient market. *Research is needed to explore the effect of energy constraints on industrial location patterns and the corresponding availability of nonagricultural employment opportunities in rural areas.*

Rural Service Provision

Among the most persistent problems facing rural America is a relatively inadequate service infrastructure to meet health care needs and provide services to persons who are disadvantaged or otherwise in need of special services and programs. On a per capita basis, rural areas have far fewer physicians, dentists, nurses, and other health care providers than urban areas, despite a higher incidence of illness, disease, and other health problems. Many rural residents are elderly or poor, compounding the need for health care as well as other social services.

To an extreme, rural residents are dependent on individual private transportation to provide access to both jobs and services, for public transportation is virtually nonexistent in most rural areas. Energy restrictions may significantly reduce the mobility of many rural residents and thus their access to services that are often available only in larger communities. Energy constraints will also increasingly restrict group service delivery organizations, such as "Meals-on-Wheels" programs for the handicapped and elderly, group transportation programs for medical treatment, shopping, and recreation, and similar service provision programs. In the 1980s, *researchers must assess: (1) the existing service needs and capabilities of rural areas; (2) the effects of energy shortages and rising energy costs on residents' access to nonlocal services, and the viability of dispersed service provision systems; and (3) the potential for alternative strategies to enhance the availability of special services and programs for rural residents.*

Impacts on Agriculture

Modern commercialized agriculture requires substantial energy resources for the operation of mechanized equipment such as tractors, milking machines, and heating and cooling equipment. Production of pesticides and fertilizers also requires extensive energy use. The historic trend toward larger farms and corporate agriculture has resulted in increasingly energy-intensive farming practices (see Buttel and Larson, 1979). Modern agriculture, like other capital-intensive industries, is highly vulnerable to potential energy shortages and cost increases.

In the short term, energy constraints could result in reduced agricultural production. Some operators might quit farming altogether, others might shift their production to less energy-intensive crops, others might join the growing number of part-time farmers. Over the long term, the energy-intensive character of large-scale commercial farming may encourage a reversal of current trends and a shift back toward smaller, family-operated farms, coupled with less energy-intensive agricultural practices. However, given the high costs of initiating a viable farming operation, such a reversal would probably be slow if not altogether improbable. Such a reversal would require the development of policies and programs that encourage such changes rather than supporting large, energy-intensive agricultural units.

An additional effect of restricted supplies of conventional energy sources could be the development of an energy-producing agricultural industry. Technologies that convert biomass to methane or alcohol fuels could lead to a new and rapidly expanding form of agriculture focused on cultivation of "energy crops." Of course, large-sale application of such technologies would appear reasonable only if a net increase in energy resulted, rather than simply an energy-consumptive conversion process. Other alternative technologies, such as extensive solar collector facilities in rural areas, could also affect the nature of agriculture by preempting or modifying certain types of agricultural land uses. In the 1980s, *research is needed that addresses the effects of energy constraints and alternative energy production options on agricultural productivity, farm tenure trends, cultivation practices, and production costs.*

Quality-of-Life and Equity Issues

As a result of energy restrictions, some rural areas may experience a decline similar to that which occurred between 1940 and 1970. High rates of unemployment and underemployment, deteriorated community life, declining service availability, and general economic underdevelopment could combine with out-migration to result in a self-perpetuating spiral of rural stagnation and decline. Changes in population, employment, income, service provision, and other indicators of material well-being comprise major components in most quality-of-life measures. In a society highly dependent on energy use, a scenario of future energy shortages would suggest corresponding declines in the general quality of life. Such consequences become more probable in the absence of policies and programs that encourage development of nonconventional energy systems. It has also been suggested that energy depletion might necessitate a shift toward a steady-state society, which, though radically different from the present "growth society," could present opportunities for enhanced human welfare, greater equality, and a generally improved quality of life (see Anderson, 1976).

While energy scarcity may exert major effects on all members of society, existing inequities would place a greater share of the burden on some segments of the population who are at a competitive disadvantage. Among the rural population, we would expect elderly, poor, unemployed, and undertrained people to experience the greatest difficulties. Such people are less able to move freely toward areas of enhanced life chances and less likely to share in advantages that may accrue to others in a given area. They are less able to absorb added energy costs, yet are highly dependent on the mobility that energy provides to satisfy basic life needs.

Unless a shortage of energy supplies can be avoided or counteracted, residents of rural America may once again be described as the "people left behind." In the 1980s, *researchers should consider the possible effects of shortages, energy allocation policies, and alternative production options on various quality-of-life indicators in rural America, focusing particularly on the potential for such issues to either reduce or exacerbate inequities that presently confront many rural residents.*

Impediments to Conservation in Rural Areas

In order to prevent widespread social and economic disruptions that may accompany energy shortages and rapidly escalating energy costs, it will be necessary to enhance energy supplies, both by encouraging expanded production of conventional energy resources and by developing alternatives. Alternatively, it is often stated that energy conservation represents one of the best means of ensuring an adequate energy supply. While this observation has a certain legitimacy, there are several important impediments to effective energy conservation, particularly in rural areas.

First, the housing in rural areas is to a large extent old and substandard in terms of energy efficiency. Moreover, many rural homes rely on fuel oil or propane for heating, both of which are delivered by truck and therefore are inefficient from a delivery standpoint. In order to facilitate energy conservation in rural areas, extensive resources in the form of home improvement and construction grants and subsidies might be required to provide improved insulation, efficient heating, on-site alternative energy-producing facilities, and reduced home energy consumption.

Second, some rural citizens commute long distances to secure employment and obtain consumer goods and services. To a degree, this source of energy inefficiency may be alleviated by programs that encourage car pooling and rural mass transportation. A more effective resolution might include provision of employment opportunities and services in growth centers more accessible to more rural residents.

A third impediment to rural energy conservation involves the aforementioned trend toward increasingly energy-intensive agriculture. Other impediments include attitudinal and behavioral patterns that influence the reluctance of residents to adopt energy conservation practices or invest in energy efficiency. Unless these and other obstacles are overcome, the immediate role of energy conservation as a means of buffering the effects of energy shortages on rural society will be limited at best.

Over the long run, however, restricted energy availability will necessitate the active pursuit of effective conservation measures. In order to facilitate an orderly and minimally disruptive transition to an energy-conserving society, *researchers in the 1980s need to consider characteristics of rural society that impede energy conservation. They also need to identify and evaluate policy alternatives that might encourage conservation while diluting the painful social adjustments that may accompany such practices.*

Costs and Benefits of Energy Development

One reaction to energy supply shortages will be the more rapid development of energy resources in our society. Such energy development has particularly important implications for rural areas. Whether the energy resource to be exploited is coal, oil shale, synthetic fuels, or a nuclear, coal, or hydroelectric power plant, it is generally safe to assume that both energy production facilities and waste storage depositories will be located in rural areas, and that such developments will be of increasingly large scale (Santini, et al., 1979).

Thus, rural areas are and will continue to be required to bear the environmental, economic, and social burdens of energy development and, in many cases, may receive relatively few of the benefits which derive from such large-scale developments (see Murdock and Schriner, 1978; and Krannich, 1979). In terms of taxes, for example, some states have dispersion programs that return virtually nothing to communities that serve as host for a power plant or mine. Other states allow local taxing authorities to reap what amounts to a "tax bonanza" from energy development. Even then, tax revenues may appear long after the area has encountered increased demands for public services and has expended considerable front-end resources in attempting to expand what may already be an inadequate infrastructure.

Local support for energy development may exist primarily as a result of expectations of enhanced employment opportunities and general economic progress. However, a mismatch between rural labor force characteristics and energy development demands may at times result in limited employment benefits for area residents (Little and Lovejoy, 1979) despite the fact that many rural residents suffer from unemployment or underemployment. Particularly in relatively isolated energy development locales, the inadequate supply of a local skilled labor force generally results in an influx of construction and support workers, which may lead to a boom growth situation. Unless properly managed, such rapid growth may overwhelm the capacity of the local service infrastructure, transform the social structure of the host community, replace traditional cultural elements, and give rise to a host of accompanying social problems (Cortese and Jones, 1977).

Despite these potential problems, energy developments generally can be expected to contribute diverse economic benefits to the host community (Murdock and Schriner, 1978). A leakage of economic benefits out of the development locale, however, will reduce the ability of rural areas to capitalize on energy developments as a means of improving local conditions (Clemente, 1975). Thus, while energy development appears to hold some potential as a rural development mechanism, in at least some instances rural host communities are forced to bear environmental and social costs while the benefits of enhanced energy supplies are transported to distant population centers. In the 1980s, *research is sorely needed regarding the consequences of energy development in rural areas and the types of impact mitigation strategies that could best enable rural communities to maximize the benefits of development, to minimize adverse effects, and to reduce disparities inherent in the allocation of energy development costs and benefits.*

REFERENCES

Anderson, Charles H. 1976. *The Sociology of Survival: Social Problems of Growth.* Homewood, Illinois: Dorsey Press.

Buttel, Frederick H., and Oscar W. Larson, III. 1979. "Farm size, structure, and energy intensity: An ecological analysis of U.S. agriculture." *Rural Sociology* 44(Fall):471–488.

Carter Administration. 1979. *Small Community and Rural Development Policy.* Washington, D.C.: The White House.

Clemente, Frank. 1975. "What industry really means to a small town." *Farm Economics* (April). University Park, Pennsylvania: Pennsylvania State University and United States Department of Agriculture.

Cortese, Charles F., and Bernie Jones. 1977. "The sociological analysis of boomtowns." *Western Sociological Review* 8(1):76–90.

Freudenburg, William R. 1976. "The social impact of energy boom development on rural communities: A review of literatures and some predictions." Paper presented at the annual meetings of the American Sociological Association, New York.

Krannich, Richard S. 1979. "A comparative analysis of factors influencing the socioeconomic impacts of electric-generating facilities." *Socio-Economic Planning Sciences* 13:41–46.

Little, Ronald L., and Stephen B. Lovejoy. 1979. "Energy development and local employment." *The Social Science Journal* 6(April):27–49.

Murdock, Steven H., and Eldon C. Schriner. 1978. "Structural and distributional factors in community development: A comparative analysis of evidence from four western states." *Rural Sociology* 43:426–449.

Santini, Danilo, David South, and Erik Stenehjem. 1979. *Evidence of Future Increases in the Impact of Conventional Electrical Facilities on Rural Communities.* Argonne, Illinois: Argonne National Laboratory.

Summers, Gene F., Sharon D. Evans, Frank Clemente, E. M. Beck, and Jon Minkoff. 1976. *Industrial Invasion of Nonmetropolitan America.* New York: Praeger Publishers.

5
Appropriate Technology

DORA G. LODWICK
DENTON E. MORRISON

Modern technology has traditionally been seen as the driving force behind economic growth and prosperity. Capital-intensive, complex, and petroleum-based, this technology has created the large-scale, highly specialized farms that have become the hallmark of U.S. agriculture (Hoffman, 1970). The result has been a high quality of life for most Americans.

During the last decade, these technologies have been criticized increasingly as inappropriate because of negative impacts on the quality of rural life. For instance, the increasing scale of farming operations has sharply reduced the opportunities for entrance into agriculture as an occupation (Rodefeld et al., 1978). Technology has also reduced the number and vitality of rural service centers (Whiting, 1974). Critics have suggested that a more appropriate technology is needed.

Conflict surrounds the appropriate technology issue (Rybczynski, 1980; Lovins, 1976, 1977; Nash, 1979; Stiefel, 1979). The basic argument is over the relationships between the level of economic development and the quality of life. "Growthists" advocate greater economic growth through capital and energy intensification of technology. The appropriate technology advocates claim that we have reached a point of diminishing, even negative, returns as shown in Figure 5.1. Several ques-

Dora G. Lodwick is a doctoral candidate in the Department of Sociology, Michigan State University, East Lansing, Michigan. She is the coauthor of a recent article on the social impacts of alternative energy systems. **Denton E. Morrison** is a professor in the Department of Sociology, Michigan State University, East Lansing, Michigan. A past fellow at the Woodrow Wilson International Center for Scholars, he has published numerous articles on environmental issues and appropriate technology.

FIGURE 5.1 Conflicting Growthist and Appropriate Technology Perspectives on the Relationship of Level of Economic Development and Quality of Life.

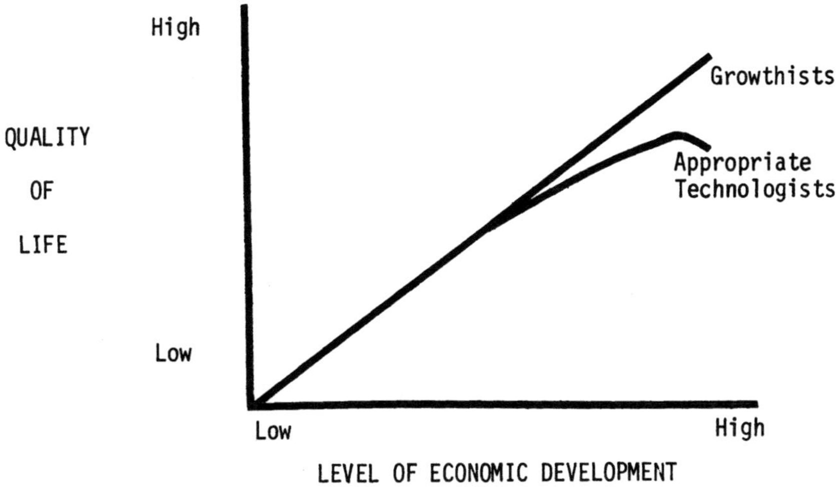

Source: Morrison, Denton E. 1978. "Equity impacts of some major energy alternatives." In Seymour Warkov (editor), Energy Policy in the United States: Social and Behavioral Dimensions. New York: Praeger Publishers. Page 183.

tions generated by this conflict are addressed in this chapter: What are the issues in this debate? What is the relevance of appropriate technology to rural America? How can rural sociological research help inform policy on appropriate technology?

THE APPROPRIATE TECHNOLOGY PROPOSAL

The appropriate technology idea became known in industrialized countries through E. F. Schumacher's seminal book, *Small is Beautiful: Economics as if People Mattered* (1973). It was developed to address the failure of Western technology transfer to reduce poverty in nonindustrialized countries. Equity was an early emphasis. An environmental

---

This is Michigan Agricultural Experiment Station Journal Article Number 9649. We wish to acknowledge the helpful comments made by Christopher Vanderpool, Craig Harris, Thomas Dietz, and Michael Price on an earlier draft.

emphasis was grafted to it by Amory Lovins (1976, 1977, 1978) with a focus on energy. Lovins argued that energy, environmental, and other societal problems have a common source in hard (i.e., large-scale and centralized) energy technologies that use nonrenewable fuels (e.g., nuclear) and are controlled by society's elites. The solution to these problems is found in soft (i.e., small-scale) technologies that use renewable energy sources (e.g., dispersed solar) and are governed by the ultimate consumers.

"Appropriate technology" is a broad political-economic critique and proposal for a fundamental revision of the sociotechnical systems of industrialized nations. Lovin's critique can be summarized as follows: Means of production that are capital-intensive, complex, large-scale, centralized, resource-intensive, resource depleting, and dependent on nonlocal resources have undesirable social impacts. These scientific-industrial technologies displace people from jobs and alienate them from society. Those who remain employed are alienated from their work. The result is overabundance for a few and deprivation of the masses. Society's social units become highly interdependent and therefore vulnerable to external events beyond their control. The technologies are environmentally destructive and ultimately destroy the affluent lifestyle they created. Judged on the basis of social equity, humane values, and ecological sustainability, they must be considered inappropriate.

Systems that are small-scale, decentralized, resource conserving, and that use local and renewable resources are considered appropriate because of desirable social impacts. These technologies create meaningful work (particularly for less skilled workers), supply basic needs, allow self-sufficiency, and create an ecologically sustainable and higher quality of life.

Thus, the *social* impacts of technology are central in the critique of appropriate technology advocates. Table 5.1 summarizes the current dialogue between appropriate technology advocates and the defenders of the dominant scientific-industrial technologies.

RELEVANCE OF APPROPRIATE TECHNOLOGY TO RURAL UNITED STATES

Rural life in the United States has changed markedly toward the following characteristics criticized by appropriate technology advocates:

- increased scale of machinery and scale of operations in farming, forestry, mining, and fishing
- increased capital requirements, with technology and energy substituting for labor

- increased complexity
- increased specialization in maintenance, manufacture, and operation
- increased centralization of ownership and control
- increased interdependence with the larger society and increased dependence on nonlocal, including foreign, resources

Some of the many negative impacts that have been attributed to these sociotechnical changes in the rural areas are:

- reduced rural, and especially farming, populations
- reduced viability of rural service centers and their economic, political, educational, health, religious, and other institutions
- centralization of services and institutions in large centers
- decreased participation of individuals in decisions affecting their fate
- persistence of rural poverty and unemployment
- prosperity and power for the few who own and control production technologies
- deterioration of land, air, and water quality as a result of farming, waste disposal, forestry, and mining practices
- increased alienation and vulnerability of rural people[1]

Do these negative impacts imply, as some claim, that the solution is to move back to small, self-sufficient farms that depend mostly on the physical labor of the family owner-operators instead of huge, expensive, petroleum-driven machinery? Do these impacts also imply that we must strive for a massive decentralization of the population and revitalization of small towns?

Advocates of appropriate technology answer these questions in different ways. Some advocate the total transformation of society (Satin, 1978; Hess, 1979). The majority, however, are moderates. They recognize that the technological types are not pure, but exist in a mixture of complex, interacting characteristics. The moderates realize that even a modest move toward appropriate technology will require important tradeoffs that result in risks and uncertainties.

In suggesting the need for changes, the moderate advocates of appropriate technology cite such studies as those by Goldschmidt (1978), which documented greater involvement, satisfaction, and higher quality of life among people who live in small-scale sociotechnical systems. Additionally, McDonald (1975) indicates that important economic efficiencies are gained for many crops through small-scale agriculture. The moderate appropriate technology advocates are interested in the specific

Table 5.1 A Comparison of Characteristics and Critiques of Appropriate Technology (AT) and Hard Technology (HT)

The Appropriate Technology Characterization and Critique of Hard Technology	The Appropriate Technology Proposal	The Hard Technology Rationale for Itself and Its Reaction to the Appropriate Technology Proposal
1. Capital intensity of HT makes it unaffordable except by an economic elite.	1. AT is affordable technology for nonelites.	1. Modern HT is expensive but also efficient and productive. AT is second-rate, inefficient, and unproductive.
2. HT involves highly concentrated capital organized in economic monocultures controlled by and benefiting mainly an elite.	2. AT is distributed capital, organized through small entrepreneurships, benefiting many social groups.	2. Concentrated capital and associated HT scale are economic imperatives of productive industry. AT brings cottage industry, craft economy, and associated low productivity and low incomes.
3. Large-scale economic organization of HT brings human and environmental costs that completely offset productivity benefits.	3. Small-scale economic organization of AT is ecologically safe, simple, sophisticated--thus promoting human and environmental benefits. "Small is beautiful."	3. Efficiency characteristics and productivity benefits of economies of large scale clearly outweigh costs. AT is romantic, risky; small is pitiful.
4. HT systems involve centralized, authoritarian decision making in which ordinary people have no control over their fate.	4. AT systems are decentralized and promote democratized decision making for production; is locally controlled by the users of the technology.	4. Rational, scientific economic planning and management requires expert, centralized decision making and control. AT is economic chaos.
5. Centralized innovation by experts creates an elite; "trickle-down" of benefits tends not to reach the poor while culturally disruptive costs do.	5. Local innovation, development, and "bottom-out" diffusion of technologies related to basic needs guarantees compatibility with local cultures and benefits reach the poor.	5. Rationally programmed R & D by experts, backed by basic science, has demonstrated productive merits. AT is haphazard, "tinker-tech."
6. Automated, large-scale HT displaces people, especially underdogs, from jobs and is exploitive and dehumanizing for the employed.	6. Labor-intensive technology provides meaningful jobs--especially for low-skilled workers.	6. HT is labor saving. AT is backward, back breaking.

7. Specialization around HT separates, isolates, and alienates. The resulting "interdependence" is in fact hierarchical and adversarial dependence.	7. AT reduces segmentation of work roles, allowing low and fluid division of labor with little stratification in work organization. The nonadversarial relations of production allow freedom, openness, and self-fulfillment in work.	7. Specialization is the foundation of efficiency and productivity since workers organize to improve their situation and conflicts are minimized through institutionalized labor/management relations. Nonspecialization around AT guarantees inefficiency and low productivity.
8. Work in HT society is for greeds, not needs, i.e. consumer "demands" are artificially created to sustain "growth" in the economy. Such growth involves complex, fragile interdependencies.	8. The local production of AT sustains local basic needs, emphasizing quality-of-life, not economic, growth.	8. Only through demands for goods created in affluent, developed sectors will jobs be created and basic needs satisfied in the poorer sectors. Economic growth benefits all. AT involves leveling at an unacceptably low level.
9. HT creates simultaneous consumer affluence for a few and high unemployment.	9. AT promotes full employment, moderate levels of living, and minimal income differences.	9. Affluence is intrinsically good and provides surplus for meeting basic needs of even the unemployed. Full employment at a subsistence level with AT has no intrinsic merit.
10. HT wastes, depletes, and denigrates natural resources, creating dangerous environmental pollution. HT creates competition for increasingly scarce resources and the associated means for destruction via weaponry.	10. AT's sparing use of indigenous natural resources, especially nonrenewable ones, reduces the potential of conflicts over scarcities and preserves environmental quality.	10. Rational management, development, and utilization of natural resources brings sustained productivity. The "limited good" mentality of AT means economic underdevelopment and stagnation. Only <u>more</u> HT can preserve environmental quality or security.
11. HT moves society toward large, highly centralized, urbanized communities that are crowded, interdependent, vulnerable; the countryside is depopulated.	11. Decentralized, small, self-sufficient communities where production and consumption are integrated around basic needs provision through AT reduces vulnerability to outside actors and increases social resiliency.	11. Concentrated populations have well-known advantages in increasing the levels of economic, social, and cultural amenities. The AT notion of community self-sufficiency is romantic; rural communities are inevitably backward, isolated, and poor.

Source: Morrison, Denton E. 1980. "The soft cutting edge of environmentalism: Why and how the AT notion is changing the movement." In Robert G. Mitchell (editor), <u>Natural Resources Journal</u> 20(2, April):275-298, pages 290-291.

impacts of appropriate technologies on rural people. They realize that practical economic problems will be the driving force shaping the decisions of rural citizens to opt for appropriate technologies. Further, they see appropriate energy technologies as an important part of the answer to the current petroleum-based economic squeeze. Rural Americans, especially those on farms, use more energy per capita than other Americans. They are especially dependent on liquid fuels, which are the most costly and in shortest supply (Perelman, 1972). They also have strong economic incentives to seek energy alternatives because their incomes are lower than those of other citizens.

In addition, rural America's dispersed, small-scale social units are well suited for implementing appropriate technologies. Rural people have a wealth of do-it-yourself skills and practical ingenuity. Generous supplies of wood, land, sunshine, wind, water, tools, and other materials also exist. Thus, appropriate energy technologies, such as the following, are seen as promising:

- solar space-heating of agricultural buildings (e.g., animal shelters)
- solar grain-drying
- solar water-heating for food processing (e.g., dairy operations)
- solar space-heating and water-heating of residences, businesses, schools, churches, and hospitals
- space-heating and water-heating from wood
- burning of agricultural or municipal wastes to generate electricity
- biogas from manure and other agricultural residues
- use of municipal sludge for fertilizer on forests, crops, and pastures
- wind power for electricity, pumping, and other mechanical needs
- small-scale hydroelectric generation from streams and rivers
- aquaculture integrated to utilize solar heating and wind pumping
- district heating from local industries and utilities
- organic substitutes for fossil fuel-based fertilizers and agricultural chemicals
- pedal power for small-scale grinding, plowing, and pumping
- underground living shelters

RESEARCH ISSUES

Rural sociological research can inform policy on appropriate technology by determining: (1) to what extent, at what rate, and under what conditions life in rural America improves as a result of a change to appropriate technologies; (2) what functions (e.g., agriculture, shelter, transportation) are best performed by appropriate technologies; and (3) for which group of people (e.g., small farmers, larger farmers, minorities, the elderly) do the life conditions in rural America improve as a result of a change to appropriate technologies?

Because the concept of appropriate technology is quite new, there is very little research on it. There is much advocacy and theory, compiled descriptions of hardware, encouraging anecdotes, and action programs.[2] However, there is very little scientific examination of the social dimensions of appropriate technology. Many experiments with technologies like the examples listed above will continue to develop. Informed debate and decision making on technological policy require that the social impacts of these technologies be examined carefully.

If small-scale and decentralized technologies do not fulfill their promise to improve rural life, there is in fact little basis for calling them more appropriate than the competing technologies. There are many renewable energy technologies, for example, that do not have the characteristics of appropriate technologies but rather share the characteristics of the currently dominant technologies. Some of these are solar power towers, wind farms, sun satellites, large-scale hydroelectricity, and large-scale gasohol. Their attractiveness will increase if the appropriate technologies fail to fulfill their promise.

Two additional research needs are to determine: (1) the financial, cultural, and institutional barriers to the invention, development, and diffusion of appropriate technologies; and (2) the policies that will reduce these barriers. Answers to these questions are important for achieving systematic deployment of appropriate technologies that would, in turn, allow their in-depth study. In particular, it will be important to do research on the means of reducing the risk to early adopters of appropriate technologies and to make possible their adoption by low-income groups (e.g., the elderly, small farmers).

Initially, social scientists must specify the appropriate technology claims in some detail in order to make them testable as hypotheses and to identify those that are not testable. This in itself will inform and sharpen policy debate. Next, concepts must be sharpened and measurement methods developed. What kinds of data will serve as indicators of notions like scale, centralization, and equity? The ambiguities of these notions must be reduced if research is to take place. Finally, the claims must be tested in careful research designs to allow maximum assurance of causality.

The debate over technological alternatives is a central social-policy struggle of our time. The social impacts are the key issue and thus the central criterion for policy decision. Therefore, it is critical to obtain a greater factual base for such policy choices. Wrong policy decisions or policy indecisions at this historical period—the worldwide energy crisis – may eventually result in irreversible trajectories and foregone opportunities.

The type of research needed will be costly and time-consuming if it is to scrutinize objectively the conflicting claims about the social impacts of alternative technologies. But this is a necessary investment to reduce the large risks inherent in policy making in the absence of such systematic information.

NOTES

1. General sources of information documenting these impacts are Ford (1978) and Rodefeld et al. (1978).

2. Among the main advocates of appropriate technology are Schumacher (1973) and Lovins (1976, 1977, 1978). Although Jequier (1976) wrote primarily for an international audience, he presents an excellent overview and some case studies of appropriate technology. Dunn (1978) and Eckhaus (1977) represent the hardware focus among appropriate technology advocates. Anecdotes and articles are reported in the publications of several groups, including the *A. T. Times* (published by the National Center for Appropriate Technology, Butte, Montana) and *Rain–Journal of Appropriate Technology* (published by a group in Seattle, Washington).

Other groups who are active appropriate technology advocates include Friends of Appropriate Technology (Washington, D.C.), The New Alchemy Institute (Woods Hole, Massachusetts), and the Ozark Institute (Eureka Springs, Arkansas). In addition many federal agencies now have appropriate technology programs (see U.S. Congress, Office of Technology Assessment, 1978), and the state of California has an Office of Appropriate Technology.

REFERENCES

Dunn, P. D. 1978. *Appropriate Technology: Technology with a Human Face.* New York: Schocken Books.

Eckhaus, Richard S. 1977. *Appropriate Technologies for Developing Countries.* Washington, D.C.: National Academy of Sciences.

Ford, Thomas R. (editor). 1978. *Rural U.S.A.: Persistence and Change.* Ames, Iowa: Iowa State University Press.

Goldschmidt, Walter. 1978. *As You Sow: Three Studies in the Social Consequences of Agribusiness.* Montclair, New Jersey: Allanheld, Osmun, and Co.

Hess, Karl. 1979. *Community Technology.* New York: Harper and Row.

Hoffman, A. C. 1970. "Trends in the food industries and their relationship to agriculture." In J. R. Brake (editor), *Emerging and Projected Trends Likely to Influence the Structure of Midwest Agriculture, 1970-1985.* Iowa City, Iowa: Agricultural Law Center, University of Iowa, Monograph 11.

Jequier, Nicolas (editor). 1976. *Appropriate Technology: Problems and Promises.* Paris, France: Development Centre, Organization for Economic Cooperation and Development.

Lovins, Amory. 1976. "Energy strategy: The road not taken?" *Foreign Affairs* 55(1, Fall): 65-96.

———. 1977. *Soft Energy Paths.* New York: Harper and Row.

———. 1978. "Soft energy technologies." In Jack M. Hollander, Melvin K. Simmons, and David O. Wood (editors), *Annual Review of Energy,* Volume 3. Palo Alto, California: Annual Reviews, Inc.

McDonald, Angus. 1975. "The family farm is the most efficient unit of production." In P. Barnes, (editor), *The People's Land.* Emmaus, Pennsylvania: Rodale Press.

Morrison, Denton E. 1978. "Equity impacts of some major energy alternatives." In Seymour Warkov (editor), *Energy Policy in the United States: Social and Behavioral Dimensions.* New York: Praeger Publishers.

Morrison, Denton E. 1980. "The soft, cutting edge of environmentalism: Why and how the AT notion is changing the movement." In Robert C. Mitchell (editor), *Natural Resources Journal* 20(2, April):275–298. Special symposium entitled "Whither environmentalism?"

Nash, Roderick. 1979. "Problems in paradise." *Environment* 20(6, July/August):25–27, 39–40.

National Center for Appropriate Technology. 1979. *Energy and the Poor: An Imperative for Action.* Butte, Montana: National Center for Appropriate Technology.

Perelman, Michael. 1972. "Farming with petroleum." *Environment* 14(8, October):8–13.

Rodefeld, Richard D., Jan Flora, Donald Voth, Isao Fujimoto, and Jim Converse (editors). 1978. *Change in Rural America: Causes, Consequences, and Alternatives.* St. Louis, Missouri: C. V. Mosby Co.

Rybczynski, Witold. 1980. *Paper Heroes: A Review of Appropriate Technology.* Garden City, New York: Anchor Press.

Satin, Mark. 1978. *New Age Politics: Healing Self and Society.* West Vancouver, British Columbia: Whitecap Books.

Schumacher, E. F. 1973. *Small is Beautiful: Economics as if People Mattered.* New York: Perennial Library.

Stiefel, Michael. 1979. "Soft and hard energy paths: The roads not taken." *Technology Review* 82(1, October):56–66.

U.S. Congress (Office of Technology Assessment). 1979. *Selected Federal Programs in AT.* Washington, D.C.: U.S. Congress.

Whiting, Larry R. (editor). 1974. *Communities Left Behind: Alternatives for Development.* Ames, Iowa: Iowa State University Press.

Part 3
THE PEOPLE

An academic colleague once asked, "What do you rural sociologists mean when you say a person is provincial?" After listening to a labored attempt at definition, he answered his own question: "In other words, you mean the people in New York City are more provincial than the people in Wahoo, Nebraska, because the people in Wahoo would have less difficulty getting along in New York City than the people of New York City would have getting along in Wahoo." He went on to explain his observation in a way that provides insight into the nature of the people of rural America. His first observation was that, because of affluence and the incorporation of most of rural America into a national consumption community, many of the residents of Wahoo had spent considerable time in New York City. His second observation was that we are all increasingly dependent on the national media for our images and self-perceptions; the media, and television in particular, have been far more accurate in portraying life in New York City and similar urban centers than they have in portraying rural America through such shows as *The Beverly Hillbillies, Mayberry RFD, Sheriff Lobo,* and *Little House on the Prairie.*

Through a variety of means, more rural people have been brought into the arena of urban America than urban people into the arena of rural America. There is no region in rural America without cosmopolitan and affluent people. Many of America's most successful citizens, from presidents of the United States to corporation executives, are either rural Americans or go out of their way to point out their natural heritage. Yet the quaint and provincial image of the people of rural America persists.

The chapters in this section are *not* focused on those affluent rural residents who, by virtue of lifestyle, patterns of consumption, and greater mobility, really belong to cosmopolitan America despite their choice of rural residence. Their lifestyle is not constrained by the adequacy or inadequacy of local services, resources, and opportunities. Theirs is a wider world. Most chapters in this sector are concerned with those who, because of a lack of personal or family resources, are limited in their life chances to what their localities can or do provide. The difference between the rural residents who are full participants in the larger society and those who are constrained by the more limited opportunities of locality is not restricted to any age group. There are some very affluent rural elderly in possession of time, experience, and financial resources who reside in the same communities where other elderly live at the margin of existence. Some rural youths will go to the best colleges and ride an easy path into the affluent society regardless of the quality of their rural education, while their classmates will consider the pros and cons of dropping out of school to go to work in a local factory. Similarly, sex is no guarantee of either opportunity or deprivation in rural communities. Rural communities, because they are small, sometimes offer greater opportunities for the female entrepreneur or manager than do urban communities. Offsetting this, however, are more traditional norms that serve to limit aspirations and curb the opportunities of many rural women simply because they are women.

The following eight chapters are less concerned with the advantaged than with the disadvantaged because, in many respects, the advantaged have the resources to go where they want in search of whatever services they desire. The resource limitations of the rural environment do not constrain them. These chapters are concerned with identifying research questions that, if resolved, would help reduce the constraints facing the rural disadvantaged.

This section begins with a look at who lives in rural America now compared to who used to live there, and contrasts the population composition with that of urban America. The theme of Chapter 6, by Johnson and Beegle, is that rural America continues to be a place of change. The demographic research issues they identify complement those identified by Wardwell.

Chapter 7, by Willits, Bealer, and Crider, is also concerned with rural/urban differences, but the primary focus of this chapter is on values and attitudes. The authors note that rural/urban differences continue to exist and call for research to better document the reasons for their existence.

The belief that rural family life is simple and free from stress is brought into question by Coward and Smith in Chapter 8. They describe special problems facing rural families and the difficulties that ruralness implies for providing needed family services.

Chapter 9, by Lee and Lassey, describes the life of the rural elderly as being both advantaged and disadvantaged. Among the research priorities they identify for the 1980s is sorting out how various segments of the elderly are affected differently by living in a rural locale. The substantial movement of early retirees into rural places, an important component of the population turnaround, gives a certain urgency to addressing some of the research issues identified in this chapter.

The research literature on rural youth produced by rural sociologists is enormous and has been quite influential in the design of programs to put opportunities for rural youth on a par with those for urban youth. In Chapter 10, Falk recognizes this contribution, which has, for the most part, focused on individual aspirations and achievements. He suggests the need for other research that focuses on whether the life chances of rural youth are being thwarted by structural characteristics of the labor market. Some penetrating questions concerning the desirability of certain types of industrialization in rural areas are posed in this chapter.

Chapter 11, by Kuvlesky and his associates, points out that minorities are as much a part of rural America as they are of urban America and are not concentrated in a single region. The need to understand their individual as well as their collective situations constitutes an important issue for the 1980s.

Chapter 12, by Haney, notes that rural women have often been researched, but most often as a factor in, for example, farm production. The lack of appropriately focused research has contributed to a substantial void in our knowledge of the total roles, activities, and concerns of rural women. Haney recommends a broad program of research.

Finally, the brief chapter on poverty by Moland and Page (Chapter 13) provides an appropriate conclusion to this section. Poverty is the result of unresolved issues covered in each of the preceding five chapters. An important part of the agenda for rural sociologists in the 1980s must be to research the people-problems covered in these chapters.

6
The Rural American People: A Look Backward and Forward

NAN E. JOHNSON
J. ALLAN BEEGLE

In order to understand the policy needs of rural Americans, it is important to consider their unique social and economic characteristics. It is also critical to understand how these characteristics have developed. In the following three sections of this chapter we portray three periods in the peopling of rural America. The historical discontinuity of some recent trends and the research issues therein raised are explored in this chapter.

THE PRIMARY SUSTENANCE PHASE: THE AGE OF THE FARMER

In 1790, 95 percent of the nearly four million residents of colonial America lived in rural settings.[1] For the next century, the rural population grew rapidly, the rate of increase generally exceeding 25 percent

---

Nan E. Johnson is an assistant professor in the Department of Sociology, Michigan State University, East Lansing, Michigan. She is the author of numerous articles pertaining to the sociology of human fertility. **J. Allan Beegle** is a professor in the Department of Sociology, Michigan State University, East Lansing, Michigan. A past president of the Rural Sociological Society, and past editor of *Rural Sociology,* he has written several rural sociology textbooks and many articles.

every ten years. High fertility was one important cause of rural population growth. The availability of low-cost farm land may have led to high fertility on the rural frontier by enhancing the economic value of children, by reducing the age at which couples could marry, and by enabling rural parents to bequeath land to their descendents (Stokes et al., 1979). In addition, since contagious diseases, the most prominent causes of death, were more quickly spread in densely settled environments, mortality rates were lower in rural places. As a result, the net rate of natural increase (the birth rate minus the death rate) was more positive in the countryside than in the city.

Nonetheless, the net migration rate (the immigration rate minus the out-migration rate) was higher for urban than for rural places during the nineteenth century. The mechanization of agriculture made farming less labor-intensive, while the growth of manufacturing drew many rural people to the city. The net rural-to-urban internal migration of young adults became the most important source of nineteenth century urban population growth (Lee, 1964). Because the effect of natural increase in rural population was tempered by net out-migration to urban places, the decade rates of rural population growth were less than urban rates during the nineteenth century, except for the 1811–1820 decade.

Net migration also produced regional differences in urban population growth. In 1790, 95 percent of the U.S. population was concentrated east of the Appalachian Mountains along the Atlantic Seaboard. The population was almost evenly divided between northern and southern states. Although urbanites were a minority in both regions, they comprised 8.1 percent of the Northeast's population and 2.1 percent of all southerners. Because the South was the region of lower urbanization, the migration of rural white Southerners to urban industrial centers produced a net flow of whites from south to north. In 1880, urbanites numbered over seven million in the Northeast and had become the majority (50.8 percent) in that region. In contrast, urbanites did not attain a majority in populations of the north-central and the western regions until 1920 (52.3 percent and 51.8 percent, respectively) or in the South until 1960 (52.7 percent). Moreover, a net interregional flow of migrants from east to west led to boomtowns. After its first appearance in the census of 1850, the West

This chapter is Michigan Agricultural Experiment Station Journal Article Number 9684. This research was supported under Projects 1062 and 3243-S, Michigan Agricultural Experiment Station, and by a grant from the U.S. Department of Agriculture to study community impacts of nonmetropolitan growth in northern Michigan. We thank Calvin Beale, Kenneth Keppel, Merwyn Nelson, and two anonymous reviewers for constructive comments on an earlier draft.

had the most rapid rate of interdecade urban population growth of all regions in the nineteenth century.

THE CENTRALIZATION PHASE: URBANIZATION, SPECIALIZATION, INDUSTRIALIZATION

A new phase in population distribution appeared in the 1880s. For the first time, the 1880 census showed that urbanites comprised a majority of the population in the Northeast. In that year, New York officially became the nation's first city of one million people.

The 1880s witnessed a change in both origin and destination of most foreign immigrants. Whereas the old immigrants (those arriving before the 1880s) had come from rural areas of northern or western Europe, the new immigrants were from rural parts of southern, eastern, or central Europe (Taeuber and Taeuber, 1958). However, since most frontier farm land had already been acquired, most new immigrants settled in the Northeast or the Midwest, where they typically took jobs in mines and factories. Because of these historic settlement patterns, the majority of family farm owners were then, as today, white Protestants of northern or western European ethnicity.

Unlike many old immigrants, the new immigrants had to undergo two simultaneous processes of assimilation: that of a foreigner to an American, and that of a rural dweller to an urbanite. These processes were rendered all the more difficult by religious differences: the old immigrants had been largely Protestants, but the new immigrants were mainly Catholics. The ethnic antagonism that arose was an important reason for several attempts to restrict further immigration from southern, eastern, or central Europe. The first was the Immigration Act of 1921, which limited the annual number of legal immigrants from a particular country to 3 percent of that nationality enumerated in the 1910 census. A more deliberate attempt was the Immigration Act of 1924, which limited the quota of legal immigrants to 2 percent of that nationality counted in the 1890 census, when the numbers declaring ancestry from southern, eastern, or central Europe were smaller than in 1910. Consequently, foreign immigration declined as a source of both rural and urban population growth (Peterson, 1961; Keely, 1974).

Because the quota laws reduced the volume of new immigrants to American cities, rural-to-urban migration was the prime source of urban population growth in the 1920s. The 1920–1921 crash in land values robbed farm families of purchasing power; in fact, the real gains in purchasing power during the 1920s were made by the top 7 percent of nonfarm families (Lindert, 1977). Increased inequality in the distribution of real income probably stimulated rural-to-urban migration of whites during that decade.

Economic subsistence could be eked out more easily on the farm than in the city, so some urbanites returned to their farm origins during the Great Depression. Reduced employment opportunities in the city also led to greater retention of potential farm out-migrants. As a result, net farm migration was approximately zero between 1930 and 1935. Much scholarly attention was then focused on this unprecedented phenomenon. However, subsequent studies showed that most urban-to-rural migrants during that period chose rural nonfarm destinations (Taeuber and Taeuber, 1958:108).

The outbreak of World War II in Europe led to military mobilization in the United States and stimulated new movement out of rural areas. Between 1940 and 1944, approximately eight million people left the farm (Beale, 1978). Further mechanization of agriculture, improvements in seeds, and use of fertilizers and pesticides added impetus to this cityward movement after the war ended. Therefore, the rural population declined from 57.5 million in 1940 to 54 million in 1950 and stabilized at that level for the next two decades. The farming element of the rural population, on the other hand, declined from 30.5 million in 1940 to 23 million in 1950 and to only 9.7 million in 1970 (Beale, 1978).

The stability in size of the total population during the 1950s and 1960s was possible only because the heavy losses to out-migration were replaced through natural increase. At the end of World War II, total fertility rates implied 2.7 live births per rural white woman and 1.8 live births per urban white woman by age 45 (Rindfuss and Sweet, 1977). However, the historic rural/urban fertility differential narrowed significantly during the postwar baby boom, for two reasons. First, although the total fertility rates rose for both rural and urban white populations, the percentage increase was greater for urban white women. By 1957, the total fertility rate was 37 percent above 1945 for rural white women, but 64 percent higher for urban white women. Second, the timing of peak total fertility rates during the baby boom was different for rural and urban white populations. The highest total fertility rate was recorded for rural whites in 1957 but for urban whites in 1959. As a result, the difference in rural/urban total fertility rates converged between 1945 and 1959, but became constant in the 1960s. Hence, by 1969 the total fertility rate represented 2.5 live births per rural white woman and 2.2 live births per urban white woman by age 45. Why the rise in the total fertility rate during the baby boom was slower and briefer for rural than for urban white women is not well understood.

Rural/urban differentials in mortality also narrowed substantially during the centralization phase. The advent of public sanitation programs increased control of infectious diseases and greatly reduced the mortality rates in urban environments. Thus, by 1970 degenerative diseases had replaced infectious ones as the principal causes of mortality, cardiovascular disease becoming the leading cause. Kitagawa and Hauser's (1973) analysis of 1960 data from census schedules and death certificates showed that metropolitan areas had age-adjusted death rates only 5 percent above those in nonmetropolitan places. Moreover, Preston's (1976) analysis of data from forty-three nations gathered between 1960 and 1964 showed that residence in large cities was associated with higher male mortality but lower female mortality. He suggested that cardiovascular diseases may raise the mortality rates of males in large cities through cigarette and alcohol consumption, low physical exercise, and stressful "mental" occupations more characteristic of men in metro environments. This interpretation may partially explain the failure of the national male age-adjusted death rates to decline despite declines in the national female death rates during 1955–1968, a period of heavy net rural-to-urban migration (see discussion by Bogue, 1969:590–602; and Smith and Zopf, 1976:445–447).

The centralization phase saw a significant interregional migration of rural southern Blacks. Even after the Emancipation Proclamation freed all southern black slaves in 1863, the volume of net migration of Blacks from the South to North was low. A major reason was that illiteracy prevented most southern Blacks from learning job opportunities in the North (Uhlenberg, 1973). However, industrial expansion associated with the outbreak of World War I created a demand for new sources of unskilled labor. As a result, northern manufacturing firms sent representatives to recruit black workers from the South. Between 1916 and 1918, over one million black people left rural areas in the South to settle in the industrial centers of Michigan, Illinois, Ohio, Pennsylvania, and New York (Campbell et al., 1974). Once in the North, these immigrants became an additional source of aid and information to rural southern Blacks desiring to follow. The net out-migration of Blacks from the South continued until 1970.

THE POSTINDUSTRIAL PHASE: CHANGES IN THE 1970s

The 1970s ushered in a new phase of American population redistribution (discussed in detail by Wardwell in Chapter 3). Between 1970 and 1977, the population of metro counties grew by 8.3 million (or .7 percent annually), whereas nonmetro residents increased by 4.8 million (or 1.2 percent annually) (U.S. Department of Commerce, 1979). Approximately half of this average annual percentage of growth in nonmetro counties resulted from natural increase, and half from net-migration. These patterns signalled a significant departure from those of the centralization phase in two ways: the nonmetro population was increasing faster than the metro population, and the net out-migration from nonmetro to metro areas was reversed. The in-migration to nonmetro counties did not signify a resurgence in the farm population; rather, the number of persons living on farms declined from 9.7 million in April 1970, to 8 million in April 1978 (U.S. Department of Commerce, 1979:28).[2]

The exchange of migrants between metro and nonmetro counties between 1970 and 1975 did not significantly alter metro/nonmetro differences in population composition. Zuiches and Brown (1978) found that the two migration streams between metro and nonmetro counties for 1970–1975 had younger ages, higher occupational statuses, and more years of formal education than did the nonmetro nonmovers. In a similar vein, Lichter et al. (1979) found that, for 1955–1975, the nonmetro-to-metro stream and its counterstream were more alike in age, education, and occupational status than like the nonmoving populations at either destination. Although the post-1970 stream from metro to nonmetro counties had somewhat older ages, lower occupational statuses, fewer years of schooling, and higher proportions of whites and males than did its counterstream (Zuiches and Brown, 1978), very little change occurred in the composition of metro and nonmetro populations between 1970 and 1975 (Lichter et al., 1979).

For these reasons, we present data from the 1970 census to illustrate salient social, economic, and demographic differences between urban and rural populations (see Table 6.1). The historic out-migration of young, better educated adults from rural areas contributed to the higher proportion of persons aged sixty-five years or over (10.1 percent) there than in the urban population (9.8 percent). The selective pattern of out-migration also led to a smaller proportion of persons aged fourteen years or more in the rural population who had completed high school (28 percent) as compared to persons of the same age in urban settings (30.2 percent). The median age of persons in rural areas (27.9 years) remained below that of urbanites (28.1 years) because of the larger number of children born per thousand rural farm (2,591) and rural nonfarm females (2,362) aged fifteen years or over as compared to numbers born per thousand urban women (1,863).

More rural women than men migrated to urban places, which raised the sex ratio in the rural population and lowered the ratio in urban environments. There were one hundred males for every one hundred females in rural America in 1970, but only ninety-three males per one

Table 6.1 Selected Characteristics for Urban and Rural Residence, 1970[a]

Characteristics	Urban	Rural
Median years of age	28.1	27.9
Percent 65 years and over	9.8	10.1
Percent Negro and other nonwhite races	13.8	9.1
Males per 100 females	93.0	100.1
Persons 14 years and over--Percent married		
Male	65.0	67.7
Female	59.5	66.7
Persons 14 years and over--		
Percent high school graduates[b]	30.2	28.0
Percent foreign-born[c]	5.7	1.7

[a]Source: U.S. Department of Commerce (Bureau of the Census). 1971. United States Census of Population, 1970, Number of Inhabitants, Final Report PC(1)-A1, United States Summary. Washington, D.C.: U.S. Government Printing Office. Table 52 and 54, pages 269-275 and 278-280.

[b]Source: U.S. Department of Commerce (Bureau of the Census). 1973b. United States Census of Population, 1970, Detailed Characteristics, Final Report PC(1)-D1, United States Summary. Washington, D.C.: U.S. Government Printing Office. Table 199, pages 627-633.

[c]Source: U.S. Department of Commerce (Bureau of the Census). 1973b. United States Census of Population, 1970, Detailed Characteristics, Final Report PC(1)-D1, United States Summary. Washington, D.C.: U.S. Government Printing Office. Table 189, pages 591-592.

hundred females in the urban population. The less balanced sex ratio in urban areas was associated with a smaller percentage of people currently married there than in the rural population, a tendency that was more pronounced among women than among men (see Table 6.1). Largely because of the net out-migration of Blacks from rural areas, which had begun in World War I, a higher proportion of the urban (13.8 percent) than of the rural population (9.1 percent) in 1970 was composed of racial minorities. In addition, the concentration of foreign immigrants in urban areas during the centralization phase contributed to the larger proportion of urbanites (5.7 percent) than of rural dwellers (1.7 percent) in 1970 who were foreign-born. The smaller proportion of currently married persons and larger proportion of racial and ethnic minorities contributed to the greater diversity of lifestyles found in urban than in rural society; this heterogeneity was shaped in part by historic patterns of migration.

A second new trend in population redistribution in the 1970s was a reversal of the net out-migration of Blacks from the South. For example, between 1970 and 1973, a total of 166,000 Blacks left the South, while 247,000 Blacks arrived from other regions (U.S. Department of Commerce, 1973a). This trend was accompanied by a reversal from population losses to gains for Blacks in nonmetro counties. While the number of Blacks in nonmetro counties declined by 5.3 percent between 1960 and 1970, their number increased by 10.2 percent (580,000 persons) between 1970 and 1978 (U.S. Department of Commerce, 1979).

RESEARCH ISSUES

Two approaches have dominated demographic research during the last decade. One of them is historical demography, in which a detailed analysis of a demographic phenomenon is made from a longer time perspective. This permits a study of social change processes that most demographic research does not address. The other emphasis is social demography, which takes the empirical findings of population studies and relates them to social theories. Both of these approaches raise a number of important research issues, answers to which offer a better understanding of future demographic shifts.

Research is needed on the historical association between population movements and concomitant social changes. From a historical perspective, the issue of how long-term rural-to-urban migration has impacted both communities of origin and destination has not been well delineated. Did the movement of people from rural farming areas to urban places prevent the development of a peasant agriculture in the United States? Was the urban unrest of the 1960s and early 1970s traceable to the earlier migration? To what extent is migration now taking the form of life cycle migration? Is there historical evidence to support an observed tendency for youth to migrate to urban areas and then return to rural areas later in life?

Research is needed that distinguishes the demographic and economic characteristics before and after a mobility period for first-time in-migrants, return migrants, and nonmigrants. The migration system typology developed by Goldscheider is applicable to this issue (1971:44–54). These distinctions could suggest how in-migration to a nonmetro area might change economic statuses and how such changes would differentially accrue to newcomers, returnees, and nonmigrants. While such comparisons could suggest some reasons for migration to nonmetro counties, this research has been hampered by a scarcity of longitudinal data for studies of mobility, as noted by Wardwell (see Chapter 3).

Research is also needed on how newcomers to nonmetro counties adjust to service-deprived hinterland areas. Some research suggests that a conflict between the interests of oldtimers and newcomers is an inevitable consequence of nonmetro in-migration, while other studies find that newcomers are readily accepted (Sokolow, 1977; Beegle and Rathge, 1980). More research on the consequences of population growth for the rural community is needed because of its relevance to policy. Associated questions are: Will urban-origin migrants to nonmetro areas make a satisfactory adjustment? To what extent will the skills of newcomers be recognized and utilized in rural communities characterized by an entrenched power elite?

Another issue in need of research is the extent to which net in-migration alters fertility and mortality patterns of nonmetro areas. For example, in-migrants from metro areas introduce knowledge, attitudes, and behaviors causally related to the lower fertility of the urban environments of origin; they can thereby become agents of fertility decline in rural settings (Goldstein, 1976). However, as Beale (1978) noted, some of the nonmetro in-migrants have been those seeking a more suitable environment for child rearing. To the extent that this motivation has been dominant, no narrowing of nonmetro/metro fertility differentials might be expected. The lack of consensus among these scholars points to a need for further research on this issue.

Research is needed on the effects of race on nonmetro in-migration. To date, the increased migration of Blacks to rural areas that has occurred since 1970 has not generated much interest among rural sociologists or demographers. Although two studies have examined the social and economic characteristics of Black migrants returning to the South (Campbell et al., 1974; Long and Hansen, 1977), no published research has analyzed this migration with data subsequent to 1970. The lack of research is regrettable, for Ritchey (1976) argued that racial minority status contributes an independent influence on the rate and the direction of migration. Since 1960 and 1970 census data suggested that Blacks were less migratory than whites (even after the effects of education, occupation, and age had been accounted for), Ritchey concluded that Blacks must be more reluctant than whites to migrate from areas affording economic opportunity (e.g., from urban or non-Southern residences). Yet Black net in-migration occurred during the 1970s to nonmetro counties and to the South, where the racial disparities in income were greater than those elsewhere. These phenomena suggest that Ritchey's interpretation may have been in error and illustrate current limitations of migration theory. Future research should compare the factors precipitating Black and white in-migration to non-metro counties and to the South. Racial differences in residential choice could then inform migration theory and public policy.

NOTES

1. For purposes of this historical review, the census definition used from 1910 to 1940 has been applied to all preceding censuses. The urban population for 1790–1940 was thus defined as all persons living in incorporated areas of twenty-five hundred or more inhabitants or in areas classified as urban under special rules about population density. The rapid rural-to-urban migration occurring during the 1940s, concomitant with urban sprawl, made this definition less useful, and it was modified for the 1950 census. The new definition was reemployed in the 1960 and 1970 censuses with only minor changes. A new concept introduced was that of an "urbanized area," having a central city/twin cities with a total/combined population of fifty thousand residents (if there are twin cities, the smaller must have at least fifteen thousand people) and surrounding environs having incorporated places of twenty-five hundred or more people, closely settled areas of at least one hundred housing units, or parcels of land with a density of at least one thousand inhabitants per square mile. Thus, in 1970, the urban population was extended to include persons living in urbanized areas or in unincorporated places of at least twenty-five hundred residents.

2. The Census of Population and Housing has classified the rural population (whether in metro or nonmetro counties) into farm and nonfarm groupings since 1930. Although the definition of "farm" has changed subsequently, it was held in the 1960 and 1970 censuses to be a place of ten or more acres from which the sale of "farm products" had amounted to $50 or more in the preceding year, or a place of less than ten acres from which the sale of "farm products" had amounted to $250 or more in the preceding year.

REFERENCES

Beale, Calvin L. 1978. "People on the land." In Thomas R. Ford (editor), *Rural U.S.A.: Persistence and Change.* Ames, Iowa: Iowa State University Press.

Beegle, J. Allan, and Richard Rathge. 1980. "Consequences of population growth for the nonmetropolitican community: Osceola County, Michigan." Paper presented at the Fifth World Congress for Rural Sociology, Mexico City, Mexico.

Bogue, Donald J. 1969. *Principles of Demography.* New York: John Wiley and Sons.

Campbell, Rex R., Daniel M. Johnson, and Gary J. Stangler. 1974. "Return migration of Black people to the South." *Rural Sociology* 39(4):514–528.

Goldscheider, Calvin. 1971. *Population, Modernization, and Social Structure.* Boston: Little, Brown, and Co.

Goldstein, Sidney. 1976. "Facets of redistribution: Research challenges and opportunities." *Demography* 13(4):423–434.

Keely, Charles B. 1974. "Immigration composition and population policy." *Science* 185 (August):587–593.

Kitagawa, Evelyn M., and Phillip M. Hauser. 1973. *Differential Mortality in the United States: A Study in Socio-Economic Epidemiology.* Cambridge: Harvard University Press.

Lee, Everett S. 1964. "Internal migration in the United States." In Ronald Freedman (editor), *Population: The Vital Revolution.* Garden City, New York: Basic Books.

Lichter, Daniel T., Tim B. Heaton, and Glenn V. Fuguitt. 1979. "Trends in the selectivity of migration between metropolitan and nonmetropolitan areas: 1955–1975." *Rural Sociology* 44(4):645–666.

Lindert, Peter H. 1977. "American fertility patterns since the Civil War." In Ronald Demos Lee (editor), *Population Patterns in the Past.* New York: Academic Press.

Long, Larry H., and Kristin A. Hansen. 1977. "Selectivity of Black return migration to the

South." *Rural Sociology* 42(3):317–331.

Peterson, William. 1961. *Population.* New York: Macmillan Co.

Preston, Samuel H. 1976. *Mortality Patterns in National Populations.* New York: Academic Press.

Rindfuss, Ronald R., and James A. Sweet. 1977. *Postwar Fertility Trends and Differentials.* New York: Academic Press.

Ritchey, P. Neal. 1976. "Explanations of migration." In Alex Inkeles (editor), *Annual Review of Sociology.* Palo Alto, California: Annual Reviews, Inc.

Smith, T. Lynn, and Paul E. Zopf, Jr. 1976. *Demography: Principles and Methods.* Port Washington, New York: Alfred Publishing.

Sokolow, Alvin D. 1977. "California's new migration to the towns of the 'cow counties.'" *California Journal* (October).

Stokes, C. Shannon, Wayne A. Schutjer, and Merwyn R. Nelson. 1979. "Land availability and human fertility: Toward a synthesis of agricultural and demographic development policy." University Park, Pennsylvania: Pennsylvania State University. Unpublished manuscript.

Taeuber, Conrad, and Irene B. Taeuber. 1958. *The Changing Population of the United States.* New York: John Wiley and Sons.

Uhlenberg, Peter. 1973. "Noneconomic determinants of nonmigration." *Rural Sociology* 38(3):296–311.

U.S. Department of Commerce (Bureau of the Census). 1971. *United States Census of Population, 1970, Number of Inhabitants, Final Report PC(1)-A1, United States Summary.* Washington, D.C.: U.S. Government Printing Office.

U.S. Department of Commerce (Bureau of the Census). 1973a. *Population Characteristics.* Washington, D.C.: U.S. Government Printing Office, Current Population Report, Series P-20, 256.

U.S. Department of Commerce (Bureau of the Census). 1973b. *United States Census of Population, 1970, Detailed Characteristics, Final Report PC(1)-D1, United States Summary.* Washington, D.C.: U.S. Government Printing Office.

U.S. Department of Commerce (Bureau of the Census). 1979. *Population Characteristics.* Washington, D.C.: U.S. Government Printing Office, Current Population Report, Series P-20, 336.

Zuiches, James J., and David L. Brown. 1978. "The changing character of the nonmetropolitan population, 1950–1975." In Thomas R. Ford (editor), *Rural U.S.A.: Persistence and Change.* Ames, Iowa: Iowa State University Press.

7
Persistence of Rural/Urban Differences

FERN K. WILLITS
ROBERT C. BEALER
DONALD M. CRIDER

Contrary to the idea that modern methods of transportation, rapid communication, national mass media coverage, and extensive internal migration have led to the formation of a single, homogeneous society, important distinctions between rural and urban sectors of the United States continue to exist. If effective and efficient action programs are to be designed and carried out to meet the needs of all citizens, such differences must be explicitly recognized. Failure to do so can lead to policies that are relevant only to the dominant urban society or that cannot be adequately implemented in the less densely populated countryside.

DIFFERENCES IN PERSPECTIVE

Rural/urban differences have been of major interest to rural sociologists for many years. Commonly, rural sociologists take *rural* and *urban* to denote opposite ends of a conceptual continuum, with real people and communities falling somewhere between the two hypothetical

Fern K. Willits is a professor in the Department of Agricultural Economics and Rural Sociology, Pennsylvania State University, University Park, Pennsylvania. She is the author of numerous articles on values, rural youth, migration, and longitudinal research issues. **Robert C. Bealer**, also a professor in the Department of Agricultural Economics and Rural Sociology at Pennsylvania State University, University Park, is currently president-elect of

extremes. Thus, any specific instance in the real world is viewed as demonstrating relative degrees of "rurality" or its opposite, "urbanity." Moreover, the meanings given to the extremes of the continuum have been neither simple nor unambiguous. Characteristics of physical areas and/or attributes of people are often used in making rural/urban distinctions. Similarly, ecological, occupational, and sociocultural criteria are used either separately or in combination in making distinctions. Ecologically, rural areas have low population density, settlements of small absolute size, and communities that are relatively isolated from other segments of society. Occupationally, rural areas involve extractive-types of industries. Agriculture is the most widespread such industry in rural America, although mining, forestry, and fishing are also included. Socioculturally, rural areas are characterized by a predominance of personal, face-to-face social relationships among similar people and a comparative slowness in altering traditional cultural heritage.

In the past, it was assumed, with justification, that these three aspects of rurality were closely linked. For the United States, however, time has eroded the simple connections among them. Today, ruralites and their urban counterparts can read the same newspapers, magazines, and books; hear the same radio and television programs; and attend the same kinds of schools, churches, and clubs. Persons raised in the city have sought housing in the open country interspersed with farmers who often work part-time in urban industry. The nature of farming itself has been dramatically altered by technological advances.

Given such changes, many observers have proclaimed the demise of a distinctive rural culture. It has become popular to picture the United States as a mass society where earlier internal differences have waned or disappeared altogether, being replaced by increasingly standardized lifestyles. Such a perspective emphasizes the shared, undifferentiated aspects of the culture. Admittedly, *rural* and *urban* do not form entirely distinct or separate subpopulations. There are many overlapping characteristics. Similarities are clearly present, and they are important. However, an emphasis on similarities ought not to be at the expense of the demonstrable diversity still characteristic of American society.

To some degree, each of the chapters in this book deals with rural/ur-

---

the Rural Sociological Society. He is a past editor of *Rural Sociology* and has written extensively on issues of rurality, metasociology, and the uses of sociological theory in research. **Donald M. Crider** is an associate professor in the Department of Agricultural Economics and Rural Sociology, Pennsylvania State University, University Park. He has written many articles on values, the rural church, and social-psychological changes in the life cycle.

ban differences. We need only to look at a few examples to emphasize that point. There are important demographic distinctions as described by Johnson and Beegle in Chapter 6. In rural areas (as contrasted with urban) the ratio of males to females is generally higher; incomes are lower and proportionately more families live in poverty; women are less likely to be employed outside the home; adults tend to have less formal schooling; and older persons are overrepresented in the population. As significant as these differences are, they do not exhaust the range of important rural/urban distinctions.

Historically, rural people have been disadvantaged in regard to the quality and quantity of many public services that contribute to their well-being or a full life: fire and police protection; educational, religious, and transportation facilities; welfare activities; health care; water, refuse, and sewage systems; organized recreational opportunities; and shopping outlets (see Chapter 14). Such rural disadvantage stems largely from the relatively small, scattered populations that contribute to a high cost per person of providing services. Generally lower incomes and the traditional system of financing such services by local taxation also contribute to the problem.

Rural and urban governments continue to operate with different internal organization and administrative style. Traditionally, small government, local control, and indigenous support were inherent in rural political structures. Typically run by part-time officials lacking professional managerial skills, these governments were expected to be simple, accessible, and protective of local values. Today, policy making in rural areas continues to be the responsibility of elected governing boards with a preponderance of part-time or volunteer workers. Rural government services are dominated by traditional functions such as policy protection and road maintenance, with less concern for planning, parks and recreation, and environmental control. Public officials tend to be products of their communities and are sensitive to local values and expectations. Serious political conflicts are often avoided by using decision-making styles that emphasize consensus and support for the status quo. Thus, regardless of financing capacity, rural governments are less likely to become involved in activities to bring about change or planning. Moreover, because these units generally lack strong elected executives, hired professional managers, and knowledge of grantsmanship, they may be unable to respond to federal and state programs that require local initiative.

DIFFERENCES IN PEOPLE'S OUTLOOKS

Related to the rural/urban differences discussed above, whether as causes or consequences, are distinctions between rural and urban residents' outlooks, e.g., values, beliefs, attitudes, and goals. An understanding of these differences is important in formulating effective policy for rural areas.

For a political democracy to be true to its ideals, the wishes of the entire constituent citizenry must be honored. Programs need to address how rural values and beliefs may differ from those of the larger society and how they should be taken into account in program formulation and implementation. Failure to do so may lead to an imbalance of the methods and goals of policy programming and the needs, desires, and lifestyles of rural dwellers. For example, welfare programs designed to aid the poor in our society have often excluded rural persons because of a failure to understand the dimensions of rural poverty and the values of the people involved. In accord with traditional values that emphasize the virtues of physical work and the importance of the family, the rural poor are frequently employed (although often part-time or at substandard wages) and live in households with a male head (see Chapter 13). Yet welfare programs are often geared to the unemployed and/or limited to households with a female head. In such cases, rural persons may fail to qualify for aid for reasons that have nothing to do with their legitimate needs.

Other rural values may similarly detract from the effectiveness of intervention programs designed to help the poor, the elderly, and the handicapped. The modern philosophy that government and voluntary agencies have a social responsibility to provide for their welfare is often foreign to rural persons, conflicting sharply with their ingrained values of independence and self-sufficiency. Many pride themselves on "never having taken a handout," no matter how difficult their circumstances or how great their need.

RESEARCH ISSUES

Assessing Differences in Outlook

Value, belief, and attitude differences between rural and urban residents have been documented in past as well as contemporary American society. The research evidence is neither as extensive nor systematic as one might wish, but certain patterns can be identified. For example, rural dwellers, in comparison with urban people, generally tend to be more traditional in their moral orientation, less accepting of minority rights, more ideologically religious and conservative in their practices, more likely to oppose federal government, and, though evaluating their community facilities less favorably, more satisfied with their lifestyle.

However, the existing evidence is fragmentary. In a dynamic society such as ours, the existence and nature of rural/urban distinctions need to be assessed periodically so that their persistent and changing aspects can be charted and understood. *Research is needed to identify more specifically the overall nature of rural/urban differences in values and beliefs and to continue to monitor the changing and stable aspects of these distinctions.*

Ascertaining Reasons for Differentiation

There is little evidence that rural/urban differences in outlook are waning. Some differences have narrowed while others have become more pronounced. Why did such differences arise in the past? What circumstances foster their persistence? Answers to these questions could enable the policy maker to better anticipate the future.

A number of explanations can be offered. It seems plausible that the larger and more diverse urban setting fosters the generation and acceptance of new ideas. Densely settled areas, if they are also occupationally and organizationally diverse, are more likely to provide a "critical mass" productive of innovations and supportive of changes in norms, which can then be spread or diffused into the hinterland. If this is true, individuals in sparsely settled regions would be likely to lag behind urban areas in the acceptance of new ideas and to continue to express more traditional viewpoints. In addition, while the geographic isolation once characteristic of rural areas has obviously declined, social and psychological isolation may still continue. Similar television, radio, movie, magazine, and newspaper availability does not guarantee similar impact. Individuals can be selective–watching, listening to, and reading those materials that are most in keeping with their prior values, beliefs, and interests. Selective exposure to alternative ideas also may be brought about by other circumstances. A sense of both superiority and inferiority may provide a kind of psychological isolation to set the rural dweller apart from his nonrural counterparts. On the one hand, many ruralites may see themselves as embodying the traditional virtues of America–independent, self-reliant, God-fearing–and hence superior to their urban cousins. On the other hand, the ruralite may feel inferior in coping with secular, modern, or worldly pursuits. This type of isolation could operate as effectively as geographic separation to preserve traditional patterns of thought and behavior among ruralites and to maintain rural/urban differences. The validity of these suggestions–and others as well–needs to be researched further. Descriptions of existing rural/urban distinctions can provide a useful picture of the current situation, but an understanding of *why* such differences arose and continue to exist requires more complex analysis. What circumstances lead to the emergence and persistence of different values, attitudes, beliefs, and actions? Do changes in these conditions serve to alter the values and beliefs of the people? *Additional research is needed to determine why there are continuing rural/urban differences in values and beliefs.*

Understanding Heterogeneity within Rural Society

The persistence of rural/urban value differences has been documented by rural sociologists and should be taken into account by policy makers. However, just as the view of a mass society can restrict our perception of differences within the society, emphasis on rural/urban distinctions can cause us to overlook the tremendous diversity that occurs *within* the rural sector. Rural persons and communities are not all alike. They do not present a single, united, or undifferentiated position on any characteristic.

What are the bases of this sociocultural heterogeneity within the rural category? Partly, the distinctions depend on the degree of ecological or occupational rurality. We know that farmers stand considerably apart, on the average, from the aggregation of other groupings in their responses to public opinion polls. Still, within the category *farmers* there can be wide differences between full-time and part-time operators, among those with different sizes of farms, by the type of farm enterprise, and by the length of time a person has been in farming. Similarly, answers to many questions on public opinion polls show differences by size and relative isolation of place even among communities classified as rural.

Differences among rural people may also be related to personal characteristics such as age, income, education, sex, race, and ethnicity. These characteristics have been shown to relate to behavioral differences among people in other settings as well. It seems likely that some of the rural/urban differences in our society result partly from the differential distribution of these characteristics in the two subpopulations (e.g., a higher percentage of elderly in rural areas). However, even when the effects of such variables are controlled, rural/urban disparities have been found to persist.

Geographic regions provide still another possible area of useful differentiation within the rural population. A tobacco farmer in the Deep South seems likely to differ in many ways from a Midwestern corn grower, a Northeastern dairyman, and a West Coast fruit farmer. These differences may result from ethnic, racial, or religious variations. Others may be linked directly to geography or types of farming or other industrial pursuits that predominate in the region; these regional characteristics include the economic well-being of the area, whether the population is declining, stable, or growing, the ease of access to metropolitan areas and facilities, and the extent and type of industrialization.

Data that document heterogeneity within rural society is limited. For example, information on value differences *among* farmers is critical to programs directed to farmers, but it is often lacking. Because farm people constitute a small and declining fraction of the U.S. population, many data sources (e.g., the Gallup Poll and similar national surveys) that could provide evidence for inferring values no longer routinely use a farm/nonfarm distinction, let alone provide for analysis of differentiation within this group.

To determine the extent to which policy designed for one segment of rural society is likely to meet the needs of other rural groups, the nature of differences among rural dwellers in regard to values, attitudes, and beliefs needs to be carefully studied. Specifically, *we need to explore the extent and types of pluralism that exist within American rural society and ascertain the bases of that heterogeneity.*

Creating a New Research Scope

Much that is known of the attitudes, values, and beliefs of people in rural America is based on two types of data sources: national public opinion polls, and past research studies of specific geographic areas. Both types of studies are severely limited in providing important data for policy makers interested in rural people.

Existing national surveys of the general population are too limited in specific data for rural inhabitants. Regardless of how the term *rural* is defined, the number of cases available for analysis is frequently too few to provide opportunities for differentiation *within* rural society and hence for studying its heterogeneity. Moreover, national opinion surveys do not provide for systematic and detailed assessment of values and beliefs. Such surveys tend to rely on a single question to obtain information on how the respondent feels about a certain situation. Such simple responses are unlikely to be valid and reliable indicators of the more abstract and generalized ideas of values and beliefs that could be useful to policy makers.

Regional, state, or local studies often use samples of rural persons and carefully constructed instruments to measure social-psychological attributes, but they seldom present information that can be synthesized to focus on the commonalities and diversities within rural America. Lack of comparability among such efforts in the sample designs, instrumentation, and even in the meaning given to *rural,* make it impossible to generalize across studies or to highlight specific differences in their findings.

If information on rural values and beliefs is to be utilized most effectively by national policy makers, more complete and systematic data need to be available than currently exist. *We need periodic national surveys of rural Americans devised to assess both attitudes toward current issues and their underlying values and beliefs.*

Particular attention must be given to sampling all regions of the country and, within each, obtaining sufficient data to allow for regional and subregional comparisons. The use of similar periodic studies could provide information on the changing nature of rural values and beliefs and allow for the monitoring of the effects of particular policies and programs directed toward targeted populations.

REFERENCES

Anderson, Clay, Ronald M. Fisher, Stratford C. Jones, Bill Peterson, and Cynthia Russ Ramsey. 1974. *Life in Rural America.* Washington, D.C.: National Geographic Society.

Bealer, Robert C., Fern K. Willits, and William P. Kuvlesky. 1965. "The meaning of rurality in American society: Some implications of alternative definitions." *Rural Sociology* 30(September):255–266.

Coward, Raymond T. 1979. "Planning community services for the rural elderly: Implications from research." *The Gerontologist* 19(June):275–282.

Deavers, Kenneth L., and David L. Brown. 1979. *Social and Economic Trends in Rural America.* Washington, D.C.: Economics, Statistics, and Cooperatives Service, U.S. Department of Agriculture, The White House Rural Development Background Paper.

Fischer, Claude S. 1976. *The Urban Experience.* New York: Harcourt Brace Jovanovich, Inc.

Ford, Thomas R. (editor). 1978. *Rural U.S.A.: Persistence and Change.* Ames, Iowa: Iowa State University Press.

Glenn, Norval D., and Lester Hill, Jr. 1977. "Rural/urban differences in attitudes and behavior in the United States." *The Annals* 429(January):36–50.

Olson, Philip (editor). 1963. *America as a Mass Society.* New York: Free Press.

President's National Advisory Commission on Rural Poverty. 1967. *The People Left Behind.* Washington, D.C.: U.S. Government Printing Office.

Shover, John L. 1976. *First Majority–Last Minority.* Dekalb, Illinois: Northern Illinois University Press.

Whiting, Larry R. (editor). 1974. *Communities Left Behind: Alternatives For Development.* Ames, Iowa: Iowa State University Press.

8
Families in Rural Society

RAYMOND T. COWARD
WILLIAM M. SMITH, JR.

Many Americans continue to hold a largely nostalgic and romantic image of rural living. The myth that is perpetuated portrays country living and family life as simple, pure, and wholesome; slower paced; free from pressures and tensions; and surrounded by pastoral beauty and serenity. In reality, rural life seldom matches this popular characterization and many family scholars believe that it rarely ever did.

The harsher reality of rural family life is that economic conditions have forced millions of families to leave agriculture (Wilkening, 1981). Nonmetropolitan families, like other families, demonstrate rising rates of divorce, family violence, and adolescent pregnancies (Brown, 1981; Cedar and Salasin, 1979). Rural schools are judged to be less adequate than their urban or suburban counterparts, and human services for the family are less abundant and more expensive than in urban areas (Coward, 1977; Nelson, 1980; Sher, 1977). Rural poverty is not uncommon, many rural elderly live in deplorable conditions, and, like their urban and suburban counterparts, rural families are experiencing significant increases in substance abuse, stress, and mental health problems (Christopherson et al., 1980; Coward, 1979; Coward and Kerckhoff, 1978; Rosenblatt and Anderson, 1981). Despite this sobering list, we should not conclude that rural families are in a shambles. Rural families,

---

Raymond T. Coward is a research associate professor at the Center for Rural Studies, University of Vermont, Burlington, Vermont. He has written numerous articles on child and family development. **William M. Smith, Jr.** is a professor emeritus in the Department of Agricultural Economics and Rural Sociology, Pennsylvania State University, University Park, Pennsylvania. A past president of the National Council on Family Relations, he is the author of nearly one hundred bulletins and articles on youth, family, and the community.

like other families, have many strengths and, to paraphrase Mark Twain, the notice of their demise is greatly exaggerated. At the same time, the popular romantic image of rural family life must be reshaped to reflect more accurately the current reality. Scholars, social service providers, and policy makers must begin to understand and respond to families in rural society who are experiencing significant internal changes while simultaneously adapting to a remarkably altered rural America.

From a policy perspective, the rural family is caught, unfortunately, at the axis of two policy voids—the absence of a coordinated federal policy for rural America *or* a policy for American families—and thus rests in a particularly vulnerable position (Coward, 1980). Without an overarching policy framework or a comprehensive federal agenda for these two areas, legislative actions often appear capricious, contradictory, counterproductive, and narrow.

THE CHANGING FAMILY IN A CHANGING RURAL AMERICA

During the 1970s, social scientists documented many important structural changes that had occurred in rural families, including a rising number of single-parent families, increased divorces, smaller family sizes, and more dual-employment families (Brown, 1981). The direction of these changes parallel similar trends in urban families, although the magnitudes remain significantly lower. The effects of these changes on the quality of rural family life have not been fully documented but are of vital interest and concern to scholars of the rural family (Smith and Coward, 1981). On the surface, research seems to indicate that rural and urban families are similar in many respects. Yet it is unclear if the antecedents of those familial changes that have been experienced are the same or different for urban and rural families. Research in the next decade, therefore, must focus on the changing nature of families in rural society while treating residence as a potential intervening variable—not as a constant.

For scholars and policy makers concerned with rural communities, the changes that have occurred in families are but one side of the coin. The 1970s also produced a significantly altered rural environment characterized by a migration turnaround, an increase in industrializa-

---

Coward and Smith are the coeditors of two books, *The Family in Rural Society* and *Rural Family Services: Status and Needs.*

Appreciation is expressed to Gordon Lewis, Robert Jackson, Russell Mullens, and four anonymous reviewers for their insightful comments on earlier drafts of this chapter.

tion, continued decline in the number of family owned and operated farms, land use debates, economic fluctuations, rising interest costs, increased environmental consciousness, and an energy crisis. These significant changes in both families *and* rural America have rendered much of our previous knowledge of rural families outdated or, at best, suspect. There is an immediate need to create a more accurate understanding of rural family functioning to serve as the foundation of public policy development. The mobilization of resources to address the research issues outlined below would permit scholars and policy makers to join forces in a creative effort to support families in rural society in the 1980s.

RESEARCH ISSUES

Research priorities for the 1980s can be grouped into three broad categories. Within each, there is much to do and much to understand. The categories are expanded below.

Internal Family Dynamics

There is a need for a better and more comprehensive understanding of internal family dynamics and the family life cycle as it is manifested in rural society. We believe it is fair and accurate to characterize much of what we know about families as being *suburban* based. Too often the conclusions reached from such data are generalized for inappropriate populations and, perhaps more damaging, they serve as an empirical basis for wide-ranging public policy development.

It is not that we believe rural families function in ways that are totally different than their more urban counterparts. Indeed, there is nothing in the research literature that would lead us to believe that the major conceptual frameworks of family sociology are not applicable to rural environments. Rather, we support the proposition that rural residence operates as an intervening or mediating influence. When this perspective is adopted, investigators reduce their focus on simple bivariate comparisons between rural and urban samples and direct more attention to illuminating the differential effects of residence on particular variables.

This should not be misconstrued as a plea to repeat in rural America every piece of research ever completed on urban or suburban families. Certain areas of family research would not appear to be significantly changed by examining the intervening effect of the macroenvironment. In contrast, there are other areas where a sensitivity to the rural environment and its changing nature would lead social scientists to be interested in certain styles of family functioning or particular stages of family development.

For example, rural lifestyles are often characterized by a greater interdependency and intertwining of family living with the major economic pursuits of the individual members. Despite the decline in family owned and operated farms, significant numbers of rural families are still engaged in self-directed and self-operated businesses that are often in close proximity to the home. Weekly newspapers, small restaurants, hardware and general stores, machine shops, boutiques, craft outlets, wood-cutting operations, and recreational enterprises are but a few of the wide-ranging "microentrepreneurial" businesses located in rural America. Although such businesses hold much potential for positive family life and functioning (Ploch, 1981), they can also be stress-producing for families (Rosenblatt and Anderson, 1981; Wilkening, 1981). Rosenblatt and Anderson (1981) have speculated that certain personal and family stresses may be a direct result of economic and work characteristics that they believe are more common in those rural families that are engaged in farming. Although these characteristics are not unique to farm families, the clustering of them in the agricultural environment may increase their importance in understanding the dynamics of family life on farms.

Within this broad research area, there is a specific need for a greater exploration of the major transitional phases of family development (e.g., marriage, parenthood, middle age, retirement, death). Such transitions often produce stress in families, and research has indicated that social support and social networks, both formal and informal, can be mediating influences in the family's ability to cope (McCubbin et al., in press). Since the availability, accessibility, and quality of such support can vary as a function of residence, families in sparsely populated areas may employ different mechanisms for contending with developmental transitions, with perhaps different end results, than their counterparts in more urban surroundings.

For example, research suggests that the transition into widowhood can often be facilitated if the widow becomes engaged in meaningful activities outside the home. Many elderly create these outside activities for themselves, but for many others more formal helping agencies must assist in making the connections with individuals, groups, or institutions. The RSVP program, the Retired Executives program, the Big Grandfather program, and elderly volunteers in day-care centers, hospitals, and rest homes are all examples of retirees, widows, and widowers seeking meaningful outlets for their time and creative energies. We know that the availability of formal, organized opportunities for such involvement is less in rural areas when compared to suburban communities and even less in farm or open country. What we do not know is what mechanisms the individuals in these environments use to make positive transitions into widowhood. Is there a consistent pattern that is adopted by many individuals? What is the role of relatives, neighbors, and the church in these transitions? Place of residence will be an intervening factor in such transitions, one that facilitates positive transitions or one that acts as an obstacle to coping. Family scholars and public policy makers need to have a better understanding of the role of rural society in such transitions.

Lastly, American families are increasingly characterized by a plurality of lifestyles and this diversity is also reflected in families in rural society. Ploch (1981) has captured some part of this range of lifestyles in his case studies of in-migrant families living in rural Maine. But his pioneering work needs to be built upon and expanded by others. We must remember that the majority of rural families in the 1980s will not be farm families; *farm* and *rural* are no longer synonymous. Additionally, rural America remains characterized by a rich ethnic diversity and heritage. When analyzed collectively, these factors create a diversified portrait of family life in rural society that must be the cornerstone of future public policy development.

Relationships to Institutions

There is a need for a more comprehensive exploration of the relationships of rural families to major external institutions. The family is not a closed system, but rather part of a larger system that involves other institutions. Through interactions, these other social institutions (e.g., schools, churches, hospitals, government, banks, markets) assume a major role in the lives of families. Indeed, many family sociologists believe that these external forces now exert a more prominent influence on the quality of family life. In order to develop public policy that is supportive of family living, it is necessary to understand the relationships between rural families and these major institutions.

There is an inadequate understanding of such interactions. For example, although there has been a renewed scholarly and policy emphasis on rural education, very few, if any, of these explorations have included an examination of the interaction between families and rural schools. The focus has been on functions within local school systems or between local school systems and the larger educational milieu, i.e., the state and federal educational bureaucracies. These perspectives are important in their own right, but their focus fails to promote a better understanding of the influence of such institutions on the family. Similarly, although the economic and production aspects of the alarming decline in the number of family farms and the rise of corporate agriculture has been debated extensively, very little attention has been given to the ramifications for family life of this significant change in the structure of agriculture.

Perhaps the most compelling of the institutional relationships to be explored is that between families and government policy. Legislative policies directed at rural issues are routinely adopted at local, state, and federal levels. Farm product subsidies, land use laws, environmental protection legislation, farm inheritance laws, rural job creation programs, tax reductions for farm land, and numerous other actions have been adopted or revised in the last decade, and the pace of such governmental intervention will likely continue into the 1980s. Yet the impact of these actions on families is frequently *not* considered by the policy makers. Furthermore, social scientists have not pursued the impact of such policies on families in a timely or systematic manner. Some reformers have demanded that family impact statements, analogous to environmental impact statements, be prepared for each piece of legislation. The viability and usefulness of such a strategy is debatable. It is clear, however, that there is an inadequate understanding of the impact of government initiatives on rural families and that rectifying the situation will require designating such research as a priority.

Service Delivery

There is a need to identify strategies that are effective for developing and delivering human services in rural environments. In the past decade, small towns and rural communities have experienced a significant growth in human services. Where once there was almost nothing, now there are Meals-on-Wheels programs, day-care services, visiting nurses, welfare, CETA, and myriad other interventions. However, these significant increases have failed to erase the rural/urban differences in the range and number of human services available to support families and individuals in crisis (Cedar and Salasin, 1979; Nelson, 1980).

Early attempts by practitioners to develop and deliver family social services in rural areas soon demonstrated one important fact: Rural areas would require more than simply a watered-down version of big city programs. Scale was not the only, and perhaps not even the most significant, difference between rural and urban social service delivery. Aspects of program delivery that had been of little concern when developing models for urban areas suddenly became major obstacles to rural implementation (Coward, 1979). Program location, transportation, anonymity, delivery costs, limited physical facilities, and staff burnout are but a few of the major logistical issues confronted by rural practitioners and service recipients. There is still a limited understanding among the human service professionals of what works and what does not work in rural communities. There is a significant need for a greater understanding and dissemination of program delivery strategies that have been successfully implemented in rural areas. Furthermore, where necessary, new and innovative program delivery strategies that are applicable to a wide range of rural social services must be developed.

A systematic and concerted effort is needed to uncover those aspects of rural human service practice that truly are unique. We need to identify program delivery strategies or models that are successful in rural communities and define the skills, attitudes, and knowledge that facilitate the success of human service practitioners in rural areas. Until such an empirical base is built, rural social service delivery will too often be haphazard and serendipitous.

Currently, attention needs to be directed at identifying successful preventive strategies that utilize existing community strengths and resources (e.g., formal and informal educational agencies, natural helping networks, self-help organizations). The struggle to obtain the appropriate balance of prevention and amelioration will continue into the next decade and, perhaps, intensify as fiscal resources become more scarce. Nevertheless, to the best of their abilities, academicians and policy makers must pursue the advantages of both strategies.

CONCLUSION

Changes in both families and rural America during the past quarter of a century have accentuated the need to renew research interests in the families that live in such environments. Categorization of the research needs of practitioners and policy makers into the three broad areas discussed above should not obscure the range of specific issues subsumed in each. It is critical that citizens, scholars, service providers, and policy makers collectively recognize the growing significance of these issues and mobilize the resources necessary to address them.

REFERENCES

Brown, David L. 1981. "A quarter century of trends and changes in the demographic structure of American families." In Raymond T. Coward and William M. Smith, Jr. (editors), *The Family in Rural Society*. Boulder, Colorado: Westview Press.

Cedar, T. and J. Salasin. 1979. *Research Directions for Rural Mental Health*. McLean, Virginia: MITRE Corp.

Christopherson, Victor A., Barry R. Bainton, and Monika C. Escher. 1980. *Alcohol Usage Patterns Among the Rural Aged in Arizona*. Tucson, Arizona: Office of Human Development and Family Research, University of Arizona.

Coward, Raymond T. 1977. "Delivering social services in small towns and rural communities." In Raymond T. Coward (editor), *Rural Families Across the Life Span: Implica-*

tions for Community Programming. West Lafayette, Indiana: Cooperative Extension Service, Purdue University.

______. 1979. "Planning community services for the rural elderly: Implications from research." *The Gerontologist* 19(June):275–282.

______. 1980. "Rural families changing but retaining distinctiveness." *Rural Development Perspectives* 3:4–8.

Coward, Raymond T., and Richard K. Kerckhoff. 1978. *The Rural Elderly: Program Planning Guidelines.* Ames, Iowa: North Central Regional Center for Rural Development, Iowa State University.

McCubbin, H. I., C. B. Joy, A. E. Cauble, J. K. Comeau, J. M. Patterson, and R. H. Needle. In Press. "Family stress and coping: Decade review." *Journal of Marriage and the Family.*

Nelson, G. 1980. "Social services to the urban and rural aged: The experience of area agencies on aging." *The Gerontologist* 20(2):200–207.

Ploch, Louis A. 1981. "Family aspects of the new wave of in-migrants to rural communities." In Raymond T. Coward and William M. Smith, Jr. (editors), *The Family in Rural Society.* Boulder, Colorado: Westview Press.

Rosenblatt, Paul C., and Roxanne M. Anderson. 1981. "Interaction in farm families: Tension and stress." In Raymond T. Coward and William M. Smith, Jr. (editors), *The Family in Rural Society.* Boulder, Colorado: Westview Press.

Sher, Jonathan P. (editor). 1977. *Education in Rural America: A Reassessment of Conventional Wisdom.* Boulder, Colorado: Westview Press.

Smith, William M., and Raymond T. Coward. 1981. "Images of the future." In Raymond T. Coward and William M. Smith, Jr. (editors), *The Family in Rural Society.* Boulder, Colorado: Westview Press.

Wilkening, Eugene A. 1981. "Farm families and family farming." In Raymond T. Coward and William M. Smith, Jr. (editors), *The Family in Rural Society.* Boulder, Colorado: Westview Press.

9
The Elderly

GARY R. LEE
MARIE L. LASSEY

Increasing life expectancies, higher rates of mobility, and reform measures such as social security and Medicare have combined to greatly increase the relative and absolute numbers of "senior citizen" families in the United States. The proportion of elderly persons who share their homes with adult children has decreased markedly since the turn of the century. The elderly have simultaneously gained greater visibility, accompanied by the realization that many older people are disadvantaged by whatever criteria are employed.

Evidence accumulated since the pioneering work of Youmans (1967) shows that many social and economic difficulties afflict the rural elderly more severely than their urban counterparts. These problems include lower incomes, poorer health, fewer medical services, more limited transportation, and lower housing quality, all of which indicate that the "objective" quality of life is markedly lower among the rural than the urban elderly. However, the rural elderly fare no worse, and perhaps somewhat better, than the urban on indicators of emotional well-being or adjustment. Any study of the rural elderly must be concerned with the problems faced by this group as well as with the positive aspects of rural life for older people.

Gary R. Lee is associate professor in the Department of Sociology, associate rural sociologist in the Department of Rural Sociology, and director of Aging Research, Social Research Center, at Washington State University, Pullman, Washington. He is author of the book *Family Structure and Interaction: A Comparative Analysis* and has written articles on family sociology and social gerontology. **Marie L. Lassey** is an associate professor in the Department of Sociology and Anthropology, University of Idaho, Moscow, Idaho. She

The importance of research on the rural elderly will, if anything, increase in the near future. Despite numerous predictions to the contrary (Atchley, 1980), this population category is increasing numerically and proportionally. This is due in part to the aging of the general population, attributable to increasing life expectancies and, especially, declining birth rates. However, recent evidence (Deavers and Brown, 1980; Lee and Lassey, 1980a) indicates that the proportion of the elderly population residing in rural areas is also increasing. An increase in the proportion of rural people who are elderly, and in the proportion of elderly people who are rural, may exacerbate existing problems and create new ones for the elderly themselves and for the rural communities that must absorb them.

CURRENT KNOWLEDGE

Several earlier reviews of research (for example, Youmans, 1967) have determined quite conclusively that the rural elderly are disproportionately disadvantaged on a variety of social and economic dimensions (Youmans, 1977; Coward and Kerckhoff, 1978; Lee and Lassey, 1980b). Among persons aged sixty-five and over, a much higher proportion of the rural than the urban elderly fall below the poverty level (Lee and Lassey, 1980a). Older rural residents also tend to be in poorer health than comparable urban dwellers, according to both medical and self-report data (Youmans, 1977; Lassey et al., 1980), although this does not necessarily translate into lower life expectancies (Kwan and Bertrand, 1978). The rural elderly spend a lower proportion of their incomes for housing (Lawton, 1980) but the quality of their housing is much lower in virtually all dimensions (Struyk, 1977). Transportation is simultaneously more necessary for, and less available to, the rural elderly (Patton, 1975; Lassey et al., 1980). This may be particularly crucial because public services that are designed to benefit the elderly are usually more distant and thus less accessible in rural areas (Nelson, 1980). On these dimensions at least, life would seem to be much more difficult for older people who live in rural areas.

However, there are at least two indicators that rural/urban differences

---

is coauthor of the rural sociology textbook *Rural Society and Environment in America.* Lee and Lassey are also coeditors of the Western Rural Development Center (Oregon State University) monograph *Research and Public Service with the Rural Elderly.*

This chapter is Scientific Paper Number 5889, Project 0406, Agricultural Research Center, Washington State University.

in the quality of life of the elderly cannot be analyzed this simply. One is that the rural elderly consistently score as high as, or slightly higher than, the urban elderly on measures of emotional or subjective well-being. The studies that report this finding (Hynson, 1975; Sauer et al., 1976; Donnenwerth et al., 1978) disagree rather dramatically concerning its cause, for gerontological theory clearly predicts that the urban elderly, with their many "objective" advantages, should show a comparable advantage in terms of subjective adjustment (see also Lee and Lassey, 1980a, 1980b).

A second indication that rural life may offer some currently undocumented advantages to older persons involves the recent increase in urban-to-rural migration. The elderly constituted a higher proportion of urban-to-rural migrants in the 1970s than their proportion of the total rural population (Deavers and Brown, 1980). The elderly have never been a highly mobile segment of the population, but they are now becoming more mobile and are proportionally more likely to move from urban to rural locations than the reverse.

Both the high levels of emotional adjustment among the rural elderly and the rural direction of elderly migration suggest that there are perceived advantages as well as disadvantages of rural life for older people. Existing research, sparse as it is, has been much more successful in documenting and explaining the disadvantages, perhaps because they are easier to conceptualize and measure. This bias should be rectified in future research.

RESEARCH ISSUES

Many of the important unanswered questions regarding the rural aged involve the recent increase in urban-to-rural migration noted above. The long-term effects of this trend are still unknown but may be of great importance to the elderly migrants and to their destination communities. The phenomenon thus deserves thorough attention.

Research is needed on the social and economic characteristics of elderly urban-to-rural migrants. We have documented the magnitude of this trend but know little about its nature (also see Chapter 3). What kinds of resources are the migrants bringing to their new communities? These people are probably the "young-old," recently retired with sufficient health and financial resources to enable them to live where they choose. Thus, the new migrants may bring substantial resources to their new communities, contributing to local economies. On the other hand, as time passes, the migrants may require more health and other services that are normally less available in rural areas. Will the economic resources that the migrants bring to rural communities counterbalance the resources these communities will need to expend for the support of their new residents? Less tangible resources are also relevant: Are these people experientially prepared for rural life? Are they life-long urban residents or were they part of the rural-to-urban migratory flow of earlier generations? Answers to these questions will be important in facilitating the adjustment of elderly migrants and their new communities to one another.

Research on the motivations of these migrants is equally important. To what kinds of rural communities are they attracted? Are they moving *toward* perceived advantages of rural life or *away* from perceived disadvantages of the city? If the former, are they moving toward children, recreational opportunities, and greater perceived safety from crime, or are they moving toward a lower cost of living? If the latter, what is it about the city that they hope to escape? Will they find what they are searching for and, if so, will they be able to remain in rural areas throughout old age, or will they be forced to return to the city as the decrements of age increase their need for the services and amenities the city can offer? Knowledge of the motivations of these migrants will enable prediction of the kinds of rural communities toward which they will move, which will allow more effective preparation for future migration. It will also improve our demographic models (see Chapters 3 and 24).

Research is needed on the ability of rural communities to absorb elderly migrants. Are elderly migrants to rural areas moving to the same rural areas as younger migrants? If so, these areas will face problems involving relatively straightforward population growth; this is unlikely, however, since motivations for residential mobility and thus destinations are likely to vary by age. If not, then the age structure of rural communities attractive to elderly (but not younger) migrants may rapidly become imbalanced. This will occur particularly if elderly persons are attracted to rural areas that have experienced, or are still experiencing, net out-migration of young adults. The implications of a disproportionately elderly population for rural communities could be very serious. To name just two obvious examples, the elderly need more hospitals and fewer schools than do younger populations. We thus need research not only on the extent of urban-to-rural migration but also on likely destinations and the relationship of destination to age. Such research will not solve problems in itself, but will at least indicate where and when these problems are likely to arise and thus allow more effective planning and preparation.

We must also ascertain the consequences of migration for the individuals involved. What costs and benefits actually accrue to those who move? What are the implications of disrupted friendship and family ties for the migrants? How rapidly and thoroughly are immigrants to rural areas integrated into their communities? What factors promote or impede such integration and what are the consequences of differential integration for the adjustment and well-being of the immigrants? How will their presence affect indigenous elderly residents in terms of community integration as well as economic status and access to services? The problems of aging have historically been more visible and more amenable to programmatic intervention in urban areas, due to higher concentrations of persons in need of services. This means that elderly urban-to-rural migrants will generally be moving away from appropriate services (Nelson, 1980) and increasing the pressure on whatever services are available. What services will need to be provided or expanded in rural communities and at what cost to these communities? How can available resources be redistributed to deal with expansion of the elderly population? Will the immigrants contribute to or detract from the resource base of their new communities, and what implications will this have for existing elderly residents? These questions lead to issues involving the social and economic characteristics of the indigenous rural elderly.

Much more research is needed on the economics of aging in rural areas. As established above, the rural elderly have markedly lower incomes than the urban elderly; this is true in spite of the fact that rural males, at least, are likely to continue working until later ages than are urban males (Powers et al., 1977). What supplemental income sources are available to the rural elderly? Do rural men postpone retirement longer because they want to or because it is financially necessary? How is retirement different in rural areas than urban, and do the causes and consequences of retirement differ by residence? We do not know the extent to which the lower incomes of rural elderly translate into a lower level of living. The rural elderly may be more self-reliant and may have greater access to nonmonetary sources of subsistence, such as growing their own food. Are there opportunities unique to rural communities that allow the elderly to remain reasonably independent and self-supporting even on low incomes? Further attention should be given to variation in income and other resources among the rural elderly. The elderly are no more homogeneous than any other segment of the population and the fact that average income is low does not imply that all older rural persons live in poverty. We need a more complete understanding of both the causes and consequences of variation in financial resources. What are the consequences of low income in terms of health, nutrition, access to services, transportation, and housing for the rural elderly? How can these consequences be most effectively ameliorated? Are intervention strategies employed in urban areas equally appropriate in rural settings? If not, how might these strategies be modified to increase their effectiveness?

In this connection, research on the relationship between income and expenditure patterns among the rural elderly would be enlightening. How do the expenditures of the low-income elderly differ from those with higher incomes? In what areas do older persons with few resources cut expenses in order to make ends meet? What economic needs can be satisfied, or partially satisfied, by nonmonetary resources? What are these resources, and to whom are they available? To what extent do family and friends contribute to the economic support of the rural elderly? We know that, while the rural elderly as a category are economically disadvantaged in objective terms, they do not perceive themselves to be particularly disadvantaged (Coward and Kerckhoff, 1978). Why not? What opportunity structures or support systems allow them to subsist as well as they do with such limited financial resources?

The nature, effectiveness, and availability of service delivery systems for the rural elderly also require careful scrutiny. We know that the delivery of services is more difficult in rural areas due to low population density and other factors (Nelson, 1980). The means by which delivery systems could be improved with available resources are not clear. In this connection, there is some evidence that other nations, particularly western European countries, do a better job than the United States, especially in terms of health care delivery (Kane and Kane, 1976). Study of how other industrialized nations provide information on alternative delivery models, their effectiveness, and their efficiency would be useful for designing or modifying our own rural delivery systems.

We have concentrated thus far on the relative deprivation of the rural elderly on several objective dimensions of quality of life. While the disadvantages faced by these people should certainly be the primary focus of social policies and programs, the positive side of rural aging must not be ignored. The evidence that the rural elderly score at least as high as their urban counterparts on measures of subjective well-being shows that there must be advantages in rural life that counteract the negative effects of generally lower income, poorer health, less adequate housing, and the limited availability of services.

Research should examine the factors responsible for the higher morale of the rural than the urban elderly. Previous research has paid little attention to the identification or explanation of the advantages of rural residence for older people. We may infer that such advantages exist from the higher scores of the rural elderly on measures of subjective well-being. There are at least three factors that may contribute to the perceived well-being of the rural elderly, i.e., community integration, family support, and crime.

Further research is needed on community, neighborhood, and friendship relations among the rural elderly. There is some evidence that social participation and community integration may be higher among the rural than the urban elderly (Lawton et al., 1975; Donnenwerth et al., 1978; Coward and Kerckhoff, 1978; Lassey et al., 1980), although reported differences have not been large. Further documentation is clearly needed, but even more important is our need to know what characteristics of rural persons and communities facilitate social integration. The advantage of the rural elderly in this regard is, in all probability, substantially exaggerated by popular culture, perhaps leading to the belief that they need little in the way of programs and services because their needs are met by natural support systems. Many common stereotypes about the rural elderly have proven fallacious and misleading; the dangers of overestimating the prevalence and potentials of informal support networks among this population are substantial. We need to know the extent to which they exist, where and for whom they exist, and precisely what needs they are capable of fulfilling.

Additional research is also needed on the nature and functions of family and kinship relationships. One of the more persistent beliefs about rural life in both social science and popular culture is that family relationships are stronger in rural than in urban populations; the "isolated nuclear family" is believed to be largely a consequence of urbanization (see Lee, 1980). However, research has provided little support for this belief, particularly in terms of intergenerational relations (Lee and Cassidy, 1981). Evidence is also accumulating that shows that interaction with kin is unrelated to subjective well-being among the elderly (Lee and Ihinger-Tallman, 1980). This does not mean that family relations among the rural elderly are unimportant, but it does mean that their presumed strength may be overestimated as a contributing factor to well-being. We need to know a great deal more about the kinds of assistance that the rural family is capable of providing: economic support, long-term care, transportation, social integration, and so forth. But we clearly cannot assume that the rural family is able to deal with any and all problems of its elderly members, nor can we assume that all rural elderly have families on which they can depend.

Further research should also be directed toward the implications of crime and fear of crime for the well-being of the rural elderly. Crime rates are, of course, higher in urban than rural areas, but even more important is the fact that the urban elderly are much more fearful of crime than are their rural counterparts (Lebowitz, 1975). Fear, anxiety, and distrust of others may well produce feelings of alienation and vulnerability among older persons in urban, high-crime areas, which could have substantial negative effects on emotional adjustment and mental health. The lower crime rates in rural communities may be a major factor in enhancing the perceived quality of life for the rural elderly and could be a motivating force in the flow of urban-to-rural migration. It is thus critical to increase our knowledge of the real extent of this advantage and of how it might be maintained in the face of possibly rising rural crime rates (see Chapter 23).

CONCLUSION

There is relatively little solid information regarding any aspects of the lives of the rural elderly. Such knowledge should be systematically developed prior to the formulation of policies and programs designed to minimize the problems of old age for rural residents. We must ascertain the factors that affect the quality of life of the rural elderly, which of these factors are susceptible to programmatic intervention, and at what cost. These issues will become simultaneously more important and more complex if the migration of the elderly to rural areas continues.

Perhaps the greatest danger in future research on the rural elderly is that researchers and funding agencies may unduly narrow the focus of inquiry. Few questions about the rural elderly can be successfully answered by studying the rural elderly alone. Any attempt to determine the unique problems of aging in rural areas that begins with observations on only older rural persons is doomed to failure for two reasons. First, the effects of rural residence on the elderly can only be identified by comparison across types of communities, including urban as well as rural. Second, not all the problems of older rural Americans are attributable to the fact that they are old; many of the difficulties they face are common to rural residents in general. Both residence and age must be treated as variables, not as conditions, if we hope to understand how the lives of the rural elderly may be improved.

REFERENCES

Atchley, Robert C. 1980. *The Social Forces in Later Life.* Belmont, California: Wadsworth Publishing Co.

Coward, Raymond T., and Richard K. Kerckhoff. 1978. *The Rural Elderly: Program Planning Guidelines.* Ames, Iowa: North Central Regional Center for Rural Development, Iowa State University.

Deavers, Kenneth L., and David L. Brown. 1980. "The rural population turnaround: Research and national public policy." In David L. Brown and John M. Wardwell (editors), *New Directions in Urban-Rural Migration.* New York: Academic Press.

Donnenwerth, Gregory V., Rebecca F. Guy, and Melissa J. Norvell. 1978. "Life satisfaction among older persons: Rural/urban and racial comparisons." *Social Science Quarterly* 59(December):578–583.

Hynson, Lawrence M., Jr. 1975. "Rural/urban differences in satisfaction among the elderly." *Rural Sociology* 40(Spring):64–66.

Kane, Robert L., and Rosalie L. Kane. 1976. *Long-Term Care in Six Countries: Implications for the United States.* Washington, D.C.: National Institutes of Health, U.S. Department of Health, Education, and Welfare, Publication 76-1207.

Kwan, Yui-huen, and Alvin L. Bertrand. 1978. *Mortality and Longevity in Louisiana: The Relationship of Rural Residence to Survival After Age 65.* Baton Rouge, Louisiana: Center for Agricultural Sciences and Rural Development, Louisiana State University, Bulletin 707.

Lassey, Marie L., William R. Lassey, and Gary R. Lee. 1980. "Elderly people in rural America: A contemporary perspective." In William R. Lassey, Marie L. Lassey, Gary R. Lee, and Naomi Lee (editors), *Research and Public Service with the Rural Elderly.* Corvallis, Oregon: Western Rural Development Center, Oregon State University.

Lawton, M. Powell. 1980. *Environment and Aging.* Monterey, California: Brooks/Cole Publishing Co.

Lawton, M. Powell, Lucille Nahemow, and Joseph Teaff. 1975. "Housing characteristics and the well-being of tenants in federally assisted housing." *Journal of Gerontology* 30(September):601–607.

Lebowitz, Barry D. 1975. "Age and fearfulness: Personal and situational factors." *Journal of Gerontology* 30(November):696–700.

Lee, Gary R. 1980. "Kinship in the Seventies: A decade review of research and theory." *Journal of Marriage and the Family* 42(November):923–934.

Lee, Gary R., and Margaret L. Cassidy. 1981. "Kinship and extended family ties." In Raymond T. Coward and William M. Smith, Jr. (editors), *The Family in Rural Society.* Boulder, Colorado: Westview Press.

Lee, Gary R., and Marilyn Ihinger-Tallman. 1980. "Sibling interaction and morale: The effects of family relations on older people." *Research on Aging* 2(September):367–391.

Lee, Gary R., and Marie L. Lassey. 1980a. "Rural/urban differences among the elderly: Economic, social, and subjective factors." *Journal of Social Issues* 36(Spring):62–74.

———. 1980b. "Rural/urban residence and aging: Directions for future research." In William R. Lassey, Marie L. Lassey, Gary R. Lee, and Naomi Lee (editors), *Research and Public Service with the Rural Elderly.* Corvallis, Oregon: Western Rural Development Center, Oregon State University.

Nelson, Gary. 1980. "Social services to the urban and rural aged: The experience of area agencies on aging." *The Gerontologist* 20(April):200–207.

Patton, Carl Vernon. 1975. "Age grouping and travel in a rural area." *Rural Sociology* 40 (Spring):55–63.

Powers, Edward A., Patricia M. Keith, and Willis J. Goudy. 1977. *Later Life Transitions: Older Males in Rural America.* Ames, Iowa: Department of Sociology, Iowa State University, Sociology Report 139.

Sauer, William J., Constance Sheehan, and Carl Boymel. 1976. "Rural/urban differences in satisfaction among the elderly: A reconsideration." *Rural Sociology* 41(Summer): 269–275.

Struyk, Raymond J. 1977. "The housing situation of elderly Americans." *The Gerontologist* 17(April):130–139.

Youmans, E. Grant (editor). 1967. *Older Rural Americans.* Lexington, Kentucky: University of Kentucky Press.

Youmans, E. Grant. 1977. "The rural aged." *Annals of the AAPSS* 429(January):81–90.

10
Rural Youth and the Labor Force

WILLIAM W. FALK

Since the 1920s, there has been a succession of reports dealing with the youths of America. Although the majority of these reports have dealt with youth generally (Coleman et al., 1972), the special case of rural youth has not gone unnoticed (Burchinal, 1965). A common theme to all of the reports has been problems encountered by youths in the labor market. The focus of this chapter is on selected aspects of career orientations and achievements of rural youths, on the structure of labor markets as a factor in employment, and on the opportunities created by rural industrialization. My concern is with rural youths in their late teens and early twenties and with what Mills (1957) called public issues as opposed to private troubles.

RESEARCH ISSUES

Human Capital Theory and Status Attainment

Rural sociologists have long been interested in studying career orientations of young people, a direct outgrowth of the long-standing fact that large numbers of rural youths leave rural areas for urban ones. Indeed,

---

William W. Falk is an associate professor in the Department of Sociology and Rural Sociology, Louisiana State University, Baton Rouge, Louisiana. He is the author of a wide range of articles on labor market segmentation and other labor force issues.

Development of this chapter was sponsored by the Louisiana Agricultural Experiment Station, Project H-1780. The author wishes to acknowledge the clerical assistance of Karen

several presidents of the Rural Sociological Society, including William Sewell, Archibald Haller, Lee Coleman, Walter Slocum, Harry Schwarzweller, and Robert Bealer, have conducted considerable research on this topic. Ten years ago, Kuvlesky and Reynolds (1970) marshalled hundreds of rural aspiration studies that made residential, sex, race, and other such comparisons. In the past ten years, this research tradition has been extended considerably (Shea, 1976; Spenner and Featherman, 1978).

The most widely cited studies have been done by a small group of researchers at the University of Wisconsin. They advanced the study of career orientations (aspirations) from simple comparisons of aspirations to a sophisticated social-psychological model for analyzing the aspiration formation process and the transferral of aspirations into behaviors. This model posits a flow of influence from background factors (parental statuses) through a set of intervening factors (grades, school track, IQ, parental and others' influence) to early attitudes and behaviors (primarily educational and occupational aspirations and attainments). The results of this research show that rural/nonrural differences in aspirations are slight and seem to have diminished over time. Similarly, the processes by which early parental background statuses and influences affect the outcomes for children are similar across rural and nonrural groups. The processes are also similar for males and females but somewhat mixed for racial groups.

The research on career orientations and the processes by which these orientations were formed and transferred into adult outcomes has been called by the researchers *status attainment.* This perspective in sociology has been paralleled in economics by what is called human capital theory (Horan, 1978; Beck et al., 1978; Lord and Falk, 1980a). The assumption is made that the individual invests (capital) in him/herself by such things as choice of school track and school attainment for occupational and income attainment. The success of the investment is ascertained by the prestige of one's occupation and/or income.

Status attainment research findings can be summarized as follows: The effects of parental statuses on the child's statuses are severely reduced over time. For the child, the important early influences are primarily school grades earned (although these also decrease considerably over time), school track, and significant others' influence (the effect that

---

Olivier and Lori Olivier. He also wishes to acknowledge the helpful comments of F. A. Deseran, D. Haas, William Kuvlesky, G. F. Lord, and one anonymous reviewer to whom he is especially indebted.

parents and others have through their encouragement of the child). The most important effects on the child's early statuses come from the child's own educational and occupational aspirations; these directly influence the child's early educational and occupational attainments, which in turn affect income, although the degree to which this is true during the life cycle is unclear. In addition, sex and race differences are highly pronounced for income determination, with white males consistently getting greater return from education and occupation.

Despite extensive research literature on status attainment, important questions remain. How does the economy influence one's orientations and eventual attainments? How does on-the-job training in some ways supercede the influence of other variables that occur prior to it? How is migration into or out of an area influenced by the health of that area's economy? Also, how do people displaced by shifts in labor markets in one geographic area search for new jobs in that same area? Are there benefits as well as costs which accrue to the individual from this type of shift (a very different issue from benefits to firms having available labor for employment)? What impact does individual behavior in the labor market have on the affected families? And, as Cramer (1979), Stolzenberg and Waite (1977), and Smith-Lovin and Tickamyer (1978) have brought to our attention, how do marital and fertility plans and behavior affect the status attainment process? Do these things occur prior to, after, or along with career orientations and attainments? And, not unrelated to these issues, how do familial considerations affect sex roles within families as well as in the labor market? *Perhaps the most important status attainment research issue is determining to what degree the rural youth is accountable for his/her fate versus the degree to which particular corporate policies and practices impede or enhance the chances for success.*

Labor Market Segmentation and Class Attainment

Unlike human capital and status attainment researchers, labor market segmentation and class researchers are more explicitly concerned with the form of the economy, i.e., capitalism per se. They believe that the structural variable of capitalism must be studied if we are to gain a full understanding of individual accomplishments within a society. Segmented labor market and class researchers argue that contemporary capitalism has entered an era of monopoly capital, i.e., fewer and fewer corporations controlling more and more industrial production. The theoretical underpinnings to this literature are clearly Marxian. This perspective conceptualizes the individual relative to the means of production, i.e., a class focus as opposed to a prestige hierarchy, i.e., the status focus.

Labor market segmentation theorists hold that the labor market is divided along industrial and occupational dimensions. For the U.S. economy, O'Connor has stated that there now exist "two subgroups: competitive industries organized by small business, and monopolistic industries organized by large-scale capital" (1973:13). The competitive sector is labor-intensive. It is more likely to have local or regional markets with pricing dependent on supply-and-demand functions, to have underdeveloped labor, to be dependent on growth in employment for higher production, and to have unstable product and labor markets. In contrast, the monopoly sector is capital-intensive. It is more likely to have large-scale production with national and international markets, highly developed and organized labor with unions, and to depend on increases in capital and technological progress for greater production (Lord and Falk, 1980a). Occupationally, the division is essentially between "good" and "bad" jobs.

The most advantaged jobs are those primary jobs in the monopoly sector. These jobs have the advantage of high wages and good working conditions; they are in capital-intensive industries. For these industries, the retention of one's job is not strictly dependent on supply and demand in the market. The least advantaged jobs are those in the competitive sector. There, workers have low-paying jobs with a high turnover. Above all, these workers and their industrial sector are characterized by instability. It is in these jobs that we are most likely to find the young.

As Bowers has pointed out, "Most young people work in . . . jobs with low wages, requiring menial work, and with little prospect or incentive for continuous employment" (1979:5). Of course, this may be only a temporary, transitory thing associated with being young. Returning to the human capital position, further schooling may offer *the* way to improve one's lot in life. Thus, the investment that the individual makes in education comes back to him or her in terms, ultimately, of financial rewards. The better the education, the better the job–hence the better the income. However, this equation may not be as linear as is commonsensically thought. As demonstrated by Carnoy and Rumberger (1975), Gordon (1972), and Osterman (1975), this equation does not apply well to the competitive sector with its secondary jobs. These researchers have also noted the problematic aspect of the relationship between wages and age. One would assume that wages would rise with age, but this has been found to be untrue in secondary jobs. As Edwards notes about these jobs, "these are dead-end jobs. . . . Neither seniority nor education seems to pay off. And, since employers have little investment in matching workers and their jobs, they feel free to replace or dismiss workers as their labor needs change" (1979:170).

This kind of analysis is highly applicable to rural America with its preponderance of competitive industries and secondary jobs, a point made by Bluestone et al. (1973) and more recently by Beck et al. (1978) and Nilsen (1979). Nilsen shows the contrast between metropolitan and nonmetropolitan in terms of industrial distribution, and also the concentration of nonmetro workers in "low-earnings occupations," the jobs most readily available to rural youths. This places rural youths at a disadvantage that is hard to overcome. This has been graphically illustrated by Fratoe (1979), whose analysis shows rural youths disadvantaged in school district expenditures per pupil and in the more crucial factors such as educational progress in reading, writing, mathematics, and science. For young ruralites, the incentives appear to be for entering the labor market early. As Hobbs and Hobbs have shown in research on rural Missouri youths, it is clear that deferring labor force entry will only result in a general loss of wages as opposed to an enhancement of them (1979). It would seem that the question that some rural youths ask themselves is, "If I remain at home, what difference will another year or two of education make, since the local job opportunities do not require much education anyway?"

The complexity of the linkages between available industries and available jobs in rural areas and their effect on the rural young raise a number of important research and policy issues. For example, to what degree is the rural labor market segmented along industrial, firm, occupational, and regional lines? Is there a type of bifurcation, as argued by the dual economists, or is there a more complex picture with a much larger number of sectors to it? Only recently have any of these issues been addressed and, clearly, much remains to be done (see Tolbert et al., 1980; and Hodson, 1978). How does labor market segmentation relate to the structure of agriculture? As small farms have been displaced by larger corporate farms, what product market changes have occurred? How have corporate farms altered the occupational opportunities in rural areas? Do larger farms exhibit a type of kinship with capital-intensive industry, offering some of the employment advantages found among primary, monopolistic firms? Can the segmentation thesis help to explain individual earnings? How are the findings of Lord and Falk (1980b) on fringe benefits and segmentation extended when examining rural labor markets? Do unionized rural workers have considerable advantages over their nonunionized counterparts? *For rural youths, the research issue is whether their life plans and life chances are enhanced or impeded by the structural characteristics of the local labor market.*

If we adopt a class perspective that ignores the status dimension and instead asks about one's relationship to the means of production, what new things do we find about rural society? At a minimum, we shift the analytical focus away from the concern with the prestige of one's occupation and the process by which that occupation was attained; we ask instead about the implications for a society that is more and more characterized by workers and less and less characterized by owners. The results will have broad implications for a society historically founded on an entrepreneurial work ethic that is being replaced via industrialization with a substitute ethic involving one's working for someone else. In Marxian terms, it involves selling one's labor power to the owner class. And, as Wright and Perrone (1977) have shown, in contemporary capitalism this can also have a managerial class, which is "contradictory" in that it lies completely within neither the owner nor the worker class. How does rural society reflect this type of class structure and what is its impact on rural youths? What is the role of rural schools in all of this? Do schools perpetuate or alter the class structure? (For a critical review, see Bowles and Gintis, 1976; for a more positive view, see Rutter et al., 1979.) How do changes in authority and control in the work place affect the perceived life chances of rural youths? How is the societal trend toward bureaucratization reflected in rural society and what are the implications for rural youths?

The Rural Industrialization Dream

In 1972, the U.S. Congress passed a Rural Development Act so that the American hinterlands could be improved for "those left behind." At the same time, industry more or less discovered rural areas as a potential sanctuary against higher labor costs, energy costs, and so forth. It is safe to say that the rural industrialization movement has been heavily encouraged by southern states. They have offered as incentives indigent labor forces of largely unskilled workers anxious for steady work, state legislatures that are largely antiunion, and low or no corporate income taxes.

This potential boon for rural areas was originally received with considerable enthusiasm. As the important work of Summers et al. (1976) has shown, however, rural people are not always the greatest beneficiaries of rural industrialization. In fact, their lot in life improves comparably little, relative to those who own or manage the immigrant industries. Rural people, especially the young, are likely to be successful only insofar as that means getting what we have described as secondary jobs, albeit, if lucky, in primary industrial firms (hence getting steadier employment than would otherwise be the case).

Beale (1977) reported that, by 1970, people were moving back to rural areas faster than they were moving out of them. In 1970, 53.8 million people were classified as rural. Of this group, "Nearly one-half (46.4 percent) . . . was less than twenty-five years of age" (Cosby and McDermott, 1978:6), and 42 percent of all rural youths lived in the South. We can add to this the remarkable statistic that 96 percent of rural black youths live in the South. Since this group is the single most disadvantaged and also the most likely to find employment in secondary jobs and industries (see Thomas and Scott, 1978; also see Bonacich, 1976, on markets split along racial lines), it would seem that this group is especially likely to benefit from in-migrant industries to the rural South.

However, as Till has noted, "Industry tends to bypass certain rural areas almost entirely. The most notable areas bypassed by the growth of manufacturing employment had been those with heavy Black populations. Indeed, if we superimposed maps showing heavy Black population concentration, there would be an almost perfect mismatch–industry tends to avoid heavy Black population concentrations" (1974:18). Till explores the reasons why employers do not choose to locate in certain heavily black areas. The reasons include difficulties in finding Blacks who meet hiring standards, Blacks being more likely to join unions, exacerbating affirmative action problems, and the lack of nonfarm work experience. The result is a self-fulfilling prophecy; as industry avoids heavily black areas, the relatively unskilled indigent labor force remains unskilled.

As rural youths become old enough to enter the labor force, they are faced with a difficult choice: to stay and search locally for whatever work is available, or to move to a more urbanized area, thereby broadening the range of work possibilities. It is obvious that rural industrialization could serve to provide greater job opportunities for rural youths. *The research issue for the 1980s is to find out what kinds of jobs are provided for rural youths by rural industrialization and whether some types of industries are more responsive to local, especially employment, needs than others.*

This research issue grows out of Summers' findings that rural areas suffer a type of financial hardship in providing services for in-migrant industries. In rural industrialization, is it the case that "bigger is better," i.e., are larger industrial firms better "corporate citizens?" Does rural industrialization open up avenues for upward social mobility that would otherwise be absent? Does it offer on-the-job training programs and educational opportunities for rural youths? Or are jobs offered that are largely secondary in nature, capable of being done by almost anyone? And how do rural youths feel about industrialization in rural America? Would they rather see rural America retained pretty much as it is (the conservationist view) or changed by such means as industrialization (the developmentalist view)? Recent events in Alaska over both the offshore oil industry and the use of interior forests are examples of how people get polarized over such issues. For the rural young, this issue entails making judgments about the "quality of life" they hope to have.

Conclusion

The theme of this chapter has been that, above all else when analyzing rural youth, researchers and policy makers must examine issues pertaining to the labor force. Labor force activity is central to other aspects of a rural youth's life, including marital and fertility behavior. Traditionally in rural areas, farming has offered a primary means of employment that was tied to quality-of-life considerations such as entrepreneurship and desirable man/land relationships. As later chapters (see Chapters 30, 32, and 33) point out, U.S. agriculture is increasingly corporate and mechanized. A central issue for the 1980s is to understand how, as the form of rural economy changes, the young people residing in rural America change with it.

REFERENCES

Beale, Calvin L. 1977. *The Revival of Population Growth in Nonmetropolitan America.* Washington, D.C.: Economics, Statistics, and Cooperatives Service, U.S. Department of Agriculture, ERS-605.

Beck, E. M., Patrick M. Horan, and Charles M. Tolbert, III. 1978. "Stratification in a dual economy: A sectoral model of earnings determination." *American Sociological Review* 43:704–720.

Bluestone, Barry, William M. Murphy, and Mary Stephenson. 1973. *Low Wages and the Working Poor.* Ann Arbor, Michigan: Institute of Labor and Industrial Relations, University of Michigan.

Bonacich, Edna. 1976. "Advanced capitalism and Black/White race relations in the United States: A split labor market interpretation." *American Sociological Review* 41:34–51.

Bowers, Norman. 1979. "Young and marginal: An overview of youth employment." *Monthly Labor Review* 102:4–18.

Bowles, Samuel, and Herbert Gintis. 1976. *Schooling in Capitalist America.* New York: Harper and Row.

Burchinal, L. G. 1965. *Rural Youth in Crisis: Facts, Myths, and Social Change.* Washington, D.C.: U.S. Department of Health, Education, and Welfare.

Carnoy, Martin, and Russell Rumberger. 1975. *Segmented Labor Markets: Some Empirical Forays.* Palo Alto, California: Center for Economic Studies.

Coleman, James S., R. H. Bremner, B. R. Clark, J. B. Davis, D. H. Eichorn, Z. Griliches, J. F. Kett, N. B. Ryder, Z. B. Doering, and J. M. Mays. 1972. *Youth: Transition to Adulthood.* Chicago: University of Chicago Press.

Cosby, Arthur G., and Virginia P. McDermott. 1978. "Rural youth in context." In Arthur G. Cosby and Ivan Charner (editors), *Education and Work in Rural America: The Social Context of Early Career Decision and Achievement.* College Station, Texas: Texas A & M University.

Cramer, James C. 1979. "Fertility and female employment: Problems of causal direction." *American Sociological Review* 45:167–190.

Edwards, Richard C. 1979. *Contested Terrain.* New York: Basic Books.

Fratoe, Frank A. 1979. *The Educational Level of Farm Residents and Workers.* Washington, D.C.: Economics, Statistics, and Cooperatives Service, U.S. Department of Agriculture,

Rural Development Research Report 8.

Gordon, David M. 1972. *Theories of Poverty Underemployment.* Lexington, Massachusetts: D.C. Heath and Co.

Hobbs, Daryl J., and Vickie Hobbs. 1979. "A research and development approach to rural education: A case study." Presented at the annual meetings of the American Education Research Association, San Francisco, California.

Hodson, Randy. 1978. *Labor in Monopoly, Competitive, and State Sectors of Production.* Madison, Wisconsin: Center for Demography and Ecology, University of Wisconsin, CDE Working Paper 78-2.

Horan, Patrick M. 1978. "Is status attainment research atheoretical?" *American Sociological Review* 43:534–541.

Kuvlesky, William P., and David H. Reynolds. 1970. *Occupational Aspirations and Expectations of Youth: A Bibliography of Research Literature: Volume I.* College Station, Texas: Department of Agricultural Economics and Rural Sociology, Texas A & M University, Departmental Information Report 70-5.

Lord, George F., and William W. Falk. 1980a. "An exploratory analysis of individualist versus structuralist explanations of income." *Social Forces* 59:376–391.

______. 1980b. "Hidden income and labor market segmentation." Paper presented at the National Science Foundation's Conference on the Structure of Labor Markets and Socio-Economic Stratification, Athens, Georgia.

Mills, C. Wright. 1957. *The Sociological Imagination.* New York: Oxford University Press.

Nilsen, Sigurd R. 1979. *Assessment of Employment and Unemployment Statistics for Nonmetropolitan Areas.* Washington, D.C.: Economics, Statistics, and Cooperatives Service, U.S. Department of Agriculture, Rural Development Research Report 18.

O'Connor, James. 1973. *The Fiscal Crisis of the State.* New York: St. Martin's Press.

Osterman, Paul. 1975. "An empirical study of labor market segmentation." *Industrial Labor Relations Review* 28:508–523.

Rutter, Michael, Barbara Maughan, Peter Mortimore, and Janet Duston. 1979. *Fifteen Thousand Hours: Secondary Schools and Their Effects on Children.* Cambridge: Harvard University Press.

Shea, Brent M. 1976. "Schooling and its antecedents: Substantive and methodological isues in the status attainment process." *Review of Educational Research* 46:463–526.

Smith-Lovin, Lynn, and Ann R. Tickamyer. 1978. "Labor force participation, fertility behavior, and sex role attitudes." *American Sociological Review* 43:541–556.

Spenner, Kenneth I., and David L. Featherman. 1978. "Achievement ambitions." *Annual Review of Sociology* 4:373–420.

Stolzenberg, Ross M., and Linda J. Waite. 1977. "Age, fertility expectations, and plans for employment." *American Sociological Review* 42:769–782.

Summers, Gene F., Sharon D. Evans, Frank Clemente, E. M. Beck, and Jon Minkoff. 1976. *Industrial Invasion of Nonmetropolitan America.* New York: Praeger Publishers.

Thomas, Gail E., and Will B. Scott. 1978. "Black youth and the labor market: The unemployment dilemma." *Youth and Society* 11:163–189.

Till, Thomas E. 1974. "Industrialization and poverty on the nonmetropolitan labor markets." Paper prepared for the Task Force on Southern Rural Development, Nashville, Tennessee.

Tolbert, Charles, Patrick M. Horan, and E. M. Beck. 1980. "The structure of economic segmentation: A dual economy approach." *American Journal of Sociology* 85:1095–1116.

Wright, Eric O., and Luca Perrone. 1977. "Marxist class categories and income inequality." *American Sociological Review* 42:32–55.

11
Minorities

WILLIAM P. KUVLESKY
CLARK S. KNOWLTON
THOMAS J. DURANT, JR.
WILLIAM C. PAYNE, JR.

William P. Kuvlesky, the principal organizer of this team effort, invited colleagues with particular expertise on specific racial and ethnic minorities to develop short sections as contributions to this overview chapter. The principal authors of each section are: "Native Americans"—Clark S. Knowlton; "Black Americans"—Thomas J. Durant, Jr.; "Mexican-Americans"—William P. Kuvlesky; "Amish"—William P. Kuvlesky; and "Mormons"—Clark S. Knowlton.

The section on U.S. Department of Agriculture policies and programs was prepared by William C. Payne, Jr., of the Office of Equal Opportunity, U.S. Department of Agriculture. The views expressed in this section are those of the authors and do not necessarily represent the views of the U.S. Department of Agriculture or its Office of Equal Opportunity.

This chapter was derived from a much more detailed and extensive list of references and sections on two rural ethnic groups not treated here—Cajuns and Southeast Asian immigrants. The original manuscript has been organized into a monograph and is available upon request: write to

---

William P. Kuvlesky is a professor in the Department of Rural Sociology and Sociology, Texas A & M University, College Station, Texas. A past president of the Southwest Sociological Association and the Association for Humanist Sociology, he has written widely on rural youth, rural ethnic groups, and intergroup relations. **Clark S. Knowlton** is a professor in the Department of Sociology, University of Utah, Salt Lake City, Utah. A past president of the Rocky Mountain Social Science Association, he is the author of numerous

William P. Kuvlesky, Editor, for Portraits of Rural Ethnic Minority Groups in the U.S.: Quality of Life, Social Problems, and Policy Needs. *Texas Agricultural Experiment Station, Department of Rural Sociology, Texas A & M University, College Station, Texas.*

The racial and ethnic variability of rural United States has been largely ignored by both social scientists and a majority of the population. As a result, both the society at large and the rural ethnic and racial populations suffer a loss of human potential (Cosby, 1980). In this chapter, we call attention to the present circumstances and most important problems facing some of the many American rural ethnic and racial minorities.

Ethnic minority groups in any society evolve in one of two ways: as a result of one culture coming in contact with another culture on a continuous basis, or as a result of internal cultural and social differentiation. All but one of the rural minorities considered here evolved in the first of these ways. The Blacks and Amish evolved from migrant populations. Mexican-Americans evolved initially as a result of colonization produced by territorial expansion of the United States and have been expanding through migrant flows. American Indians represent a colonized people. Only the Mormons represent an internally generated ethnic minority, differentiated initially by religious ideology and practices. All of the above minorities evolved in the United States first as rural rather than urban populations. However, in recent times, all except the Amish have undergone substantial urbanization.

Minority group status implies negative social ranking reinforced by prejudices and/or discrimination (Kuvlesky, 1980). All of the groups treated here have experienced stigmatization and ill treatment. But these phenomena change with time and are altered by historical events; for instance, some might question whether or not the Mormons or Amish should now be viewed as ethnic minorities. To what extent any of these groups receives pejorative treatment is partly determined by the context of intergroup relations, i.e., whether one is viewing them in the context of the larger society, a region, or a local community.

Negative statuses and their consequences are accumulative (Kuvlesky, 1980:10–12). Being identified as rural in our highly urbanized society can

---

publications on rural poverty and rural minorities in the Southwest. **Thomas J. Durant, Jr.** is an associate professor in the Department of Sociology and Rural Sociology, Louisiana State University, Baton Rouge, Louisiana. His research work has focused on problems of rural Blacks and the elderly in the South. **William C. Payne, Jr.** is deputy chief of the Civil Rights Division, U.S. Department of Agriculture, Washington, D.C.

have negative social implications (Cosby, 1980; Kuvlesky, 1977:7–15). Combining rural status with ethnic or racial minority status generally produces an "ethclass" (Gordon, 1964) that is substantially more disadvantaged than their urban counterparts. Much recent research supports this broad assertion (Fratoe, 1980:3–15; Kuvlesky and Boykin, 1977; Durant and Knowlton, 1978; Kuvlesky and Juarez, 1975:280–284). We will assess the particular problems faced by these minorities and the response of the U.S. Department of Agriculture to their problems. We will suggest general research issues for meliorating their disadvantaged statuses and improving their quality of life. In doing this, we are committed to providing a perspective that takes into account the internal diversity within these rural ethnic categories (Kuvlesky, 1979a).

AMERICAN INDIANS

We tend to think of American Indians as a social category of relatively homogeneous and similar people. However, the American Indians are incredibly diverse. This minority includes tribes that have mixed extensively with other races and ethnic groups as well as tribes that have mixed little. There are tribes that have largely acculturated at the expense of native cultures and languages, and tribes in which both are flourishing. Reservations exist where the land is tribally owned and used by tribal members; in other reservations most of the best land has passed into the hands of white owners or lessees. Strong tribal governments are coming into existence that are pressing hard for complete autonomy, while other tribal governments are factionalized, weak, and ineffective. The heterogeneous nature of both rural and urban American Indians makes it difficult to discuss them briefly with any degree of precision. However, certain common problems do exist.

The American Indian population is one of the fastest growing ethnic minorities in the United States. Although American Indians diminished in number from the start of the European migration until the first decade of the twentieth century, in the last half century their numbers have increased three-fold: from 224,437 in 1920 to 792,730 in 1970 (U.S. Department of Commerce, 1970:XI). Also, they are probably the most rural ethnic minority in the United States: 55.4 percent lived in rural areas in 1970, compared with fewer than 20 percent of Blacks and Mexican-Americans.

Although the majority of American Indians are rural residents, few engage in commercial agriculture despite unrelenting government pressures for almost a century. Only 6.2 percent of the American Indians lived on farms in 1970. Proportionately, this approximates the rate for whites but is substantially higher than the rates for Mexican-Americans (1.6 percent) and Blacks (3 percent) (Sorkin, 1971:67–74).

Most successful Native American commercial farms or ranches are operated by tribal governments or producer cooperatives (Sorkin, 1971:67–74). Subsistence agriculture is common and livestock operations are an important source of income among many Indian tribes and pueblos; however, few American Indians have land, technology, credit, or marketing facilities to succeed in commercial agriculture. Many tribes do not have tribally owned land or reservations. On many reservations, most of the good land has passed into the hands of white operators or is divided into numerous small plots with multiple owners as a result of inheritance. Sorkin (1971:72) holds that "It will be impossible to solve the problem of land use on many reservations until the heirship problem is resolved." He urges that all land in heirship status be returned to tribal ownership. The dimensions of the land problem are stressed by Meyer (1967:332), who writes that "93 percent of the land at Sisseton (a Santee Sioux reservation in South Dakota) is in heirship status, most of it so fractionated as to be virtually useless to its owners or anyone else."

The American Indian population is among the youngest of American minorities: a median age of 20.4 years in 1970 as compared with 28.9 for whites and 19.3 for Mexican-Americans. High birth rates and large family size promise continued rapid growth of the American Indian population.

As the rural Indian population is increasing rapidly, unemployment is becoming more serious. Lack of education, skills, health services, and housing are still critical problems among most rural Indian populations. Many reservations and Indian populations are located far from industrial and urban centers. During the past decade, many Indians from such tribes as the Navajo and Kickapoo have moved into the migrant labor stream. Urban relocation, in spite of government assistance, has not worked well; consequently, some Indian leaders are urging economic development of reservations and employment of Indians closer to them.

Although many larger tribes, such as the Navajo and Utes, are developing successful tribal governments, the governments of other tribes are being paralyzed by factionalism, lack of a land base, and small numbers. At a time when private industry and state and federal governments are pressing for development of energy resources on western Indian reservations, weak tribal governments open many Indian tribes to continued exploitation and loss of natural resources.

On many reservations, serious conflicts exist between more acculturated mix-bloods and poorer, more traditional pure-bloods. Although poverty is chronic among rural and urban Indians, militancy among all Indian groups is increasing. Tribal leaders and governments have come together to exert pressure on federal and state agencies for more tribal autonomy. Pan-Indian movements are developing among urban Indians and among those whose tribal identity has weakened. On many reservations, groups of militant Indian youths, often in alliance with older Indian groups, are in conflict with their own tribal governments as well as with the federal government and the surrounding white society.

Modern American Indians tend to be rural, poor, with little education, few skills, and suffering from health problems. But the apathy created by white conquest is coming to an end. Indian adolescents have generally high aspirations for social attainment (Kuvlesky and Edington, 1976). Traditional or mixed-blood, militant or conservative, most Indian groups are pressing for more autonomy, more freedom to manage their own affairs, more economic development of reservation resources where such exist, greater participation in political and economic decision making, and are developing a greater interest in their native cultures and languages. One can safely predict that, with continued rapid growth, increased ethnic pride, improved organization within and among tribes, and increasing activism in attacking institutionalized forms of discrimination, the American Indians will play an important role in the future of rural America, particularly in those states where they are now concentrated.

BLACK AMERICANS

Almost 6.5 million Black Americans lived in nonmetropolitan areas of the United States in 1977, mostly in the South. Nonmetro Blacks constituted about one-fourth of the total U.S. black population in 1977. Their numbers increased by 10 percent, or more than 600,000 people, from 1970 to 1977 (Fratoe, 1980:2). Southern, nonmetro Blacks constitute the largest ethnic minority group in rural America; they are also one of the most disadvantaged ethnic minorities, severely afflicted by social and economic deprivation, negative social prejudices, and patterns of negative personal and institutionalized discrimination (Fratoe, 1980:3–5; Durant and Knowlton, 1978:145–152; Kuvlesky and Boykin, 1977; Kuvlesky et al., 1972).

The descriptive research on rural Blacks that has dominated past studies plays a useful role in knowledge building. Consequently, we know much about the situational problems confronting rural Blacks. However, we do not know enough about the institutional sources of change that are influencing the status of rural Blacks. We do not know the extent to which local, state, and federal authorities understand the complex interplay of factors that influence socioeconomic status among various elements of the rural black population. Nor do we know the extent to which situational circumstances and diversity of the rural black population produce special needs and call for unique approaches and solutions. The extent to which socioeconomic problems affecting rural Blacks are institutional rather than individual is another area in which knowledge is lacking. It is unclear how the "Black experience," historically characterized by relative deprivation and inequality in rural society, is linked to the current social status of rural Blacks. We also lack knowledge about the extent to which the relationship between racial "status" and social class of rural Blacks is influenced by institutional discrimination, prejudice, inequality, and ethnic or cultural patterns unique to rural society (Kuvlesky et al., 1972).

The perennial sources of socioeconomic problems currently affecting rural American Blacks are lodged in the nature of rural *and* urban institutions. The many causes of these problems include: (1) conflict and lack of coordination among rural development projects of local, state, and federal governments and enterprises (Clinton, 1979); (2) lags in institutional development and neglect of the problems of rural Blacks (Hightower, 1973; Frazier, 1978; President's National Advisory Report on Rural Poverty, 1967); (3) institutional racism and discrimination, including unequal application of financial resources (Howze, 1970); (4) lack of a strong grass-roots movement by rural Blacks to promote their welfare; and (5) lack of black political representation in granting institutions where their needs and interests could be promoted. These factors suggest that there is need for research that focuses on institutional sources of problems that affect rural Blacks as opposed to research that focuses on the symptoms that affect individuals and communities.

As we enter the 1980s, there are many research questions that need to be asked. Here are a few concerns that emerge from past research as unanswered questions:

- How do relationships within the family, the system of farming, credit availability, and the effectiveness of community development agencies influence the status of black farmers? To what extent is the cooperative farm system a viable means of enhancing attitudes toward farming, community solidarity, farm productivity, and organizational bargaining power of small black farmers? (Smith, 1969; Linder, 1976; Frazier, 1978; Davis, 1978)
- To what extent does racial status influence social class in rural areas? (Wilson, 1978)
- What are the institutional factors related to maintenance or widening of the income gap between rural Blacks and rural

whites, e.g., differential training opportunities, union requirements, seniority systems? (Levitan et al., 1972)

- What effect does rural industrialization have on the employment of rural Blacks? (Durant, 1974; Terry and Charlton, 1974; Brown and O'Leary, 1979)
- What is the impact of educational opportunities, school consolidation, school desegregation, and busing on the educational and occupational opportunities of rural black youths? (Kuvlesky and Boykin, 1977; Kuvlesky et al., 1979; Fratoe, 1979, 1980)

As the number of Blacks in the rural areas of America increases, they are becoming more diverse in their values, life goals, and attitudes toward relations with whites. The passivity once thought to characterize southern rural Blacks toward prejudice and discrimination has passed. In fact, many rural Blacks are explicitly rejecting perceived injustices at the hands of local white populations. Evidence suggests that southern rural Blacks exhibit more hostility and prejudice toward whites than their metropolitan counterparts and that this might be expected to produce periodic events of explicit intergroup conflict (Kuvlesky, 1978; Durant and Knowlton, 1978). Changing institutional arrangements, increasing impact of mass media, and altered social climates are influencing rural Blacks' perceptions of life chances and quality of life (Kuvlesky et al., 1979; Stanley and Kuvlesky, 1978). It is imperative that we gain a better understanding of these processes and how they interact if we are to evolve effective policies and workable programs to encourage rural Blacks in their struggles for human and social betterment.

MEXICAN-AMERICANS

Mexican-Americans are the fastest-growing large ethnic minority group in the United States. Estimates of the number of Mexican-Americans residing in the United States are notoriously questionable: in 1970, estimates of the population ranged from a conservative four to five million up to eight million (Miller, 1974:2–4; Durant and Knowlton, 1978:154). According to the Bureau of the Census, which provided a 1970 estimate of five million Mexican-Americans, the 1973 population had increased by about 39 percent over the 1970 count to 6,293,000. This represents a dramatic rate of growth for such a short period of time (Durant and Knowlton, 1978:154). Approximately 85 to 95 percent of our Mexican-American population is concentrated in Texas and California. Most of the remainder reside in Arizona, Colorado, and New Mexico.

The proportion of Mexican-Americans residing in nonmetro locations in five southwestern states decreased markedly between 1950 and 1960

(Grebler et al., 1970:113–114). However, the increasing urbanization of Mexican-Americans may have slowed during the 1970s. A 1976 estimate by the Bureau of the Census (U.S. Department of Commerce, 1977:10-Table H) indicated that about 23 percent of all Mexican-American families were living in nonmetro areas. Whatever the case, proportionately more Mexican-Americans than Anglos or nonwhites live in nonmetro settings (Miller, 1974:2–3). Because the vast majority of rural Mexican-Americans reside in the Southwest (mostly in Texas, California, and New Mexico), the remainder of this section will focus on that region.

Since the mid 1960s, an extensive body of research knowledge has been accumulated by rural sociologists about southwestern United States Mexican-American populations (Knowlton, 1962, 1965, 1970; Eastman, 1971, 1972; Hawkes, 1973; Medina and Kuvlesky, 1976; Miller, 1975, 1978a, 1978b; Kuvlesky and Juarez, 1975; Kuvlesky, 1979a, 1979b).

Historically, Mexican-Americans' economic progress has been impeded by low income, which is at least partially determined by very low levels of formal education and magnified in its consequences by large family sizes. In all of these respects, rural Mexican-Americans have been historically worse off than their urban counterparts (Stoddard, 1973:126, 157–175; Miller, 1974:5–13).

The proportional rate of poverty among rural Mexican-Americans in 1970 (38.5 percent of rural nonfarm and 32.7 percent of rural farm households) was roughly twice the rate of poverty experienced by rural people in general and over three times the rate of the U.S. urban population (Durant and Knowlton, 1978:158). Even compared with urban Mexican-Americans, who also have a high incidence of poverty (22 percent), rural Mexican-Americans suffer much higher rates of socioeconomic deprivation. Even more extreme deprivation was experienced by rural Mexican-Americans in Texas and New Mexico. According to 1970 census data, their incomes average \$4,192 and \$4,765, respectively, compared to \$5,229 in Arizona, \$5,365 in Colorado, and \$6,291 in California (Durant and Knowlton, 1978). Clearly, strong policy measures and funded development programs aimed at meliorating extreme rates of poverty among rural Mexican-Americans should receive high priority.

The ethnic composition in rural areas including Mexican-Americans varies dramatically in the Southwest and thus represents different adaptive requirements for particular Mexican-American communities and families. Many of the Rio Grande Border areas of Texas are predominantly Mexican-American accompanied by small proportions of Anglos. Similar areas exist in Arizona, New Mexico, and, to a lesser extent, California. In some rural areas of Arizona and New Mexico, inhabitants are predominantly Mexican-American with a smaller number of Native Americans. In central, northern, and eastern parts of rural Texas, Mexican-Americans are usually a small or very small numerical minority of the population. Consequently, the nature and quality of intergroup relations can be expected to vary markedly (Miller, 1975; Kuvlesky, 1979a, 1979b).

Mexican-Americans and Anglos in the rural Southwest have lived through dynamic times during the past fifteen years as Mexican-Americans aggressively used their rights as citizens to move out from under the yoke of paternalistic Anglo dominance. Rural Mexican-Americans played a highly visible role in the Chicano movement of the 1960s (Rivera, 1978). While most Americans were paying attention to the glamorized protest movements of Cesar Chavez in California and Tijerina in New Mexico (Stoddard, 1973:187–207), hundreds of small communities were undergoing interethnic power struggles that transformed many of them. The outcomes of these local struggles have produced a wide range of variously structured interethnic relations. These range from rather conspicuous "Chicano take-overs" (Miller, 1975) to a continuation of the traditional, oppressive Anglo-dominant system (Jennings, 1980). Where Mexican-Americans are dominant, it is more likely that they have achieved substantial political control of community institutions and some economic power. These communities still exhibit patterned interethnic prejudice and discrimination; however, the intensity of negative intergroup feelings and resentment has diminished markedly (Kuvlesky, 1979a). In other rural communities where Mexican-Americans are in substantial numbers but do not constitute a numerical majority, the intergroup struggle proceeds unevenly as the Mexican-American minority moves toward social and economic parity with the dominant Anglo population. In many of these cases, one can expect continued aggressive action on the part of Mexican-Americans seeking civil rights (Wright et al., 1973; Durant and Knowlton, 1978:158–159). In other communities, a pluralistic social situation has or will develop, where the ethnic groups involved live in relative social isolation from each other but not demonstrating strong, overt reciprocal hostility (Kuvlesky, 1979a).

Evidence from recent studies indicates that rural Mexican-American youths vary in desire for cultural and social assimilation with Anglos; however, most appear to strongly favor a bicultural lifestyle, including bilingualism, coupled with full formal social integration with Anglos. This is the most probable future state of interethnic relations between Mexican-Americans and Anglos in the rural Southwest.

Mexican-Americans, rural and urban, are a diverse people (Miller, 1974). The old stereotyped notions of the Mexican-American subculture consisting of a tradition-oriented people clinging to a strong extended kinship system grounded in strong familial, religious, and moral values does not hold up under the glare of hard facts produced by social scientists. Evidence supports the assertion that rural Mexican-Americans are tremendously diverse in patterns of social behavior (Miller, 1974; Kuvlesky, 1978, 1979a), values and aspirations (Marshall and Miller, 1977; Kuvlesky and Juarez, 1975; Kuvlesky and Edington, 1976), family structure (Hawkes, 1973; Miller, 1978b), religious participation (Kuvlesky, 1978, 1979a), their feelings about full assimilation into the core U.S. culture (Kuvlesky, 1979b), and their sense of ethnic identity (Miller, 1976, 1978a).

The disproportionately high rate of poverty of Mexican-Americans is not due to a monolithic, homogeneous, "pathological," and distinct subculture, but rather to social inequalities rooted in institutionalized discrimination and widespread negative social prejudices (Kuvlesky and Juarez, 1975; Miller, 1974; Miller and Maril, 1979; Durant and Knowlton, 1978:158–159; Kuvlesky, 1979b). Any attempt to assist Mexican-Americans in improving their life chances and quality of life will have to take into consideration the quality of intergroup relations.

Beyond the obvious need of a large proportion of poor Mexican-Americans for better income and opportunities, one should be cautious about making general presumptions about categorized attributes or needs of "the rural Mexican-American." Development policy should be instructed by knowledge of local situations and involve from the outset information and advice from local Mexican-Americans.

AMISH

The Amish are a small but easily identifiable ethnic group, numbering about 75,000 people (Kephart, 1976:6–51). They are clearly the most rural of American ethnic groups. Principally, the Amish are farm families who maintain a distinct culture based on religiously rooted ultraconservative social orientations and beliefs in agriculture as a way of life. They believe they are God's chosen people and emphasize isolation from others. They maintain strong ethnic community boundaries that limit contact of their young people with outsiders.

Hostetler (1977:352) reports that there are 109 Amish settlements spread over twenty states. However, 75 percent of the Amish are concentrated in Pennsylvania, Ohio, and Indiana (Hostetler, 1977:352). Hostetler estimates that they have grown ten-fold in seventy years, doubling their population every ten years. This rapid growth, combined with their commitment to farming, creates great pressure on available farm lands of constantly higher value in the vicinity of their settlements (Martineau and MacQueen, 1977:383). Thus, the number of settlements have increased dramatically in this century and will continue to increase.

The Amish have also adapted to the shortage of farm land by entering other occupations. In recent decades, with increased tourism in Amish areas, this has taken the form of small business enterprises producing handcrafted products for sale from the farm. In Holmes County, Ohio, most Old Order Amish families have been running businesses in addition to their farms – selling oak rocking chairs, operating gun shops, making decorative windmills, crafting large clocks, and doing leather work (Kuvlesky, 1978:17–29). Martineau and MacQueen (1977) have also noted increasing Amish employment in off-the-farm jobs.

Most Amish dislike the disturbances the tourists bring to their communities. Buck (1978:232–233) concludes from a recent study in Lancaster County, Pennsylvania, that this outside intrusion is meliorated by the fact that tourism is "structured" or regulated to keep the tourists away from "direct contact" with the Amish people. In fact, Buck (1978:233) speculates that, in Lancaster County, the tourist enterprise might even strengthen the Amish identity. Whether this is true in other areas of Amish settlement is open to question.

The Amish strongly value the separation of their communities from the outside world, although they do use some outside services, such as stores, banks, and medical services. Still, they are the subject of negative prejudices and periodic acts of personal and small-group hostility (Kuvlesky, 1978:25–28). However, they seem to have won some of their battles against institutionalized discrimination, i.e., forced participation in public schooling, social welfare programs, and local restrictive regulations (Kephart, 1976:39–41, 46–47).

The Amish are not a combative people. They will not even fight to protect themselves. From their point of view, the best thing that we, the non-Amish, can do for them is leave them alone to live in peace. Almost all observers of the Amish believe that they face serious problems due to "land pressure," impact of tourism, and the constant threat to the young of competing sources and agencies of socialization (Kephart, 1976:44–49; Martineau and MacQueen, 1977:328–330; Hostetler, 1977:359–361). Yet the Amish have survived worse threats and retained their way of life. It appears to this author, as well as to other observers, that they will adequately cope with current pressures and problems (Buck, 1978; Hostetler, 1977:360–361).

MORMONS

The concentration of Mormons in the western United States was stimulated by severe prejudice and acts of discrimination by non-Mormons. Mormon Church settlement in Utah and surrounding states was carefully organized and directed by church leaders from 1847 to almost the turn of the century. Groups of Mormon settlers composed of men with occupational skills essential to successful settlement were called to settle wherever mountain water could be applied to valley, desert, or piedmont soils in Utah; southern, southwestern, and northern Idaho; eastern Nevada; northwestern New Mexico; northern and southern Arizona; and even northern Mexico and western Canada. Each settlement received full economic, social, and cultural support from the central church. As a result, the failure rate was low (Arrington, 1958:1–234, 293–323).

Immigrant converts from Europe were carefully intermingled with Anglo-Mormons to facilitate assimilation. Most of these immigrants came from the industrial and mining towns of Europe. They had to learn farming and ranching skills on the nineteenth century Mormon frontiers (Mulder, 1956:416–433).

Almost every Mormon settlement was constructed according to a master plan devised to colonize new lands. The plan stressed grouping the population into farm villages. Each farm family received enough land to support the family, and little more. Most farms ranged from ten to one hundred acres. Each farm included plots of good, medium, and poor land. Although farms could be bought and sold once the initial phase of settlement was over, efforts to develop large farm holdings were discouraged. All water, timber, and grazing lands were held in common. Many farm villages even held their farm lands in common for years. Irrigation projects were communally developed. The church, through sponsorship of local village industries, regional banking, and mercantile companies, provided capital, markets for local farm commodities, and off-the-farm employment (Nelson, 1952:1–65; Hunter, 1973:59–92; Allen and Leonard, 1976:257–388).

The initial Mormon regional economic system collapsed under severe federal pressures in the late nineteenth century and left the small Mormon farmer ill-equipped to survive in a competitive national economic system (Arrington, 1958:353–414). Farms were very small, limited by a scanty supply of water. Although federal irrigation and reclamation projects from the 1900s to the 1950s increased water supplies in certain favored areas such as the Wasatch Front in Utah and the Phoenix-Mesa section of Arizona, the extra water was soon diverted to urban and industrial use. Before 1950, the majority of Mormons in the Rocky Mountains were rural; now a majority of the over three million Mormons in the United States are urban dwellers (Allen and Leonard, 1976:563). Many farmers turned to subsistence agriculture, selling small surpluses for low prices in regional markets. Many rural Mormon farming areas in southern and central Utah began to exhibit the pathology of depressed agricultural regions during the 1930s (Nelson, 1952:275–285; Arrington, 1963:353–414).

During World War II, the federal government established many defense plants and military installations in the Rocky Mountain states that provided off-the-farm employment, turning many small farmers into part-time farmers. This laid the foundation for the accelerated urbanization and industrialization now characteristic of the entire region. Urban sprawl already has devoured most of the farm land along the Wasatch Front in Utah. Energy and missile developments threaten the land and water supply of many more farmers in the region.

The future of the small Mormon farmer is in doubt. But agriculture is still a major industry in the Mormon region and large numbers of Mormon farmers hang on because Mormon values exalt agriculture. Many urban Mormons exhibit these agrarian values: they garden, buy up small farms, or develop small ranches. Also, most Mormon stakes, urban or rural, have purchased farms to produce agricultural commodities for the church's welfare system. Undoubtedly, a shadowy Mormon economic system with an agricultural base still exists despite economic and government pressures. Rural-agrarian values continue to be widespread among rural and urban Mormons alike.

Mormons have a long history of intergroup hostilities and conflicts with other ethnic groups (Tyler, 1978:23–24; Ulibarri, 1978:629–650). Their westward migration was spurred in part by strong prejudices that others held toward them and they often experienced vicious acts of social discrimination. Even after their settlement in Utah, there were political attempts to destroy the church, which continued until they formally gave up the practice of polygamy. From that time on, institutionalized discrimination toward Mormons has decreased. In many ways, most Mormons are today culturally and socially assimilated into the larger society.

Mormons tend to take pride in having treated the Indians better than others did; however, Mormon relations with particular American Indian tribes have a long, uneven history. Their early expansion into Ute territory, pushing these people off their land, and the colonization of the Payutes, producing an uneven symbiotic relationship, has left a residual intergroup hostility that could develop into open conflict over political control of areas and water rights. Also, there appears to be some current degree of reciprocal prejudice and discrimination between white Mormons and Mexican-Americans and Blacks in Utah, even though some Mexican-Americans and Blacks are Mormons (Ulibarri, 1978:629–650).

Today, most of rural Utah except the mining areas is still inhabited predominantly by Mormons. A similar situation prevails in some portions of adjacent states. Their dominance provides a basis for social conflict with other ethnic groups, especially those whose lifestyle conflicts with Mormon moral norms. The continued development of energy-based industry and military installations in heavily Mormon-populated areas will probably lead to more pronounced and open intergroup hostility and conflict, particularly in reference to political dominance of local areas.

THE U.S. DEPARTMENT OF AGRICULTURE AND RURAL MINORITIES

The record of federal policy and programs regarding rural minorities is not enviable. At various times, Indians, Hispanics, and, at a later time, Asian-Americans were evicted from land they lived on, placed on reservations or in internment camps, or had their land expropriated through military actions, treaties, and homesteading settlements. Blacks were transported to this country as slaves to provide labor for an agricultural economy (U.S. Department of Commerce, 1960:74, 79). The past treatment of rural minorities has very much influenced their present condition.

For a variety of reasons, many associated with race and national origin, minorities have not been able to adapt to change and retain association with land they once had. As a result, some minorities have disappeared from the land at a much higher rate than nonminorities.

Prior to the civil rights legislation of the mid-1960s, the U.S. Department of Agriculture (USDA) generally acquiesced to local custom regarding race relations and treatment of minorities. Many of its offices were segregated (U.S. Commission on Civil Rights, 1965:24). The relatively few minority employees of the USDA were generally relegated to service occupations. Local programs were administered along racial lines. Fewer and more poorly trained minority employees meant that minority rural residents were not served equally, if at all.

Minorities were also either excluded or underrepresented on local boards and committees established to administer or advise on agricultural programs. Although Blacks comprised a substantial portion of southern farm operators, no Black ever served on an Agricultural Stabilization and Conservation Service (ASCS) county committee in that region until 1969 (U.S. Commission on Civil Rights, 1969:26). Credit programs available to minorities through the Farmers' Home Administration (FmHA) generally were limited to current expense loans, while whites were much more likely to receive capital expense loans (U.S. Commission on Civil Rights, 1965:87). Racial and ethnic discrimination has promoted a cycle of poverty that feeds upon itself with the result that few minorities escape the cycle through agriculture.

Change has been slow. Segregated USDA offices have been eliminated. Minority employment as well as minority participation in USDA programs and on boards and committees have increased. The USDA has established mechanisms to enforce nondiscrimination policies, such as affirmative action plans, data collection and evaluation, compliance reviews, outreach, public notification, and investigation of complaints. Many problems remain, however. In one state, an audit determined that one of every three 4-H clubs organized in areas with potential for interracial membership were nonetheless segregated by race. Reviewers in the USDA concluded that this state had not substantially improved its civil rights compliance over similar findings a decade earlier.

Minorities are still underrepresented on many boards and committees that are adjuncts of agricultural programs at the local level. Less than 3 percent of ASCS county committee members, less than 2 percent of soil and water conservation district board members, and less than 4 percent of Rural Electrification Administration board directors are minorities. In the entire South, there are only five black ASCS county committee members, out of a total of more than twenty-seven hundred members in the region.

There are still problems of low minority participation in USDA programs. Although minorities received nearly 15 percent of all FmHA rural housing loans in 1979, the minority proportion of substandard rural housing is 31 percent. Many FmHA-financed rural rental housing projects are in segregated living areas. While FmHA farm ownership loans to minorities have increased dramatically over the last two years, they still account for only 4 percent of all farm ownership loans made.

The record regarding minority participation in USDA programs is not all bleak, however. Minorities comprise 55 percent of the persons who participate in food programs – a figure that compares favorably with the minority proportion of the low-income population nationally. There was a 73 percent increase in the number of FmHA farm ownership loans to minorities in 1979. The USDA's aid to the sixteen historically black land grant colleges and Tuskegee Institute – aid that was very modest to nonexistent in the 1960s – has been increasing. The USDA's procurement from minority business firms tripled between 1977 and 1979.

Minorities represent about 12 percent of all USDA employees. This compares with about 21 percent minority employment in the federal government as a whole. In USDA-assisted programs staffed by nonfederal employees, minorities account for just over 4 percent of ASCS county office employees and a little less than 9 percent of professional extension workers at the state and local level.

In each of sixteen southern states there are still two land grant colleges, one primarily for whites established by 1862 legislation and one originally for Blacks established by 1890 legislation. For years, the 1890 schools suffered from discriminatory patterns of federal, state, and private funding, yet they managed to survive. A study of 1968 funding showed that, on a proportional enrollment basis, combined federal and state aid to the predominantly white land grant schools was approximately twice that of the aid to the predominantly black land grant schools in the same states (U.S. Commission on Civil Rights, 1970:17). Nearly all of the USDA's funds went to the white schools. Under pressure from Congress, the USDA began providing research and extension funds to the 1890 schools in substantial amounts in 1971. By 1979, USDA funding for the sixteen 1890 schools and Tuskegee Institute amounted to $26.7 million. In 1970, it had been less than $1 million.

Early in this century, Blacks owned more than fifteen million acres of farm land in the United States. In 1954, they owned 10.6 million acres. In 1969, they owned 5.6 million. Today, the number of farm acres owned by Blacks is estimated at about three million acres. The disappearance of the Black farmer – there were more than 900,000 in 1920 and only about 40,000 today – is one of the effects of rapidly changing economic forces, agricultural policy, and racial discrimination. Much of the loss of Blacks from farming is in reaction to economic forces, but some is the product of exploitative and marginally legal means by whites who take advantage of unsophisticated black land owners. Partition sales, tax sales, foreclosures, and adverse possession are several means by which this is done (Ball, 1980).

The main barrier to Indian participation in USDA programs is that programs have been established with the individual farm operator or rural resident in mind. Indians on reservations are members of tribes with land and property held by the tribe. Thus, Indians on reservations have difficulty obtaining much-needed agriculture credit and services that non-Indians are able to obtain. The USDA's policies and programs need to be altered to take into account the modes of Indian social organization.

In order to improve federal policies and programs affecting rural minorities, the USDA needs first to enforce vigorously national equal opportunity law and policy. There is simply no excuse, more than fifteen years after the Civil Rights Act of 1964 prohibiting racial discrimination in the benefits and services of government programs, for inequities of the kind mentioned here to exist. To rectify the situation may involve more resources, but mainly it requires, at all levels where agricultural policy is formulated and implemented, committed leadership and more efficient and effective use of present resources.

Much of the USDA's current civil rights activities are predicated on assuring nondiscriminatory treatment from the time of the Civil Rights Act forward. That is not enough. The effects of decades of prior discriminatory treatment of minorities in education, employment, housing, and services have left a scar that cannot be removed by the mere absence of further discriminatory treatment. This nation has an obligation to act in ways that will enable minorities to compete equally with nonminorities.

RESEARCH ISSUES

The racial and ethnic minority groups located in the nonmetro areas of the United States defy easy generalization: They differ in location, the extent of cultural homogeneity, in the manner and degree to which they are organized, in the degree to which they experience pejorative treatment from dominant groups in society, and in their desires for autonomy and cultural and social pluralism rather than assimilation.

There are important and significant research problems and issues associated with each of the limited number of rural ethnic minority groups discussed in this chapter. For example, although rural Blacks and Mexican-Americans are both found in heavily disproportionate numbers among the rural poor, their problems and circumstances differ on such fundamental factors as language and culture. Space prevents a delineation of all the important and relevant research issues. The following are offered as generic issues that span most, if not all, rural ethnic groups.

Research is needed on the extent to which patterned discrimination imposed on ethnic peoples influences their life chances in such fundamental areas as education and employment. Research is also needed on the extent to which the social class structure places limitations on the aspirations and social and physical mobility of rural ethnic populations. Comparative research is needed on the extent to which race is a factor that causes differentiation among ethnic groups' relative opportunities within the larger society. Most important is the need for research on the extent to which rurality and the rural community enhances or impedes the aspirations of ethnic minorities in comparison with urban members of the same ethnic populations.

CONCLUSION

Policy makers, social developers, and humanists concerned with helping the rural disadvantaged should clearly understand two things about these rural minorities before they try to help them:

- They are too diverse as social groups for a singular meliorative program aimed at all to be of much good.
- In most cases, the ethnic groups themselves are not well organized beyond the community level and embrace a wide diversity of cultural and social patterns and definitions of what the "good life" is or should be.

The best programs to assist rural minority group members will be developed at a local level first, using members of the ethnic groups themselves to define problems and needs and to establish ways of meeting these. At the same time, the USDA should take on an explicit advocacy role for these groups as a whole to make sure their interests are represented in national policy priority setting and program development.

REFERENCES

Allen, James B., and Glen M. Leonard. 1976. *The Story of the Latter Day Saints.* Salt Lake City, Utah: Deseret Book Co.

Arrington, Leonard J. 1958. *Great Basin Kingdom.* Cambridge: Harvard University Press.

_____. 1963. *The Changing Economic Structure of the Mountain West, 1950–1960.* Logan, Utah: Utah State University Press.

Ball, Howard G. 1980. "Black landownership in the rural South: A thing of the past." *Newsline* (Rural Sociological Society) (November):37–39.

Brown, David L., and Jeanne M. O'Leary. 1979. *Labor Force Activity of Women in Metropolitan and Nonmetropolitan America.* Washington, D.C.: Economics, Statistics, and Cooperatives Service, U.S. Department of Agriculture, Rural Development Research Report 15.

Buck, Roy C. 1978. "Boundary maintenance revisited: Tourist experience in an Old Order Amish community." *Rural Sociology* 43(2):221–234.

Clinton, Charles A. 1979. *Local Success and Federal Failure: A Study of Community Development and Educational Change in the Rural South.* Cambridge, Massachusetts: Abt Associates.

Cosby, Arthur G. 1980. "The urban context of rural policy." *The Interstate Compact for Education* 14(Fall, 3):38–39.

Davis, Leroy. 1978. "The relationship of farm size on rural poverty." *Journal of Social and Behavioral Sciences* 24(Winter, 1):6–16.

Durant, Thomas J., Jr. 1974. "Work orientation attitudes of rural low-income residents of three south-central Virginia counties." Paper presented at the annual meetings of the Southern Association of Agricultural Scientists, Memphis, Tennessee.

Durant, Thomas J., Jr., and Clark S. Knowlton. 1978. "Rural ethnic minorities: Adaptive responses to inequality." In Thomas R. Ford (editor), *Rural U.S.A.: Persistence and Change.* Ames, Iowa: Iowa State University Press.

Eastman, Clyde. 1972. *Assessing Cultural Change in North-Central New Mexico.* Las Cruces, New Mexico: Agricultural Experiment Station, New Mexico State University, Bulletin 592.

Eastman, Clyde, Garrey Carruthers, and James A. Liefer. 1971. *Evaluation of Attitudes toward Land in North-Central New Mexico.* Las Cruces, New Mexico: Agricultural Experiment Station, New Mexico State University, Bulletin 577.

Fratoe, Frank A. 1979. *The Educational Level of Farm Residents and Workers.* Washington, D.C.: Economics, Statistics, and Cooperatives Service, U.S. Department of Agriculture, Rural Development Research Report 8.

______. 1980. *The Education of Nonmetro Blacks.* Washington, D.C.: Economics, Statistics, and Cooperatives Service, U.S. Department of Agriculture, Rural Development Research Report 21.

Frazier, James. 1978. *Equal Opportunity Report, USDA Programs, 1978.* Washington, D.C.: Office of Equal Opportunity, U.S. Department of Agriculture.

Gordon, Milton M. 1964. *Assimilation in American Life.* New York: Oxford University Press.

Grebler, Leo, Joan Moore, and Ralph Guzman. 1970. *The Mexican-American People: The Nation's Second Largest Minority.* New York: Free Press.

Hawkes, Glenn R., Minna Taylor, and Beverly E. Bastian. 1973. *Patterns of Living in California's Migrant Labor Families.* Davis, California: Department of Applied Behavioral Science, University of California, Research Monograph 12.

Hightower, James. 1973. *Hard Tomatoes, Hard Times: A Report of the Agribusiness Accountability Project on the Failure of America's Land Grant College Complex.* Cambridge, Massachusetts: Schenkman Publishing Co.

Hostetler, John A. 1977. "Old Order Amish survival." *The Mennonite Quarterly Review* 4:352–361.

Howze, Glenn R. 1970. "The Black farmer and the USDA." Paper presented at the meetings of the Association of Southern Agricultural Workers, Memphis, Tennessee.

Hunter, Milton R. 1973. *Brigham Young, the Colonizer.* Santa Barbara, California, and Salt Lake City, Utah: Peregrine Smith.

Jennings, Paul. 1980. "Class and national division in south Texas: The farm worker strike in Raymondville." *Humanity and Society* 4(February, 1): 52–69.

Kephart, William H. 1976. "The Old Order Amish." *Extraordinary Groups.* New York: St. Martin's Press.

Knowlton, Clark S. 1962. "Patron-peon pattern among the Spanish-Americans of New Mexico." *Social Forces* 40:12–17.

______. 1965. "Changes in the structure and roles of Spanish-American families of northern New Mexico." Paper presented at the annual meetings of the Southwest Social Science Association.

______. 1970. "Violence in New Mexico: A sociological perspective." *California Law Review* 58(October).

Kuvlesky, William P. 1977. *Rural Youth in the U.S.A.: Profile of an Ignored Minority.* College Station, Texas: Department of Rural Sociology, Texas A & M University, DTR 77-3.

______. 1978. "A tri-ethnic comparison of the religious involvements and orientations of Texas rural youth: A study of Black, White, and Mexican-American adolescents." *South Texas Journal of Research and Humanities* 2(1):87–122.

______. 1979a. "Minority group orientations: Are rural Mexican-American youth assimilations prone or pluralistic?" Paper presented at the annual meetings of the Association for Humanist Sociology, Johnstown, Pennsylvania.

______. 1979b. "Youth in northern Taos County, New Mexico: No one cares." *Humanity and Society* 3(3).

______. 1980. *Brooks County Youth: Their Self-Defined Quality of Life, Problems, and Needs. A Report of Preliminary Findings.* College Station, Texas: Department of Rural Sociology, Texas A & M University.

Kuvlesky, William P., and William C. Boykin. 1977. *Black Youth in the Rural South: Educational Abilities and Ambitions.* ERIC Clearinghouse on Rural Education and Small Schools.

Kuvlesky, William P., and Everett D. Edington. 1976. "Ethnic group identity and occupational status projections of teenage boys and girls: Mexican-American, Black, Native American, and Anglo youth." Paper presented at the annual meetings of the Southwest Sociological Association, Dallas, Texas.

Kuvlesky, William P., and Rumaldo Juarez. 1975. "Mexican-American youth and the American dream." In Picou and Campbell (editors), *Career Behavior of Special Groups.* New York: Charles E. Merrill.

Kuvlesky, William P., John Dunkelburger, V. A. Boyd, Melvin Knapp, and George Ohlendor. 1979. "Historical change in educational aspirations and expectations of rural Black youth in the South." *Sourcebook of Equal Educational Opportunity.* Chicago: Marquis Academic Media.

Kuvlesky, William P., Richard Warren, and George Ragland. 1972. "Orientations toward racial prejudice among nonmetropolitan and metropolitan Blacks." Paper presented at the annual meetings of the Rural Sociological Society.

Levitan, Sar A., Garth L. Mangum, and Ray Marshall. 1972. *Human Resources and Labor Markets.* New York: Harper and Row.

Linder, William. 1976. *The Progress and Promise of Title V in the South: A Synopsis of Progress Reports on Title V Rural Development Programs in the Southern States.* State College, Mississippi: Southern Rural Development Center, Mississippi State University.

Marshall, Kimball P., and Michael V. Miller. 1977. "Status and familial orientations of rural Mexican-American youth: Integration and conflict within aspirational frames of reference." *Journal of Vocational Behavior* 11:347–362.

Martineau, William H., and Rhonda Sayres MacQueen. 1977. "Occupational differentiation among the Old Order Amish." *Rural Sociology* 42(3):383–397.

Medina, Dennis, and William P. Kuvlesky. 1976. *Mexican-Americans: A Survey of Research by the Texas Agricultural Experiment Station, 1964–1976.* College Station, Texas: Texas Agricultural Experiment Station, Progress Report 3194.

Meyer, R. W. 1967. *History of the Santee Sioux.* Lincoln, Nebraska: University of Nebraska Press.

Miller, Michael V. 1974. "An assessment of the current status of the Mexican-American population." Paper presented at the annual meetings of the Southwest Sociological Association.

______. 1975. "Chicano community control in south Texas: Problems and prospects." *Journal of Ethnic Studies* 3(Fall):70–89.

______. 1976. "Mexican-Americans, Chicanos, and others: Ethnic self-identification and selected social attributes of rural Texas youth." *Rural Sociology* 41(Summer, 2):234–247.

______. 1978a. "'Chicanos' and 'AntiChicanos': Ethnic identity polarization and selected status indicators." *South Texas Journal of Research and Humanities* 2(Fall, 2):125–139.

______. 1978b. "Variations in Mexican-American family life: A review synthesis of empirical research." *Aztlan* 9:209–231.

Miller, Michael V., and Robert Lee Maril. 1979. *Poverty in the Lower Rio Grande Valley of Texas: Historical and Contemporary Dimensions.* College Station, Texas: Department of Rural Sociology, Texas A & M University, DTR 78-2.

Mulder, William. 1956. "Immigration and the Mormon question: An international episode." *Western Political Quarterly* 9(June):416–433.

Nelson, Lowry. 1952. *The Mormon Village.* Salt Lake City, Utah: University Press.

President's National Advisory Commission on Rural Poverty. 1967. *The People Left Behind.* Washington, D.C.: U.S. Government Printing Office.

Rivera, Julius. 1978. "Power and symbol in the Chicano movement." *Humanity and Society* 11(February, 1):1–17.

Smith, Joyce Louise. 1969. "The social organization of small farmers: A case study analysis of interaction, satisfaction, and cooperative behavior." Baton Rouge, Louisiana: Louisiana State University. Doctoral dissertation.

Sorkin, A. L. 1971. *American Indian and Federal Aid.* Washington, D.C.: Brookings Institution.

Stanley, William D., and William P. Kuvlesky. 1978. *The Impact of the T.V. Event, "Roots": A Case Study of East Texas Nonmetropolitan Black Women.* College Station, Texas: Department of Rural Sociology, Texas A & M University, DTR 78.

Stoddard, Ellwyn R. 1973. *Mexican-Americans.* New York: Random House.

Terry, Geraldine B., and J. L. Charlton. 1974. *Changes in Labor Force Characteristics of Women in Low-Income Rural Areas of the South.* Fayetteville, Arkansas: Arkansas Agricultural Experiment Station, Bulletin 185.

Tyler, S. Lyman. 1978. "The earliest people." In Richard D. Polls (editor), *Utah's History.* Provo, Utah: Brigham Young University Press.

Ulibarri, Richard O. 1978. "Utah's unassimilated minorities." In Richard D. Polls (editor), *Utah's History.* Provo, Utah: Brigham Young University Press.

U.S. Commission on Civil Rights. 1965. *Equal Opportunity in Farm Programs.* Washington, D.C.: U.S. Government Printing Office.

U.S. Commission on Civil Rights. 1969. "One in four thousand or a federal farm agency makes progress." *Civil Rights Digest* (Spring). Washington, D.C.: U.S. Government Printing Office.

U.S. Commission on Civil Rights. 1970. "The Negro land grant colleges." *Civil Rights Digest* (Spring). Washington, D.C.: U.S. Government Printing Office.

U.S. Department of Commerce (Bureau of the Census). 1960. *Historical Statistics of the United States, Colonial Times to 1957.* Washington, D.C.: U.S. Government Printing Office.

U.S. Department of Commerce (Bureau of the Census). 1970. *Subject Report, American Indians.* Washington, D.C.: U.S. Government Printing Office.

U.S. Department of Commerce (Bureau of the Census). 1977. *Persons of Spanish Origin in the United States.* Washington, D.C.: U.S. Government Printing Office.

Wilson, William. 1978. *The Declining Significance of Race.* Chicago: University of Chicago Press.

Wright, David E., Esteban Salinas, and William P. Kuvlesky. 1973. "Ambitions and opportunities for social mobility and their consequences for Mexican-Americans as compared with other youth." In Kruszewski et al. (editors), *Chicanos and Native Americans: The Territorial Minorities.* New York: Prentice-Hall.

12
Women

WAVA G. HANEY

The women's movement of the past two decades has heightened national awareness of sexual inequalities and stimulated research into the origins and perpetuation of patriarchy and women's inferior social position. This research – an impressive volume in little more than a decade – has already invalidated many traditional assumptions on which family, labor, tax, and other public policies have been based and has provided new insights into the position of women. For certain groups of women, however, study of policy-related issues remains quite limited. In particular, we are relatively ignorant about the everyday world of rural women and how their lives are specifically circumscribed by social processes and public policies.

To be sure, research has given us scattered information about rural women, but little of it has made women and their activities a central focus. This paucity of research results in part from the historically narrow conceptualization of the roles of women in our dominant research paradigms. Leading theories in the social sciences consider women's activities and their positions in society as subsidiary to those of men. Consequently, many studies overlook women completely. In other studies, women are "there" but analytically invisible. Even when incorporated into research studies, typically only those aspects of their lives that relate to men and children are included. As Joyce and Leadley (1977:35–52)

Wava G. Haney is a visiting associate professor at the College of Community Sciences, University of Wisconsin, Green Bay, Wisconsin. She has previously written articles on women and work, women and development, and neighborhood perception.

The present version of this chapter has benefited by critical comments from Polly Fass-

point out, research often treats women as a "factor" (e.g., wife's cooperation, nonparticipation, nonsupport) which, implicitly at least, explains the success of men. Because women are perceived as occupying peripheral or supportive positions, substantive questions about many facets of their traditional roles remain uninvestigated. Viewed simply as occupants of traditional roles—wife, mother, and housewife—much about the lives of rural women remains unexplored.

The way in which researchers have handled the work of women is a notable example of how models can inhibit the collection of policy-relevant data. Limiting productive activity to paid labor has led social scientists to ignore or misinterpret the economic impact of housework and community service activities, not to mention the work that women perform on farms and in other rural family businesses. Hence, the literature tends to understate the contribution of rural women to family and community well-being. A policy consequence of these imbalanced perspectives is the reinforcement of traditional sex role stereotypes and the perpetuation of discrimination against so-called "economically inactive" housewives in tax and social security legislation and employment. As long as researchers do not document the nature and scope of women's work, their studies will contribute little to reform an employment system that places classroom credentials and formal work experience far ahead of experiential knowledge gained in the home or family business. Researchers are not likely to contribute to debates on inheritance and estate laws—a vital issue for farm women today—or the extension of social benefits to housewives.

Also characteristic of our dominant research orientations are explanations for such social outcomes as delayed entry into the paid labor force and wage discrimination in terms of personal and family attributes (e.g., traditional sex role attitudes, marital status, discontinuous work record). Fewer studies investigate the impact of structural factors. Continuous reorganization of agricultural production, the spread of labor-intensive industries to the countryside, expansion of extractive industries, and the migration turnaround are profoundly reshaping the social and physical landscape of rural America. These forces are bringing deep-seated changes to the work, family, and community life of rural women and increasing the demand for additional human services in rural areas (see Chapters 8 and 14). To deal adequately with policy issues important to

---

inger, Cornelia Butler Flora, Sally Hacker, Emil Haney, Judith Heffernan, and Eugene Wilkening.

rural women, structural consequences of these major social changes must become a central focus of research.

A PORTRAIT OF RURAL WOMEN

Although the existing literature is limited in both the range of issues addressed and the types of women studied, there are encouraging developments. Several current studies clarify many conceptual issues and enable us to grasp a partial picture of the lives of rural women.

As is true of the general female population, age at marriage and divorce rates are increasing among rural women while fertility and household size are declining. Compared with their urban counterparts, however, "rural women are still more likely to be married, have more children, live in larger families . . . complete their families earlier" and they are less likely to divorce (Whitener-Smith, 1979:3). At the same time, studies reveal lower levels of marital and personal satisfaction among rural, especially farm, residents (Flora and Johnson, 1978: 169–171).

We also know that rural women are entering paid employment in increasing numbers. Not only has the declining number of farm wives taken more off-the-farm jobs (Sweet, 1972; Wilkening and Ahrens, 1979; Fassinger and Schwarzweller, 1980; Bokemeier and Coughenour, 1980) but the expanding population of rural nonfarm women is entering the paid labor force in record numbers (Bokemeier et al., 1980). During the 1960s and 1970s, women accounted for nearly all of the employment growth in nonmetropolitan counties (Brown and O'Leary, 1979). Labor force participation for metropolitan women remains higher, but the gap between metro and nonmetro women is narrowing. Especially evident in the past few decades is the increased participation of women who previously were seen as least likely to work outside the home, i.e., young mothers with preschool children (Almquist, 1977). In a Michigan sample of farm families, except for the large-scale farms, one-half or more of mothers with dependent children at home were employed off the farm (Fassinger and Schwarzweller, 1980).

Rural industrialization has increased the rate of labor force participation among nonmetro women, but the jobs are concentrated in low-skill and low-wage occupations and industries (Brown and O'Leary, 1979; Bokemeier et al., 1980; Sweet, 1972). Among both metro and nonmetro women, the majority of those employed are in low-level white-collar occupations, especially clerical jobs. The blue-collar workers are disproportionately service workers or operatives, especially in nondurable goods manufacturing. However, a difference in the type of industries in metro and nonmetro areas, as well as occupations within industries, leads to an overall inferior economic situation for employed nonmetro women (O'Connor, 1973; Brown and O'Leary, 1979). Moreover, nonmetro women tend to have a more limited range of occupational choice and employers, fewer chances for promotion, greater likelihood of part-time employment, and greater vulnerability to fluctuations in economic cycles.

Earning differentials between nonmetro men and women are not reported in these studies, but inferences can be drawn from national data. Featherman and Hauser (1976) found that the female/male earnings ratio for married men and women did not improve from 1962 to 1973; in 1973, the gap was $6,942. As Almquist (1977:850) puts it, "Throughout the last two decades, most full-time women workers have taken home paychecks only 60 percent as large as those of their husbands, brothers, and lovers." Wright's (1979:221) comparison of the income gap between sexes and races in the United States suggests that "sexual inequality is greater than racial inequality."

Subsidization of farm income by off-the-farm female employment is not new for American farm families—we need only recall who staffed early New England factories. What has changed is that increasing numbers of married farm women are selling their labor off the farm (see Chapter 34). Recent studies clarify the work of farm women in two ways: the different ways in which farm family households integrate farm and off-the-farm work, and the different ways farm men and women integrate farming activities. When work patterns of both spouses are included, it is apparent that part-time farming, in the sense of farm couples combining farm and off-the-farm work, is even more common than assumed (see Bokemeier and Coughenour, 1980). Many men may be able to remain full-time operators because of women's labor on and off the farm. Indeed, women's work is vital to the survival of family farms. In a Michigan study, households managing large-scale farms were less likely than small-scale farm families to have off-the-farm income, but women were more often the sole source of off-the-farm earnings. Compared with women on moderate-scale and hobby farms, women on large-scale farms were "more likely to be doing farm work, putting in the longest hours on the farm, and helping with the farming activities year round" (Fassinger and Schwarzweller, 1980:23). In a longitudinal study of a sample of Wisconsin dairy farms, Dorner and Marquardt (1979) found that the labor input of farm wives was a significant factor in expansion of the farm operation.

Studies recording farm work performed by wives of full- and part-time farmers challenges the census figure that 60 percent of farm women are "economically inactive." On large-scale farms in Michigan (Fassinger and Schwarzweller, 1980) and Wisconsin (Wilkening and Ahrens, 1979), on Oklahoma beef and grain, Colorado fruit, and Vermont truck and dairy farms (Boulding, 1979), and on Colorado grain farms (Pearson, 1979), data suggest that husband and wife are partners in the farming operations. The presence of younger children does not reduce work activities of farm women. Wilkening and Ahrens (1979) found that women with dependent children were more likely to be involved in farm work. Not until children were old enough to take over did the amount of farm chores and field work decrease for farm women. Farm women engage in a great variety of work activities, labor long hours (one study reports sixteen-hour days and 113-hour work weeks, excluding community volunteer work), and operate at a high skill level. Women are also substantially involved in decision making (Wilkening and Bhradwaj, 1967, 1968; Wilkening and Guerrero, 1969; Salamon and Keim, 1979), coordination (Boulding, 1979), and management (Boulding 1979; Wilkening and Ahrens, 1979). A consistent finding on family farms is that women tend to be the accountants, the personnel and equipment managers, and the purchasing agents. Despite the labor, management, and capital contributions that farm women make to family farms, participation in government programs under their signature is still often not possible. And, under a legal system that assigns the husband as head of the household, wives are obligated to perform household services without legal right to the property their labor helps to amass.

Studies on the work life of rural women are still in the exploratory stage; research on their community and political life is practically nonexistent. Earlier research at the community level noted their service roles in major community institutions such as church, school, and farm organizations. Except for extension homemaker groups, there have been few women's organizations in rural America. Rural community organizations have tended to be organized around family membership, with men typically holding the offices and making decisions. Salamon and Keim (1979) argue that limited freedom of movement and restricted opportunities to meet with women other than extended family members have retarded the development of female solidarity groups that could exert power at the community level. Others have suggested that low levels of political participation by rural women may be attributable to limited support services such as child care facilities (Lynn and Flora, 1977).

On the other hand, there is some evidence of increased participation by rural women in political and community affairs. Farm women's groups have been organized in several states as well as nationally, and rural women's workshops, seminars, and task forces appear with some frequency. A longitudinal study of community decision making in two rural midwestern communities documents a significant increase in the proportion of women identified as community power holders (Bokemeier and Tait, 1980). They suggest that this change is explained by increased saliency of "women's issues," more public experience, and greater access to communication and information networks.

RESEARCH ISSUES

Together with emerging anthropological and historical literature, sociological studies challenge previous interpretations of rural women's insignificance in the life of rural families and communities. This research undermines the assumed supremacy of traditional values in guiding rural women's behavior. Past shortcomings notwithstanding, new approaches and renewed commitments to the study of rural women are needed. To generate data relevant to public decision making and policy formulation, research on rural women in the 1980s should systematically look at women as workers and as economically active family members and give attention to the involvement of rural women in politics, community service, and national policy.

Sociological research should address two central issues. First, studies should make clear how social processes and current policies circumscribe the lives of the very heterogeneous group of women who reside in rural America. Research that exposes how and why current conditions of specific groups of rural women have emerged is a prerequisite to changing the mechanisms that have institutionalized women's subordinate positions. Second, research on rural women in the 1980s should examine both individual and social consequences of maintaining and changing sexual inequalities. In addition, research must continue to examine important differences between rural farm and nonfarm women, whites and minorities, different social classes, and women in different family roles. Unmarried daughters, single women who head households, and widows are vastly underrepresented foci of the literature.

Work and the Work Place

Top priority should be given to studying the work of rural women. Research is needed to disentangle the multiple and complex ways in which rural women are involved in the production process; to document the social processes that produce job and wage discrimination and the resulting preponderance of rural women in low-skill, low-wage jobs or as unpaid family laborers; and to identify consequences for women of the changing nature of work in agriculture and industry.

Research is needed to document the division of rural women's work among child care, production for household use, production for family status, and production for sale or wage. Detailed information about the economic contribution of women is paramount in answering questions about family and marital property reform. Research that documents the multiple work roles of rural women can also be instrumental in showing the degree and range of women's skills. Such data would contribute to rural women's self-images and self-esteem. They could also increase employers' awareness of the inadequacy of current methods of assessing skills and enhance the development of new procedures for evaluating job skills of women. Likewise, knowledge of the amount and range of farm women's work activities is potentially important to development of family farm policy. Studies are needed to determine the extent to which families have been able to enter or stay in family-centered production because of women's farm and off-the-farm work.

Research needs to consider carefully the benefits and problems of women's new patterns of work. We need to explore more fully any change in the proportion of time devoted to various types of production activities and to assess the impact of women's entry into the labor force on length of work days, definition of necessary housework, work patterns within the family, commercialization of household services, women's health, family relationships, and community and political involvement.

Research should also examine the sex segregation of occupations and industries that employ rural women. Research is needed on entry and nonentry, career mobility and immobility, and wage differentials for rural women across the occupational spectrum. Within the agricultural sector, for example, research needs to examine exclusionary processes in production (e.g., barriers to women as independent producers or farm managers), processing and marketing, input manufacturing and distribution, and recruitment into traditionally male professions such as agricultural education, journalism, and veterinary medicine. We need to determine if attitudes and actions of employers thwart women's occupational attainment. Pilot programs to change discriminatory policies of decision makers could follow. Studying job and wage discrimination issues in a variety of work settings has the potential for affecting policy making at several levels, from industrial firms and academic departments to the nation's capital.

A third research priority is to consider the consequences of the changing nature of work in agriculture and industry for women. We need research on the impact of continued rationalization of production in agriculture (Friedland et al., 1980) and in industry (Braverman, 1974) on work opportunities for rural women and on the type of jobs available. For example, have women disproportionately joined the ranks of the unemployed as a result of the mechanization of fruit and vegetable production? Have new jobs replaced those supplanted by machines? The impact of rationalization of production on place and variety of work and on human relationships where rural women are employed also needs systematic study. Research on these relationships is important to resolving occupational health and safety, sexual harassment, and other work place issues. Moreover, because of the potential link between work environment, mental health, and family relations, this research can be important to decisions about the types of human service agencies needed in rural communities (see Chapters 8 and 14).

The Family

Research needs to examine contributions of various members of rural families to the household and family economy and to relate these work and economic patterns to family decision making and authority relations. For example, in farm families, we need to examine whether women's contributions to the economy of the household and farm have led to more egalitarian relationships between husbands and wives.

Research also needs to examine connections between public policies and interpersonal relations within the family (see Glazer-Malbin, 1976). Rather than view the family as isolated from society, we need to determine the impact of public policy on family members and learn what changes are necessary in our social institutions to reduce personal and interpersonal conflict. Accommodation of work and family, a challenge in family-centered production units, takes on new dimensions when either or both spouses are employed outside the family. Our concern is how different work schedules, stressful working conditions, extensive travel, low salary, limited benefits, and frequent moves contribute to family conflict. The more general issue is the implication for individuals and families of an employment system that typically demands that individuals accommodate employers' needs. Similarly, the impact of family law and state welfare policy on family relationships should be investigated.

Family farm and rural development policy formulation depends in part on understanding what emerging integration of different types of employment by rural men and women has meant for the social and economic position of rural families. It is important to examine for various regions and agricultural commodity groups how public policies reduce the number of family farms and increase the ranks of rural families in the agricultural or industrial working class (see Wright, 1979). We also need to know whether these policies and processes contribute to the growth of a small employer group in agriculture. Such research might suggest economic strategies that would help to stabilize the continued rapid disintegration of family-centered agricultural production.

Politics

Research needs to determine if existing patterns of authority restrict rural women's ability to organize effectively and represent their interest in the economic and political arena. Two types of relations, patriarchal relations between men and women (see, Hartmann, 1976) and paternal relations between employer and employee (see Newby, 1977), need to be investigated in a variety of settings. If such studies unite research and social action (see Hacker, 1980), the potential exists to merge strategies for overcoming barriers at the individual level with policies to change institutionalized relations.

Documentation of the nature and amount of involvement by rural women in local government, social movements, and occupational and political interest groups is overdue. As repeatedly suggested in recent literature, it may be that women's involvement in politics has been less visible because of the failure to ask relevant research questions. Studying rural women's protests and their social movements is vital to understanding social change in rural America and to developing change strategies.

Community Services

Research should document the extent to which rural communities rely on the voluntary efforts of women for the delivery of many community services. If rural women's voluntary labor is as instrumental as generally assumed, it is important to determine the impact on service delivery in rural communities of greater labor-force participation by rural women.

Research is also needed on the availability of services that are of particular importance to rural women, such as health and child care, welfare, and low-cost legal aid. As evidence mounts on the amount of violence in the family (see Chapter 8), research needs to look not only at the normative causes of wife battering and sexual, child, and elderly abuse in rural areas, but also at the availability of such services as safe houses, support and therapy groups, and community mental health centers for rural residents. We also need to look at the relationship between access to community-based reproductive health services and fertility rates of rural women. The relationship between the differential effects of poverty on women and children and the availability of a range of community services such as literacy and nutrition programs and displaced homemaker and single-parent services needs to be examined. With more women entering the paid labor force, pilot studies are needed to develop cooperative preschool-age and school-age child care and recreational facilities in rural communities. The delivery of low-cost legal services to rural women by law firms knowledgeable in women and family issues also needs to be perfected through field experiments.

State Policy

Finally, to complement research that takes a disaggregated approach, we need to consider the overall consequences of social processes and state policy for rural women. A critical research focus is whether emergent federal policies may arrest those changes that in the past few years apparently have tempered some of the most blatant sexual inequalities. In the past, conditions such as war, peace, and rapid economic expansion have influenced the gains and losses of women. In the decade ahead, our concern is the implication for rural women of "stagflation," local, state, and federal fiscal crises, natural resource constraints and energy shortages, and increased military spending. Research must ask in what ways rural women's movement away from a position of structured disadvantage may be thwarted by new cold war policies (see Buttel, 1980) and recently manifested economic conditions.

CONCLUSION

The research agenda that we have outlined for the 1980s should allow us to enter the 1990s with a greater understanding of the dynamics of modern rural America and with knowledge of more effective ways to change some of its greatest contradictions. At the very least, however, this chapter is a request for greater awareness of women's issues in the academic and public policy circles and a call to expand the amount of research and the range of research questions dealing with women.

REFERENCES

Almquist, Elizabeth M. 1977. "Review essay: Women in the labor force." *Signs* 2(Summer): 843–855.

Bokemeier, Janet, and C. Milton Coughenour. 1980. "Men and women in four types of farm families: Work and attitudes." Paper presented at the annual meetings of the Rural Sociological Society, Ithaca, New York.

Bokemeier, Janet, Verna Keith, and Carolyn Sachs. 1980. "Whatever happened to rural women?" Paper presented at the annual meetings of the Rural Sociological Society, Ithaca, New York.

Bokemeier, Janet L., and John L. Tait. 1980. "Women as power actors: A new trend in rural communities." *Rural Sociology* 45:238–255.

Boulding, Elise. 1979. "The labor of farm women in the United States: A knowledge gap." Paper presented at the annual meetings of the American Sociological Association, Boston, Massachusetts.

Braverman, Harry. 1974. *Labor and Monopoly Capital: The Degradation of Work in the Twentieth Century.* New York: Monthly Review Press.

Brown, David L., and Jeanne M. O'Leary. 1979. *Labor Force Activity of Women in Metropolitan and Nonmetropolitan America.* Washington, D.C.: Economics, Statistics, and Cooperatives Service, U.S. Department of Agriculture, Rural Development Research Report 15.

Buttel, Frederick H. 1980. "The 'new cold war' and rural America." *Newsline* (Rural Sociological Society) 8(March):59–68.

Dorner, Peter, and Mark Marquardt. 1979. *Economic Changes on a Sample of Wisconsin Farms: 1950–1975.* Madison, Wisconsin: University of Wisconsin, Agricultural Economics Staff Paper Series 135.

Fassinger, Polly A., and Harry K. Schwarzweller. 1980. "Exploring women's work roles on family farms: A Michigan case study." Paper presented at the annual meetings of the Rural Sociological Society, Ithaca, New York.

Featherman, David L., and Robert M. Hauser. 1976. "Sexual inequalities and socio-economic achievement in the United States, 1962–1973." *American Sociological Review* 41(June):462–484.

Flora, Cornelia, and Sue Johnson. 1978. "Discarding the distaff: New roles for rural women." In Thomas R. Ford (editor), *Rural U.S.A.: Persistence and Change.* Ames, Iowa: Iowa State University Press.

Friedland, William H., Mena Furnari, and Enrique Pugliese. 1980. "The labor process in agriculture." Paper presented at the Working Conference on the Labor Process, Santa Cruz, California.

Glazer-Malbin, Nona. 1976. "Review essay: Housework." *Signs* 1(Summer):905–922.

Hacker, Sally L. 1980. "Women and agribusiness." *Human Services in the Rural Environment* 5(Spring).

Hartmann, Heidi. 1976. "Capitalism, patriarchy, and job segregation by sex." *Signs* 1(Spring):137–169.

Joyce, Lynda M., and Samuel M. Leadley. 1977. *An Assessment of Research Needs of Women in the Rural United States: Literature Review and Annotated Bibliography.* University Park, Pennsylvania: Pennsylvania State University.

Lynn, Naomi, and Cornelia Butler Flora. 1977. "Societal punishment and aspects of female political participation: 1972 national convention delegates." In Marianne Githens and Jewel L. Prestage (editors), *A Portrait of Marginality: The Political Behavior of the American Woman.* New York: David McKay Co.

Newby, Howard. 1977. "Paternalism and capitalism." In Richard Scase (editor), *Industrial Society: Class, Cleavage, and Control.* London: George Allen and Unwin, Ltd.

O'Connor, James. 1973. *The Fiscal Crisis of the State.* New York: St. Martin's Press.

Pearson, Jessica. 1979. "Note on female farmers." *Rural Sociology* 44(Spring):189–200.

Salamon, Sonya, and Ann Mackey Keim. 1979. "Land ownership and women's power in a midwestern farming community." *Journal of Marriage and the Family* 41(February):109–119.

Sweet, James A. 1972. "The employment of rural farm wives." *Rural Sociology* 37(December):553–577.

Whitener-Smith, Leslie. 1979. "The changing family roles of rural women." Paper presented at the annual meetings of the Rural Sociological Society, Burlington, Vermont.

Wilkening, E. A., and Nancy Ahrens. 1979. "Involvement of wives in farm tasks as related to characteristics of the farm, the family, and work off the farm." Paper presented at the annual meetings of the Rural Sociological Society, Burlington, Vermont.

Wilkening, E. A., and Lakshmi K. Bhradwaj. 1967. "Dimensions of aspiration, work roles, and decision-making of farm husbands and wives in Wisconsin." *Journal of Marriage and the Family* 29(November):703–711.

______. 1968. "Aspirations and task involvement as related to decision-making among farm husbands and wives." *Rural Sociology* 33(March):30–45.

Wilkening, E. A., and Sylvia Guerrero. 1969. "Consensus in aspirations for farm improvement and adoption of farm practices." *Rural Sociology* 34(June):182–196.

Wright, Erik Olin. 1979. *Class Structure and Income Determination.* New York: Academic Press.

13
Poverty

JOHN J. MOLAND, JR.
ALMA T. PAGE

The National Advisory Commission on Rural Poverty was created in 1966 to study economic situations adversely affecting rural people and to make recommendations for action by all levels of government and private enterprise. Programs designed to reduce rural poverty were a major feature of the years that followed. Fifteen years later, we are continuing to search for evidence of the effectiveness of these programs.

A general conclusion is that poverty has been lessened in some nonmetropolitan areas, but in others, pockets of poverty remain unabated. The existence of poverty is especially persistent in depressed areas of the South, the Coastal Plains, Appalachia, Western Indian reservations, and areas of high Mexican-American concentration.

CURRENT KNOWLEDGE

A brief examination of some poverty statistics for the years of 1969 to 1976 will provide the basis for considering the extent of reduction in poverty and for raising relevant issues for which research investigation is needed. Of the twenty-seven million persons in the nation with incomes below the poverty level in 1969, 44 percent lived in nonmetro areas, a percentage far greater than the nonmetro proportion of the total popula-

John J. Moland, Jr. is professor in the Department of Sociology and director of the Center of Social Research, Southern University, Baton Rouge, Louisiana. A past president of the Southwestern Sociological Society and the Association of Social and Behavioral Scientists, his articles and book reviews have appeared in a number of professional journals. **Alma T.**

tion. Persons below the low-income threshold represented 19.3 percent of the nonmetro population and 11.2 percent of the metropolitan population. In the nonmetro areas of the South, nearly 28 percent of all persons lived in poverty and, in the most rural counties, 35 percent of the population was in poverty. Of all nonmetro Blacks, 52.6 percent were classified as being in poverty; in the most rural nonmetro counties, 56.1 percent were below the poverty level.

Seven years later, in 1976, there were twenty-five million persons with incomes below the poverty level, two million less than in 1969; 39 percent lived in nonmetro areas. People in poverty represented 14 percent of the nonmetro population and 10.7 percent of the metro population. Although this represented a 5 percent decline in the nonmetro poverty population between 1969 and 1976 compared to 1 percent in the metro areas, the nonmetro areas still have a higher percentage of persons in poverty. Of all nonmetro Blacks, 38.2 percent were below the poverty level in 1976, a drop of 14.4 percent from 1969. We know very little about what factors have contributed to the decline in the percentage of rural Blacks with income below the poverty level. Was it because of outmigration? Or was it because of an increase in employment opportunities for Blacks? Was the percentage drop influenced by minimum wage laws, transfer payments, or by a combination of these and other factors? These questions call attention to the constant need for research data relevant to monitoring changes in nonmetro poverty, for evaluating the effectiveness of action programs, and for providing input for program planning and implementation.

Despite the overall decline in rural poverty, low earnings and a low standard of living persist in many rural counties (see Table 13.1). Persistent low-income (PLI) counties in 1975 have been identified in a study by Thomas F. Davis as those that appeared in the bottom quintile of the national rankings of nonmetro counties on per capita income. The average per capita income for the 255 counties with PLI status was $3,299 in 1975. No PLI county had a per capita income above $3,853.

In 1969, 94 percent of the 298 PLI counties were located in the southern region, followed by 5 percent in the north-central region, 1 percent in the West, and none in the Northeast. These PLI counties are associated with a relatively high concentration of minorities (Blacks, Hispanics, and Native Americans) and with the mostly white areas of Appalachia and the Ozarks. By 1975, the number of PLI counties had

---

Page is a professor in the Department of Sociology, Southern University, Baton Rouge, Louisiana.

Table 13.1 Regional Distribution of Persistent Nonmetro Low-Income Counties (PLI) in 1969 and 1975

	PLI Counties by Region				Counties Shedding PLI Classification	
	1969		1975			
Region	N	%	N	%	N	%
United States	298	100	255	100	43	100
North-east	0	0	0	0	0	0
North-central	15	5	14	5	1	2
East-north-central	3	1	2	1	1	2
West-north-central	12	4	12	4	0	0
South	279	94	237	93	42	98
South Atlantic	82	28	62	24	20	47
East-south-central	140	47	128	50	12	28
West-south-central	57	19	47	18	10	23
West	4	1	4	2	0	0
Mountain	4	1	4	2	0	0

Source: Davis, Thomas F. 1979. Persistent Low-Income Counties in Nonmetro America. Washington, D.C.: Economics, Statistics, and Cooperative Service, U.S. Department of Agriculture, Rural Development Research Report 12, page 4.

declined by 14 percent. Forty-two of the forty-three counties that lost their PLI designation were in the South. Growth in agriculture and mining industries, coupled with growth in wage and salary income, were major factors contributing to overall income growth in those counties that shedded their PLI status.

The findings from this study raise a number of questions: What role did various institutions play in bringing about the conditions and support for positive income change? To what extent did people in poverty benefit from the income growth of their county of residence? Who were the beneficiaries by age, sex, education, and minority status? To what extent, if any, did out-migration have a positive effect on county income? What is the combination of inputs that should be exercised in program planning and economic development by federal, state, and local governments and by private enterprise? How should these inputs vary from one location to another in order to realize the greatest effectiveness in bringing about income growth and reducing poverty?

RESEARCH ISSUES

The Working Poor

In 1969, almost 50 percent of the income of poor people was from wages and salaries. Relative to the metro poor, incomes of the nonmetro poor included a slightly larger percentage of wages and social security. Among poor nonmetro minorities, nearly two-thirds of their incomes came from wages and salaries. Thus, a substantial number of nonmetro poor persons were employed (see Chapter 17). Unlike the unemployed or those who have dropped from the labor force, the prevalence of the working poor is less documented and their plight is less understood. Yet their problems may be more complex in that their poverty status cannot be explained by such frequently proposed explanations as illiteracy, sickness, laziness, and unwillingness to work. To what extent and in what ways is the plight of the working poor attributable to underemployment and failure of the economic system to provide adequate jobs for talented and capable workers?

Like poverty, the concept of the working poor is not clear-cut except that income is plainly inadequate. Given today's high cost of living and related problems of energy and changing technology, the relativity and ambiguity of the concepts become increasingly evident. Many explanations have been given for the high poverty rates that characterize nonmetro areas and the nation in general. These explanations, largely singular in nature, can be summarized under two basic concepts of the nature and causes of poverty: Poverty is sometimes attributed to characteristics of the individual or group, including elements in the personality, in the family structure, or in a subculture. Poverty has also been blamed on the operation of economic and social circumstance imbedded in the social system at a point beyond the control of the individual (Peet, 1972).

Longitudinal studies are needed of the personal and familial characteristics of the working poor, but even more important is how these characteristics are influenced by situational and structural conditions of the economic system that adversely affect their life chances. Thus, the needed research for rural youth outlined by Falk in Chapter 10 applies also to other segments of the rural population. *Research is needed on the institutional structures of society—the political, educational, and economic, including the dynamics of the market place and the linkage between technology, production, supply, and demand—as they impact the labor market forces and produce the structure of jobs and wages available in nonmetro areas of the nation.*

The problem encountered in defining the poor means that there is no universal characterization that encompasses all the poor. Some are poor because they cannot find employment, others are poor even though they are employed. Consequently, poverty must be studied in the context of the total social system and societal change. Research is needed to acquire better leverage on the relationships between poverty and the various conceptions of its meaning and causes. In addition, research should be directed toward answering several other questions.

Research needs to determine the available opportunities for escaping from poverty in nonmetro areas by region and by state. To what extent are these opportunities equally accessible to different groups? What are the social forces that restrict opportunities and limit access to opportunities for escaping from poverty? How do these forces differ by nonmetro locality?

Research needs to evaluate the effectiveness of rural institutions in reaching and meeting the needs of the poor. Problems of the nonmetro poor may be the result of institutional lag, such as excessively slow adjustments to an aging population and changing educational needs. To what extent are institutional means limited to coping with poverty rather than providing a comprehensive program for preventing and eliminating poverty?

Research is also needed on the implications for the nonmetro poor of technological change, automation, energy shifts, and changes in international markets. We need to know how these implications vary by region.

Finally, we need to know whether nonmetro poverty areas are sufficiently different with respect to conditions responsible for poverty to justify different tailor-made antipoverty programs. Despite the war on poverty begun in the 1960s, there is much we do not know about what makes programs to alleviate poverty successful. Such knowledge is essential for the development of future antipoverty efforts.

REFERENCES

Bird, Ronald, and Ronald Kampe. 1977. *Twenty-Five Years of Housing Progress in Rural America.* Washington, D.C.: Economics, Statistics, and Cooperatives Service, U.S. Department of Agriculture, Agricultural Economic Report 373.

Davis, Leroy. 1978. "The relationship of farm size and rural poverty." *Journal of Social and Behavioral Sciences* 24:6–16.

Davis, Thomas F. 1979. *Persistent Low-Income Counties in Nonmetro America.* Washington, D.C.: Economics, Statistics, and Cooperatives Service, U.S. Department of Agriculture, Rural Development Research Report 12.

Ford, Arthur M. 1973. *Political Economics of Rural Poverty in the South.* Cambridge, Massachusetts: Ballinger Publishing Co.

Fratoe, Frank. 1978. *Rural Education and Rural Labor Force in the Seventies.* Washington, D.C.: Economics, Statistics, and Cooperatives Service, U.S. Department of Agriculture,

Rural Development Research Report 5.

Garfinkel, Irwin, and Robert H. Haveman. 1977. *Earning Capacity, Poverty, and Inequality*. New York: Academic Press.

Hansen, Niles M. 1970. *Rural Poverty and the Urban Crisis*. Bloomington, Indiana: Indiana University Press.

Hines, Fred K., David L. Brown, and John M. Zimmer. 1975. *Social and Economic Characteristics of the Population in Metro and Nonmetro Counties, 1970*. Washington, D.C.: Economics, Statistics, and Cooperatives Service, U.S. Department of Agriculture, Agricultural Economic Report 272.

Kampe, Ronald. 1975. *Household Income, How It Relates to Substantial Housing in Rural and FHA Areas by State and Race, 1970*. Washington, D.C.: Economics, Statistics, and Cooperatives Service, U.S. Department of Agriculture, Agricultural Economic Report 287.

Louisiana State Advisory Council for Vocational/Technical Education. 1977. "The availability of vocational/technical education to Blacks, other minorities, and women." Unpublished study prepared by investigators at Southern University, Baton Rouge, Louisiana, and Grambling State University, Grambling, Louisiana.

Marshall, Ray. 1978. "The old South and the new." In Ray Marshall and Virgil L. Christian, Jr. (editors), *Employment of Blacks in the South*. Austin, Texas: University of Texas Press.

Moland, John, Jr. 1980. "The Black population." Prepared for the Future of Rural America Advisory Group, Farmers' Home Administration. Washington, D.C.: U.S. Department of Agriculture.

Page, Alma Thornton. 1979. "Attitudes of plant and nonplant employees toward rural industrialization." Baton Rouge, Louisiana: Louisiana State University. Doctoral dissertation.

Peet, Richard. 1972. "Some issues in the social geography of American poverty." *Geographical Perspectives on American Poverty*. Worcester, Massachusetts: Antipode Publishers.

Rogers, David L., Brian F. Pendleton, Willis J. Goudy, and Robert O. Richards. 1978. "Industrialization, income benefits, and the rural community." *Rural Sociology* 43:250–264.

Sampson, Joylean P. 1979. *Inequality of Human Services: The Rural Tennessee Dilemma*. Nashville, Tennessee: Tennessee State University.

Southern Growth Policies Board. 1974. *The Future of the South*. Research Triangle Park, North Carolina: Southern Growth Policies Board.

Southern Regional Council. 1972. *Hungry Children: A Special Report*. Atlanta, Georgia: Southern Regional Council.

Tamblyn, Lewis R. 1973. *Inequality: A Portrait of Rural America*. Washington, D.C.: Rural Evaluation Association.

Thomas, John K., and William W. Falk. 1978. "Career attitudes and achievement." In Arthur G. Cosby and Ivan Charner (editors), *Education and Work in Rural America: The Social Context of Early Career Decision and Achievement*. College Station, Texas: Texas A & M University.

Tweeten, Luther, and George L. Brinkman. 1976. *Micropolitan Development*. Ames, Iowa: Iowa State University Press.

U.S. Department of Commerce (Bureau of the Census). 1977. *Social Indicators, 1976*. Washington, D.C.: U.S. Government Printing Office.

______. 1978. *Social and Economic Characteristics of the Metropolitan and Nonmetropolitan Population, 1970 and 1977*. Washington, D.C.: U.S. Government Printing Office, Current Population Report, Series P-23, 75.

______. 1973. *United States Census of Population, 1970, Characteristics of the Population,*

Volume 1, United States Summary Section 1, General Social and Economic Characteristics. Washington, D.C.: U.S. Government Printing Office.

______. 1979. *The Social and Economic Status of the Black Population in the United States: An Historical View, 1790–1978.* Washington, D.C.: U.S. Government Printing Office, Current Population Report, Series P-23, 80.

Part 4
THE PEOPLE'S NEEDS

In the nostalgic view of many Americans, the rural community was self-sufficient; it was the place that people depended on to satisfy most of their needs. That self-sufficient community of one-room country schools, general stores, butcher shops, and family doctors, if it ever really existed, has long since given way to federal, state, and local partnerships in the provision of many services. The services themselves are usually provided through large-scale organizations, which have become increasingly specialized and centralized. Consolidated schools serve many communities, physicians are concentrated in clinics in the larger towns, and areawide "growth centers" supply much of the shopping and entertainment for large rural areas whose people are purchasing much the same market basket as their urban and suburban counterparts. With the concentration of services, transportation has become a necessity rather than a luxury. Rural people, who long ago gave up the prospect of a doctor for their town, urge instead better roads and public transportation for the elderly. Whether for shopping, going to school, going to work, visiting a doctor, or doing business with government, individual private transportation has become an essential way of life in rural communities.

Providing services has increasingly become the business of government bureaucracies at all levels, and great attention has been devoted to needs assessments. Robert Nisbet, in the book *Quest for Community,* calls attention to how, in an earlier and less complex era, voluntary associations at the community level were usually able to get things done. However, as the delivery of services has become the business of government, such community-based organizations are less effective in fulfilling the needs of the citizens they represent. Fulfillment of many community needs now requires a proposal that must be supported by evidence documenting the need. Meeting the people's needs is now a complex business involving not only needs assessment but also knowing where the means to meet the needs can be identified.

In Chapter 14, Rogers discusses the present context of service delivery in rural areas. He describes how providing services to rural people is different from providing them to urban people. A broad array of research issues are identified, and underscoring most of them is the belief that considerable change is taking place in how services reach rural people. Research must respond to this change.

Kaye (Chapter 15) notes that nothing is more central to the development of rural areas than transportation. Transportation has been the tradeoff for the lack of local services in many rural communities. The near void of past sociological research coupled with more expensive energy makes this a very important area for future research. The results may determine whether some rural areas get needed community services or must do without.

Farming is no longer the major source of rural employment in any region of the country. In recent years, paralleling the population turnaround, there has been a significant increase in industrial employment and relocation in nonmetropolitan America. This has not, however, proved to be a panacea, as noted in the chapters by Summers and Tweeten. In Chapter 16, Summers calls for additional research on the costs and benefits of rural industrialization. In Chapter 17, Tweeten describes the important need for better measures of manpower utilization in rural areas. He contends that unemployment is an inappropriate measure of underused human resources and should be replaced by a measure of underemployment.

Chapter 18, by Parks, Ross, and Just, describes the present disadvantaged position of rural schools. They explain the need for experimenting with alternative forms of organization to provide rural students with access to quality education without incurring the numerous costs of further consolidation.

Rural housing traditionally shows up in statistical data as an area of need. Morris and Winter, in Chapter 19, contend that what constitutes satisfactory housing is heavily affected by well supported social norms, and that just any type of housing will not necessarily satisfy the needs of rural people. The research agenda they propose is broad, developed around the overriding issue of how to provide housing that people want while preserving the rights of future generations to do the same.

Outdoor recreation is an integral part of the lives of most Americans but is supplied mostly by rural America. As the country has become more devoted to outdoor recreation, it has produced a number of conflicts of interest that will require policy attention as described by Bultena in Chapter 20. The effects of changing energy costs is one of the most pressing research needs.

The major problem that rural people have with health care is the increasing centralization of medical services, which are less accessible and more costly to the rural resident. Chapter 21, by Miller, also describes some of the research issues related to environmental and other hazards to health from rural living. A closely related concern is the nutritional status of the rural population. In Chapter 22, Purtle describes some of the norms associated with food production and consumption in rural areas and how these contribute to substandard nutrition among many rural people. The research issues that are identified range from food production to the cultural meaning of food.

Although rural America has traditionally been regarded as a haven from rising crime rates, that assumption, like so many others, is not supported by current data. In Chapter 23, Phillips, Donnermeyer, and Wurschmidt describe the current rapid increases in rural crime, especially crimes against property, and propose a number of areas of research needed to address the problem and its probable causes.

14 Community Services

DAVID L. ROGERS

Rural United States has a preponderance of private drinking water systems, a relative absence of modern sewage disposal methods, limited garbage collection and solid waste disposal sites, and higher fire fatality rates than urban places (Warner and Burdge, 1979). Comparisons also reveal that rural places have lower but accelerating crime rates, greater fire losses and higher insurance rates, lower survival of private transit companies, and fewer physicians, nurses, dentists, and hospital beds (U.S. Department of Justice, 1975; Rainey and Rainey, 1978; American Medical Association, 1972; Hines et al., 1975; Williams et al., 1975). Many differences in the level and quality of local services between rural and urban places are increasing.

Comparison of per capita expenditures by local governments also reveals a widening gap in public service expenditures between rural and urban places. In 1957, rural governments spent 86 percent as much per capita as did urban governments; in 1967, they spent 74 percent as much; and, in 1972, they spent 69 percent as much. Nonmetropolitan public service expenditures are generally lower, except for highways, than are metropolitan expenditures (U.S. Department of Commerce, 1977). During the same period, however, nonmetro government revenues were almost identical with those in metro counties, suggesting that per capita expenditures were relatively unaffected by available revenue (U.S. Department of Agriculture, 1975).

David L. Rogers is a professor and chairperson in the Department of Sociology, Colorado State University, Fort Collins, Colorado. A coeditor of the book *Rural Policy Research Alternatives*, he has published numerous articles on voluntary associations and organizational relations in community development.

RESEARCH ISSUES

During the 1970s, expenditures by rural governments remained relatively unchanged, with major commitments going to education, highways, public welfare, police protection, and sewerage. Local government services receiving lower per capita expenditures included fire protection, health, parks and recreation, and libraries (U.S. Department of Commerce, 1977). These differences in per capita expenditures, plus the higher per unit costs of providing services in small governments, suggest that rural services are more limited and that their position relative to urban areas is getting worse (Deavers and Brown, 1979). Is this pattern a reflection of lower value to rural residents of certain services, or is it because it costs less to produce comparable service in rural areas? *More research is needed on cost effectiveness of service delivery in rural areas (not just in smaller places) compared to urban places.*

Subjective assessments of the quality of services reveal that rural residents rate services as less satisfactory than urban residents do. Whatever standards are used in evaluation, the data reveal that needs are not being met in some important areas. Lower satisfaction ratings in rural areas are given to streets, roads, and education. The highest ratings are given to air quality, safety from crime and violence, and as a place to raise children (Dillman and Tremblay, 1977). Several studies using subjective indicators reveal that rural residents are worse off than their urban counterparts (Williams et al., 1975; Warner and Burdge, 1979; Christenson, 1976; Rojek et al., 1975; Miller and Crader, 1979; Christenson and Sachs, 1980). *Research is needed to determine which services are perceived as declining in quality and to determine whether rural and urban residents hold the same expectations for local government services. Research is also needed to determine which rural services are stable and which are falling behind in urban places in an objective sense (e.g., availability) and to determine what actions could be taken to reduce any gaps in service delivery.*

Community Services and Quality of Life

Quality of life is a product of a composite of factors including work, family, health, community, neighborhood, and other experiences. Satisfaction with community has been shown to be a major element in quality of life and satisfaction with services is a major determinant of community satisfaction (Campbell et al., 1976; Christenson, 1976; Ladewig and McCann, 1979). Other research has shown that other life experiences play a larger role in satisfaction than one's place of residence (Goudy, 1977). Whatever the conclusion, community services do play a role and continue to be used as indicators of the quality of life in a community. *More research is needed on the role that satisfaction with services plays in determining community satisfaction.*

Factors that influence feelings of satisfaction with community services have sometimes been classified into four major, although not exhaustive, categories: size of place, status of residents, political efficacy, and use of services. A relatively unexplored but potential source of satisfaction is the amount a service is used. Greater use could dispose a person in either of two ways. Through more exposure to a service, users might identify more problems. Or greater use could produce greater benefit and therefore greater satisfaction. What direction to expect is not clear. Research has shown a positive relationship between use and satisfaction with libraries, recreation, transportation, fire protection, and cultural programs (Brouillette and Rogers, 1979). This suggests support for the "benefit" rather than "critical eye" hypothesis. Perhaps it is the aesthetic qualities of the service, or the manner in which it is delivered, or the accessibility that influence satisfaction. Whatever these factors are, they should be important to local policy makers. *More research is needed on what factors influence feelings of satisfaction with community services.*

How will increased satisfaction with services affect the behavior of residents? Will it "cause" them to remain in the community, be more supportive of private efforts to improve the community, and support increased funding of existing or new public services? Up to now, research attention has been focused more on predicting levels of satisfaction than on concern with the impact of higher or lower levels of satisfaction with services. *Research is needed on the consequences of satisfaction with services for local community stability or growth.*

Impact of Population Changes on Rural Service Delivery

Community service needs are changing rapidly because of the population shifts described in Chapter 3. Nearly 350 nonmetro counties grew by 16.7 percent or more between 1970 and 1976. This rapid rate of growth in selected areas is associated with new service problems. Typically, a growth rate of 2.5 percent or larger puts strains on a local government's ability to provide needed facilities and services (Deavers and Brown, 1979). It is in the rapid growth areas that levels of dissatisfaction with community services reach their highest peak (Murdock and Schriner, 1979).

Rapid growth overburdens existing facilities and programs, creates new expectations from in-migrants, and produces a lag between new service demands and the new tax base needed to pay for expansion. Many local governments are not equipped to handle the impact of growth coming after decades of decline (Deavers and Brown, 1979). Strains on existing facilities are often felt first in areas of housing, recreation, and medical services (Murdock and Schriner, 1979). New residents, especially those from urban areas, may press for new services. Public officials are caught in a fiscal bind when residents want more than can be provided. Local governments may be faced with establishing new services with current revenues because the tax base will usually not reflect growth for several years. This is especially true when property taxes are the main source of local revenue. Other forms of taxation (e.g., sales tax) could be implemented sooner, but require a referendum and are frequently turned down by the public. At the same time that officials search for new sources of revenue, they are often pressured to expand services. Developing new services and reexamining old programs are difficult tasks for local governments because traditional community values and individual lifestyles often are challenged by new people. *Research is needed on what service needs will develop with community expansion and what new service needs should be anticipated.*

Population decline also affects services. The typical pattern of change with population decline is that youth leave, the average age rises, the birth rate falls, and income declines (Beale, 1974). This selective movement of people increases the burden on remaining residents through extra costs and lower levels of service (Williams et al., 1975). As the number of persons employed in an area declines, the number of persons to be serviced and the number of persons who share in the cost of the service also decline. More than five hundred nonmetro counties experienced a decline in population between 1970 and 1977.

All rural places face similar problems that set them apart from urban places. One of these distinctions is a smaller revenue-generating capacity. Rural areas have always had less financial resources to draw from than urban areas (Stoker, 1977). Other special obstacles include small overlapping governments, service to heterogeneous populations, geographic dispersion of residents, and more units of government per capita (Bish, 1977). Small size means higher cost per capita and a lack of efficiencies of scale. Heterogeneous populations are also harder to serve because of the different needs and expectations of various segments of the population.

Rural areas, no less than urban areas, have felt the impact of inflation, but they have less flexibility in responding to it. The problem of increased costs is compounded by a more limited financial base from which to draw resources. Although revenues from property taxes have increased, much of this difference is due to inflation, which leaves governments with little financial relief. Also, growth in taxable property (associated with location of mineral extraction industries, for example) does not always occur in the area impacted by residential growth. Consequently, one local government may realize the tax benefits of growth and another the expenses of service expansion. *Research is needed to identify the impact of population shifts on services and the alternatives available to local governments for dealing with these shifts. Research is also needed on the cost of supplying public services in sparsely populated areas.*

Funding Strategies Used by Local Governments

The major sources of revenue used to pay for services include local taxes, intergovernmental revenue transfers, and nontax revenues such as user fees. Each of these funding sources has a potential impact on who controls community services. The origin of funds is closely tied to who will make decisions about service provision.

As noted earlier, taxes as a source of revenue complicate covering rapidly expanding service needs. Federal and state intergovernmental transfer payments, on the other hand, have increased substantially over the years. These transfer payments come in the form of grant-in-aid and revenue-sharing programs. In 1977, 43 percent of the revenue of nonmetro areas came from intergovernmental transfer. This is up from 39 percent in 1972. Metro areas increased during the same time from 33 percent to 38 percent (U.S. Department of Commerce, 1977). Thus, rural governments rely more heavily than urban governments on state and federal funds to finance services. But at the same time, they often have a greater problem gaining access to federal dollars because they lack the grantsmanship skills needed to develop proposals (Deavers and Brown, 1979).

Relationships with state and federal agencies have both positive and negative consequences for community services. On the positive side, transfers provide a major source of revenue needed for services. Without federal funds, certain programs would never be provided. Federal and state programs can also provide new ideas about program design and relevant technologies. The negative consequences are largely associated with increased dependency of local governments on the federal government. There is some indication that grants-in-aid have influenced local priorities and local service programs (Rainey and Rainey, 1978). *Research is needed on what determines the types of new rural services and, specifically, the possible influences of changes in objective needs, information about federal programs, and progressive local leadership on rates of service innovation.*

A second impact of federal assistance is federal government control over local services. For example, some service problems are aggravated by federal performance standards based on the "best available technology." This technology is often capital-intensive and inappropriate for smaller local governments. Rural officials often argue that these standards are not realistic for small towns (Deavers and Brown, 1979).

Research is needed to determine whether federal standards are excessive, thus unnecessarily raising the cost of services for rural areas.

There is variation between rural and urban areas in their reliance on user fees and miscellaneous revenues. Nontax revenues are especially important in financing rural community services (Hitzhusen, 1977). In rural areas, the relative proportion of revenues raised through user charges has been increasing since World War II. These nontax sources of revenue tie the benefits and costs of a service more closely together.

Broadening the revenue base and turning to nontax revenues shifts the costs to two major groups. First, user fees shift costs more directly to consumers. As a result, some categories of consumers may be placed at a real disadvantage and find their access to critical services significantly limited. Shifting costs to consumers is regressive and moves away from the equitable provision of services to a system in which access to basic community services is dependent upon a person's wealth. Second, costs might be shifted to public-minded citizens who participate as volunteers in service programs, making it possible for "free-loaders" to take advantage of services without contributing. The role of volunteers is very important in the organization and provision of rural services (Hitzhusen, 1977; Williams et al., 1975). Areas that typically receive volunteer efforts are fire protection, ambulance service, and libraries. Volunteerism substitutes free labor for paid labor and is an important nontax basis for providing services in rural communities. *Research is needed to determine the impact of increased use of nontax revenues in rural areas and to determine which services are likely to be impacted the most. Research is also needed to determine the contribution of volunteers to public service delivery in rural areas. The consequences of this time and energy expenditure on other activities (e.g., family, private business, leisure time) should be determined.*

Unexplored Organizational Options

To reduce service costs and increase efficiency, policy makers are using centrally located communities as delivery points for several services (Gessaman, 1975). Efforts to reduce administrative and overhead costs propel services toward central locations. Police and fire protection, which have traditionally been delivered by communities, are being transferred to county governments in some areas.

The time spent by the user in securing a service, however, is often ignored in calculating the costs of services. This is especially critical in rural, low-density areas. User costs are primarily a function of distance to the service. The cost of time and transportation to cover that distance becomes critical as energy costs rise. One implication of the present locational trend is that rural Americans living outside of these centers are going to be asked to carry a disproportionate burden of service delivery costs. These costs may assume many forms. An example is the drop in standardized test scores associated with the amount of time a student spends riding a bus to and from school (Lu and Tweeten, 1973).

Other organizational innovations for service delivery might involve taking services to rural residents or providing public transportation to move clients into service centers. Still another option might be to improve public transportation *and* decentralize services so that not only are the costs of transportation shared by all but the opportunity costs of one's time is also shared among a larger portion of the population. Another option that is becoming more important when a service is primarily informational is to transport information through electronic technology rather than to transport people. *Research needs to determine the relative net social and economic costs and benefits to consumers, as well as to providers, of alternative rural delivery systems; whether certain portions of the rural population enjoy greater access to services than others; and the effect of current trends toward centralization on equity.*

The most frequent approach to achieve provider efficiency is to locate services in growth centers. One of the largest increases in government growth is the expansion of local governments in county seat towns (Capener, 1974). These locational decisions worked better for providers and consumers when fuel costs were relatively low and people could afford to travel to service centers. However, with spiraling fuel costs, this approach should be reexamined. One implication of the centralization trend is that some remote and lower-income rural citizens will be denied access to services.

A variation of geographic centralization is organizational consolidation. This strategy has never been popular among rural citizens. Early successes were achieved in the consolidation of rural schools, but consolidation of city/county governments has been much slower. The 1970s was a period of referenda activity with few consolidations (eight out of forty-five referenda were passed) (Glendening and Atkins, 1980). *Research is needed to determine which services are moving to central places and the impact of this movement on population distribution, service access, and service quality.*

Competition has been a predominant paradigm for the analysis of relations between communities (e.g., the central place perspective as it applies to private retail goods and services) (Haga and Folse, 1971). Communities are viewed as being in direct competition with one another for scarce resources (i.e., selected private services). The placement of services is determined by threshhold values, by appropriate infrastructure, and by costs of transportation for the consumer. Competition blends with conflict as larger places are shown to dominate neighboring towns:

large places get larger, and small places get smaller. This competitive model pits one community against another in their efforts to secure needed resources.

An alternative has been neglected. It focuses on the interdependence among communities that occurs when individual governments cannot supply local needs and therefore must join with other governments to share their capabilities. Every local government cannot provide every service needed by its residents, but through recognition of their common interdependence governments can enter into sharing agreements that reduce costs because of increased scale. Under conditions of scarcity, the importance of cooperative intergovernmental agreements increases. *Research is needed to determine whether local governments can successfully negotiate intergovernmental agreements among themselves to provide for basic services, and whether these agreements affect service delivery.*

In most multi-county regions, some governments are growing while others are declining. Through cooperative intergovernmental agreements, a system of tradeoffs could be developed. Public officials should be helped to understand how the economy of their government is tied to the economy of its region and that they are interdependent. *Research is needed to document this interdependency and demonstrate the need for governments to work together.*

An alternative that should receive greater attention by officials and by researchers is interlocal agreements. The Lakewood Plan, in which smaller governments contract with a larger central government (Los Angeles County), has received some attention but its application to rural areas needs further study (Bish, 1971). It is difficult to anticipate the negative consequences of this alternative. The potential positive outcomes are easy to identify: increased efficiency from larger size, interdependent relations between units with similar resources, and continued control by local officials.

Establishing linkages with other local governments is used less often by local goverment officials and has been given less attention by scholars than vertical linkages. *Research is needed to document how much intergovernmental activity occurs between local governments, the forms it takes, and the resources involved.*

REFERENCES

American Medical Association. 1972. *Health Care in Rural America.* Chicago: American Medical Association.

Beale, Calvin L. 1974. "Quantitative dimensions of decline and stability among rural communities." In Larry R. Whiting (editor), *Communities Left Behind: Alternatives for Development*. Ames, Iowa: Iowa State University Press.

Bish, Robert L. 1971. *The Public Economy of Metropolitan Areas*. Chicago: Markham Publishing Co.

______. 1977. "Public choice theory: Research issues for nonmetropolitan areas." In Committee on Agriculture, Nutrition, and Forestry, U.S. Senate (editors), *National Conference on Nonmetropolitan Community Service Research*. Washington, D.C.: U.S. Senate.

Brouillette, John, and David L. Rogers. 1979. *Public Satisfaction with Quality of Life and City Services*. Fort Collins, Colorado: Department of Sociology, Colorado State University.

Campbell, Angus, Philip Converse, and Willard Rodgers. 1976. *The Quality of American Life*. New York: Russell Sage Foundation.

Capener, Harold R. 1974. "Enhancing social opportunity." In Larry R. Whiting (editor), *Communities Left Behind: Alternatives for Development*. Ames, Iowa: Iowa State University Press.

Christenson, James A. 1976. "Quality of community services: A macro-unidimensional approach with experimental data." *Rural Sociology* 41(4):509–525.

Christenson, James A., and Carolyn E. Sachs. 1980. "The impact of size of government and number of administrative units on the quality of community services." *Administrative Science Quarterly* 25:89–101.

Deavers, Kenneth L., and David L. Brown. 1979. *Social and Economic Trends in Rural America*. Washington, D.C.: Economics, Statistics, and Cooperatives Service, U.S. Department of Agriculture, The White House Rural Development Background Paper.

Dillman, Don A., and Kenneth R. Tremblay, Jr. 1977. "The quality of life in rural America." *The Annals of the American Academy of Political and Social Science* 429:115–129.

Gessaman, Paul H. 1975. "Delivery systems and decision-making for rural community services: Some implications for research." In Great Plains Agricultural Council (editors), *Public Services for Rural Communities: Some Analytical and Policy Considerations*. College Station, Texas: Great Plains Agricultural Council, Publication 70.

Glendening, Parris N., and Patricia S. Atkins. 1980. "City/county consolidations: New views for the eighties." In International City Management Association (editors), *Municipal Year Book, 1980*. Washington, D.C.: International City Management Association.

Goudy, Willis J. 1977. "Evaluation of local attributes and community satisfaction in small towns." *Rural Sociology* 43(Fall):371–382.

Haga, William J., and Clinton L. Folse. 1971. "Trade patterns and community identity." *Rural Sociology* 36:42–51.

Hines, Fred K., David L. Brown, and John M. Zimmer. 1975. *Social and Economic Characteristics of the Population in Metro and Nonmetro Counties, 1970*. Washington, D.C.: Economics, Statistics, and Cooperatives Service, U.S. Department of Agriculture, Agricultural Economics Report 272.

Hitzhusen, Fred J. 1977. "Nontax financing and support for 'community' services: Some policy implications for nonmetropolitan governments." In Committee on Agriculture, Nutrition, and Forestry, United States Senate (editors), *National Conference on Nonmetropolitan Community Service Research*. Washington, D.C.: U.S. Senate.

Ladewig, Howard, and Glenn C. McCann. 1979. *Perceptions of Life Quality: A Study of the Southern Rural Environment*. Raleigh, North Carolina: Southern Cooperative Series Bulletin 239.

Lu, Tao-Chi, and Luther Tweeten. 1973. "The impact of busing on student achievement." *Growth and Change* 4(October):44–46.

Miller, Michael K., and Kelly W. Crader. 1979. "Rural/urban differences in two dimensions of community satisfaction." *Rural Sociology* 44:489–504.

Murdock, Steve H., and Eldon C. Schriner. 1979. "Community service satisfaction and stages of community development: An examination of evidence from impacted communities." *Journal of the Community Development Society* 10(Spring):109–124.

Rainey, Kenneth D., and Karen G. Rainey. 1978. "Rural government and local public services." In Thomas R. Ford (editor), *Rural U.S.A.: Persistence and Change*. Ames, Iowa: Iowa State University Press.

Rojek, Dean G., Frank Clemente, and Gene Summers. 1975. "Community satisfaction: A study of contentment with local services." *Rural Sociology* 40(Summer):177–192.

Stoker, Frederick D. 1977. "Fiscal needs and resources of nonmetropolitan communities." In Committee on Agriculture, Nutrition, and Forestry, U.S. Senate (editors), *National Conference on Nonmetropolitan Community Service Research*. Washington, D.C.: U.S. Senate.

U.S. Department of Agriculture (Economics, Statistics, and Cooperatives Service). 1975. *The Economic and Social Condition of Nonmetropolitan America in the 1970s*. Washington, D.C.: Economics, Statistics, and Cooperatives Service, U.S. Department of Agriculture.

U.S. Department of Commerce (Bureau of the Census). 1977. "Compendium of government finances." In Bureau of the Census, U.S. Department of Commerce (editors), *Census of Governments*. Washington, D.C.: U.S. Government Printing Office.

U.S. Department of Justice (Federal Bureau of Investigation). 1975. *Crime in the United States, 1974*. Washington, D.C.: Federal Bureau of Investigation, U.S. Department of Justice.

Warner, Paul D., and Rabel J. Burdge. 1979. "Perceived adequacy of community services: A metro/nonmetro comparison." *Rural Sociology* 44:392–400.

Williams, Anne S., Russell C. Youmans, and Donald M. Sorensen. 1975. *Providing Public Services: Leadership and Organizational Considerations*. Corvallis, Oregon: Western Rural Development Center, Oregon State University, Special Report 1.

15 Transportation

IRA KAYE

Perhaps nothing is more crucial to the development of rural areas than transportation. Transportation facilitates the emergence of markets for goods that provide the basis for the existence of communities in industrialized nations. The economic and geographic history of rural United States has been heavily influenced by the available means of transportation. Initially, the availability of water transportation circumscribed the location of agriculture, extraction, and commercial enterprise. Later, railroads extended production and marketing even further. More recently, highways, trucks, and private automobiles have further removed the constraints of space on the distribution of population and economic activity.

Before the 1970s, the prevailing, though often challenged, perception of the future of the rural United States was one of diminished population and opportunities. Its exploitative potential was buttressed by inexpensive and virtually inexhaustible fossil fuel. It was assumed that each rural household had access to a private automobile, which was within the means of most to acquire and operate. These perceptions contributed to the demise of most forms of rural public transit; they also encouraged the consolidation and centralization of many services that made everyday life in rural America even more dependent on individual private transportation. The relatively self-sufficient community of the past gave way to rural people depending on multiple towns to meet their needs. The connecting thread of the economic and social

Ira Kaye was formerly a rural development specialist in the Office of Transportation, U.S. Department of Agriculture, Washington, D.C. His writings include articles and chapters on diverse aspects of transportation in rural areas.

service system became the private automobile.

Recent evidence and changed circumstances have shaken these perceptions. During the 1970s, a population turnaround occurred simultaneously with higher energy prices and uncertain supplies. The percentage of rural households without access to an automobile is much higher than urban households: In low-income rural counties, over 20 percent of the households are without private transportation. Lack of transportation may be the major barrier to obtaining and holding a job in rural areas, especially for minorities and other disadvantaged households. This barrier, however, is not limited to jobs. Medical care, education, food stamps, senior citizens' activities, and almost every other form of social service is not available to large components of our rural population if they lack transportation. The movement of goods to and from rural America faces similar obstacles. The rush toward deregulation, affecting all modes of transportation, has not afforded time for proper consideration of the impact of such deregulation on rural economy or development.

With rural America so heavily dependent on transportation, it is disquieting to note some of the features of the transportation profile of rural America:

- in the next few years, 37,000 kilometers (nearly 23,000 miles) of rail lines face abandonment or discontinuation of service; this does not include rail service affected by bankruptcies, mergers, or technological obsolescence
- the realignment of the rural road system required by federal aid-to-highway legislation removed one-third of such roads from eligibility for federal assistance; this accelerated a decline of suitability for the requirements of modern transportation; recent legislation has only slightly modified this condition
- one-third of our rural bridges are structurally deficient, 38 percent are functionally obsolete, 9 percent are collapsed, and 24 percent are posted against excessive weight
- since 1965, over 114 small cities have lost their scheduled air service and 189 others have had service suspended; since the air line deregulation, this trend has accelerated and rates to and from smaller communities have risen sharply
- passenger rail service is available in very few rural communities; intercity bus lines serve only 40 percent of towns between 2,500 and 10,000 population and only 15 percent of towns and places under 2,500; both rail and intercity bus service is not geared to serve rural areas, and scheduling is such that, even where

available, it is often not feasible for people to use it
- construction of the interstate highway system consumed so much of the fiscal, technological, and available human resources that rural roads and bridges were ignored or became victims of what railroad managers called "deferred maintenance"

Despite the centrality of transportation to the rural way of life, it has been a relatively neglected area of research. The Current Research Information System, which is the scientific research project classification system used by the U.S. Department of Agriculture, includes over 21,000 research projects involving 10,400 scientific man years of effort. Of these, only 42 projects, involving thirty-three scientific man years of effort, were devoted to transportation.

In addition to a relatively small amount of rural transportation research in relation to the significance of the problem, much past research has been too narrowly focused; for example, only a specific use of a general mode of transportation has been researched as if the vehicle had a dedicated use. In rural United States, transportation is the largest consumer of energy. Inefficient or uncoordinated use of transportation wastes energy and complicates the development of an energy policy to assure nontransportation users the energy they require.

Only recently have rural social scientists recognized that a rural region injures its potential for development if its basic economy lacks competitive transportation for inputs and outputs and if a significant percentage of its population lacks access to job sites, basic services, and social interaction. Both farm and nonfarm sectors are affected. Rural areas accounted for 40 percent of the nonfarm jobs created between 1970 and 1977, but rural workers who commute across county lines travel about one-third farther than urbanites commute. A large percentage of the family budget thus becomes devoted to commuting. The consequences of this trend will become more severe if the need for rural transportation is not dealt with more creatively in the coming years.

RESEARCH ISSUES

The centrality of transportation to the rural way of life is reflected in the various chapters in this book. Of the forty-one chapters, at least twenty-seven have a direct relationship to transportation. Consequently, we will not be concerned in this chapter with the specific issues of how the presence or absence of transportation influences access to health care (see Chapter 21) or the implications of more expensive travel for the location of schools and educational programs (see Chapter 18). We will attempt instead to identify general transportation issues that have implications for most aspects of rural life and service delivery. We will identify transportation issues under demographic, technological, behavioral, economic, institutional/fiscal, and transportation/communication tradeoffs.

The research issues we face for the 1980s include the mobility needs of people, the movement of goods, and the options available to rural communities to provide both. Perhaps of equal importance is the possible substitution of communication for transportation, a prospect just appearing over the horizon, which has been superficially studied and little understood.

Demographic Considerations

Research is needed that will provide us, state-by-state, information about the availability of private transportation to rural households in each rural county. The results would provide the private sector with potential market information and state and federal governments with insights on the areas of greatest need. This research will be facilitated by the 1980 census, which, for the first time, will provide data on the total private transportation resources by household, including pickup trucks and other farm vehicles.

Technological Issues

Present experience suggests that full implementation of the recently enacted nonurbanized area public transit program is blocked or delayed because of the absence of an efficient, safe, and comfortable vehicle. High operating and maintenance costs and the hesitancy of potential users combine to increase costs and reduce revenues. All known research and development in this field has been based only on requirements of metropolitan areas. The 1980s should see the development of a multipurpose vehicle, the prototypes of which can be modified to meet a variety of market needs. Optimally, it should be designed for no more than twenty passengers, carry mail and small packages, and be quickly converted for emergency transportation purposes. The engines should be able to use efficiently the type of fuels that will come on line in the 1980s.

Similar development for rail transit purposes is required. Prototypes like the Swedish Rail Bus should be tested for suitability to rural America. Thousands of kilometers of otherwise abandoned or underused rail lines could become useful and revenue producing.

Even implementation by the Civil Aeronautics Board of the Small Community Air Service provisions of the Airline Deregulation Act of

1978 flounders because of the absence of a suitable aircraft for shorter, lower-density market flights providing service to small towns. To date, American industry for the most part sees no market for such a plane. The smaller air lines, mostly fledgling commuters, use antiquated, uncomfortable equipment or have acquired English or even Brazilian craft. If a suitable plane were developed, capable of carrying freight as well as passengers, fuel efficient, safe, and comfortable, the potential market could explode. The profitability of such service would increase and long-distance driving to a hub would decline. *More research is needed on the extent and type of rural transportation needs in order to provide design criteria for new technology and to determine the magnitude of potential demand if alternative technology were available.*

Both rapidly growing and declining rural communities complain of the lack of public transit. There are many reasons why public transit in rural areas has not been widely used except for such specific functions as school transportation. *Research is needed to determine the extent to which an effective rural public transit system is inhibited by the absence of appropriate equipment.*

Behavioral Implications

Public transit in small towns and rural areas once was widespread. Its reintroduction confronts many psychological barriers. The types of resistance include, but are not limited to, the reluctance of the elderly to ride with the young, the well with the ill, the affluent with the poor, and vice versa. Urban transit does not question the suitability of its service to the affluent even though the system is heavily subsidized. Rural communities tend to want to limit the service to those who cannot afford any alternative. Without analysis and answers, rural public transportation may not get off the ground. *Research is needed to identify the attitudinal and behavioral barriers of rural people to using public transit.*

Economic Effects

There is one overriding economic issue for the coming decade: the economics of deregulation. Early trends point to sharp increases in fares and rates following deregulation. This issue encompasses such subsets as the effect of changes in transportation costs on agriculture and other forms of rural-based production and the general impact on rural consumers. However, there is need for research in a more conceptual frame. Will our transportation configuration in the closing decades of this century conform to rural economy (agriculture, forestry, mining, power generation), or will the rural economy be required to adapt to the transportation configuration? *Research is needed to discover how rural com-*

munities can sustain transportation services no longer provided by the private sector at reasonable rates.

Institutional Participation

A characteristic of rural transportation systems is that they are often confined to a single use. For any rural household, there may be multiple publicly supported vehicles passing each day picking up school children, delivering mail, picking up senior citizens, and so forth. Each of these vehicles is supported, managed, and operated by separate institutions with separate purposes. Greater attention will probably be directed toward this redundancy of publicly supported transportation systems in rural areas during the coming decade.

There are prototypes of multiple use systems. Analysis should be made of the European experience with the post/bus system and its applicability to rural America. In Scandinavia, Switzerland, and Scotland, the rural delivery of mail and parcels is combined with a public transit function. It varies in form but seems to be adaptable to many cultures and topographies.

Increasing attention is being devoted to the possibilities of multiple transit use of school buses whose primary function is limited to a few hours per day, five days a week, and no more than nine months per year. Employing such vehicles for the transport of older citizens to physicians or providing transportation for factory workers could serve a needed purpose and result in lower fixed costs of operation of school transportation.

There are many possibilities, but there are also a number of institutional and fiscal restraints. *Research is needed to determine the feasibility of multiple use transportation systems for rural areas and the institutional problems that such multiple use would create.*

Since transportation serves the needs of not only individuals and localities but also the nation, there are important questions about what kinds of transportation-related costs should be borne by users, what portion by communities and local units of government, and what portion by state and nation. *Research is needed on the proportionate sharing of costs for new transportation developments between users, communities, states, and the nation.*

At present, most transportation is supplied by individuals, by the private sector, or by various units of government. One prospect for reducing costs of transportation and increasing accessibility would be various types of collective ownership, such as cooperatives and other institutional arrangements. *Research is needed on the kinds of organizational structures that would be most appropriate for supplying the transportation needs of rural America.*

Transportation/Communication Tradeoff

While it may be jarring to raise the issue of substituting communications for transportation in this chapter, history reveals that a more rational relationship between communications and transportation does not mean diminution of transportation; it only changes the nature of transportation. Failure to research the many-faceted relationship between the two technologies may result in the proliferation of chaotic, single-purpose communication systems such as those developed in the transportation field with its client-oriented minisystems that dot the countryside. However, once expensive communication systems are in place, the battle over turf will make coordination and consolidation more difficult. In such a struggle, the disregard for rural concerns that already afflicts both technologies would be exacerbated. The human factor must always be before us. Rural people are not likely to choose to be "wired," and they will always insist on some degree of mobility. *Research by multidisciplinary teams must determine which needs are best served by transportation and which by communications.*

REFERENCES

Brown, David L. 1977. "Passenger transportation in nonmetro America." In Economics, Statistics, and Cooperatives Service, U.S. Department of Agriculture (editors), *Looking Forward: Research Issues Facing Agriculture and Rural America.* Washington, D.C.: Economics, Statistics, and Cooperatives Service, U.S. Department of Agriculture.

Burkhardt, Jon E. 1979. *Planning Rural Public Transportation Systems: A Section 147 Demonstration Program Technical Manual, Number 2.* Washington, D.C.: U.S. Department of Transportation.

Cook, Allen R. 1979. *Paratransit Resource Guide.* Springfield, Virginia: National Technical Information Service, U.S. Department of Commerce.

Hayes, Jack. 1979. *Rural Public Transportation Vehicles: A Section 147 Demonstration Program Technical Manual, Number 4.* Washington, D.C.: U.S. Department of Transportation.

Ketola, H. N. 1979. *Rural Public Transportation Coordination Efforts: A Section 147 Demonstration Program Technical Manual, Number 3.* Washington, D.C.: U.S. Department of Transportation.

McGillivray, R., U. Ernst, J. L. Olsson, and F. Tolson. 1979. *Rural Public Transportation Services and Performance: A Section 147 Demonstration Program Technical Manual, Number 1.* Washington, D.C.: U.S. Department of Transportation.

Panebianco, T. S. 1979. *Marketing Rural Public Transportation: A Section 147 Demonstration Program Technical Manual, Number 5.* Washington, D.C.: U.S. Department of Transportation.

Public Technology, Inc. and Urban Consortium for Technology Initiatives. 1979. *Elderly and Handicapped Transportation: Local Government Approaches.* Washington, D.C.: U.S. Department of Transportation.

U.S. Department of Transportation (Office of Technology Sharing). 1976. *Rural Passenger Transportation/Technology Sharing: State of Art Overview*. Washington, D.C.: Office of Technology Sharing, U.S. Department of Transportation.

U.S. Department of Transportation. 1979. *Proceedings of the Fourth National Conference on Rural Public Transportation*. Vail, Colorado.

16 Industrialization

GENE F. SUMMERS

This chapter has benefited greatly from the generous and insightful comments of several colleagues: Farnum Alston, Alvin Bertrand, Leonard Bloomquist, E. Evan Brunson, Jay Chance, Brady Deaton, D. D. Detomasi, Paul Eberts, Rodney Erickson, John Gartrell, Thomas Hirschl, Donald Johnson, Larry Leistritz, William Linder, Richard Lonsdale, Eli March, Paxton Marshall, Steve Murdock, Howard Newby, Glen Pulver, Ron Shaffer, Eldon Smith, C. Matthew Snipp, Len Wheat, Ron Wimberley, and two anonymous reviewers. Much of the material in the "New Industry" section of this chapter was previously published in Social Impact Assessment (1978) and is used here with the permission of the editor, Charles Wolf. That section also draws on an extensive review of site-specific studies (Summers et al., 1976). Finally, the material in the subsection, "Large-Scale Resource Development Projects," draws heavily from Murdock and Leistritz (1979) and from personal communications with D. D. Detomasi, John Gartrell, and Kristi Branch, all of whom have been heavily involved in impact assessments of large-scale energy developments.

Between 1970 and 1979, nonmetropolitan counties of the United States had a 23.9 percent increase in manufacturing jobs. Over the same decade, metropolitan counties gained only 3.9 percent. Regionally, the

Gene F. Summers is a professor in the Department of Rural Sociology, University of Wisconsin, Madison, Wisconsin. He is the author of several books, including *Before Industrialization, Industrialization in Nonmetropolitan America,* and *Nonmetropolitan Industrial Growth and Community Change*. He has also written extensively on issues related to industrialization.

South and West gained manufacturing employment at a much faster rate than other regions, especially in nonmetro counties (30.2 percent in the South and 62.3 percent in the West) (Smith and Deaton, 1980). These shifts in the location of manufacturing employment are the substance of rural industrialization.

For the past two decades, the U.S. Congress has tried to harness this industrial migration trend and use it as a policy instrument to deal with the issues of rural poverty and urban crisis (Hansen, 1970; Wheat, 1973). The logic behind this intervention strategy is fairly simple. Both rural poverty and urban unemployment are seen as products of a geographic mismatch between labor supply and demand. This mismatch has a history stretching back to the nineteenth century when there began a decline in economic opportunities in rural areas and an increase in urban areas: mechanization and commercialization of agriculture combined with industrial growth in cities. The subsequent rural-to-urban migration ultimately created a surplus of labor in many urban areas and left pockets of poverty in rural areas with stagnant economies. One means of correcting this imbalance was to stimulate and diversify the rural economy, thereby increasing rural job opportunities and halting the exodus of rural labor to the city. Manufacturing was chosen to execute the strategy.

Clearly, manufacturing is moving to nonmetro areas, but these location decisions are affected by fundamental economic, demographic, and social forces as well as public intervention. The South and West have higher demand/supply ratios for consumer products than older urban-industrial regions, which makes them strong regional markets (Wheat, 1973). Labor continues to be relatively cheaper in rural communities. Land for plant sites is more available and less expensive. Labor unions are likely to be less demanding and less powerful. Taxes are lower. Improved transportation and telecommunication technology permit greater spatial dispersion of component manufacturing processes. Much of America's manufacturing industry has arrived at the mature stage of the product cycle that permits spatial dispersion to take advantage of areas with lower wage rates (Erickson, 1976; Erickson and Leinbach, 1979; Averitt, 1979; Norton and Rees, 1979). Once these structural conditions make it possible for management to consider nonmetro plant locations, climatic and social amenity factors enter the matrix of decision making.

NEW INDUSTRY: ECONOMIC AND SOCIAL EFFECTS

Relief from poverty, unemployment, the fiscal crunch in government, and improvements in the quality and quantity of public services are all noble goals for rural America. Job creation, increased income, and an expanding tax base are appropriate means for achieving these goals. Manufacturing plants are regarded by many people as capable of generating jobs, income, and an expanded tax base. However, there is some myth mixed with the realities of rural industrial development.

Jobs

By its nature, new industry creates jobs. But do these jobs go to local people, especially the unemployed or underemployed and those with low incomes? Frequently, they do not. Instead, they go to in-migrants, commuters, and new entrants to the labor force. Local labor markets operate in ways that often work against the needs of people for whom industrial plant location has been promoted.

Unemployment

In two-thirds of the cases of rural plant locations, the rate of unemployment has declined. But decreases have been small, relative to the magnitude of unemployment. This reality is not surprising, for new jobs frequently go to in-migrants, commuters, and new entrants. Jobs leak out of the local community rather than going to unemployed residents. This situation often indicates that local unemployed persons do not have the skills necessary for employment in the new industry. Inadequate planning has created new jobs poorly matched to the local supply of labor.

Even in instances where the rate of unemployment is reduced, one must exercise caution. It is possible to reduce the *rate* of unemployment without providing a single job to previously unemployed workers. This occurs when the number of persons in the labor force increases faster than the number of unemployed persons. This is not uncommon when a new industry hires its work force outside the local community.

Income

For the most part, new industry increases the per capita income. But, if one examines the distribution of income gains among local residents, the positive effects are less clear. New industry may raise average income in a community while, at the same time, depressing relative income status of some residents. The increased activity in local markets benefits residents to the extent they possess the resources that are in greater demand. Some such resources are money to invest, land, retail or service business, residential or commercial property, and work skills required by the industry. Thus, the elderly, the unemployed, the low-skilled workers, and people on fixed incomes often do not receive an average share of the growth in income.

Multiplier Effects

New jobs at an industrial plant create additional jobs in other areas of employment. Some of the new firm's payroll is spent locally, creating second-round effects. Similarly, local purchases of goods and services by new industry stimulate additional employment. Consequently, there are multiplier effects. But the number of additional jobs created is much smaller than many industrial development enthusiasts apparently believe. According to actual case studies, it takes an average of three new manufacturing jobs to generate one additional job in the community.

There are at least three reasons for the low multiplier effect. Many of the new jobs and much of the payroll from the new plant are leaked out by commuting workers and shopping in regional centers. Existing facilities, such as housing, retail stores, and service businesses, have excess capacity. Much of the increased business can be handled without hiring more help or building expansion. Finally, new industries often are tied into regional and national networks of suppliers of their material and service needs. As a result, they purchase little beyond labor in the local community.

Population

New industry does halt population decline; often population growth accompanies a new manufacturing plant. The growth results from increased in-migration and unchanged or slightly decreased out-migration. Contrary to popular belief, new industry does not mean that young people will cease to leave their home towns in search of work. What it does mean is that, as they leave, other young people come to take their places. The end result is a younger population with more households containing children. The altered population structure affects the type and amount of public services needed. Thus, the long-run consequences of population changes must be examined carefully. From the perspective of local businesses, more people means more sales. But, to government, people cost money and more people cost more money.

Local Markets

Clearly, there is growth in the private sector resulting from new industry. Retail sales increases are experienced as the income gains are spent locally. Population growth usually stimulates home construction, and the inventory of residential property is enlarged. On the other hand, commercial and industrial inventories do not usually increase. This inertia probably is due to underuse of existing facilities and to the nonlocal linkages of manufacturers for materials, services, and handling of the finished products.

Assessed valuation of real property universally increases with new industry. The market value of all types of property responds positively, thus assuring capital gains to property owners. However, this fact may force some older residents out of their homes. Higher assessed valuation usually means higher taxes. Combined with other inflationary tendencies, older residents may find it necessary to collect their capital gains by selling their homes and moving to a less expensive areas. In some instances, this involves moving to another community.

Public Sector Net Gains

Private sector inventories, valuations, and volume of transactions are the primary tax base of local governments. Because new industry stimulates growth of the private sector, new manufacturing improves the fiscal base of local communities.

Increases in the tax base are only one side of the ledger from the public sector perspective. Costs of local government and school districts are also increased by additional industry where new industry has resulted in population growth. For most communities, net gains have been small. Increased fiscal base often is outweighed by increased costs. Net gains are reported more often when local government offers no subsidy to industry and when little population increase accompanies the new industry.

RESEARCH ISSUES

The structure of employment in rural areas is becoming more diversified. Consequently, the mental habit of equating rural industrialization with manufacturing is no longer appropriate. Several trends in rural areas help define the context of industrialization research issues for the 1980s.

First, regional shifts of manufacturing continue, but at a slower pace as the supply of goods increases in regional markets. Second, labor-oriented classes of manufacturing industry continue bouncing about the rural countryside in search of a cheap but adequate labor supply with a continual attrition to foreign locations. In the long run, these labor-oriented industries will diminish in *relative* importance but their continued existence supports the need for research in several respects.

Third, resource-oriented industries will be a driving force of rural industrialization in the 1980s. There is no doubt that more rural communities will be hosting energy-related developments, often very large scale projects such as coal mines with associated processing facilities, power-generating plants, and oil extraction with related processing plants. The research needs produced by expanded efforts to exploit mineral and energy resources are enormous and have only begun to attract social scientists' attention (Murdock and Leistritz, 1979).

Fourth, recent figures from the Bureau of Labor Statistics indicate the nation had a whopping 35.4 percent increase in service-producing industries between 1970 and 1979. Nonmetro counties had a higher rate of growth than metro counties: 42.4 percent compared to 33.2 percent (Smith and Deaton, 1980). Virtually nothing is known about the implications of this version of rural industrialization that have been articulated by Pulver and his associates (Pulver, 1979; Pinkovitz et al., 1979; Smith and Pulver, 1980; Smith, 1979).

Finally, many retirees are migrating from metro to nonmetro residences and bringing cash transfer payments with them. While one may be reluctant to regard social security and private pension benefits to retirees or property income as an industry, they are important additions to the economic base of many rural communities (Hirschl, 1980; Smith et al., in press; Harmston, 1979).

Manufacturing-Related Issues

Subsidies to Industry. / *One of the most pressing research issues for the 1980s is a thorough examination of the policy of subsidizing industrial location at the federal, state, and community levels.* Competition among communities for the finite and relatively small number of manufacturing plants is intense. With encouragement and some technical assistance from state and federal industrial development agencies and private developers, fifteen thousand community industrial development groups compete for the one thousand firms that locate annually (Deaton, 1974). As the bidding stakes escalate, industry appears to benefit. For example, it has been estimated that states and municipalities forfeit $40 million annually by undervaluing industrial properties (Mulkey and Dillman, 1976). Tax concessions for new and expanded industrial facilities have exempted $3.6 billion worth of property. Add to these estimates the several billion dollars of annual federal subsidy for rural industrial development, and the cost of new manufacturing jobs for rural communities becomes very large.

It is not clear that existing policy results in the creation of public goods being equal to the public expenditure. Indeed, there is some indication that subsidies intended to encourage job creation through rural plant locations are turned into greater profits for industry with little of the desired effect (Harrison and Kanter, 1978; Birch, 1979).

Foreign Competition. / *The effects on rural communities of foreign competition for the existing supply of manufacturing jobs is an important research need for the 1980s.* As rural wage rates increase, competition for the existing supply of new plants will increase further. Foreign competition will become more severe than it is now because the cheaper labor of foreign bidders will give them a competitive advantage. Further, developing nations, where cheaper labor is generally found, are acquiring the technology to produce other factor inputs at a competitive price.

Branch Plants. / *The creation of a knowledge base regarding branch plants is also an important research need.* The present information base is extremely thin. Very little is known and understood about the organizational structures within which these plants operate and the effects such structures have on the longevity and stability of locations. A modest beginning is being made, but only the tip of the iceberg has been recognized (Erickson, 1976; Erickson and Leinbach, 1979; Erickson, 1980). The fact that branch plants are a major mechanism through which industrial growth has been occurring in rural localities makes American communities particularly vulnerable to foreign competition. Many communities have had the experience of a branch plant being closed to relocate in a foreign nation.

Job Leakage. / *The process of job "leakage" needs examination in order to more effectively address the manpower, development, and utilization issues of rural workers, especially those of minority populations.* One of the reasons why local workers are not employed by new industry may be that they lack appropriate skills. They may not be hired because the firm imports workers by moving them from other locations or operations within the firm to the rural community; this is a common practice in branch plants. However, it may be that outside workers migrate to the community in response to the "market signals" about local job opportunities.

Urban Immigrants. / *Research is needed on the social, political, and cultural effects of urban immigrants on the rural community.* The effects may be dramatic or they may be negligible. We need to identify the range of effects and the conditions under which they occur. Not all labor employed by a new industry is indigenous. The resulting net migration has a number of implications for the small communities and rural areas in which they locate (Smith and Summers, 1978). These immigrants are bringing income and income-earning capacities with them. They become involved in local social, political, and educational affairs and augment the existing stock of human resources, qualitatively as well as quantitatively. They offer the potential for enhancing the area's ability to attract additional economic activities. However, they also often bring more urban lifestyles and higher expectations of public services, which may generate social and political conflict in the community.

Local Autonomy. / *Research is needed on the impact that social, political, and cultural dimensions of development have on local autonomy.* A purely economic cost/benefit analysis is not sufficient. Many social benefits and costs cannot be readily and easily translated into dollar terms. They involve human preferences for lifestyles, values, and institutional arrangements. Benefit/cost analyses of industrial development typically ignore these issues of local autonomy (see Chapter 25).

The external linkages that a new industry brings to a community appear to increase external linkages in other institutional areas of the locality. For example, state and federal intergovernmental transfer payments are positively associated with industrial growth in rural communities (Summers et al., 1979). Moreover, industry home offices make decisions about plant and community relations motivated by the interests of the firm but affecting the well-being and future of the community (Seiler and Summers, 1979). In the most extreme case, the decision may be to close the plant. The issues involved in the social costs of plant closings are extremely important, as are the economic issues.

Institutional structures in the community that are affected by externally imposed decisions of private firms and government agencies need to be studied. These structures are the mechanisms by which community capacities are activated to deal with the impacts. In instances where the imposed activity is quite large vis-à-vis the community, the resulting "boomtown" presents serious threats to the institutional structures of the host community. The storage of hazardous wastes, such as radioactive materials, is a similar situation, although, in this instance, the challenge is more to the technical capabilities and less to the magnitude of response capabilities.

The autonomy of the local community is affected by industrial development. No community is an island unto itself, but local autonomy, self-governance, and independence are deeply embedded in the culture of rural America. Externally induced, vertically controlled developments can be a threat to those cultural principles. Rural citizens may accept them, but some rural residents express feelings of resentment, alienation, and helplessness.

Multipliers. / *Research is needed to extend our understanding of conditions that affect employment and income multipliers.* The evidence is clear that multiplier effects of new industry are smaller than hoped for and expected (Summers et al., 1976; Hirschl, 1980; Smith et al., in press). The inadequacy of the local retail trade sector; access to larger, regional shopping centers; wide-area commuting of workers; the backward and forward linkages of the new industry; the presence of underused private and public facilities; and the existence of underemployment are all potential explanations that need to be examined more extensively.

Development or Exploitation. / *Another important research question is whether rural industry is contributing to rural development or "mining" rural resources.* Rural industry may be using cheap labor while investing little in the future of the community. There is limited evidence that industries actively discourage growth in the community. It is not unreasonable to expect a new industry to want limited growth, for rapid expansion in the community usually means wage rate increases and property tax escalations. This issue of political economy in rural communities is virtually unexplored.

Large-Scale Resource Development Projects

The future of rural industrialization is certain to include large-scale resource development projects. Several factors make this form of industrialization one that demands extensive and immediate attention. The contrast in size between the host community and the new industry is usually dramatic. The work force of the development project is often ten to twenty times larger than the community's indigenous population. The host community is normally selected by a combination of the forces of nature, historical coincidences that placed the community at a resource-rich site, developments in technology, world markets, and a federal government or private industry decision to develop the resource.

Consequently, local residents have little, if anything, to say about the appearance of this form of new industry on their village green. Similarly, the scope and magnitude of the project are so large that the rural community does not have resources to begin the analysis of potential impact, not to mention mitigation of those impacts. Although the basic demographic, economic, and social processes of community change probably are the same as in other communities with new industry, the difference in magnitude is so great that they appear qualitatively different. Indeed, there may be unique processes at work in these boomtowns. In any event, the existing knowledge base, which rests on incomplete and thin research into the impacts of small-scale industrial development, is inadequate to the needs of communities concerned with large-scale resource development projects.

Research is needed on how communities are impacted by these large-scale resource development projects. The issues intrinsic to these developments support the increasing attention given to social and cultural as well as economic and environmental impact assessments (also see Chapter 29). The fact that such statements are required of all proposals may itself become a factor in influencing location decisions for certain kinds of industrial development. The day may not be far ahead when an important variable in an industrial location decision will be the estimates of time and expense required to prepare a detailed environmental, economic, and social impact assessment for the proposed project. This will become especially significant when sequences or staging of multiple projects are proposed for a given location (e.g., the Alberta Oil Sands project near

Fort MacMurray in northern Alberta). We may know how to go about assessing the impacts associated with individual projects, but we know very little about the cumulative effects of a series of independent projects or the most appropriate methodology for making assessments of synergistic effects associated with a series of seemingly harmless individual projects.

Longitudinal analyses of the impacts of energy and other large-scale developments are essential. A few efforts are underway, but the time frames of two or three years are insufficient for tracking long-term effects. Longitudinal analyses must receive further emphasis.

As a partial substitute and complementary strategy, comparative analyses are essential for ascertaining the effects of specific factors in a complex process. Every community and development site is in some respects unique. Hence, there is no substitute for making comparisons of similar developments in a variety of communities. Likewise, the knowledge that can be obtained by different types of development projects in similar communities is valuable to understanding the complexities of social change.

REFERENCES

Averitt, Robert T. 1979. "Implications of the dual economy for community change." In Gene F. Summers and Arne Selvik (editors), *Nonmetropolitan Industrial Growth and Community Change*. Lexington, Massachusetts: D. C. Heath and Co.

Birch, David L. 1979. *The Job Generation Process*. Cambridge, Massachusetts: Program on Neighborhood and Regional Change, Massachusetts Institute of Technology. Report prepared for the Office of Economic Research, Economic Development Administration, U.S. Department of Commerce.

Deaton, Brady J. 1974. *Industrialization of Rural Areas: Recent Trends and the Social and Economic Consequences*. Blacksburg, Virginia: Department of Agricultural Economics, Virginia Polytechnic Institute and State University.

Erickson, Rodney A. 1976. "The filtering-down process: Industrial location in a nonmetropolitan area." *Professional Geographer* 27(3, August):254–260.

———. 1980. "Corporate organization and manufacturing branch plant closures in nonmetropolitan areas." *Regional Studies* 14(6):491–501.

Erickson, Rodney A., and Thomas Leinbach. 1979. "Characteristics of branch plants attracted to nonmetropolitan areas." In Richard E. Lonsdale and H. L. Seyler (editors), *Nonmetropolitan Industrialization*. New York: John Wiley and Sons.

Hansen, Niles. 1970. *Rural Poverty and the Urban Crisis*. Bloomington, Indiana: University of Indiana Press.

Harmston, Floyd K. 1979."A study of the impact of retired people on a small community." Paper presented at the meetings of the Midcontinental Regional Science Association, Minneapolis, Minnesota.

Harrison, Bennett, and Sandra Kanter. 1978. "The political economy of states' job creation business incentives." *Journal of American Institute of Planners* (October).

Hirschl, Thomas. 1980. "Cash transfers and the export base of rural communities."

Madison, Wisconsin: University of Wisconsin. Master's thesis.

Mulkey, David, and B. L. Dillman. 1976. "Location effects of state and local industrial development subsidies." *Growth and Change* 7(April):37–43.

Murdock, Steve H., and F. Larry Leistritz. 1979. *Energy Development in the Western United States: Impact on Rural Areas.* New York: Praeger Publishers.

Norton, R. D., and J. Rees. 1979. "The product cycle and the spatial decentralization of American manufacturing." *Regional Studies* 13(2):141–151.

Pinkovitz, William H., Glen C. Pulver, and Stephen M. Smith. 1979. *Nonmanufacturing Industry Potential in Rural Areas: An Analysis of Five Industries.* Madison, Wisconsin: College of Agricultural and Life Sciences, University of Wisconsin, Research Bulletin R2879.

Pulver, Glen C. 1979. "A theoretical framework for the analysis of community economic development policy options." In Gene F. Summers and Arne Selvik (editors), *Nonmetropolitan Industrial Growth and Community Change.* Lexington, Massachusetts: D. C. Heath and Co.

Seiler, Lauren H., and Gene F. Summers. 1979. "Corporate involvement in community affairs." *Midwest Sociological Quarterly* 20(Summer):375–386.

Smith, Eldon D., and Brady J. Deaton. 1980. "The changing industrial structure of the rural economy." Paper prepared for the National Extension Manpower Workshop, Silver Springs, Maryland.

Smith, Eldon D., Merlin Hackbart, and Johannes Van Veen. In press. "A modified regression base multiplier model." *Growth and Change.*

Smith, Eldon D., and Gene F. Summers. 1978. *How New Manufacturing Affects Rural Areas.* Mississippi State, Mississippi: Southern Rural Development Center, University of Mississippi.

Smith, Stephen M. 1979. *Export Orientation of Nonmanufacturing Businesses in Nonmetropolitan Communities.* Moscow, Idaho: Department of Agricultural Economics, University of Idaho, Research Series 224.

Smith, Stephen M., and Glen C. Pulver. 1980. *Characteristics of Nonmanufacturing Businesses in Nonmetropolitan Wisconsin.* Madison, Wisconsin: College of Agricultural and Life Sciences, University of Wisconsin, Research Bulletin R2879.

Summers, Gene F. 1978. "Rural industry: Myth and reality." *Social Impact Assessment* 34(October):4–6.

Summers, Gene F., Sharon D. Evans, Frank Clemente, E. M. Beck, and Jon Minkoff. 1976. *Industrial Invasion of Nonmetropolitan America.* New York: Praeger Publishers.

Summers, Gene F., C. Matthew Snipp, and E. M. Beck. 1979. "Coping with industrialization." In Richard E. Lonsdale and H. L. Seyler (editors), *Nonmetropolitan Industrialization.* New York: John Wiley and Sons.

Wheat, Leonard. 1973. *Regional Growth and Industrial Location.* Lexington, Massachusetts: D. C. Heath and Co.

17 Employment

LUTHER TWEETEN

In spite of considerable socioeconomic progress, rural areas continue to be characterized by higher rates of poverty, lower income, and poorer infrastructure and services than urban areas. Gainful employment is critical to raise earnings of individuals and communities, alleviate underemployment, and provide the means to acquire public and private services in rural areas. Gainful employment is much more than a livelihood for individuals and an economic base for communities; consider the adage, "What you are is what you do." Revitalization of the rural spirit as well as the rural pocketbook depends on jobs. Research is needed on the performance of public and private institutions in serving employment needs and opportunities of rural areas within a national context.

EMPLOYMENT BY INDUSTRY

The diverse pattern of employment in nonmetropolitan and metropolitan America is illustrated in Table 17.1. Of the 16.2 million nonmetro males employed in 1974, 27.7 percent were employed in manufacturing and 15.9 percent in the extractive industries of agriculture, forestry, fisheries, and mining. The importance of manufacturing employment to nonmetro areas is accentuated by including female workers: of 22 million rural male and female workers in 1975, 9 percent were in agriculture, forestry, and fisheries, compared to 23 percent in

---

Luther Tweeten is Regents Professor in the Department of Agricultural Economics, Oklahoma State University, Stillwater, Oklahoma. Currently president of the American Agricultural Economics Association, he is author of four books, including *Micropolitan Development*, and has written nearly 250 articles.

Table 17.1 Employment by Industry for Metro and Nonmetro Males, 1974

	U.S. employment[a] (in thousands)	Metro		Nonmetro		Nonmetro as percentage of U.S. employment[a]
		Employment (in thousands)	Distribution[a] (in percentages)	Employment (in thousands)	Distribution[a] (in percentages)	
Total Employment	51,681	35,522	100.0	16,159	100.0	31.13
Agriculture, forestry, and fisheries	2,959	767	2.2	2,191	13.6	74.1
Mining	593	220	.6	373	2.3	62.9
Construction	4,906	3,123	8.8	1,782	11.0	36.3
Durable manufacturing	9,528	6,797	19.1	2,730	16.9	28.7
Nondurable manufacturing	5,278	3,527	9.9	1,751	10.8	33.2
Transportation and other public utilities	4,448	3,247	9.1	1,201	7.4	27.0
Wholesale trade	2,597	2,080	5.9	517	3.2	19.9
Retail trade	7,041	4,873	13.7	2,167	13.4	30.8
Finance, insurance, and real estate	2,212	1,789	5.0	422	2.6	19.1
Business and repair services	1,994	1,537	4.3	456	2.8	22.8
Personal service	711	523	1.5	188	1.2	26.4
Entertainment and recreation	474	369	1.0	105	.7	22.2
Professional and related services	5,721	4,268	12.0	1,453	9.0	25.4
Public administration	3,221	2,399	6.8	822	5.1	25.5

[a]Elements may not add to totals due to rounding.

Source: U.S. Department of Commerce (Bureau of the Census). 1975. Social and Economic Characteristics of the Metropolitan and Nonmetropolitan Population, 1974 and 1970. Washington, D.C.: U.S. Government Printing Office, Current Population Report, Series P-23, 56, pages 84-89.

manufacturing (Deavers and Brown, 1979:17). Compared to metro male workers, nonmetro male workers were employed disproportionately in the extractive industries noted above, in nondurable manufacturing, and in construction.

The share of construction points to the greater economic growth in nonmetro than in metro areas. Between 1970 and 1977, nonmetro wage and salary employment increased 22 percent, double the percentage gain in metro areas.

Percentage gains in employment were larger for nonmetro than for metro areas for each industry in Figure 17.1. In nonmetro areas, the largest percentage gain was in mining, a comparatively small industry, followed by services, finance, insurance, and real estate – comparatively high-paying industries. Data for 1975 presented by Deavers and Brown (1979:22) show that nonmetro immigrants (nonmetro residents in 1975 but metro residents in 1970) were disproportionately represented in relatively high-paying trade, finance, insurance, real estate, and other professional services. Thus, although earnings of nonmetro workers averaged only 80 percent of those of metro workers in 1973 (Nilsen, 1979:15), absolute and relative employment increases in the highest-paying U.S. industries (finance, insurance, real estate, and professional services) in nonmetro counties helped to reduce the gap. Mean annual earnings in these high-paying industries in nonmetro areas averaged only 90 percent of those in metro counties, thus diminishing the contribution of growth in these industries to closing the gap between metro and nonmetro incomes.

RESEARCH ISSUES

The employment turnaround has narrowed differences in income and services between metro and nonmetro areas. The incidence of poverty on farms fell from 51 percent in 1960 (Edwards and Coffman, 1977) to 20 percent in 1975 (Hoppe, 1980:7). In the same year, the incidence of poverty among nonmetro residents as a whole, including farmers, was 11 percent and was 12 percent among metro residents (Deavers and Brown, 1979:6). The proportions of poor rural households headed by a full-time worker (25 percent) and with two or more workers (nearly one-third) are approximately double those for urban workers (Deavers and Brown, 1979:11), suggesting inadequate employment earnings and services in rural areas.

In short, after controlling for race, education level, employment, and other factors that influence poverty, the incidence of poverty remains higher in nonmetro than in metro areas. The depth and extent of rural poverty in a crescent extending from the Carolina coastal plains through

FIGURE 17.1 Change in Nonfarm Wage and Salary Employment, March 1970-77

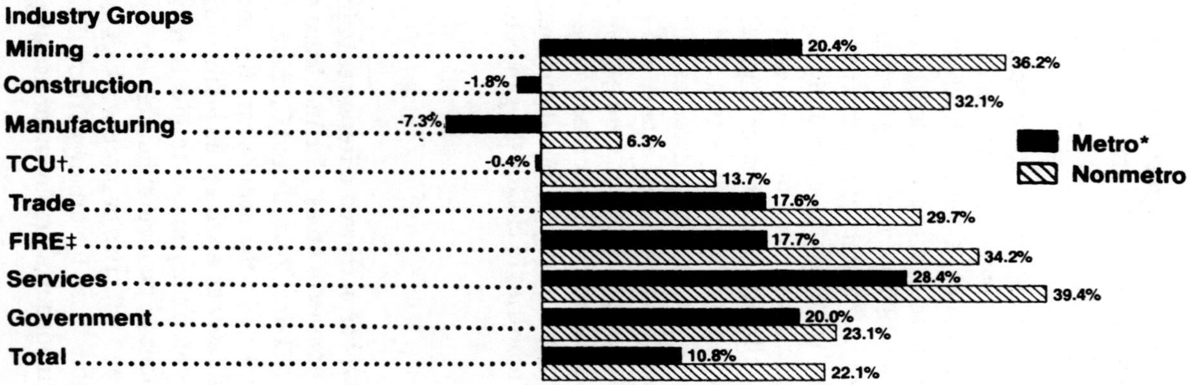

*Excludes about 50 smaller standard metropolitan statistical areas.
†Transportation, communications, and utilities groups.
‡Finance, insurance, and real estate groups.

Source: Bergland, Bob. 1979. "Rural development progress, January 1977-June 1979." Fifth Report of the Secretary of Agriculture to the Congress. Washington, D.C.: Office of the Secretary, U.S. Department of Agriculture. Page 4.

the Black Belt of Alabama to the Mississippi Delta, in the Appalachian region, and in the Four Corners region of Arizona, Colorado, New Mexico, and Utah, matches or exceeds deprivation found in metro areas despite the massive rural progress since 1960. The demographic turnaround by no means signals victory over deprivation for rural people.

Rural Cost-of-Living Index

Interpretation of the above data on earnings is muddied by differences in cost of living between rural and urban areas. Adequate comparisons of absolute or relative deprivation among sectors and areas are impossible without adjusting for cost of living. Although farm poverty levels are adjusted for goods produced and consumed in the farm household, no adjustment is made for the cost of purchasing typical items by consumers in rural and urban areas. *Research is needed to construct a cost-of-living index for rural areas suitable for comparing income and wealth between sectors.* (See Holden et al., 1979, for data required to construct index.)

Unemployment

Norwood (1977:6–11) estimates that $16 billion of federal funds were allocated to unemployment payments in 1976. If unemployment does not measure what it is intended to measure, funds miss their target. The unemployment rate is widely used to measure two principal needs for work force and social welfare programs: economic hardship or deprivation, which is a problem of economic equity, and underused resources, which is a problem in economic efficiency. The measure now serves neither purpose well.

Economic Hardship. / In the past, when each family tended to have one breadwinner, unemployment may have been a measure of economic hardship for wage and salary workers. Today, many of the unemployed are secondary or tertiary earners in multiple breadwinner families, are only briefly unemployed, or are sustained by unemployment compensation and union/company layoff supplements. The National Commission on Employment and Unemployment Statistics (1979:6) recognized this shortcoming of unemployment data used to target programs intended to alleviate economic hardship. We do not know the degree of economic hardship engendered by unemployment. *Research is recommended to determine: (1) the association between unemployment and economic hardship; (2) whether economic hardship programs (CETA, etc.) now allocated according to unemployment would better be allocated using other measures of hardship, such as poverty and median family income; and (3) whether rural and urban areas are served equally by alternative measures of hardship.*

Inefficiency. / Unemployment represents a wasted resource of people willing and able to work to produce goods and services desired by society. A large number of education and training programs, along with job creation programs (e.g., Economic Development Administration), are allocated mainly to reduce this inefficiency. Two issues are relevant: How well is unemployment measured in rural areas? If unemployment were measured accurately, would it be the appropriate concept of underutilized human resources?

The principal source of unemployment data are the current population surveys taken monthly by personal interview (see Tweeten, 1979b:534–535, for details). Because the sample is much too small to provide reliable data on each rural county, unemployment data for individual rural counties are estimated by the Bureau of Labor Statistics' "handbook method," using available data on unemployment insurance claims, public employment service registration, and other sources. The resulting estimates are inaccurate: A comprehensive personal interview survey of residents of Gadsden County, a rural county in Florida, reported by Korsching and Sapp (1977), found 20 percent of the labor force unemployed compared to the official unemployment rate of 9.2 percent.

More serious is the answer to the first issue above: After reviewing the conceptual foundation for unemployment statistics, I concluded that ". . . no amount of massaging of unemployment statistics will provide appropriate measures of employment needs in rural areas. Unemployment is simply the wrong concept" (Tweeten, 1979b:543).

The chief criticisms of the official unemployment rate as a measure of job needs include failure to measure (1) workers who are employed at jobs that do not utilize their capabilities (subemployment), (2) potential workers who either did not enter the labor force or dropped out for lack of job opportunities (discouraged workers), and (3) the degree of employment among the self-employed.

Self-Employment. / The Bureau of Labor Statistics considers a person to be employed if self-employed one hour or more per week. The incidence of self-employment in farming and small businesses is far higher in rural than urban areas. A large number of rural residents are part-time farmers. They can lose their regular nonfarm jobs, work one hour per week on their farms that may provide nominal income, and be classified as employed. Family members (e.g., sons and daughters of a farm operator) are also considered employed if they work one hour or more per week on the farm, even if they lost full-time off-the-farm jobs. Adjustment for self-employment raised the adjusted unemployment rate 1.5 percentage points for nonmetro areas and .9 percentage point for metro areas in 1975 (Nilsen, 1979:13).

Subemployment. / A worker receiving small compensation for a job relative to his potential (e.g., a mechanical engineer receiving $200 per week for a full-time job) is subemployed. So is a part-time worker picking up odd jobs, such as cutting wood, babysitting, and sporadic farm day-work, but who desires full-time employment. Neither of these examples is considered even partial unemployment by current official measures, yet each represents underused human resources.

Discouraged Workers. / Able-bodied workers who desire work but who are not actively seeking work are not classified as unemployed. These workers are expected to be especially prominent in depressed rural areas where job opportunities are scarce; where few employers exist, and hence active job search need be of short duration; and where low-income self-employment in farming allows subsistence living. Because data on discouraged workers are collected from only 25 percent of the current population survey sample, measures of discouraged workers are considered by some to be too unreliable for adjusting unemployment data (Nilsen, 1979:3).

The Bureau of Labor Statistics publishes an underemployment index comprised of full-time job seekers plus one-half the number of unemployed seeking part-time work, plus one-half of those working involuntarily part-time, as a percentage of the entire labor force less one-half of the part-time labor force (Nilsen, 1979:4). These weights are highly arbitrary, as are those on indexes of underemployment proposed by Levitan and Taggart (1974), Hauser and Sullivan (see Sullivan, 1977), and Rowe and Zimmer (1977). The Rowe and Zimmer approach is otherwise attractive because it measures underemployment by how far county income falls below national norms. With modifications suggested by Tweeten (1979b:553–554), it has promise for a reasonably objective measure of underused human resources. *Research is needed to compare and refine measures of underemployment until a suitable measure is devised for official acceptance as a basis for measuring labor market performance and for allocating work force programs to make use of human resources.*

Other Research Issues

A host of additional research issues relate to rural employment. Some, such as problems of migrant farm workers, have been researched extensively. Others, such as problems of undocumented aliens, are so new that it is difficult to determine the proper questions to ask. These, along with the following selected topics, are likely to be of research concern for some time.

Inadequate Work Force Services. / The literature abounds with references to the urban orientation of the U.S. Department of Labor and failure to provide rural workers with adequate employment and training programs. Ray Marshall, before he became Secretary of Labor, stated, "By whatever standard we judge manpower experiences, the evidence seems to support the conclusion that rural areas have been shortchanged in manpower efforts" (1974:119). The massive farm-urban exodus was largely unattended by labor force services. Rural people make little use of the public employment service when they need jobs according to data presented by Tweeten and Brinkman (1976:105–108). After reviewing a large number of federal work force pilot programs for rural areas, we concluded: "On the one hand, the long list of work force programs depicts the image of a public labor effort that is alert, imaginative, and bold. On the other hand, the image is a labor policy that is barren of proved, solid, comprehensive delivery systems" (1976:119).

Federal legislation has implications for the location of federal offices, facilities, and installations, and hence of employment in rural areas. Section 601 of the Rural Development Act of 1972 required heads of all executive departments and agencies to give first priority to the location in rural areas of all new offices, facilities, and installations. The 1972 act and the Agricultural Act of 1970, which preceded it and required similar action, contained escape clauses that permitted easy circumvention. The 1970 act provided that federal structures only be placed in rural areas "in so far as practicable," and the 1972 act's Senate-House Conference Report made clear that a new structure need not be located in a rural area "if there is an overwhelming reason" for locating it elsewhere. Appropriate research can be coincidental with clearer definition of federal intent relating to location of facilities.

The failure to provide a comprehensive employment delivery system is undoubtedly the result of complex economic, political, and social factors. Additional research can help to sort issues of political will from issues of inadequate program performance. *Research is needed to determine the economically justified level of labor force services (including service delivery systems) for rural areas. Research is also needed to determine the nonpecuniary social costs and benefits associated with labor programs such as those that result in migration.*

Social Programs. / A number of social programs, including minimum wage laws, social security, and collective-bargaining legislation exempting unions from antitrust laws and allowing a union shop, have benefited many rural and urban workers. But the public is increasingly concerned over the contribution of the programs to national inflation, unemployment (especially among marginal workers), substitution of capital for labor, creation of secondary labor markets, and slow economic growth. *Research is needed to determine the impact of social programs on performance of the national economy as it relates to employment and earnings. Research also needs to determine possible alternatives to existing programs.* For example, a wage supplement could replace minimum wage as a means to provide marginal workers with socially acceptable earnings while encouraging employment and substitution of labor for capital.

Rising Energy Prices. / The mass rural-urban exodus prior to 1970 and the urban-rural exodus in the 1970s were possible in no small part because of cheap energy for transportation. At issue is what higher energy prices will do to location decisions of people and industries (also see Chapters 3, 4, and 15). Opinion surveys indicate that rural people favor bringing jobs to people, not people to jobs, and favor commuting over migration if jobs cannot be found within the community. As a consequence, the commuting field for large metro areas, extending as far as seventy-five miles, reaches into many rural areas. In a brief analysis, I earlier concluded that "energy constitutes only a small portion of the cost of commuting. The major cost of commuting is time. If the commuter averages 30 miles per hour, gasoline is $1.00 per gallon, and gas mileage is 15 miles per gallon, the energy cost is $.067 per mile or $2.00 per hour. This . . . is unlikely to have much influence on commuting decisions" (1979a:13). The optimal residence location is where the tradeoffs from greater marginal productivity from a job in a densely populated area just offset additional dissatisfactions from residing in (or commuting to) that area. *Research is needed to explore in greater depth the impact of energy prices on commuting, migration, and the comparative advantage of locating jobs and residences in rural rather than urban areas.*

REFERENCES

Bergland, Bob. 1979. "Rural development progress, January 1977–June, 1979." *Fifth Report of the Secretary of Agriculture to the Congress.* Washington, D.C.: Office of the Secretary, U.S. Department of Agriculture.

Deavers, Kenneth L., and David L. Brown. 1979. *Social and Economic Trends in Rural America.* Washington, D.C.: Economics, Statistics, and Cooperatives Services, U.S. Department of Agriculture, the White House Rural Development Background Paper.

Edwards, R., and George Coffman. 1977. *Farm Poverty: A Current Assessment and Research Focus.* Washington, D.C.: Economics, Statistics, and Cooperatives Services, U.S. Department of Agriculture, NEAD Working Paper.

Holden, Russel, Laurie Tobias, and Richard Wertheimer, II. 1979. *Differences in Living Costs between Rural and Urban Areas, Final Report.* Washington, D.C.: Urban Land Institute.

Hoppe, Bob. 1980. "Despite progress, rural poverty demands attention." In Economics, Statistics, and Cooperatives Service, U.S. Department of Agriculture (editors), *Rural Development Perspectives.* Washington, D.C.: Economics, Statistics, and Cooperatives Service, U.S. Department of Agriculture.

Korsching, Peter, and Stephen Sapp. 1977. *People and Jobs for Gadsden County. Special report to Center for Rural Development.* Gainesville, Florida: Institute of Food and Agricultural Sciences, University of Florida.

Levitan, Sar, and Robert Taggart, III. 1974. *Employment and Earnings Inadequacy: A New Social Indicator.* Baltimore, Maryland: Johns Hopkins University Press.

Marshall, Ray. 1974. *Rural Workers in Rural Labor Markets.* Salt Lake City, Utah: Olympus Publishing Co.

National Commission on Employment and Unemployment Statistics. 1979. *Counting the Labor Force.* Washington, D.C.: U.S. Government Printing Office.

Nilsen, Sigurd R. 1979. *Assessment of Employment and Unemployment Statistics for Nonmetropolitan Areas.* Washington, D.C.: Economics, Statistics, and Cooperatives Service, U.S. Department of Agriculture, Rural Development Research Report 18.

Norwood, Janet. 1977. "Reshaping a statistical program to meet legislative priorities." *Monthly Labor Review* (November):6–11.

Rowe, Gene, and John Zimmer. 1977. *Manpower Economic Utilization Indexes by Counties, 1970.* Springfield, Virginia: National Technical Information Service.

Sullivan, Teresa. 1977. "Marginal workers, marginal jobs: The underutilization of American workers." Chicago: University of Chicago. Doctoral dissertation.

Tweeten, Luther. 1979a. "Discussion: A look at major events and policy issues facing southern agriculture." *Southern Journal of Agricultural Economics* 11(July):11–14.

______. 1979b. "Rural employment and unemployment statistics." In National Commission on Employment and Unemployment Statistics (editors), *Data Collection, Processing, and Presentation: National and Local* (Appendix Volume II of *Counting the Labor Force*). Washington, D.C.: U.S. Government Printing Office.

Tweeten, Luther, and George Brinkman. 1976. *Micropolitan Development.* Ames, Iowa: Iowa State University Press.

U.S. Department of Commerce (Bureau of the Census). 1975. *Social and Economic Characteristics of the Metropolitan and Nonmetropolitan Population, 1974 and 1970.* Washington, D.C.: U.S. Government Printing Office, Current Population Report, Series P-23, 55.

18
Education

GAIL ARMSTRONG PARKS
PEGGY J. ROSS
ANNE E. JUST

Rural education research needs seem to us very clear and straightforward in contrast to a policy world generally characterized by both complexities and ambiguities. After an extensive period of neglect by both researchers and policy makers, enough good research has been completed during the past five years or so to tell us fairly emphatically what the problem is: Various pressures have forced rural schools into almost universal adaptation of urban models of education. Rural places are generally unsuited for such models. The result has often been devastating for country schools, eroding both their unique rural characteristics (which are often strengths) and their capacity-building abilities. It is also questionable whether this practice has resulted in equal educational opportunity for rural students. *What research should do in the next few years, therefore, is evaluate alternatives that work in rural places and develop distinctively rural models for providing students with adequate curricula and services.* Many educators and researchers in rural settings know that–it is no secret to the initiated.

Nevertheless, there remain some doubting Thomases, many of whom occupy high-level positions. Because they make decisions influencing the future of America's rural schools, it is important that they recognize the following facts:

Gail Armstrong Parks is Education Program Director at the National Rural Center, Washington, D.C. She has written several publications on rural education and rural development.

Peggy J. Ross is a rural sociologist in the Economics and Statistics Service, U.S. Department of Agriculture, Washington, D.C. She is the author of many articles on social in-

- rural districts number approximately 11,000 and make up 70 percent of all the nation's school districts; but research at most federal, state, and university levels reflects a highly disproportionate focus on urban school problems (U.S. Department of Commerce, 1978)
- rural students are from poor families, out of proportion to their numbers; almost 20 percent of rural children are poor, and 40 percent of the nation's poverty is concentrated in nonmetro places having only one-third of the nation's population (National Rural Center, 1979)
- rural communities are too diverse and rural circumstances vary too much for "the one best system" (or urban model) of education to be adopted equally in rural schools throughout the nation; it is now clear that reorganization of rural schools on urban models has not been the panacea envisioned by school reformers seventy-five years ago
- environmental conditions and energy costs have, for the foreseeable future, produced a need to reappraise the economic and educational costs and benefits of massive busing of students to achieve a so-called "critical mass" of pupils.

Because the future of many rural students (and their communities) is significantly affected by the quality of their schools and where they are located, it is important that policy makers understand how this situation came about. It may help them understand better why we should explore new models of education for sparsely populated, small, and culturally diverse communities; why relevant agencies in the federal government should amend their data collection procedures and their program regulations to accommodate the rural sector; and why major national studies should be undertaken in the areas of rural school transportation, school finance, and rural student outcomes.

Historically, the "rationalizing" of rural education was simply one more reflection of a rationalizing process that served as the operating principle of government and business in the early years of this century. When David Tyack (1974) examined the school reform movements of that era, he concluded that the inclination to think of schools as functionally equivalent to factories characterized virtually everyone working on the

dicators, rural education, and program evaluation.
Anne E. Just is on leave as a grants management specialist, U.S. Department of Education, Washington, D.C. She is currently with the Department of Education at the University of California, Berkeley, California.

problem—indeed, schools were seen as the "work places" of little people, "efficiency" was viewed as a major goal of education, and schools (like factories) were seen as needing to consolidate large numbers of people in one place and to stratify their organizations along hierarchical lines in order to become efficient.

Every aspect of that argument has since been discounted. It was done very notably, of course, by Tyack himself, whose major point was that the "one best system" has failed on many occasions to serve all groups of students—rural, urban, and suburban—especially those who are poor and culturally different from the mainstream. Other aspects of the conventional wisdom have been questioned by researchers examining it from different angles.

After looking at educational results in small and large schools, Barker and Gump (1964) concluded that small schools often have distinct educational advantages and that policies should favor maintaining small community schools, which are capable of responding to individual differences and community needs in a way that large schools are not. In *Education in Rural America: A Reassessment of Conventional Wisdom* (1977), Jonathan Sher and four other authors examined several elements of the "conventional wisdom" about rural schools and found each one wanting. A basic problem, the authors argued, was that claims about practices intended to improve rural schools lacked supporting research. The result, they maintained, was the wholesale implementation of practices that have been of questionable educational value to a majority of rural students. Alan Peshkin (1978) did an intensive analysis of a small school in a small town and concluded that the school does indeed work for the community and socialize the students, fostering and maintaining a close school/community relationship. But he also concluded that under existing arrangements students are not getting the best possible range of educational offerings.

Thus there is an ambivalence toward the rural schools problem of the 1980s that tends to confuse questions about them. It is not really a matter of "rural advantages" versus "urban advantages," nor is it a question of choice between school/community closeness (and a poor curriculum) and a curriculum of high quality (and poor community rapport). It is, rather, a question of what resources and arrangements are necessary to provide students in all circumstances and places with a good education. Fundamentally different conceptions are necessary.

There is evidence that many problems and policies reflect an unconscious "one best model" bias. Sher and others argued in 1977 that rural students are discriminated against in federal programs. When Bass and Berman (1979) examined selected federal programs, they found that rural schools sometimes win and sometimes lose on financial resources but are nearly always hurt by federal program *designs and regulations.* Tom Gjelten's study (1980) expands and supports their conclusions emphatically. Herriott and Gross (1978) and Nachtigal (1980) reached the same conclusion after studying, respectively, the rural experimental schools sites and an array of reform efforts. Rural realities, Nachtigal insists, dictate the need for alternatives and different change strategies.

Nachtigal has also emphasized marked differences among three types of rural settings: those that are at least modestly prosperous and "Middle-American" (mainly in the Midwest and Northeast), those that are areas of rapid growth (mainly in the West), and those that are extremely poor and have high concentrations of minorities (overwhelmingly in the South). Most of the research cited above was done in "Middle-American" settings; thus, the need to study southern and western rural education problems seems a priority at this time.

With further analysis of the problems, insights necessary to develop educational models more appropriate to rural communities in the 1980s can be produced. But it will be necessary to take immediate action and begin simultaneous engagements on three fronts. These are specified below.

RESEARCH ISSUES

Rural School Demonstrations

First and foremost, a national commitment should be made to support long-term demonstration and evaluation of alternative models for rural education. The greatest need is for reliable information about what will work for students in a variety of settings (Nachtigal, 1980). Education has seldom been improved by a process where theoretical studies are conducted in isolation from school settings and the findings then somehow applied. School improvements occur when those with the highest stakes – students, teachers, administrators, parents, and concerned citizens – are the ones who choose, plan, and participate in experimental innovations. It simply is not the character of education to be changed fundamentally by a knowledge process that ignores issues of power and participation. The failure of the "one best system" has amply demonstrated that truth; people simply tend to say, "We are different and it won't work here." Yet experimentation, coupled with participation, has often paved the way for improvement. Failures seem to occur when one or both of two conditions exist: local people do not perceive the problem that reformers identify, or there is inadequate national support for innovations until they are firmly in place.

A few questions are of paramount importance and should be addressed through a flexible but intellectually rigorous research plan. A plan of national demonstrations with state and local participation should be designed to provide answers to general questions about what works, and to allow participating districts to choose one or more of the demonstrations described below.

Demonstrations are needed that emphasize local capacity building and the use of local resources. There is a model that has had outstanding success: the Foxfire concept that Eliot Wigginton, a teacher in Southern Appalachia, began developing in the mid-1960s. (Wigginton, 1975; Parks, 1981). Foxfire projects emphasize building a student's competence and self-esteem by involving him or her in real work and by using the community as a setting for acquiring necessary skills and knowledge. Foxfire projects, which emphasize the use of local people as experts on various matters and treat local knowledge as inherently worthy, have the distinct educational advantages of enhancing student esteem and motivation, teaching students useful skills, and fostering good relations between the school and the community. These projects have the additional advantage of being workable in both isolated and consolidated settings. Although many are known to be quite successful, no national agency or state (except Alaska) has ever provided formal support for more widespread experimentation. If supported nationally, locally relevant adaptations of the Foxfire approach could be designed to foster educational improvement through capacity building.

Demonstrations are needed that emphasize improving education for rural minorities by exploring new desegregation models for rural places. No group suffers the effects of discrimination, including racial isolation, more than rural minorities. Yet existing regulations for the Elementary and Secondary Education Act (ESEA) Title VI (desegregation) program discriminate against rural schools by favoring districts with large numbers of minority students and by concentrating on districts under recent court order. Experimentation with new methods is badly needed because rural districts are often small, because many of the schools in the rural South remain de facto largely segregated, and because there is an urgent need for educational models that accommodate improved race relations. In 1983, the ESEA Title VI legislation will be revised and new regulations will be written. Projects that demonstrate effective alternatives will help address existing biases in the program and the information gained can help in formulating new policies and provisions.

Demonstrations are needed that emphasize the use of different technologies to provide specialized education services. Small, isolated districts that try to operate in a conventional fashion cannot meet the mandate to provide adequately for students who are gifted, handicapped, bilingual, or poor–or who simply have special interests and talents such as foreign languages or physics. Schools that are *very* small and isolated have difficulty providing even the minimum curriculum considered necessary for getting into college or getting a decent job. The technology exists, however, to link the only student in a small school who wants a physics class with the best physics teacher in the state. Similarly, the technology exists to put teachers untrained in special education in touch with experts who can diagnose problems and prescribe appropriate learning exercises (this model has existed for some time in the field of rural health). More research and demonstrations are needed on the potential and limitations of new technology as a means of supplementing the programs of many small rural schools.

For example, during the mid 1970s the National Aeronautics and Space Administration (NASA) conducted a one-year demonstration program in the use of satellite delivery of educational and health services in Alaska, the Rocky Mountains, and Appalachia. Expanding upon such efforts can afford rural schools opportunities to meet the varied but often singular needs and interests of students without having to sacrifice general course offerings.

Demonstrations are needed of school/work-place collaboration. Since the announcement of President Carter's Youth Initiative in January 1980, much attention has been given to the question of what kind of relationship between education and work would benefit students and relevant institutions. For rural places, the question has other dimensions because of a frequently encountered rural need for long-term development, immediate job opportunities, and the capacities of talented, enterprising young people to enhance rural community viability.

As Stuart Rosenfeld (1980) has noted, "planners become mesmerized by labor market projections and match them faithfully to programs without respecting the difference between the urban and rural work place." Of paramount importance is the question of what vocational education programs prepare rural students to do. Do they tend, as some have suggested, to teach students how to work *for* other people, primarily in large hierarchical organizations? If so, what are the results of such a practice for rural places, some of which have a greater potential for job creation through small-scale entrepreneurial enterprises than through attracting a factory? Various entrepreneurial models need to be tested, including those models that go beyond the vocational curriculum in linking schools and work places. The question of whether or not enduring school/work-place linkages will evolve in the absence of total curricular reform will need examination, as will the conditions under which various forms of entrepreneurship are possible.

The categories above are not mutually exclusive, of course; nor are they all-inclusive. Local expertise and school/work-place collaboration, for example, might well be blended in many rural settings, just as new "small" technologies could probably be used effectively in most small rural schools. Until we begin exploring alternatives that address unique local conditions, however, we cannot gain the systematic information we need about rural education models that work.

Federal Rural Education Data and Program Regulations

Demonstrations must be supplemented with needed changes in federal data collection procedures and regulatory provisions. As Parks and Sher (1979) have pointed out, an antirural bias is endemic in published federal data sources. At a minimum, existing educational data on rural schools should be reported, stratified by various criteria of rural categories; data sources should begin immediately to collect and publish data on schools and districts with enrollments under 300; and those sources should prepare biannual reports on the status of rural education. Until we begin to cross-tabulate rural place of residence with "disadvantaged" categories, we will lack the data we need to formulate policies to address the severe problems of disadvantaged rural students and communities.

The urban bias in federal education program regulations is also endemic (Gjelten, 1980)—and painfully familiar to the rural school administrators who must compete for limited resources with large metropolitan districts and their array of administrative specialists. It should be a "research" task of each federal program concerned with public education to conduct a careful, systematic analysis of its programs' legislative authority and program regulations to determine if and where bias in favor of large size exists and to suggest corrective action wherever necessary.

Transportation Costs and Alternatives

Disproportionately rising costs for rural school transportation are directly related to questions about appropriate models for rural education and should be the subject of intensive research during the next few years. Most rural schools are confronted with dramatically rising student transportation costs, and those costs will probably continue to rise. Although many states now subsidize student transportation, the fact remains that a rural school's budget is likely to reflect proportionately more expenditures for transport and proportionately less for staff salaries than an urban school's budget. The need to evaluate cost-cutting alternatives is greater in rural areas. Possibilities might include transporting populations in addition to students, evaluating whether or not busing is accomplished in the most effective way, or even determining how much of existing transportation can be economically and educationally justified. The use of minibuses to transport students to a central location, for example, has been proposed but does not appear to be practiced widely. Elderly and handicapped persons might also benefit from school buses as public transportation, and costs of operation might be shared if persons other than students could ride. In addition, the question should be asked: Which costs more in any given situation–using fewer buses and more buildings or using more buses and fewer buildings?

School Finance

Research is needed on how rural equity can be assured in the matter of school finance. There is probably no single best system in a state's financing of its schools; yet there are special rural considerations. One of the problems is that we do not know enough about cost differences between urban and rural places, or among different types of rural places, to devise appropriate formulas. Although recent school finance reforms in some states have alleviated the problems of poor rural districts by increasing proportions of the state aid they receive, the issue of financing high-quality education in rural settings remains largely unaddressed.

School finance laws have characteristically responded to rural district "differences" by sparsity provisions, by adjustments for small schools, and by pupil transportation allowances. In 1978–1979, twenty-two states accommodated sparsity in their provisions for education support (Tron, 1980). Rachel Tomkins (1977) contends, however, that rural schools still face financing inequities from cost-of-living plans, categorical aid for capital outlay, and transportation. The inequities arise from favoring districts that claim a high cost of "doing business" and from providing financial incentives to consolidate, whether or not such action makes sense in the total context. Thus, researchers need to address certain finance questions and policy makers need to test alternative strategies if we are to gain a better understanding of how to assure "rural equity." For example, we need to:

- conduct a nationwide analysis across rural districts that are faced with a wide range of local bases for financial support
- study special provisions in the funding formulas (e.g., municipal overburden formulas), for similar provisions might be applied in rural places; study incentives to consolidate because of rising transportation costs; and study provisions for equal access
- recognize the diversity of rural places and test alternative ways to

provide rural students with full curricular opportunities to use the special circumstances of their local communities

- test the alternative strategy of giving rural schools the buying power to shop for needed services, which would encourage service agencies to respond to client needs rather than offer what someone else believes is needed
- develop separate funding criteria for aid to rural, urban, and suburban districts as one way to increase flexibility and incentives in rural education delivery

Educational Outcomes

A national research agenda should be developed that will ascertain precise factors that inhibit the upward mobility of rural students, and provide for locally relevant studies on rural youths' status with respect to education and work. There is no complete national portrait of rural students–their educational achievement, their attainment, their rate of leaving school early, and their later "success" as adults (also see Chapter 10). Fratoe's reports (1978, 1980) have begun the outlines of such a portrait but data are confined to nonmetropolitan rather than rural categories and are in aggregate form that do not adequately reflect local differences. Similarly, the status attainment work of rural sociologists (Cosby and Charner, 1978; Falk, 1975; Haller and Portes, 1973; Kuvlesky and Reynolds, 1970) suggests a strong need to study specific local conditions to determine more precisely what inhibits the advancement of poor and minority rural youth. It appears that rural and urban youths, regardless of sex, race, ability, or socioeconomic condition, want a college education and positions with money and status. But proportionately few rural youths are currently achieving such a goal. Levels of educational performance and attainment are lower for rural youth than for urban youth, although these differences diminish or disappear when socioeconomic status is considered.

CONCLUSION

Rural education, long neglected at all levels, appears to be facing an uneasy time over the next decade. Some modest resources may be allocated or at least redirected to aid rural schools; we suspect that the amounts provided for research will be modest indeed. It will be essential, therefore, to develop an agenda providing the kind of information, analysis, and knowledge useful in addressing the key issues of appropriate, high-quality rural education at an affordable cost, and of equitable and appropriate opportunities for disadvantaged rural populations. The agenda we have proposed in this chapter can, if implemented, contribute to enhancing the potential of the nation's rural schools.

REFERENCES

Barker, Roger G., and Paul V. Gump. 1964. *Big School, Small School: High School Size and Student Behavior*. Stanford, California: Stanford University Press.

Bass, Gail, and Paul Berman. 1979. *Federal Aid to Rural Schools: Current Patterns and Unmet Needs*. Santa Monica, California: Rand Corporation.

Cosby, Arthur G., and Ivan Charner (editors). 1978. *Education and Work in Rural America: The Social Context of Early Career Decision and Achievement*. College Station, Texas: Texas A & M University.

Falk, W. W. 1975. "An integrative model of the occupational choice process." In J. Steven Picou and Robert Campbell (editors), *Career Behavior of Special Groups: Theory, Research, and Practice*. Columbus, Ohio: Merrill Publishing.

Fratoe, Frank A. 1978. *Rural Education and Rural Labor Force in the Seventies*. Washington, D.C.: Economics, Statistics, and Cooperatives Service, U.S. Department of Agriculture, Rural Development Research Report 5.

_____ . 1980. *The Education of Nonmetro Blacks*. Washington, D.C.: Economics, Statistics and Cooperatives Service, U.S. Department of Agriculture, Rural Development Research Report 21.

Gjelten, Tom. 1980. "The rural experience with federal education aid." Washington, D.C.: National Rural Center. Unpublished paper.

Haller, Archibald, and A. Portes. 1973. "Status attainment processes." *Sociology of Education* 46:51–91

Herriott, Robert E., and Neal Gross (editors). 1978. *The Dynamics of Planned Educational Change*. Berkeley, California: McCutchan Publishing Corp.

Kuvlesky, William P., and David H. Reynolds. 1970. *Occupational Aspirations and Expectations of Youth: A Bibliography of Research Literature I, DTR 70-4*. College Station, Texas: Texas A & M University.

Nachtigal, Paul M. 1980. *Improving Rural Schools*. Washington, D.C.: National Institute of Education.

National Rural Center. 1979. *The Rural Stake in Public Assistance*. Washington, D.C.: National Rural Center, NRC Publication Series.

Parks, Gail A. 1981. "The Foxfire concept: Experiential education in rural America." In Jonathan P. Sher (editor), *Rural Education in Urbanized Nations*. Boulder, Colorado: Westview Press.

Parks, Gail A., and Jonathan P. Sher. 1979. *Imaginary Gardens? Real Problems: An Analysis of Federal Information Sources on Rural Education*. Las Cruces, New Mexico; ERIC/CRESS.

Peshkin, Alan. 1978. *Growing Up American: Schooling and the Survival of Community*. Chicago: University of Chicago Press.

Rosenfeld, Stuart A. 1980. "Shaping a rural vocational education policy." *Voc Ed* (March):17.

Sher, Jonathan P. (editor). 1977. *Education in Rural America: A Reassessment of Conventional Wisdom*. Boulder, Colorado: Westview Press.

Tomkins, Rachel. 1977. "Coping with sparsity: A review of rural school finance." In Jonathan P. Sher (editor), *Education in Rural America: A Reassessment of Conventional Wisdom*. Boulder, Colorado: Westview Press.

Tron, Ester. 1980. *Public Schools' Finance Programs, 1978–1979*. Washington, D.C.: U.S. Government Printing Office.

Tyack, David B. 1974. *The One Best System: A History of American Urban Education*. Cambridge: Harvard University Press.

U.S. Department of Commerce. 1978. *1977 Census of Governments, Volume 1, Number 1*. Washington, D.C.: U.S. Government Printing Office.

Wigginton, Eliot. 1975. *Moments*. New York: Star Press.

19 Housing

EARL W. MORRIS
MARY WINTER

The rural housing situation differs from the urban situation in a number of significant ways. Both the housing stock and the households are different from those in urban areas.

Rural areas have higher percentages of single-family detached dwellings, higher rates of home ownership, higher percentages of mobile homes, a higher percentage of seasonal units such as vacation homes, and more crowding in terms of persons per room (even though there are more rooms per dwelling) than in urban areas (U.S. Department of Commerce, 1979). Housing units in rural areas are more likely to lack plumbing, a private bath, a complete kitchen, an adequate water supply and sewage disposal system, and are more likely to have electrical and structural defects than urban units (U.S. Department of Commerce, 1979). Furthermore, owner-occupied rural units have lower median values, lower property taxes,and lower monthly housing expenditures than urban units (U.S. Department of Commerce, 1979).

Rural households, as a group, differ from urban households in that they are more likely to be white families with husband, wife, and children, and more likely to be headed by an elderly person. They are less likely to be headed by a female or to consist of a young single in-

Earl W. Morris is an associate professor in the Department of Family Environment, Iowa State University, Ames, Iowa. He has written extensively on the sociology of housing, mobility, migration, and fertility. **Mary Winter** is an associate professor in the Department of Family Environment, Iowa State University, Ames, Iowa. She has published numerous articles in the area of the sociology of housing. Morris and Winter are coauthors of *Housing, Families, and Society*.

dividual than are urban households; they also have lower incomes and education levels than their urban counterparts (U.S. Department of Commerce, 1979).

Rural and urban differences in the characteristics of households and the characteristics of the housing stock gain significance when evaluated in terms of housing needs.

THE APPROACH

The approach we take to the study of rural housing is developed from Rossi's (1955) notion of housing as an adjustment process and is outlined in detail in Morris and Winter (1978). In this approach, housing needs and desires are expressed in cultural norms prescribing appropriate housing conditions for American families. Norms indicate the kind of housing that is socially valued and that produces the respect of others and adds to individual well-being.

When a family's housing does not meet the norms, a deficit exists. If the family is aware of the deficit and feels that it is important, they will be dissatisfied. Dissatisfaction, in turn, produces a propensity to remove the deficit. Given such a propensity, the family would choose between alternative adjustment behaviors: moving to a new residence, or altering or adding to the current dwelling. Constraints may inhibit perception of deficits, appearance of dissatisfaction, development of an adjustment propensity, or completion of adjustment behaviors. These constraints include predispositions such as apathy, resource constraints such as low income and discrimination (racial, ethnic, sexual, etc.), and market constraints, including the supply of housing and mortgage money and their prices.

In the past, housing, including rural housing, has been studied primarily in the "social conditions" tradition. Objective conditions such as incomplete bathrooms, incomplete kitchens, crowding, and dilapidation have been treated as directly and intuitively recognizable as undesirable and therefore to be eradicated (see, for example, Beyer, 1949; Bird, 1979). With notable exceptions (Green, 1953; Montgomery and Kivlin, 1962; Montgomery and McCabe, 1973), the objective conditions have been analyzed descriptively and atheoretically.

Assessment of objective housing conditions in rural areas is of obvious importance. It has become increasingly apparent, however, that rural

This is an Iowa Agriculture and Home Economics Experiment Station Journal Article Number J-9952, Project 2341.

housing research is in need of additional concepts that go beyond the measurement of current conditions. One of the most important concepts needed refers to the standards through which housing conditions can be judged adequate or inadequate. Given knowledge of the standards and the conditions, the concept of a housing deficit (a gap between a norm and a condition) can be applied. In addition, a concept is needed that denotes the constraints that inhibit the achievement of those standards and inhibit the removal of deficits as they appear. Using these additional concepts, it is possible to make sense out of otherwise puzzling situations. Objectively undesirable conditions can produce satisfaction and objectively desirable conditions can be unsatisfactory. For example, a family of modest income may be quite satisfied renting a deteriorating rural dwelling that provides sufficient indoor and outdoor space for their family. The same family could be very dissatisfied with an urban apartment in a new, well-contructed building that they could rent for the same price. Given their standards and their constraints, their choice of conditions is satisfactory. Our approach, therefore, requires that we relate rural housing conditions to the housing standards and needs of American families.

HOUSING NEEDS OF AMERICAN FAMILIES

It is quite clear from previous research that American housing norms prescribe that families should live in owned, single-family detached dwellings with sufficient interior space to maintain standards for bedroom sharing and family activities and private outdoor open space (Morris and Winter, 1976; Montgomery and McCabe, 1973; Belcher, 1970; Dillman et al., 1979; Hanna and Lindamood, 1979). Beyond a fairly low minimum level, housing quality norms are determined by a family's economic resources. A family should live in the quality of housing that they can afford.

The content and intensity of the housing norms, except for quality, have been found to be nearly pervasive throughout society. Those norms cut across class, racial, ethnic, and age categories (Morris and Winter, 1978). Differences among groups tend to be produced by constraints that force people to compromise rather than by the holding of different housing norms (Morris and Winter, 1978).

When constraints prevent the achievement of the first choice, there are norms that govern the making of second choices. For residents of rural areas, the most favored second choice seems to be a mobile home on an owned private lot or a rented single-family detached dwelling. For urban residents, owned townhouses or rented single-family detached dwellings are the most favored second choices. The least favored choices are apartments in high-rise buildings (more likely to be located in urban areas) and mobile homes on rented lots in mobile home parks (more likely to be located in rural areas) (Dillman et al., 1979; Gladhart, 1973; Williams, 1971). The compromise least willingly made by both urban and rural residents is to give up private outdoor space (Dillman et al., in press).

RURAL HOUSING AND AMERICAN HOUSING NEEDS

Census data and annual housing survey data, along with survey data on preferences, indicate that the housing stock of rural areas is more closely attuned to the first-choice housing norms of families than is the urban housing stock. Thus, a part of the movement back to rural areas may be related to the fit between the rural housing stock and the housing norms of families (also see Chapters 3 and 24). The housing available in urban areas requires compromises for a higher percentage of people than does rural housing. There is a greater prevalence of rental apartments and a corresponding absence of private outdoor space in urban areas. Rather than suggest that there has been a change in norms for housing location, it seems more likely that there have been shifts in the constraints inhibiting rural living.

Urban families with housing norms that are more readily met in rural areas are likely to move to rural areas when the constraints are removed. Changes in housing norm priorities may be involved as well. Underlying preferences to open space that were submerged by the effects of urban employment opportunities in the past may now be surfacing.

RESEARCH ISSUES

Research issues in rural housing can be subsumed under a single overriding issue: How can our society provide the types of housing that American families need and desire in the locations they prefer while preserving the rights of other families (including future generations) to do the same (Morris and Winter, 1971)?

The overall research question is one of preserving the normative housing stock of rural areas in the face of far-reaching societal changes. Within this context, it is appropriate to outline some research issues that focus on the effects of six factors on the fit between American families and their housing: demographic change, economic change, natural resource availability, technological change, government intervention, and cultural change.

Demographic Change

Research is needed on the effect of demographic trends on rural housing needs. Key demographic research issues involve the effects on housing needs of changes in: the birth rate, the rate of family formation, migration rates within the United States, and the rate of immigration into the United States. Their combined influence on the composition of the population in housing market areas also needs to be examined. Of particular interest are the effects that in-migration may have on the housing markets of specific rural areas. The decline in the rate of family formation that results from a falling birth rate eventually may offset the impact of net in-migration to rural areas. A decline in the family formation rate could be expected to result in general decreases in the demand for housing units. Population booms in particular areas, however, may produce conditions that require quick responses, such as mobile home parks and modular housing complexes. Research could help to anticipate population changes and to develop more thoughtful responses.

As noted earlier, there is currently a higher percentage of households headed by elderly individuals in rural areas than in urban areas. The in-migration of younger families to rural areas and the decline in the out-migration of young people from rural areas may result in a decreasing percentage of elderly households in rural areas, but the elderly will continue to be a sizable subgroup. This factor is important not only in terms of overall demand for housing but also because of implications for type of housing.

Economic Change

Research is needed on the effect of the economy on rural housing choices and modes of finance. Since about 1974, there has been an interrelated set of factors with which the public and policy makers have been preoccupied. Inflation, especially as it affects housing prices and interest rates, and governmental attempts to facilitate housing construction and home ownership, have been of particular concern. The rapid and seemingly unpredictable changes in these factors have produced constraints as well as fears of a crash of house values.

Predicting economic trends is a risky endeavor. The key to sociological understanding of trends that do occur is predicting whether the society can continue to provide housing that meets the needs of its members without undue sacrifice of other needs, such as food, clothing, and recreation. For some time now, the situation has required considerable sacrifice for many, including young first-time home owners, to own the kinds of housing currently being produced (Winter, 1980). In particular, the two-income household has become commonplace in part as a response to more expensive housing.

The rapid rise in interest rates from 1974 through 1979, a rapid drop in mid-1980, and even higher rates at the beginning of 1981 have fed fears about the stability of the values of existing homes. A rapid drop in house values probably would not be a disaster, however. Many people would lose some paper equity, some people would find themselves making payments on a house worth much less than when they bought it, but others would find housing easier to afford. In addition, it would be beneficial to have a stable housing market even with house values at lower levels than they are currently.

The key economic question is the effect of the state of the overall economy on the ability of families to obtain housing in rural areas. What are the effects of inflation or recession on the ability of families to realize their (constrained) housing desires? When faced with increasing economic constraints on their housing choices, what choices are made? One likely result is an increase in purchases of mobile homes, of homes bought on land contracts, and other nonstandard choices. What are the ramifications of such behavior?

Natural Resource Availability

There is a need for research on the effects of the energy situation and land use patterns on the ability to live and vacation in rural areas. The most timely resource availability question is the effect of petroleum prices and supplies on housing. Of particular interest is whether locational choices will change. Will the price of gasoline make rural living unattractive, assuming that job locations continue to be largely urban, or will urban housing prices continue to make the less expensive rural housing attractive (also see Chapters 3, 4, and 15)?

A related question involving natural resource availability is the balance between residential and agricultural land use (see Chapter 36). Our premise is that current housing problems must be solved in a way that does not endanger the well-being of future generations. Thus, an understanding of the effects of the provision of rural housing on the supply of high-quality agricultural land would be valuable.

An additional concern is the share of land and rural housing stock devoted to second homes. The effect of the prices of petroleum on the number of second homes in rural areas, like its effect on first homes, is not obvious. Higher costs of energy might reduce the demand for second homes or, on the other hand, higher costs could increase the demand for second homes. Airline trips to Europe or South America or nationwide tours in gasoline-wasting recreational vehicles might be foregone in favor of a trip in the family's subcompact car to their home in the country. Either possibility is logically predictable. Research will be needed to monitor the response and the pattern of substitutions that occur.

Technological Change

Research is needed on the effect of technological development on economic and energy costs of housing. Illustrative of the kind of research needed is an analysis of the effect of technological innovation, such as the mobile home in the 1930s, on housing in rural areas. Has the mobile home made it possible for a higher proportion of families to realize their housing desires while not endangering others' rights to do so? Many people have used mobile homes as temporary or permanent housing choices. Were they better off than they might have been if, for instance, the "no-frills" house or a suitable apartment had been a choice? The readiness with which mobile homes have been adopted in rural areas may suggest that other innovations may also find a receptive climate in rural areas where codes and ordinances are less structured.

Government Intervention

Research is needed on the effects of government programs on housing finance and housing supply. Governmental intervention can produce altered conditions whose effects need to be understood. There has been little research on the effects of the Farmers' Home Administration and Federal Housing Administration's financing policies on the amounts and types of housing available. It could be hypothesized that the evolution of policy since the 1930s to raise loan-to-value ratios, lengthen terms, and raise ceilings on loan amounts has had the effect of reducing the number of dwelling units that have been financed, thus decreasing the number of families served. With a fixed amount of mortgage money available, the *number* of mortgages that can be made is obviously less if the maximum length of term and the maximum loan amounts are larger and the minimum down payment is smaller. Even though the amount of mortgage money available has increased, in a given year the amount available is fixed. Furthermore, it is *not* obvious that liberalization of mortgage terms was a factor in the inflation of housing prices. The effect of government programs on housing prices needs to be better understood.

A second question concerns the effect of housing finance policies on growth in numbers of mobile homes. Historically, it seems that mobile homes have been used in times of high demand and tight supplies in a cyclical manner partly because they were financed by a supply of money different from that for conventional housing. In rural areas, government activity in support of financing mobile homes has been virtually absent.

Other questions have to do with the effect of police-power measures—housing codes, building codes, zoning ordinances, and subdivision regulations—on rural housing. In an effort to preserve farm land, some communities have enacted zoning ordinances that require large minimum acreages for building new dwellings. Blackhawk County, Iowa, for example, requires a minimum of ten acres for a home built outside city limits. Do such regulations preserve farm land or convert it more quickly to residential use?

Building codes, housing codes, and zoning regulations that require unusually high standards for housing quality or for the amenities in a mobile home park or private lot may have a deleterious effect on the supply of inexpensive housing. Families served by mobile homes or lower-quality housing may no longer be able to meet their housing needs satisfactorily because quality costs too much.

Cultural Change

There is a need for research on the effect of the failure of society to effectively deal with the other issues. The usual response to a mismatch between socially based needs and desires is to attempt to increase the availability of that which is needed. Thus, an appropriate response to a housing shortage is to supply more housing. While we are convinced that such responses are of immediate importance for policy development and implementation in the near future, an alternative is to reduce the level of intensity of the desire directly. If people could be taught that they need less energy, the subjectively experienced shortage would be reduced as clearly as if the supply of energy were to be increased.

Thus, a basic research issue is whether cultural change, either spontaneous or "guided," might produce a better fit between housing desires and actual housing. If American housing norms were to change so that they no longer prescribe owner-occupancy of a single-family dwelling, many of the rural housing issues would be greatly altered. Many policy analysts suggest that change in housing norms is feasible. Although the authors are not sanguine about the feasibility of culture change programs, research to evaluate the consequences of policies that attempt to change housing preferences is greatly needed.

REFERENCES

Belcher, John C. 1970. "Differential aspirations for housing between Blacks and Whites in rural Georgia." *Phylon* 31:231–243.

Beyer, Glenn H. 1949. *Farm Housing in the Northeast*. New York: Macmillan Co.

Bird, Ronald. 1979. "The status of housing in nonmetropolitan areas." *Family Economics Review* (Spring):21–24.

Dillman, Don A., Joye J. Dillman, and Michael Schwalbe. In press. "Strength of housing norms and willingness to accept housing alternatives." *Housing and Society* (proceedings issue).

Dillman, Don A., Kenneth R. Tremblay, Jr., and Joye J. Dillman. 1979. "Influence of housing norms and personal characteristics on stated housing preferences." *Housing and Society* 6:2–19.

Gladhart, Peter M. 1973. "Family housing adjustment and the theory of residential mobility: A temporal analysis of family residential histories." Ithaca, New York: Cornell University. Doctoral dissertation.

Green, James W. 1953. "The farmhouse-building process." Raleigh, North Carolina: North Carolina State University. Doctoral dissertation.

Hanna, Sherman, and Suzanna Lindamood. 1979. "Housing preferences of Blacks and Whites in Montgomery, Alabama." *Housing and Society* 6:39–47.

Montgomery, James E., and Joseph E. Kivlin. 1962. "Place of residence as a factor in housing desires and expectations." *Rural Sociology* 27:483–491.

Montgomery, James E., and Gracia S. McCabe. 1973. "Housing aspirations of southern Appalachian families." *Home Economics Research Journal* 2:2–11.

Morris, Earl W., and Mary Winter. 1971. "Community ecology: A new approach to housing consumption." *Human Ecology Forum* 2(Autumn):4.

______. 1976. "Housing and occupational subcultures." *Housing Educators' Journal* 3 (September):2–15.

______. 1978. *Housing, Family, and Society*. New York: John Wiley and Sons.

Rossi, Peter H. 1955. *Why Families Move*. New York: Free Press.

U.S. Department of Commerce (Bureau of the Census). 1979. *Urban and Rural Housing Characteristics for the United States and Regions, Annual Housing Survey*. Washington, D.C.: U.S. Government Printing Office, Current Housing Reports, Series H-170-77.

Williams, J. Allen, Jr. 1971. "The multi-family housing solution and housing type preferences." *Social Science Quarterly* 52:543–559.

Winter, Mary. 1980. "Managerial behavior of young families in pursuit of single-family home ownership." *Journal of Consumer Affairs* 14(Summer):82–95.

20
Outdoor Recreation

GORDON L. BULTENA

Outdoor recreation is an integral part of the life of most Americans. By the millions, we sightsee, picnic, swim, fish, boat, hike, camp, bicycle, hunt, jog, golf, play tennis, and walk for pleasure. Each year, we make hundreds of millions of visits to the nation's parks, forests, and seashores. We annually contribute tens of billions of dollars to the economy through purchases of recreational equipment, vacation travel, licenses, and admission fees. We commit additional billions of dollars to the public acquisition, development, and management of recreational facilities.

Americans' penchant for outdoor recreation has received considerable study, especially by rural sociologists. Beginning with their research of wilderness recreation in the late 1950s, rural sociologists have pioneered in the study of many topics such as recreational demand, motives, and characteristics of recreationists, substitutability of recreational activities, and recreational carrying capacity. Findings from this research have contributed to the growth of theoretical knowledge about outdoor recreation and have led to more informed recreation management policies.

The 1980s will bring a continued demand for scientific inquiry into the outdoor recreational preferences and activities of Americans. Given the swiftness of societal changes today, it is important that public decision makers be sensitive to changes in the public's use and demand for outdoor recreation. Further study is vital, among other things, to ensure that the public's recreational demands remain competitive with other growing pressures on the nation's resources. Objective information about out-

Gordon L. Bultena is a professor in the Department of Sociology and Anthropology, Iowa State University, Ames, Iowa. He has written a variety of articles on outdoor recreation, public values, and environmental issues.

door recreation will also help government officials plan for the types of recreational opportunities that are desired.

RESEARCH ISSUES: RECREATION AND SOCIETAL CHANGE

Demographic Change

Changes in the size, distribution, and composition of the national population during the 1980s will provide an important context for outdoor recreation research. Continued population growth will undoubtedly contribute to the already large recreational demand. But more important to future recreational demands than added numbers of people are ongoing changes in the distribution and composition of the population.

Change in Population Distribution. / Substantial differences are found in the growth rates of various regions of the country. Whereas some areas (e.g., the Northeast and Midwest) have recently experienced static or declining populations, other areas (e.g., the Sun Belt) are growing rapidly. An especially important trend is the recent population turnaround (see Chapter 3). *Research is needed on the role played by recreational considerations in regional and urban-rural population shifts. Research is also needed into consequences of these shifts for the nature of future recreational demands in rural areas.*

Many questions need answers. For example: How important are outdoor recreational amenities today (versus financial, health, and other considerations) in people's residential decisions? How and where is the in-migration of permanent residents, as well as that of transient recreationists, affecting the demand for outdoor recreation in rural areas? How can the growing demand for recreational opportunities in rural areas best be met, especially in the face of tight fiscal resources and competitive demands for the use of public land? How is the population turnaround affecting the character of leisure values and lifestyles in rural communities?

Change in Population Composition. / Changes in the composition of the population during the 1980s will have considerable impact on future demand for outdoor recreation. An example is the rapid growth of some racial and ethnic populations, such as Blacks and Mexican-Americans (see Chapter 11). Minority groups are often underrepresented in some recreational activities and overrepresented in others. Blacks, for instance, are comparatively infrequent participants in such activities as backpacking, camping, canoeing, sailing, and golf, but tend to be well represented among picnickers, swimmers, and spectators at outdoor sporting events. Improvement during the decade in the economic status of minority populations could bring a substantial boost in their demand for outdoor recreation, especially in activities where cost has been a barrier to past participation. It should not be assumed, however, that an underrepresentation of minorities in some recreational activities is solely a result of economic deprivation. Social and cultural factors may be as important, or more important, than economic considerations in affecting their recreational pursuits. *The recreational preferences and activities of minority groups need to be systematically surveyed, giving special attention to the relative importance of economic versus sociocultural factors for their recreational profiles.*

Another important compositional change is the growing prevalence of older persons in the population. As with ethnic and racial minorities, the aged are underrepresented in many outdoor recreational activities, especially those entailing much physical exertion. Larger numbers of older persons could serve to dampen some of the current demand for such activities as backpacking, skiing, sailing, bicycling, and swimming, thus perhaps alleviating present use pressures at some recreation sites. But an aging population can also be expected to generate increased demand for other outdoor recreational pursuits such as picnicking, fishing, park use, bird-watching, golf, and sightseeing. As with racial and ethnic minorities, *there is a need to better determine influences on the recreational activity patterns of older persons.*

Age-related differences in outdoor recreational participation could be a function of diminished energy and mobility levels of older people (the "physiological hypothesis"), differences in the socialization and life experiences of varous age cohorts (the "generational hypothesis"), and/or role changes that accompany chronological aging (the "deprivational hypothesis"). Demonstration of the relative merits of these explanations is important to projecting shifts in the level and types of recreational demand resulting from further aging of the population.

Energy

Americans' use and enjoyment of the outdoors has been greatly facilitated by the automobile. Summer and winter alike, millions take to the nation's highways in pursuit of recreational experiences. But this mobility, and the recreation outlets it permits, may be jeopardized by changes in the future costs and availability of energy. Adverse impact on recreation could be mitigated if growth in personal income were to offset rising energy prices, if there were more use of energy-efficient automobiles, or if alternative modes of vacation travel, such as trains and buses, were to become popular.

There is a need to systematically identify and assess the impact of energy changes on outdoor recreation. Several types of impacts can be anticipated: changes in the places where people recreate, changes in characteristics of persons visiting recreational sites, and changes in the popularity of recreational activities.

Change in Locales. / *Research is needed on how changes in energy cost and availability influence choice of recreation locale.* Increased energy prices and/or shortages could severely curtail travel to more remote recreational settings. Traditionally popular places that are distant from population concentrations, such as many western forests and national parks, could experience sharp declines in visitation. But other recreational areas closer to cities, such as rural Pennsylvania, parts of the Eastern Seaboard, the Santa Monica Mountains, and Upper Michigan, could become more popular. The Black Hills and Missouri Ozarks illustrate these differences. Whereas there has been a recent slackening of vacation travel to the Black Hills, the Ozarks, which are near several metropolitan areas, have continued to draw large numbers of visitors.

Numerous research questions are emerging. For example: Is a possible eclipse of everyone's dream of frequent and distant vacation travel likely to prove erosive to the perceived quality of life in American society? What types of destination changes in recreation travel will occur as a result of the energy situation? How seriously will local economies be disrupted by shifts in vacation travel? What types of intergroup conflicts are likely to be produced, or exacerbated, by reduced opportunities for travel? Will snowmobilers, for example, find themselves increasingly thrust into competition with ski tourers for scarce environmental resources? What types of land use conflicts will grow out of intensified recreational demands? Mounting recreational pressures on rural areas adjacent to cities, coupled with the low priority often given recreation by rural residents, could create controversy in many communities.

Change in Visitor Profiles. / *Research needs to assess the impact of the energy situation on user profiles at recreational sites.* The energy situation could bring an alteration not only in numbers of travelers but also in their characteristics. Perhaps there will be increased "elitism" in the clientele of some of the more remote recreational settings. At one time, the well-to-do were overrepresented among visitors to many of our parks, forests, and seashores, but recent years have brought an increasing "democratization" of recreational use as the middle and lower-middle classes have been able to travel to many of these places. With increased energy costs, this trend could reverse and some of the nation's most attractive–but remote–recreational settings could again become largely "playgrounds for the rich." In fact, a decline of the "hoi polloi" from some areas could provide an inducement for the wealthy to again frequent these places.

Change in Recreational Activities. / *Research is also needed on how the changed energy situation will affect Americans' choices of recreational activities and their ability to secure desired recreational experiences.* Substitutions between activities may increasingly occur, especially replacement of energy-consumptive activities by those that are less fuel-dependent (e.g., speedboating replaced by sailing and canoeing). Substitutions could be especially prevalent in situations where persons have previously traveled long distances for activities, such as downhill skiing, wilderness camping, ocean fishing, and mountain climbing, but must now stay closer to home. It is important that we better understand what activities are most substitutable and the conditions under which people will willingly make substitutions. It makes little sense to create new recreational opportunities if they go unused.

Change in Work

Research is needed on how changes in the scheduling and nature of work as well as changes in the labor force are affecting participation in outdoor recreation. Many of our recreation patterns are a reflection of the five-day, forty-hour work week—a schedule that has often resulted in outdoor recreation being relegated to weekends and vacation periods. But changes in the structure of work (e.g., four-day work weeks, flex time, summer sabbaticals) could significantly alter when, and where, people recreate. The availability of enlarged blocks of free time could have diverse impacts, bringing increased use of some facilities, such as campgrounds, amusement parks, and historical places, and stimulating demand for second home development.

Changes in the nature of work may also alter future recreation demand. The meanings that people seek in their recreational pursuits often are an extension of, or a compensation for, work experiences. A continued shift during the 1980s of people into sedentary, white-collar jobs could bring greater demand for recreational activities that are more physical (e.g., bicycling, swimming, jogging). Similarly, the prevalence of more impersonalized, bureaucratic work places in our society could stimulate greater public interest in using recreational activities as a vehicle for solidifying family and friendship relations.

Changes in the composition of the work force also will influence future trends in outdoor recreation. The increased prevalence of multiworker families should be investigated for its implications for the nature and timing of family-based recreation. Similarly, the trend toward earlier retirement portends important changes in the outdoor recreation activities of the aged, as indicated in the recent popularity of retirement travel and the proliferation of planned leisure communities.

Social Change and Outdoor Recreation

Research needs to examine how various social changes affect recreation preferences and behavior. The appearance of new values, lifestyles, and social structures will influence future recreational demand. Part of the past neglect of these changes is attributable to the pronounced emphasis in recreation research on social-psychological approaches to the exclusion of more macro (societal) perspectives.

One important topic for study is the social processes by which recreational values are established, promulgated, and transmitted in the population. Information about the ways in which recreational values are diffused between social classes and regions is invaluable in the projection of recreational demand and, accordingly, the future provision of needed recreational facilities.

The impact of social movements on outdoor recreation also needs to be better assessed. Several recent social movements have altered the nature of recreational demand in this country. The civil rights movement stimulated new recreational interests among Blacks and eroded some of the traditional barriers to their participation in outdoor recreational activities. The environmental quality movement instilled new appreciative values for nature and gave impetus to increased demand for outdoor recreation, especially wilderness-oriented activities. The feminist movement may have profound impact on recreation demand by increasing the numbers of women who participate and in reshaping the roles that females have customarily filled.

RESEARCH ISSUES: EXTENDING PREVIOUS RESEARCH

Models to Explain Outdoor Recreation Behavior

Many research needs of the 1980s grow out of past research, which perhaps has stimulated more questions than it has answered; for example, the many studies of outdoor recreation that have sought to determine what types of people participate in various activities. Findings remain deficient in the small amount of variance in participation (generally less than 20 percent) that is explained. New variables and perhaps more comprehensive perspectives are needed.

Research needs to incorporate more "system-level variables" in explanations of recreational participation. This would correct for the past preoccupation of research with individual-level variables such as age and sex.

The subcultures that form around many recreational activities, such as skydiving, surfing, and mountaineering, are one type of system variable that needs investigation. Study is needed of how persons are socialized into these subcultures and how membership shapes their recreational behavior. Similarly, there needs to be more inquiry into the effect of social groups on recreationists' activities. Although most outdoor recreational activities are enjoyed with other persons (solitary participation is minimal), studies usually have treated participants as though they were autonomous, socially detached individuals. Whether a person is recreating in a family or peer group or in a mixed-sex or single-sex group could be salient for explaining their recreational behavior. Yet group type has been only infrequently used in explanatory models of recreational participation.

Understanding Participatory Motives and Benefits

Further study is needed of the motives that bring individuals to specific recreational activities and the types of social and psychological benefits they derive from participation. Although the principle is well documented that different persons may seek different experiences from the same activity, it is less well substantiated what types of experiences are sought and by whom. Improved understanding of the motives that guide participation is critical to evaluation of recreationists' social and psychological experiences. Whether or not wilderness visitors feel crowded during their back-country trips, for example, seems to be more a function of the orientations they bring to this activity than a consequence of so-called "objective" factors, such as the number of parties they encounter during their trips.

Study is also needed of the social and psychological benefits that participants obtain from outdoor recreational activities. Claims abound about the beneficial (often therapeutic) values of various types of recreational experiences, but these assertions remain, for the most part, undemonstrated.

Policy-Oriented Research

A paramount goal of much recreation research during the past decade has been improved recreation management. This goal will continue to be salient during the 1980s, especially as established policies are adapted to changes in the demands and characteristics of recreation clientele. In addition to substantive information needs, some of which are discussed below, attention should be paid to more cost-effective procedures for collection of data important to management decisions.

Economic Valuation of Outdoor Recreation. / *Research is needed that critically examines the current assumptions and practices by which public agencies gauge the economic worth of Americans' recreational pursuits.* The considerable importance placed on benefit/cost analysis by public agencies requires that more attention be paid to ways in which economic values are derived for recreational activities. Although economic appraisals of recreation are common (e.g., in calculating benefits of water development projects), they have drawn much criticism. The nonmarket character of many recreational activities renders these calculations suspect, especially when they are applied to what persons perceive as "priceless experiences" or "irreplaceable aesthetic qualities."

Orientations of Recreation Resource Managers. / *Study is needed of how public officials perceive their professional mandate in recreational management.* The personal values and beliefs of officials in some public agencies, such as the Forest Service and National Park Service, are important determinants of the ways in which outdoor recreational sites are developed and managed. What priorities, for example, do officials place on various recreational needs in the allocation of scarce resources between competing demands? What types of recreational pursuits are defined by managers as being appropriate or inappropriate for various physical settings?

Recreational Carrying Capacity. / *Study is needed of the use density expectations and preferences of visitors and whether or not crowding is experienced. The effect of perceived crowding on the quality of users' experience should also be assessed.* Imposition of optimum use levels at recreational sites will be an increasingly controversial issue in the 1980s. Continued growth in recreation demand, coupled with greater density of use at many recreational sites near metropolitan areas, will bring mounting pressures for restriction of visitation levels. Rationing policies may be deemed necessary to protect both the types of experiences that visitors are seeking and the physical qualities of the sites. To avoid capricious and legally indefensible decisions in the formulation of future carrying capacities for recreational sites, careful research will be needed.

Displacement of User Groups. / *Research needs to better document the nature and extent of displacement at recreational sites and to trace implications of this displacement for the formulation of more effective management policies.* A little-studied but important facet of outdoor recreation has been the displacement of some user groups from recreational sites by other groups. People who seek solitude and relatively undisturbed physical environments are especially susceptible to displacement when use increases. Historically, there has been considerable opportunity for persons displaced from one site to seek out other settings that are more conducive to satisfying their recreational needs. But increased energy costs may serve to make site substitutions more difficult; it is increasingly difficult to find locales that offer seclusion or retain a pristine character. An involuntary confinement of persons to certain recreational areas could greatly exacerbate recreation resource management problems, especially in situations where there is already difficulty in securing a satisfactory balance between competing recreational uses (e.g., between motorboaters and canoeists and between snowmobilers and ski tourers).

Depreciative Behavior. / A serious problem at many recreational sites is the "depreciative behavior" of visitors, such as littering, nuisance acts, vandalism, and rule violations. This behavior not only causes great financial loss but also affects the quality of visitors' experiences. The social and psychological factors that underly depreciative behavior tend to be poorly understood.

Study is needed of the factors that give rise to depreciative behavior in recreational settings. This investigation needs to be multifaceted, delving into the expectations and activities of recreationists as well as the degree to which present management programs are responsive to the needs of visitors.

There is a need to implement and objectively evaluate experimental management programs that are designed to reduce depreciative acts. Use of more visitor support services, such as interpretive efforts and campground host programs, could prove more effective in curbing depreciative behavior than the imposition of punitive sanctions, such as the closing of facilities, more regulations, and intensified police surveillance.

Impact of Planned Programs. / *Analysis is needed of how shifts in management programs might alter future use and enjoyment of recreational sites.* Policy makers often are faced with having to decide the relative merits of programs (e.g., choosing between several means of rationing recreational use without having sound information about how the alternatives will impact visitors). There is a need for researchers to clearly identify, using available evidence, the types of people-related impacts that can be anticipated from the implementation of alternative recreation management policies.

CONCLUSION

There has been an exploding demand for outdoor recreation during the past two decades, and there is reason to expect these pressures to continue. Today, large parts of the nation, like the coasts of Florida, much of southern California, national parks of the Pacific Northwest, and the Barrier Islands of the East Coast, constitute "recreationscapes" in which the prime attractions are fresh air, open space, and water. Recreational considerations have come to pervade all aspects of our lives, from residential decisions to lifestyle commitments.

Rural United States will especially bear the brunt of future changes in recreational demand. Many of our nation's most popular recreational facilities are in rural settings, and recreational expenditures often are the bedrock of local economies.

We can no longer afford to think of outdoor recreation as frivolous activities that command our attention after other needs are met. Rather, these activities have become a major element in many of our lives. It is important that public decision makers be alert to the evolving recreational goals of U.S. citizens, not only to ensure the proper management of recreational facilities but also to instruct social and economic policies at the highest political levels.

REFERENCES

Burdge, Rabel J., Roseann Hogan, Cindy Srihakim, and Joseph Donnermeyer. 1975. *A Social Science Bibliography of Leisure and Recreation Research*. Lexington, Kentucky: Department of Sociology, University of Kentucky.

Cheek, Neil H. and William R. Burch. 1976. *The Social Organization of Leisure in Human Society*. New York: Harper and Row.

Cheek, Neil H., Donald R. Field, and Rabel J. Burdge. 1976. *Leisure and Recreation Places*. Ann Arbor, Michigan: Ann Arbor Science Publishers.

Fischer, David W., John E. Lewis, and George B. Priddle (editors). 1974. *Land and Leisure: Concepts and Methods in Outdoor Recreation*. Chicago: Maaroufa Press.

Iso-Ahola, Seppo E. 1980. *The Social Psychology of Leisure and Recreation*. Dubuque, Iowa: Wm. C. Brown Co.

Jensen, Clayne R. and Clark T. Thorstenson. 1977. *Issues in Outdoor Recreation*. Minneapolis, Minnesota: Burgess Publishing.

Napier, Ted and John Pierce (editors). 1981. *Outdoor Recreation Planning, Perspectives, and Research*. Dubuque, Iowa: Kendall/Hunt Publishing.

Napier, Ted, Dean Yoesting, and Joseph O'Leary. 1975. *Bibliography of Outdoor Recreation and Leisure: A Decade of Research*. Columbus, Ohio: Department of Agricultural Economics and Rural Sociology, Ohio State University.

National Academy of Sciences. 1969. *A Program for Outdoor Recreation Research*. Washington, D.C.: National Academy of Sciences.

______. 1975. *Assessing Demand for Outdoor Recreation*. Washington, D.C.: National Academy of Sciences.

North Central Forest Experiment Station. 1977. *Proceedings: Symposium of River Recreation Management and Research*. St. Paul, Minnesota: North Central Forest Experiment Station.

Outdoor Recreation Resources Review Commission. 1962. Twenty-seven volumes on outdoor recreation are available. Washington, D.C.: Outdoor Recreation Resources Review Commission.

Schechter, Mordechai, and Robert Lucas. 1978. *Simulation of Recreational Use for Park and Wilderness Management*. Baltimore, Maryland: Johns Hopkins University Press.

Stankey, George H., and David W. Lime. 1973. *Recreational Carrying Capacity: An Annotated Bibliography.* Ogden, Utah: Intermountain Forest and Range Experiment Station.

Van Doren, Carlton S., George B. Priddle, and John E. Lewis (editors). 1979. *Land and Leisure: Concepts and Methods in Outdoor Recreation.* New York: Methuen Publishers.

21
Health and Medical Care

MICHAEL K. MILLER

In 1976, James Copp, a rural sociologist, asked the simple question: How healthy are rural people? Copp pointed out that discrepancies exist in the literature. For example, preinduction physical exams prior to World War II suggested that urban residents were more healthy than rural residents. Consistent with this interpretation is the fact that, in 1975, rural people had a lower self-reported health status than their urban counterparts (Kleinman and Wilson, 1977). Copp (1976) also reported that the infant mortality rate for the rural sector was well above that for urban areas. More recent data indicate that, as recently as 1976, the most rural areas were exhibiting higher infant mortality rates (16.9) than urban areas (15.0). However, the age/sex adjusted death rate for rural areas suggests that rural people are no worse off than their urban counterparts (9.5 versus 9.6 for the most rural and most urban counties, respectively).

The above data suggest that the rural habitat has not produced, as is often assumed, a healthier population than have our cities. What the figures do not show is the fact that rural America includes the extremes in health status. For example, the most rural counties in the northeastern United States had an infant mortality rate of 8.4 in 1976. In contrast, the most rural counties in the western part of the south-central states had a rate of 20.3. However, if one examines another criteria, the situation

Michael K. Miller is associate professor in the Department of Agricultural Economics and Rural Sociology, University of Arkansas, Fayetteville, Arkansas. He is coeditor of the book *Contemporary Issues in Theory and Research: A Meta-Sociological Perspective*, and has written numerous articles on policy and evaluation in the health care field.

The author would like to acknowledge the useful suggestions on various drafts of this

changes completely. The mortality rate for all causes of death (age/sex adjusted) for that sector was 9.1 in 1971 but 10.9 for the Northeast.

Similarly, a recent USDA publication calculates a health status index and reports the results for different populations in the country (Ross et al., 1979). An index of 106.1 (U.S. = 100) is reported for metropolitan America compared with 98.5 for nonmetropolitan. The index, however, is 107.0 for nonmetro counties of the north-central region compared with 92.0 for nonmetro counties of the South. This is not surprising in view of the strong relationship between health status and socioeconomic and minority status; black infant mortality in the United States is almost twice as high as white infant mortality (Ahearn, 1979). Both economic and minority status contribute substantially to the health status of rural southern counties. Thus, it is inappropriate to speak of the health status of rural Americans as if they were a homogeneous group; the development of health care policies must recognize these differences.

DELIVERY OF HEALTH CARE IN RURAL AMERICA

Virtually all rural Americans are at a locational disadvantage with regard to access to professional health care services. The health care industry employs approximately five million persons and boasts over seven thousand hospitals and nearly 1.7 million hospital beds (Culliton, 1978). The annual price tag for health expenditures is over $200 billion, or approximately $1,000 for every man, woman, and child in the country (Warner, 1979). The literature indicates, however, that nationally the absolute quantity of services is not the issue. Rather, the primary concern is maldistribution (Cordes, 1977; Hassinger and Whiting, 1976; Kane and Westover, 1976; Wright, 1976). Rural areas suffer from a relative lack of access to many of the central medical care resources (Hassinger et al., 1979). In 1973, for example, the physician/population ratio per thousand was 1.5 for metro areas compared with 6.7 for nonmetro areas. The differential in 1976 was even more pronounced. Core metro areas had an average of 2.7 physicians per thousand population; thinly populated counties, i.e., those with less than twenty-five hundred urban residents, had a ratio of .39. The rural ratio is substantially below recent recommendations, which set lower limits for physician/population ratios if

---

chapter offered by Donald Voth, Diana Danforth, Sam Cordes, and Bernal Green. The focus of this chapter is on physical health services and physical health. For summaries of the literature and needed research in the area of rural mental health, see Cedar and Salasin (1979), Flax et al. (1978), and Longest et al. (1977).

minimum essential services are to be provided, i.e., 1.3 according to Schonfield et al. (1972) and .83 according to the more conservative estimate of Scitovsky and McCall (1976).

The situation becomes even more critical when substantial variation among the regions of the country is noted. In 1976, sparsely populated rural counties of the Northeast had an average of 1.1 medical doctors, 4.1 registered nurses, and 8.2 hospital beds for every thousand residents. Similar populations in the eastern south-central and South Atlantic regions were served by approximately .35 physicians, 1.1 registered nurses, and 4.5 hospital beds. Clearly, there is a distribution problem not simply between rural and urban areas of the country but also among the rural areas.

Given the lack of access to services, it is not surprising that rural residents report lower rates of use than urban residents (3.9 versus 5.9) (Aday and Anderson, 1975; Slesinger, 1980) and a smaller total percentage seeing a doctor at least once a year (71 percent versus 76 percent) (Kane et al., 1979). This difference in use, however, is not proportioned to the differences in local availability of providers. This means simply that rural people are heavily dependent on transportation as a means of gaining access to professional health care, a factor that contributes significantly to the cost of obtaining care for those who have transportation and a much more desperate situation for those who do not.

RELATIONSHIP BETWEEN HEALTH STATUS AND HEALTH CARE

The quality of life of rural Americans would be improved if health status improved *and* if providers of professional health care services were more accessible. Both objectives are desirable, but the accomplishment of neither one will produce the solution to the other. They have different causes.

Good health of both urban and rural Americans is a result of nutritional, environmental, behavioral, socioeconomic, and, to an unknown extent, professional health care system contributions (McKeown, 1976). Of these factors, it is increasingly evident that the socioeconomic status of people may be the most important determinant. Nutrition, behavior, and, to some extent, one's environment, are strongly influenced by an individual's social class position.

This is not to imply that the medical care system does not contribute to the health status of rural Americans – no doubt it does (Roemer, 1976). Indeed, one of the major justifications for spending billions of dollars on health care (about $200 billion in 1980) has been the assumed validity of what Wildavsky (1977) has termed the "Great Equation," i.e., that professional health care equals health. Many government-sponsored programs designed to improve the well-being of the rural population have been based on this assumption (Shenkin, 1974). A result has been a preoccupation with the delivery of equitable quantities of professional health care resources to rural areas. The delivery of services may be a worthy end in itself and may serve a number of ancillary functions, such as economic development. However, the delivery of these services can best be described as a necessary but not sufficient condition to improve the health status of the rural population. The ability of the health care system to accomplish improved health is much less obvious than the maldistribution of the providers of care.

An examination of the "health" initiatives that have been made by the federal government show one common thread. Virtually all (and there are a fairly large number of them) have attempted to provide rural areas with additional manpower and/or resources (e.g., Health Underserved Rural Areas programs, community health center programs, emergency medical service programs) (McClure, 1976). These programs assume, at least implicitly, that there is a close functional relationship between a population's health status and the amount of available medical care. At this point, the evidence is not firm (McKeown, 1976; Miller and Stokes, 1978). Hence, while there are legitimate questions surrounding the provision and delivery of medical care to rural areas, it will be useful to keep in mind the ultimate goal of the services, i.e., improved health.

RESEARCH ISSUES

The literature dealing with rural health and health care is extensive (Mustain, 1980). There are two major inadequacies in existing research, however. One is that much of it, just like government initiatives, is addressed to the maldistribution of health care providers and facilities. The other problem is that the existing research has not been effectively integrated; the result is considerable duplication of research on the problem of maldistribution. Research on the determinants and consequences of health and ill health among rural people has been relatively neglected.

Production and Maintenance of Rural Health

Because Chapter 22 is fully devoted to research needed on the relationship between health and nutrition, that important determinant of good or bad health will not be treated here. However, beyond the obvious linkage among poverty, nutrition, and health, much more documentation is needed of the causal relationships among health, disability, and social class position. *Research is needed on the extent to which poor health and disability have contributed to an inability to participate in the labor force and community life and therefore have reinforced poverty among the rural population.*

Being poor contributes to inadequate nutrition and lowered opportunity for interesting and remunerative work. It also influences the ability to reach, afford, and take advantage of available curative and preventive care. If obtaining professional health care is difficult for all rural residents, it is even more difficult for those of lower socioeconomic status. *Research is needed on what factors constrain the rural poor from obtaining appropriate professional health care services.*

As pointed out in Chapter 7, there are distinctive rural values, norms, and attitudes. Prominent among national images of the ruralite is the taciturn and rugged individualist. Other images and identifiable differences prevail. To what extent do these different norms and behaviors contribute to, or detract from, good health? In what ways do they influence the health (and, in many occupations, the safety) of individuals? What sex, occupational, and social class differences are associated with these greater risks if indeed they are found to exist? *Research is needed on the relationship between rural-based behaviors and health and safety risks in various segments of the rural population.*

Modern industrial societies have brought to rural areas a wide range of actual and potential environmental hazards. Black lung among coal miners, potential hazards of chemicals and pesticides used by farmers, and various radioactive "accidents" are examples. Little is known of the extent of increased risk to rural populations as a result of environmental modifications. *Research is needed to further determine the extent to which the health of the rural population is adversely influenced by various environmental modifications.*

Research also needs to determine what behavior and/or environmental modifications could be implemented that would be more cost-effective and efficacious in improving health than the expansion of traditional medical services.

Delivery of Health Care to Rural Residents

Rural residents generally do not have equal *access* to needed and appropriate health care services. Given the increasing concentration of health care providers in fewer and larger towns, rural residents have had to travel to the services by their own means or do without. Data clearly support that both responses have been made.

If improved access to appropriate health care services is an important rural objective, and many community surveys show it to be a high priority, then there are many ways in which that objective can be achieved. Providers of health care services can be encouraged, recruited, and enticed to locate in smaller communities. That has been the primary emphasis of government programs to date. Alternatively, the problem can be defined as one of transportation with emphasis being placed on improving the availability and reducing the cost of taking users to the service. Yet another alternative would be to make the services mobile and bring appropriate preventive and curative health care to the users on a regular basis. That approach has been experimented with in many parts of the country. There has also been increasing emphasis on restructuring the health care system to incorporate more midlevel practitioners (midwives, nurse practitioners, emergency medical technicians) into the system. Presumably, such midlevel practitioners would be more widely dispersed and more accessible and would serve as the initial point of patient contact either for resolution of problems or for referral to more highly trained health care providers in regional medical centers. All of these approaches are being tried in different places on an experimental basis. *Research is needed to further evaluate experimental approaches to appropriate health care delivery for rural people and to evaluate the costs and benefits associated with each option.*

Impact of Population Turnaround

Rural areas of the country are currently undergoing substantial growth because of the population turnaround (see Chapter 3). Sheer increases in the number of people create the need for additional health resources. To the extent that the migration is selective (e.g., due to retirement or immigration), the need for services may be exacerbated in quantity and in type. The addition of substantial numbers of older people into a rural environment has many implications for health care. *Research is needed to identify the types of specialized health services that are most needed and to evaluate alternatives for gaining access to such services.*

Government Intervention

There is a long-standing tradition of government intervention in the arena of rural health care. Examples of past government intervention include the National Health Planning and Resource Development Act (which underpins the Health Systems Agencies) and the National Health Service Corps. Enactment of some form of national health insurance has been under review for some time. The proposed nature of such a program ranges from tax concessions for buying private health insurance (the American Medical Association proposal) to catastrophic illness coverage and, finally, to a totally comprehensive government-sponsored health insurance program (U.S. House of Representatives, 1976). Before it is possible to understand the appropriate role of federal state governments in such programs, it is first necessary to examine the success (or failure) of past efforts. *More research is needed to evaluate what impact past programs have had and to forecast what impact can be expected from programs proposed in the future.*

Clearly, the issues identified do not represent an exhaustive list. They do, however, provide a starting place from which a rational rural health care policy could be constructed.

REFERENCES

Aday, L., and R. Anderson. 1975. *Development of Indices of Access to Medical Care*. Ann Arbor, Michigan: Health Administration Press.

Ahearn, Mary C. 1979. *Health Care in Rural America*. Washington, D.C.: Economics, Statistics, and Cooperatives Service, U.S. Department of Agriculture, Agriculture Information Bulletin 428.

Cedar, Toby, and John Salasin. 1979. *Research Directions for Rural Mental Health*. McLean, Virginia: MITRE Corp.

Copp, J. H. 1976. "Diversity of rural society and health needs." In E. W. Hassinger and Larry R. Whiting (editors), *Rural Health Services: Organization, Delivery, and Use*. Ames, Iowa: Iowa State University Press.

Cordes, S. M. 1977. *Social Science Research on Rural Health Care Delivery: A Compilation of Recent and Ongoing Studies*. University Park, Pennsylvania: Pennsylvania State University Press.

Culliton, Barbara J. 1978. "Health care economics: The high cost of getting well." In Philip H. Abelson (editor), *Health Care: Regulation, Economics, Ethics, Practice*. Washington, D.C.: American Association for the Advancement of Science.

Flax, J., M. Wagenfeld, R. Ivens, and R. Weiss. 1978. *Mental Health and Rural America: An Overview and Annotated Bibliography*. Washington, D.C.: National Institute for Mental Health, U.S. Department of Health, Education, and Welfare.

Hassinger, E. W., L. Gill, D. Hobbs, and R. Hageman. 1979. *A Restudy of Physicians in Twenty Rural Missouri Counties*. Washington, D.C.: Department of Health, Education, and Welfare, Publication 79-634.

Hassinger, E. W., and Larry R. Whiting (editors). 1976. *Rural Health Services: Organization, Delivery, and Use*. Ames, Iowa: Iowa State University Press.

Kane, R. A., M. Dean, and M. Solomon. 1979. "An evaluation of rural health care research." *Evaluation Quarterly* 3(May):139–189.

Kane, R. A., and P. F. Westover. 1976. "Rural health care research: Past accomplishments and future challenges." In M. Leininger (editor), *Transcultural Health Care Issues and Conditions*. Philadelphia: F. A. Davis Publishers.

Kleinman, J. C., and R. W. Wilson. 1977. "Are 'medically underserved' areas medically underserved?" *Health Services Research* 12(Summer):147–162.

Longest, James, et al. 1977. *A Study in the Differentials of Mental Health Manpower and Facilities*. College Park, Maryland: University of Maryland.

McClure, Walter. 1976. *Reducing Excess Hospital Capacity*. Excelsior, Minnesota: Interstudy Publishers.

McKeown, Thomas. 1976. *The Role of Medicine*. London, England: Nuffield Hospital Trust.

Miller, Michael K., and C. S. Stokes. 1978. "Health status, health resources, and consolidated structural parameters: Implications for public health care policy." *Journal of Health and Social Behavior* 19(September):263–279.

Mustain, R. David. 1980. *Rural Health Care*. State College, Mississippi: Southern Rural

Development Center, Mississippi State University, SRDC Series 10.
Roemer, Milton I. 1976. *Rural Health Care*. St. Louis, Missouri: C. V. Mosby Co.
Ross, Peggy J., Herman Bluestone, and Fred K. Hines. 1979. *Indicators of Social Well-Being for U.S. Counties*. Washington, D.C.: Economics, Statistics, and Cooperatives Service, U.S. Department of Agriculture, Rural Development Research Report 10.
Schonfield, H. K., J. F. Heston, and I. S. Falk. 1972. "Number of physicians required for primary care." *New England Journal of Medicine* 286(March):571-576.
Scitovsky, A. A., and N. McCall. 1976. "A method of estimating physician requirements." *Health and Society* 54(Summer):299-320.
Shenkin, Bud. 1974. *Health Care for Migrant Workers: Policies and Politics*. Cambridge, Massachusetts: Ballinger Publishing Co.
Slesinger, Doris P. 1980. "Racial and residential differences in preventive medical care for infants in low-income populations." *Rural Sociology* 45(Spring):69-90.
U.S. House of Representatives (Subcommittee on Health of the Committee on Ways and Means). 1976. *National Health Insurance Resource Book*. Washington, D.C.: U.S. Government Printing Office.
Warner, Kenneth E. 1979. "The economic implications of preventive health care." *Social Science and Medicine* 13(December):227-237.
Wildavsky, Aaron. 1977. "Doing better and feeling worse: The political pathology of health policy." In John H. Knowles (editor), *Doing Better and Feeling Worse: Health in the United States*. New York: W W. Norton and Co.
Wright, D. D. 1976. "Recent rural health research." *Journal of Community Health* 2(1):60-69.

22 Food and Nutrition

VIRGINIA S. PURTLE

Nothing has been more central to the American lifestyle yet more taken for granted than food. It is often mentioned with pride that no country enjoys the quantity and quality of food with as low a commitment of per capita income than the United States. Despite this cornucopia, inadequate nutrition remains a major public health problem for reasons of under- and overconsumption and questionable nutritive value of many of the foods consumed. A further irony is that rural America–the producer of that cornucopia–fares no better than urban America in the nutritional status of its population.

However, there is more to the sociological aspects of food and nutrition than whether Americans get their minimum daily requirements of the necessary vitamins and minerals. Food must be produced, distributed, selected, paid for, prepared, and served. Each of these steps is associated with problems that need solving if we are to reach the ultimate goal of a well-fed population. The well-being of rural people, many of whom are the disadvantaged consumers of food, are affected not only by what they eat but by what the rest of America eats. Sudden changes in food habits help some producers and hurt others. The impact of changes vibrates throughout the rural community and may affect everything from the quality of the diet to the tax base.

CURRENT KNOWLEDGE

Rural people suffer from a higher incidence of chronic disease and experience more days lost from work due to illness or incapacity than do

Virginia S. Purtle is associate professor, Department of Sociology and Rural Sociology, and an associate dean of the College of Arts and Sciences, Louisiana State University, Baton

urban people (Deavers and Brown, 1979). Nutritional status is part of a vicious poverty cycle in that people without adequate nutrition are likely to become chronically ill, unable to work on a regular basis, and therefore unable to buy the food they need. Nutritional problems of rural as well as urban people are not limited to the poor, however. People with higher incomes often make poor food choices.

We often think of the United States as a well-fed nation, but results of the Ten-State Survey, the most comprehensive survey in recent years (U.S. Department of Health, Education, and Welfare, 1972), indicated that a significant proportion of the population surveyed was malnourished or at high risk of developing nutritional problems. Even though rural/urban comparisons were not made, many of the characteristics of the survey sample were similar to those exhibited by many rural areas (i.e., the poor, the elderly, and the minority groups were overrepresented).

Evidence of malnutrition was most common among Blacks, less common among Spanish-Americans, and least among whites. Generally, malnutrition increased as income and education decreased. Persons over sixty years of age were generally undernourished regardless of their ethnic group.

Although protein malnutrition is rare in the United States, a relatively large percentage of pregnant and lactating women had low blood serum albumen levels, suggesting marginal protein intake. Since the outcome of pregnancy for low-income groups is known to be less satisfactory than the national average, this problem demands special attention. This finding is particularly relevant because all American counties with infant mortality rates at least double the national average are rural (Deavers and Brown, 1979).

A group of people that is small in number but growing in rural areas comprise the "return-to-nature" social movement. The nutritional concepts held by them range from eating only organically grown foods to vegetarianism and other cult-like food beliefs. Their children are sometimes malnourished due to the omission of important foods, such as meat, from the diet. Adequately balanced diets can be achieved without meat; however, people who have little nutritional knowledge seldom accomplish this.

Overconsumption of food, another form of malnourishment, has been highlighted in the National Nutrition Goals established by the U.S. Senate Select Committee on Nutrition and Human Needs (1977). They

---

Rouge. A past president of Rural Sociologists in the South, she has published journal and experiment station publications on the sociological aspects of nutrition.

noted excess consumption of sugar, animal protein, fats, and alcohol. Obesity is one obvious result of overconsumption of sugar and fat. Although research data for rural areas is inadequate, the Ten-State Survey findings allow the inference that obesity is a significant problem in rural areas.

In the last decades, hard physical labor in rural areas has been reduced significantly by mechanization. It is likely that many rural people have reduced their total energy output without an equivalent reduction in energy intake. Big meals with an emphasis on dessert, potatoes, and meat are traditional in most rural areas of the United States. It is unlikely that the high value placed on this type of food has changed at the same rate as the decreased need for food. Michael Cepede (1975) noted that it is common for cultural groups that have long experienced inadequate food supplies to overcompensate when food is available and to become overweight.

Food and nutrition have long been of interest to sociologists. Writing in 1922, Sorokin (1975) described hunger as a determinant of social organization, including food production, trade, migration, collective behavior, and social change. In the ensuing years, rural sociologists have frequently conducted research on agricultural production and occasionally on distribution issues (see Chapters 30 to 34). However, a comprehensive annotated bibliography of food habit research by Wilson (1973) reveals only a few studies by sociologists. The use of food as a status symbol was studied by Bennett et al. (1942), Bennett (1943), and Masouka (1945). Adoption of new foods was studied by Dickens (1956) and Lindstrom (1958). Cussler and DeGive (1971) published an ethnographic study of food habits in the rural Southeast. Since Wilson's review, literature in this area has grown rapidly, with most of the research being published in the *Journal of the American Dietetic Association*, the *Journal of Nutrition Education*, *Food Technology*, the *Journal of Home Economics Research*, and various experiment station publications.

Several sociological publications have dealt with family structure and interaction as related to food habits (Schafer and Bohlen, 1977; Schafer, 1978; Coughenour, 1972; Hertzler and Vaughan, 1978). Attitudes and values related to food habits have been reported by Steelman (1976) and Shutz et al. (1975). Schafer and Yetley (1975) and Shifflett (1976) have studied taboos and faddism. The meanings of various foods have been reported by Steelman (1974) and Falkowski (1978). Shifflett and Nyberg (1978) have elaborated a social-psychological theoretical framework for understanding behavior related to food. These are only a few of the rapidly growing number of publications on the subject.

RESEARCH ISSUES

Policy issues related to nutrition may be divided into production, distribution, and selection issues. Production issues focus on agricultural policy with its close relationship to energy and foreign policy. Distribution of food is an important concern of both the rural and urban segments of our population and is of central concern to nutrition policy. Finally, issues related to the actual selection and consumption of food to meet physiological needs are becoming of greater policy importance.

Food Production

Research is needed to determine the impact of predicted energy and water shortages on future food supplies. There is a potential need for more variety in local food production and storage techniques during the 1980s. As energy costs increase, the production, transportation, and long-term storage of fresh food on a year-around basis will make such food less affordable to major parts of the population. More dispersed production of fruits and vegetables may be a response. Increased local fruit and vegetable production may also be stimulated by water shortages in areas where most fruits and vegetables are grown, particularly the Southwest (see Chapter 37). Rural sociologists can contribute to determining the impact of changes in the location of production on the people and communities who may face a decline in productive capacity or demand for their products as well as those who are diversifying for local consumption.

The consequences of decreasing farm land needs to be carefully studied if we are to retain adequate land for food production. Farm land is being lost to residential construction, particularly in the Sun Belt areas of Florida, Texas, Arizona, and California. Some zoning is now being attempted to protect farm land in these areas, but there is still a great demand for land for homes and other forms of urban growth. Research is needed on alternative housing and settlement patterns so that valuable farm land can be retained (see Chapters 19 and 36).

Techniques used by commercial agriculture are also related to long-term production potential. The use of large equipment for highly specialized farming is not generally compatible with many soil conservation techniques, and the erosion of farm land is decreasing the amount of land available in certain areas for agriculture production. This is especially true of marginal land. A related factor that may also lead to increasing erosion is the growing practice of land rental rather than land ownership for agricultural production. Motivation for using conservation techniques is believed to be less when a person is renting land. Information on the relationship of various land tenure systems to conservation practices and other production practices is also needed to ensure future food supplies (see Chapter 35).

Although the preceding problems are detailed in other chapters, their inclusion here is important. Conceptualization of research related to agricultural policy must consider nutritional needs if we are to ensure the future nutritional status of our people, both rural and urban.

Distribution

More research is needed to determine the long-term impact of importing and exporting food. The export and import policies of a nation affect food available to its population. We have been less concerned with these issues than many other nations because of our ability to produce large amounts and varieties of food. However, some of our own export and import policies affect the nutritional status of people in our society. The use of agricultural products to balance import deficits costs the American consumer through higher food costs. The farmer may enjoy a higher income due to the world market but becomes vulnerable to political whims (see Chapter 31). The low-income consumer is further deprived as the cost of food goes up.

Food import policies are seldom considered for their nutritional implications, but they are central concerns in our agricultural policy. Much concern has been expressed by meat-producing farmers about the import of meat, but little has been noted about the import of foods of questionable health value, such as sugar, tea, coffee, and cocoa. These items provide significant financial benefits to certain developing nations, to say nothing of the popularity of them in the diets of Americans. Consequently, they are associated with actual and potential political pressures. However, all of these items are questionable from a nutritional standpoint and their import could be discouraged in the name of improved nutrition. Both internal and international politics are so strongly related to these issues that nutritional well-being has been ignored.

Research is needed to determine nutritionally and socially acceptable alternatives for protein distribution. The worldwide shortage of food raises a question of whether grain-fed beef production and other similar meat production practices are justified at the current rate per capita. Cattle are less efficient users of grain than are other animals, such as pigs and poultry. (Cattle fed grass on marginal crop land is not an issue here.) Vegetable protein production is an even more efficient means of providing protein for the world's population. The substitution of other protein for beef will likely respond to economic changes, but particular attention needs to be given to the effects of the changes. Changes in protein production and sources will not only change diets but will likely have an economic impact on the producers of food and a subsequent impact on rural communities.

Rural sociological research can contribute information about rural people that is needed by planners of food distribution programs and welfare policies. Several programs now contribute to the distribution of food to low-income people. These programs include the food stamp program; the national school lunch and school breakfast program; the special milk program; the child-care food program; the summer food service program for children; the food distribution program; women, infants, and children program; and the national nutrition program for the elderly. These programs have had varied degrees of success, but in most cases they are more helpful to people living in urban areas than they are to people in rural areas. A lack of transportation and remoteness of administrative centers present major access problems in rural areas (see Chapter 14).

One unresolved controversy that will remain a policy issue of the 1980s is whether existing food programs should be supplemented with or replaced by a guaranteed minimum income. Deavers and Brown (1979) support the belief that welfare reform is a key element of federal rural policy. Rural sociologists can provide assistance in evaluating the needs of rural people and the effectiveness of alternatives for the well-being of rural people.

Food Selection

Research is needed on the relationship between food and lifestyles if people's food habits are to be successfully changed. Regardless of the nutritional quality and affordability of foods, many people choose to eat in ways that are detrimental to their health. People with ample incomes often have low-quality diets. However, more is known about what food and nutrients are needed in order for one to maximize opportunities for good health than is known about the social patterns that establish and maintain food habits.

Further research is needed on the relationship of demographic characteristics and group membership to food habits. Certain demographic variables, such as age, sex, ethnic group, income, occupation, education, religion, and resident locality, are somewhat related to dietary choices, but there are other variables that modify their effects. For example, changes in the structure of the family, such as divorce, may alter dietary patterns. The influence of other reference groups (e.g., peer groups and occupational groups) on dietary choices also needs further study. As the occupational structure of rural areas becomes more complex, the potential for social change increases with expected concomitant changes in dietary habits. Occupational changes not only lead to broader social contacts but also to a restructuring of time and role relationships. In addition to specific groups, cultural heritages in rural localities that are unique to these areas need to be understood in order to develop nutritional programs that will best meet the needs of the population of a given area.

Research is needed on the impact of changes in sex roles in rural areas on the production and preparation of foods. Changes in the jobs that people do in relation to food production and preparation are a concern in developing nations, but these issues have received little attention in the United States. If rural women continue to enter the labor force (and it is likely that they will), the pattern of family food consumption will likely be influenced. At a minimum, that role change may mean less time for things such as gardening and home preservation of food. These practices have often contributed to the quality and quantity of the diet of low-income rural residents. The decreasing amount of time the working person has for food preparation alone will undoubtedly affect what food is consumed and where. The diet will probably change because of shifting meal patterns. Traditionally, rural areas have been known for substantial breakfasts and noon meals and light evening meals. With family members working away from home, the emphasis will undoubtedly shift to a heavier evening meal and lighter noon meals.

Research is needed on means of motivating people who are socially isolated to eat balanced meals. Food is intimately related to social interaction patterns. For example, the elderly sometimes have inadequate diets because they are not motivated to prepare balanced meals for feeding just themselves. Some meal programs have been effective more because they offer the incentive of an opportunity to visit with people than because they offer good food. Feeding others and sharing food contributes to a healthier appetite and therefore better health. The problem of living alone and not having people available to share food is particularly important in rural areas where many elderly tend to be isolated. The Meals-on-Wheels and community meal programs for the elderly have had some degree of success in urban areas, but the transportation problems in rural areas make these programs ineffective for many rural elderly.

Research is needed on the social meanings of specific foods to specific subcultures. Researchers have long been concerned with why certain foods are of high status for different groups and low status in other groups. The status of a food in a particular community affects the way a group uses the food and therefore the diet of the individual. For example, Bennett (1943) found in an Illinois community that fish was considered a low-status food when, in fact, it would be a highly desirable, nutritious food. Because it was given low status, people did not report eating it even when they probably did. Other concepts that influence the acceptability of a given food include convenience, creativity, "good for you," "bad for you," traditional, and so forth. Highly acceptable food in one subculture may be undesirable in another.

Research is needed on the meaning that red meat has for specific groups. Decreased consumption of grain-fed beef would probably have positive health benefits to overconsumers of meat high in animal fats. The question of what people will substitute for beef often arises. It is easy to say that less expensive cuts of meat will be substituted, and this is probably true to a certain extent. However, the substitution will depend on the meaning that a given subculture associates with beef and other meats. For example, charcoaled steak is a high-status food that is used on social occasions by certain groups. If increased price forced a reduction in its use, it would likely be exchanged for a less expensive meat such as chicken, which can be prepared in the same way. Likewise, the standing rib roast and rump roast, which may symbolize a lot of loving care and time spent in the kitchen, may be exchanged for a roast turkey and similar long-term cooking items. Red meat is often mistakenly believed to be more nutritious than fish and poultry. These and other beliefs regarding meat, the need for a more equitable distribution of protein, and the need to reduce dietary fat demand special attention by sociologists because of the social and behavioral implications.

Research needs to determine the meaning of foods high in sugar content so that decreased consumption can be achieved. Certain foods of questionabie nutritional value are known to be highly valued, perhaps more so in rural areas than other places. Sweets, particularly pies and cakes, are the center of attention at rural community church suppers, school fairs, county fairs, and so forth. They are also central to many social gatherings. The high value placed on these food items is rooted deeply in subcultural values. Simply telling people that they should not eat these things does little to reduce actual consumption. More research is needed into why these foods are so highly valued. Perhaps they are symbols of success and abundance and satisfy needs beyond nutrition. However, we know little about how to decrease their desirability and how to increase the acceptance of healthier foods.

A better understanding of the basis of taboos and food faddism is an important research need. Food taboos exist among well-educated as well as poorly-educated segments of the population. Many people believe that to eat fish and milk at the same time will make you sick. Other groups believe that cornstarch consumption is important in the diets of pregnant women. Among the educated, there are people who refuse to eat meat as well as those who go on high-protein diets for weight loss. Both practices have inherent disadvantages. The belief that organically grown foods are superior to others has become widespread in recent years, even though scientific data are not available to substantiate this belief. We also know little about why people choose to use excessive vitamin and mineral supplements. All of these practices may be detrimental to one's health, but since they are so widespread we have to assume that the culture is supporting the practice.

The child-rearing practices of specific groups of people must be researched if we are going to understand how food habits are learned and how food habits may be changed. Food and its preparation serve many psychological and social needs. These needs are established through child-rearing practices and later-life experiences. For example, food preparation is a means of expressing creativity. Eating food is a pleasure in itself and may be given more attention by certain groups than by others.

Little research has been done on the reward and punishment aspects of food by subculture, even though most of us are aware that parents, teachers, and others use food this way. Reward foods are often undesirable foods from a nutritional viewpoint, but they contribute to the total food intake. Other child-rearing practices are known to affect the kind of food we choose as adults. We need a better understanding of what it is in our culture and specific subcultures that leads to these practices if we are to change them.

Research is needed to determine other societal influences, such as the mass media, on food selections. The influences of the family, peer groups, and other occupational groups have been mentioned but certainly the mass media, particularly television advertising, contribute significantly to changing food habits. Snack foods certainly owe much of their popularity to television advertising.

REFERENCES

Bennett, John W. 1943. "Food and social status in a rural society." *American Sociological Review* 80(October):561–569.

Bennett, John W., H. Smith, and H. Passin. 1942. "Food and culture in southern Illinois – A preliminary report." *American Sociological Review* 7(October):645–660.

Cepede, Michael. 1975. "Sociology and nutrition." *Food and Nutrition* 1(2):8–10.

Coughenour, C. Milton. 1972. "Functional aspects of food consumption activity and family life stages." *Journal of Marriage and the Family* 34(November):656–664.

Cussler, Margaret, and M. L. Q. DeGive. 1971. *Twixt the Cup and the Lip*. Washington, D.C.: Consortium Press.

Deavers, Kenneth L., and David L. Brown. 1979. *Social and Economic Trends in Rural America*. Washington, D.C.: Economics, Statistics, and Cooperatives Service, U.S. Department of Agriculture, the White House Rural Development Background Paper.

Dickens, P. 1956. "New dishes tried by small-town homemakers in 1954 as compared to 1943." *Rural Sociology* 21(September/December):295–297.

Falkowski, Carol Teresa. 1978. "Connotative meanings of food in a selected Louisiana subculture." Baton Rouge, Louisiana: Louisiana State University. Master's thesis.

Hertzler, Ann A., and C. Edwin Vaughan. 1978. "The relationship of family structure and interaction to nutrition." *Journal of the American Dietetic Association* 74(January):23–27.

Lindstrom, David E. 1958. "Diffusion of agricultural and home economics practices in a Japanese rural community." *Rural Sociology* 23(June):171–183.

Masouka, J. 1945. "Changing food habits of the Japanese in Hawaii." *American Sociological Review* 10:750–765.

Schafer, Robert B. 1978. "Factors affecting food behavior and the quality of husbands' and wives' diets." *Journal of the American Dietetic Association* 72(February):138–143.

Schafer, Robert B., and Joe M. Bohlen. 1977. "Exchange of conjugal power in the control of family food consumption." *Home Economics Research Journal* 6(December):131–140.

Schafer, Robert B., and Elizabeth A. Yetley. 1975. "Social psychology of food faddism." *Journal of the American Dietetic Association* 66(February):29–133.

Shifflett, Peggy A. 1976. "Folklore and food habits." *Journal of the American Dietetic Association* 78(April):347–350.

Shifflett, Peggy A., and Kenneth L. Nyberg. 1978. "Toward a social psychology of food use." *Mid-American Review of Sociology* 3(Winter):35–54.

Shutz, Howard G., Margaret H. Rucker, and Gerald F. Russell. 1975. "Food and food use classification systems." *Food Technology* 29(March):50–60.

Sorokin, P. A. 1975. *Hunger as a Factor in Human Affairs*. Gainesville, Florida: University Presses of Florida.

Steelman, Virginia P. 1974. *The Cultural Context of Food: A Study of Food Habits and Their Social Significance in Selected Areas of Louisiana*. Baton Rouge, Louisiana: Agricultural Experiment Station, Louisiana State University, Bulletin 657.

______. 1976. "Attitudes toward food as indicators of subculture value systems." *Home Economics Research Journal* 5(September):21–32.

U.S. Department of Health, Education, and Welfare. 1972. *Highlights of Ten-State Nutrition Survey, 1968–1970*. Atlanta, Georgia: Center for Disease Control, Health Services and Mental Health Administration, U.S. Department of Health, Education, and Welfare.

U.S. Senate (Select Committee on Nutrition and Human Needs). 1977. *Dietary Goals for the United States*. Washington, D.C.: U.S. Government Printing Office.

Wilson, Christina S. 1973. "Food habits: A selected annotated bibliography." *Journal of Nutrition Education* 15(January/March):41–71.

23
Crime and Its Prevention

G. HOWARD PHILLIPS
JOSEPH F. DONNERMEYER
TODD N. WURSCHMIDT

Traditionally, rural America has been portrayed as a sanctuary of security. Telling indicators of this were the often heard comments, "We have never locked our doors," and "I have no idea where to find the key to the front door." In addition, most farm buildings were constructed to secure contents from the weather rather than from theft. Today, a growing number of rural communities are experiencing a marked increase in crime. During the period from 1959 to 1979, the Federal Bureau of Investigation's crime rate index for rural areas of the United States increased nearly 450 percent (from 396.7 to 2,167.5 per 100,000 people). The largest part of the increase was a dramatic rise in occurrences of crimes against property (502 percent).[1]

Crime has always been less a problem in rural than in urban places, and to some extent this continues to be true. However, rural crime now exceeds the level recorded in the mid- to late-1960s for urban areas (U.S. Department of Justice, 1965–1968). The alarming urban crime rate at that time was a major impetus for the creation of the National Institute of Law Enforcement and Criminal Justice and the Law Enforcement Assistance Administration under the Omnibus Crime Control and Safe

---

G. Howard Phillips is a professor in the Department of Agricultural Economics and Rural Sociology and director of the National Rural Crime Prevention Center, Ohio State University, Columbus, Ohio. He has published numerous articles on rural crime and its prevention. **Joseph F. Donnermeyer** is assistant professor, Department of Agricultural Economics and Rural Sociology, and is a staff member of the National Rural Crime Prevention Center, Ohio State University, Columbus, Ohio. He has written numerous articles on

Streets Act of 1968 (U.S. Department of Justice, 1974:iii). Under this act, hundreds of millions of dollars have been committed to various crime control programs.

Crime is no longer just an urban problem. It has come of age in the hinterlands. Concern for the growing rural crime problem has been expressed by a diversity of rural leaders. A spokesman for the American Farm Bureau Federation estimated that crime costs the American farmer in excess of one billion dollars annually (Cheatham, 1979). The California Farm Bureau reported that, in 1977, farmers suffered an estimated loss of thirty million dollars from theft (Footlick et al., 1979). The Virginia Rural Electric Cooperative estimated a cost of more than one million dollars a year from theft and vandalism (Jones, 1979).

As rural communities find themselves confronted by greater amounts of crime, traditional approaches of dealing with public safety are being questioned. Rural residents are no longer able to rely solely on reactive strengths of their law enforcement agencies. Primary prevention strategies (Brantingham and Faust, 1976) requiring citizen involvement in crime control efforts (U.S. Department of Justice, 1974) are increasingly viewed as viable alternatives. However, rural reduction efforts require a greater understanding of the nature of the rural crime problem and the social forces influencing its growth.

CURRENT KNOWLEDGE

Until recently, studies of rural crime and delinquency have been limited. This paucity of literature is predictable given the historically low level of rural crime. For example, only eight articles related to rural crime appeared in *Rural Sociology* since its inception in 1936; three of these appeared in the most recent volumes of the journal (Steffensmeier and Jordan, 1978; Bankston and Allen, 1980; Fischer, 1980).

Few specialists in the field of criminology have made more than passing reference to rural crime and delinquency. Clinard (1944) found that rural offenders were less likely than urban offenders to display qualities of the "criminal social type," i.e., relying on crime as the whole means of support and possessing the self-concept of being a criminal.

Some more recent criminological studies have characterized rural

the extent and pattern of rural crime. **Todd N. Wurschmidt** is executive director of the Ohio Crime Prevention Association, and a doctoral candidate in the Department of Agricultural Economics and Rural Sociology, Ohio State University, Columbus, Ohio. Phillips, Donnermeyer, and Wurschmidt are coeditors of the book *Rural Crime: Integrating Research and Prevention*.

crime as petty and minor (Gibbons, 1972; Dinitz, 1973). Results of still other research have indicated that rural crime tends to be committed against persons, while urban crime is more likely committed against property (McCorkle and Korn, 1959; Reckless, 1967; Christiansen, 1970). These studies appear to reinforce recent reports by Bankston and Allen (1980) and Fischer (1980), both of which leave the impression that rural crime is disproportionately violent in nature. In contrast, a new wave of research has consistently found that rural crime, in fact, is more property-oriented than urban crime. These studies also confirm the impressions of many farm and rural leaders that rural crime is no longer petty in nature but is now a serious and costly problem. One such example is a study of farm retailers (i.e., roadside farm markets and "U-Pick" operations) in which it was found that two out of three experienced some type of crime problem annually (Phillips and Donnermeyer, 1980a).

The rate of forcible entry burglary occurring in rural households was found in three separate rural crime studies to be equivalent to the average for American metropolitan areas of one million or more people (Phillips et al., 1980; Smith, 1979; Phillips and Donnermeyer, 1980b). The forcible entry burglary rate for a twelve-month period from a nine-county rural crime study in Ohio was calculated at 29.2 per thousand households (Phillips et al., 1980). Smith's (1979) research in an agricultural county of northwestern Indiana determined a forcible entry rate of 36.0 per thousand households annually, while Phillips and Donnermeyer (1980b) estimated a forcible entry rate of 30.3 per thousand households in a mixed coal and agricultural county of southwestern Indiana. In comparison, the National Crime Survey found the forcible entry rate for metro areas greater than one million persons to be 34.6 per thousand households (U.S. Department of Justice, 1979).

Influences on Growth of Rural Crime

Although research on rural crime is sparse and results are often contradictory, the literature suggests an outline by which to understand trends and changing conditions that have contributed to recent increases. They include geographic, demographic, lifestyle, and institutional considerations.

Geography. / Low population density, relative to urban areas, is perhaps the most distinctive characteristic of rurality. However, remoteness and distance between homes increases the opportunity for criminal incidents because of the reduced probability that such activities will be observed. Further, improved transportation has increased accessibility to rural places. As a result, remoteness and isolation now seem to be a contributing factor rather than a deterring factor in rural crime rates.

The large geographic areas under the jurisdiction of rural law enforcement agencies also mean longer response time in emergency situations. In addition, law enforcement resources often are minimal. This reduces the deterrent effect often associated with high visibility of law enforcement.

Demography. / The composition of the rural population is changing. Many urban fringe counties have felt the considerable impact of suburbanization. Many other rural areas are, for the first time in decades, experiencing a net increase of in-migrants (Beale, 1977; Thomas and Bachtel, 1978). As a result of these trends, and coupled with increasing farm size, the farm population is today 15 to 20 percent of the total U.S. rural population (U.S. Department of Commerce, 1978:2). The remainder is rural nonfarm.

Some changes in the demographic composition of the rural population are important for an understanding of increasing rural crime rates. First, suburban areas generally experience a disproportionately high level of property crime, such as burglary and larceny. As more residential developments are located in rural areas, property crimes will probably increase. Second, in some rural areas an age-selective process of in-migration has occurred. Notably in areas such as central Michigan and the Missouri Ozarks, the recent waves of in-migrants have been older persons establishing retirement households (Dailey et al., 1977; Koebernich and Beegle, 1978). This represents a type of senior citizen suburbanization that may result in more attractive targets for burglary and larceny. Crimes that disproportionately victimize the elderly, such as fraud, may also rise.

A third change, as Polk (1969) indicated, is in work-related opportunities in such areas. A decreasing percentage of rural youths will have distinctively "agricultural" backgrounds. As nonmetropolitan areas continue to experience an influx of new households, the difference in rural and urban lifestyles will be increasingly blurred. As the studies by Natalino (1979), Donnermeyer and Phillips (1980), and Napier et al. (1980) suggest, there is growing evidence of little difference in participation between urban and rural youths in many forms of deviant behavior.

Lifestyle. / Several lifestyle changes have contributed to increased opportunity for crimes in rural areas. First, rural areas are generally experiencing increased affluence. This results from suburbanization, from the relocation of industry to rural areas, and from the expanding equipment inventories required to efficiently operate commercial farming enterprises.

Second, rural residents increasingly leave their homes vacant for longer periods of time, thereby increasing opportunity for burglary and theft. Three factors have contributed to this trend. One is the increase in nonfarm employment; thus, a greater share of the rural work force is commuting long distances to work. Another is that both spouses work in a growing number of rural households. For example, nearly one-half of all rural farm and nonfarm wives work away from home (U.S. Department of Commerce, 1978:9). A third factor is the many rural households who travel great distances for services and retail purchases. Clothes, furniture, medical services, and repair services are available only at distant urban service centers for many rural people.

Although growing affluence has increased the attractiveness of rural property targets, and the regular vacancy of many rural homes has increased the opportunity for crime to occur unobserved, there has not been a corresponding increase among most rural residents in the perceived need to adopt home security measures. For instance, Phillips (1976:14) found that 40 percent of rural Ohioans seldom or never locked their door when leaving home and 60 percent did not lock their automobiles. Two-thirds of the farm operators did not lock their fuel storage tanks. Similar results were obtained from a survey of farm operators in West Virginia (Bean and Lawrence, 1978:5–6).

Institutions. / One of the major factors associated with the growing rate of rural property victimization by rural youth is a change in the social control mechanisms within rural society. Earlier writers on rural crime, such as Gillin and Hill (1940) and Clinard (1944), found rural offenders different from urban offenders. The formation of gangs and the accouterments of gang behavior were found to be absent among rural offenders, and farm probationers exhibited lower violation rates. The differences often were attributed to the strength of informal social control mechanisms, principally through family, school, and church.

However, these institutions are less influential in contemporary rural society; mass media and peer groups have greater influence. One reason for this change is an increase in the number of single-parent households and households in which both parents work. This has resulted in less adult supervision during after-school hours. Second, occupational opportunities in rural areas have changed, including a decline of agricultural and unskilled jobs available to youths (see Chapter 10). The responsibilities associated with "growing up on the farm" are no longer salient to the vast majority of rural youths. This has led to an increase in leisure or unstructured time available and has strengthened the relative influence of peer pressure. A third trend is the consolidation of rural schools and the resultant loss of localized control over curricular and administrative procedures (see Chapter 18). Consolidated schools appear to be more conducive to the formation of peer subcultures whose normative prescriptions may conflict with those of the dominant culture, i.e., the "adult" world, (Natalino, 1979). For instance, Donnermeyer and Phillips (1980) found that vandalism by rural youths was "normatively acceptable" behavior.

A fourth trend is the increased influence of mass media. Glaser (1956), for instance, modified Sutherland's theory of differential association to account for the impact of communication. Glaser's theory of "differential identification" stipulates that role models may be acquired without the aid of direct interaction with "significant others." It also appears that television viewing in particular reduces the amount of "shared time" between parents and siblings, and therefore weakens the influence of the family (Glenn, 1979).

In summary, geographic, demographic, lifestyle, and institutional changes within rural society have been conducive to the emergence of the rural crime problem. Crime prevention specialists claim that there are three conditions necessary for a crime to occur: a suitable target or victim, an opportunity, and a motivated offender. As Cohen and Felson (1977) have noted, an increase in any one of these three conditions will result in a higher crime rate. It appears that rural America has experienced an increase in all three.

RESEARCH ISSUES

Many small towns and rural areas are, for the first time, faced with the difficult task of formulating cost-effective crime reduction strategies. At present, public officials and community leaders have little evidence on which to formulate policy in this area. Rural crime research during the decade of the 1980s should be focused upon several key problem areas.

The Pattern of Criminal Victimization in Rural Areas

Research is needed on the establishment of a national data base concerning the per capita volume of crime among the rural population. At present, knowledge about rural crime patterns is limited. An in-depth assessment of its extent and impact on the total rural population is needed and should focus upon several specific research issues.

First, it should be determined if there are regional variations in the type of criminal incidents that impact rural residents. Second, separate analyses should be conducted on the extent of crime occurring to three major subsectors of the rural population—farm residents, nonfarm residents, and rural commercial establishments. Third, Newman (1973) and Phillips et al. (1976) suggest the importance of ecological factors to the probability of victimization. Such factors would include proximity to a public road, visibility of the house to neighbors, and the arrangement of farm buildings on the farm operation. What are the relative contributions of these ecological factors to the increased probability of criminal victimization among the rural population?

A fourth area of research on the pattern of rural crime would include the effect of opportunity reduction strategies on victimization. For example, is there a difference between victim and nonvictim households (or persons) in the proportion with an outside security light, burglar alarm system, type of door and window locks, presence of a watch-dog, possession of a gun, and other security devices and practices?

A fifth set of research questions center on determination of demographic, economic, and social class differentials between victims and nonvictims within the rural population and comparative analyses of the relative similarity of these differentials among the urban population. A sixth area of study on rural victimization patterns should focus on victim response. For instance, was the incident reported to law enforcement and, if not, for what reason(s) were the police not notified? What is the relationship of the victim to the offender (i.e., is the offender an employee, friend, neighbor, or even relative)? What are the psychological and behavior consequences of crime to the rural victim and indirectly to other family members, neighbors, and friends?

Emergence of Rural Crime

Future research must construct research designs that allow for within-rural and rural/urban comparisons and that test theoretical explanations for differences that exist. Warren (1978:53–54) has outlined seven "great changes" that have occurred in American communities, the gist of which is that there has been "an increasing orientation of local community units toward extracommunity systems of which they are a part, with a corresponding decline in community cohesion and autonomy." These changes have cut across both rural and urban communities. Factors that explain both intrarural and rural/urban differentials may include many of the "great changes" outlined by Warren (1978). Such variables as urbanization, proximity to metro areas, the type and size of farm operations, and travel patterns of local residents may be important explanatory factors.

A second line of inquiry would include analysis of the rural offender. What are the social forces that influence unlawful behavior among rural youth? For instance, assuming vandalism is largely a youth crime, what has been the effect of mass media and the increased influence of the peer group on such phenomena as changing norms toward property destruction, illegal drug use, and so forth? Criminological theories are most suggestive of the dynamics surrounding the formation of deviant subcultures within an urban setting. Are these theories salient to the explanation of unlawful behavior within a rural environment? If not, how should they be modified?

Effectiveness of Crime Reduction Strategies

Research is needed on the social and economic cost-effectiveness of expanding law enforcement and criminal justice systems in response to increased rural crime. The rising crime rate in rural America will affect both law enforcement and the court system. How are law enforcement departments of small towns and rural counties reacting to increased crime? How are rural offenders being processed through the local court system?

A second important research need is the study of citizen involvement strategies for crime reduction within the rural setting. In contrast to the more punitive, formal system of response, are there viable nonpunitive, and informal, solutions? For instance, would "Neighborhood Watch," "CB Patrols," and other such response programs be effective strategies for reducing crime in rural areas? If the answer is affirmative, then we need to determine the nature of rural law enforcement's role in facilitating citizen involvement and identify their training needs relative to the principles of community structure and organization.

NOTES

1. The Federal Bureau of Investigation's crime rate index was designed as an indicator of the relative level of crime and consists of seven major offenses. These include four violent crimes: criminal homicide, rape, robbery, and assault. The three property offenses are: burglary, larceny, and motor vehicle theft. The rate consists of the number of offenses known or reported to the police per 100,000 population. The rate of violent crime in rural areas rose from 67.9 in 1959 to 187.4 per 100,000 persons in 1979. The rate of property crime grew from 328.8 in 1959 to 1,980.1 per 100,000 persons in 1979.

REFERENCES

Bankston, William B., and H. David Allen. 1980. "Rural social areas and patterns of homicide: An analysis of lethal violence in Louisiana." *Rural Sociology* 45(Summer):223-237.

Beale, Calvin L. 1977. "The recent shift of United States population to nonmetropolitan areas, 1970-1975." *International Regional Science Review* 2(2):113-122.

Bean, T. L., and L. D. Lawrence. 1978. *Crime on Farms in Hampshire County, West Virginia—Pilot Study*. Morgantown, West Virginia: Center for Extension and Continuing Education, West Virginia University, R.M. 69.

Brantingham, Paul J., and Frederic L. Faust. 1976. "A conceptual model of crime prevention." *Crime and Delinquency* 22(3):284-296.

Cheatham, Kenneth. 1979. "Crime and U.S. Agriculture." Paper presented at the Crime in Rural Virginia Conference, Blacksburg, Virginia.

Christiansen, Karl O. 1970. "Industrialization and urbanization in relation to crime and juvenile delinquency." In Daniel Glazer (editor), *Crime in the City*. New York: Harper and Row.

Clinard, Marshall. 1944. "Rural criminal offenders." *American Journal of Sociology* 50:38–45.

Cohen, Lawrence E., and Marcus Felson. 1977. "Social change and crime rate trends." *American Sociological Review* 44(August):588–607.

Dailey, George H., Jr., Gary J. Stangler, and Rex R. Campbell. 1977. "Migration to the Ozarks: The aging migrant." Paper presented at the annual meetings of the Rural Sociological Society, Madison, Wisconsin.

Dinitz, Simon. 1973. "Progress, crime, and the folk ethic: Portrait of a small town." *Criminology* 11(May):3–21.

Donnermeyer, Joseph F., and G. Howard Phillips. 1980. "The nature of vandalism among rural youth." Paper presented at the annual meetings of the Rural Sociological Society, Ithaca, New York.

Fischer, Claude S. 1980. "The spread of violent crime from city to countryside, 1955 to 1975." *Rural Sociology* 45(Fall):416–434.

Footlick, Jerrold K., Paul Brinkley-Rogers, and Chris Harper. 1979. "Crime on the farm." *Newsweek* (October 3).

Gibbons, Don C. 1972. "Crime in the hinterland." *Criminology* 10:177–191.

Gillin, John L., and Reuben L. Hill. 1940. "Rural/urban aspects of adult probation in Wisconsin." *Rural Sociology* 5(3):314–326.

Glaser, Daniel. 1956. "Criminality theories and behavioral images." *American Journal of Sociology* 61:433–444.

Glenn, Stephen H. 1979. "Education for alternative behavior." Paper presented as keynote address at the First Annual Southeast Drug Conference, Athens, Georgia.

Jones, Charles. 1979. "Crimes against Virginia rural electric cooperatives." Paper presented at the Crime in Rural Virginia Conference, Blacksburg, Virginia.

Koebernick, Tom, and J. Allan Beegle. 1978. "Migration of the elderly to rural areas: A case study in Michigan." In Agricultural Experiment Station, Michigan State University (editors), *Patterns of Migration and Population Change in America's Heartland*. East Lansing, Michigan: Agricultural Experiment Station, Michigan State University, Research Report 344.

McCorkle, Lloyd W., and Richard E. Korn. 1959. *Criminology and Penology*. New York: Henry Holt and Co.

Napier, Ted L., Timothy J. Carter, and M. Christine Pratt. 1980. "Correlates of alcohol and marijuana use among rural high school students." Paper presented at the annual meetings of the Rural Sociological Society, Ithaca, New York.

Natalino, Kathleen W. 1979. "A rural/urban comparison of delinquency, home factors, and peer group involvement." Paper presented at the annual meetings of the North Central Sociological Association, Akron, Ohio.

Newman, Oscar. 1973. *Defensible Space*. New York: Macmillan Co.

Phillips, G. Howard. 1976. *Rural Crime and Rural Offenders*. Columbus, Ohio: Cooperative Extension Service, Ohio State University, EB-613.

Phillips, G. Howard, and Joseph F. Donnermeyer. 1980a. "Extent of crime against farm retailers and suggested remedies." In M. E. Cravens and Susan Sullivan (editors), *Proceedings: Twentieth Annual Ohio Roadside Marketing Conference*.

______. 1980b. "Rural crime." Paper presented at the annual meetings of the Rural Sociological Society, Ithaca, New York.

Phillips, G. Howard, George M. Kreps, and Cathy Wright Moody. 1976. *Environmental Factors in Rural Crime*. Wooster, Ohio: Agricultural Research and Development Center, Ohio State University, Research Circular 224.

Phillips, G. Howard, Todd W. Wurschmidt, and Joseph F. Donnermeyer. 1980. "The Ohio rural victimization study." *Newsline* (Rural Sociological Society) 8(January):26–31.

Polk, Kenneth. 1969. "Delinquency and community action in nonmetropolitan areas." In Donald R. Cressey and David A. Ward (editors), *Delinquency, Crime, and Social Process*. New York: Harper and Row.

Reckless, Walter C. 1967. *The Crime Problem*. New York: Appleton-Century-Crofts.

Smith, Brent L. 1979. "Criminal victimization in rural areas: An analysis of victimization patterns and reporting trends." West Lafayette, Indiana: Purdue University. Doctoral dissertation.

Steffensmeier, Darrell J., and Charlene Jordan. 1978. "Changing patterns of female crimes in rural America, 1962–1975." *Rural Sociology* 43(1):87–102.

Thomas, Donald W., and Douglas C. Bachtel. 1978. *The Rural Turnaround in Southern Ohio: A Five-County Study*. Columbus, Ohio: Department of Agricultural Economics and Rural Sociology, Ohio State University, ESO 514.

U.S. Department of Commerce (Bureau of the Census). 1978. *Farm Population of the United States, 1977*. Washington, D.C.: U.S. Government Printing Office, Current Population Report, Series P-27, 51.

U.S. Department of Justice (Federal Bureau of Investigation). 1959–1979. *Crime in the U.S.: Uniform Crime Reports*. Washington, D.C.: U.S. Government Printing Office.

U.S. Department of Justice (Law Enforcement Assistance Administration). 1974. *A Partnership for Crime Control*. Washington, D.C.: U.S. Government Printing Office.

U.S. Department of Justice (Law Enforcement Assistance Administration). 1979. *Criminal Victimization in the United States: A National Crime Survey Report*. Washington, D.C.: U.S. Government Printing Office.

Warren, Roland. 1978. *The Community in America*. Chicago: Rand McNally and Co.

Part 5
THE COMMUNITY

Aside from the family farm, no aspect of rural life is bestowed with greater nostalgia, images of social harmony, and old-fashioned virtue than is the rural community. Because it is small, the rural community is romanticized as a place with no identity crisis. It is seen as a place where sharing and caring are a way of life and where democratic decision making has prevailed. In a world where social commentary seems devoted to the narcissistic society, the schizophrenic society, and the third wave, the "quest for community" often focuses on an idealized rural community. This quest is the response to uncertainty, change, impersonal bureaucracies, and the prevalence of acquaintanceship over friendships.

Thus, it is not surprising that residential preferences, the topic of Chapter 24 by Zuiches, has emerged as a significant area of research. Nor is it surprising that one of the important findings of this research is that given a choice, the majority of American citizens would prefer to live in smaller towns and cities. The surprise is that the research questions now being asked are so different from what they were in the early 1970s. At that time, the focus was on explaining the discrepancy between where people lived and where they wanted to live. Now, based on findings that preferences are related to migration, research has evolved into a substantial effort to incorporate preferences into models that better predict migration.

Chapter 25, by Goudy and Ryan, looks directly at the functioning of rural communities. Noting the proliferation of community studies in this century and the near demise of such research during the last two decades, they argue the case for a resurgence of community research and specify directions it should take.

Chapter 26, by Christenson, looks at community in quite a different way, i.e., as an arena for action aimed at improving the human condition. Efforts to bring about community change have given rise to the community development profession and produced a different type of research needs. The needs specified by Christenson identify the processes by which people work to improve the communities in which they live.

The remaining three chapters of this section are broader than community. The fact that they appear here is symbolic of the inner penetration of community and society that has occurred in the last half century.

Burdge's chapter on needs assessment surveys for decision makers (Chapter 27) traces the development of such surveys from within community activities to regional and statewide ventures. The methods he describes are critical for assisting local government in their capacity-building efforts and are likely to remain so. The rapid development of types of needs assessment surveys and methods for conducting them opens a host of research issues not even imagined a short ten years ago.

Eberts' chapter on social indicators of well-being (Chapter 28) describes a research area the impetus for which clearly developed at the national level but whose ramifications are being keenly felt by local communities. In this chapter, Eberts describes the progress made in measuring people's well-being throughout the country. Among the research issues placed on the agenda is the need of getting better community-by-community comparisons, which are critical to meeting research needs identified in many of the preceding chapters.

The final chapter in this section, Chapter 29, describes social impact assessment, a research area created by government. Technically, it does not have a community focus. Practically, it is responsible for much of the ongoing research on how community life is impacted by large-scale developments of a technological society – developments that are beyond the power of individual communities to resist.

Together, these five chapters consider major lines of research now underway. The results of this research will substantially influence the quality of life that communities will be capable of providing to their residents in the coming decades.

24
Residential Preferences

JAMES J. ZUICHES

Research interest in residential preferences emerged in the early 1970s, the result of a puzzling discrepancy between attitudes and behavior. Several national polls had shown that most Americans, if given a choice, would live in rural places. Analysis of migration statistics, however, showed that metropolitan areas, and especially the suburbs, were growing at the expense of most rural regions of the United States.

Research was undertaken to explain this discrepancy. Results from these studies were used in formulating population redistribution proposals aimed at directing movers away from large urban centers. The original policy thrust of these research efforts was short-lived, however. By the mid-1970s, a dramatic migration turnaround, described in Chapter 3, had occurred. Net immigration into the nonmetropolitan counties of America was beginning. Research interest then shifted to examining the role of locational preferences in migration decisions and the contribution of preferences to the turnaround. The possibility of preferences being a significant influence on individuals' decisions to migrate brought with it a sobering realization. Studies of residential preferences had only scratched the surface of an issue that would be of continued importance in shaping the population distribution pattern of the United States during the remainder of the twentieth century.

Many research issues flow from this realization. It is now clear that

James J. Zuiches is director of the sociology program of the National Science Foundation, Washington, D.C. He is currently on leave from the Department of Sociology, Michigan State University, East Lansing, Michigan, where he is an associate professor. He has published numerous articles and bulletins in the areas of demography, energy use, and community studies.

This is a Michigan Agricultural Experiment Station Journal Article Number 9790. John

analysis of community size preferences was only a first step in understanding residential preferences. In the late 1970s, researchers began to focus on a fuller range of community attributes. Now, unraveling what residential preferences mean to people, what leads to certain preferences and contributes to their achievement, and the connection of preferences to community population change are part of the research agenda for the 1980s. What are the community attributes valued by residents and nonresidents? How is community satisfaction and attachment related to stability or out-migration? Are these attitudes strongly held? Do they change? What should be the weight given idealized preferences in determining policies about community development, land use, or service delivery? Answers to these questions could help shape the kinds of communities in which Americans can realize the quality of life to which they aspire.

CURRENT RESEARCH

In an earlier effort to define the issues, Dillman (1973) suggested five research topics that organize the existing literature and provide the direction for further work. Using these topics as a basis for review provides a real sense of the research accomplishments during the 1970s.

Locational Preferences of Americans

All surveys of preferences, from the early Harris and Gallup polls to the more detailed national, regional, state, and local surveys, indicate that small towns and rural areas are the first choice of Americans; large cities are the choice of fewer people than now reside there and are the least preferred choice. The crucial addition of proximity to a large city used by Zuiches and Fuguitt (1972), Dillman and Dobash (1972), and others, dramatically clarified this result by showing that the especially desirable locations are small in size but within the commuting periphery of a larger place. Since these metro ring areas were those growing through in-migration, the discrepancy between attitudes and behavior was resolved. By considering proximity to a city, it was shown that preferences, in the aggregate, *might* be indicators of redistribution trends. Another result of these studies was that simple size-of-place ques-

Wardwell, Andrew Sofranko, Glenn Fuguitt, Edwin Carpenter, Carl Fredrickson, and other anonymous reviewers provided helpful and much appreciated suggestions. Statements in this chapter do not represent or imply any National Science Foundation policy or program interest in this research.

tions could no longer be regarded as adequate measures of locational preference.

Preferred Community Attributes

People who preferred smaller communities typically gave the following reasons: less crime, better quality air and water, better life for family and children, lower cost of living, and better community spirit, pride, participation, and friendliness. People preferring to live in larger cities gave as their reasons: higher wages, better jobs, more varied interpersonal contacts, greater availability of services, and better recreational and cultural opportunities. Research also showed that residents valued the attributes provided by their preferred location (Fuguitt and Zuiches, 1975; Dillman and Dobash, 1972; Dillman, 1979; Blackwood and Carpenter, 1978; Sofranko and Williams, 1980).

The value placed upon noneconomic amenities, defined as quality-of-life conditions or public goods in rural areas, is consistently reported in national, state, and local studies. Additionally, surveys of recent in-migrants to rural areas in Maine, Oregon, the Ozarks, and the Midwest corroborate the importance of these quality-of-life conditions as reasons for migration. Although migration is typically undertaken to improve one's economic well-being, these studies suggested that improvements in social, political, and interpersonal well-being may be of greater significance than improvements in income or occupational opportunities. Stevens (1980), for example, found that rural Oregon in-migrants sacrificed significant levels of income for air quality and public safety. People believed that these amenities were more available in rural areas. Williams and McMillan (1980) found that prior residence, proximity to friends or relatives, and other noneconomic linkages to rural areas helped to explain Midwestern rural in-migration. Models of migration which incorporate location-specific human capital variables seem to more fully capture the reasons underlying the migration turnaround than do simple economic or demographic models (DaVanzo, 1980).

Change in Societal Structure

Zelinsky (1974), in a prescient article, argued strongly that conditions had changed in postindustrial society and "the increasingly free exercise of individual preferences as to values, pleasures, self-improvement, social and physical habitat, and general lifestyle . . . may have begun to alter the spatial attributes of society" (Zelinsky, 1974:144). Wardwell (1977) and Carpenter (1977) have specified some of those structural changes: the decentralization of manufacturing and increased service sector employment in nonmetro areas, rising disposable income, earlier retirement, and greater retirement benefits. All of these changes lessen the constraints on mobility and increase the likelihood of realizing one's locational preferences.

These structural changes underpin the postmigration studies of retirees as well as youth and family mobility. If migration to rural areas is related to amenity selection or family linkages, expected stability is quite high. When migration is job-related, those migrants who are young, well educated, and employed expect to move again and often prefer an urban destination (Zuiches, 1981). While the structural conditions have been changing, Zuiches and Rieger (1978) and Cosby and Howard (1976) have also shown that preferences can change. Over the last two decades, rural youths have increased their preference for a rural residence. Rural-to-urban migrants have modified previous preferences in the wake of residential experiences and life cycle changes. Other surveys of preferences under various conditions, such as income losses, extensive commuting, inadequacy of services, and social or recreational opportunities, also show that preferences can be altered. As new in-migrants experience rural settings, commitment can be expected to vary according to the congruence of personal desires, individual and familial characteristics, and structural conditions.

Satisfaction, Preference, and Mobility

Previous research indicates that dissatisfaction with one's community is an important antecedent to an individual's desire to move. For people dissatisfied with their current residence, residential preferences and the community attributes associated with them provide the basis for searching for a new location, comparing locations, and selecting one. Many longitudinal studies of rural youth have provided clear evidence of the linkages between being dissatisfied, expecting to move, and actually moving (see Zuiches, 1981, for a review of these studies). Two recent studies have shown the connection between dissatisfaction and preferences; each attitude contributes independently to the intention to move (Heaton et al., 1979; Fredrickson et al., 1980). Longitudinal surveys of recent migration by DeJong and Sell (1977) and Zuiches and Rieger (1978) further strengthen the case that preferences are associated with destination choice. However, the short time frame and limited generalizability of these studies means that considerable work remains to demonstrate that people are acting on their preferences.

Population Distribution Policy and Public Opinion

A reason that preference surveys were first done was to link public policy on population distribution to the needs and desires of the public for community and housing options. Specific policies for community development, such as tax incentives, job relocation, and improvements in health, education, and public services, were associated with population distribution policies for dispersal, growth centers, new towns, and urban revitalization. Dispersal and growth center advocates often used results, e.g., a majority preference for rural areas and small towns in the Gallup and Harris polls, to support their case. Preference survey results with the proximity question (Zuiches and Fuguitt, 1972; Dillman and Dobash, 1972) contradicted the dispersal and growth center case. Further, it became clear that if preferences were translated into migration, cities would continue to lose population, suburban rings would experience further growth, and nonmetro areas would grow by retaining current residents and attracting new in-migrants. The dilemma of public policy, then, is that in an advanced industrial society where the structural disadvantages of rural areas have been lessened, policies must cope with voluntary migration that is increasingly influenced by attitudes about aesthetic features, amenities, and other noneconomic attributes. Similarly, the larger proportions of elderly, smaller family, and single-person households now in the United States affect policy formulation. New policies that focus on coping with particular community conditions ought to be considered. These conditions include decline as well as rapid growth, services for the aged as well as young families, and meeting the needs of the current residents as well as new in-migrants.

The use of residential preferences for policy determination and as an explanatory factor in the migration turnaround has meant increasing interest in the meaning of preferences. Knowledge of these attitudes and their association with life cycle changes and structural changes in the community and society takes on added theoretical and political significance.

RESEARCH ISSUES

The migration literature is filled with theoretical models of movement among regions, metro areas, labor markets, and communities. The community literature abounds with discussions of the "good" community. The study of residential preferences brings these two issues together, with its focus on ideal community characteristics in the context of household and individual decisions about migration. Ritchey (1976) has identified studies that include preferences, moving plans, and community attributes as "cognitive-behavioral." Very few studies have adequately integrated attributes of places in migration decisions or have used follow-up surveys to determine the adequacy of this approach; a comprehensive study needs to be done. The following discussion outlines research pertinent to such a project.

Measurement of Preferences

Research is needed on the measurement of preferences, including problems of question wording and ordering, validity and reliability, and replication. When a 1976 Gallup survey had one word changed in its standard size-of-place preference question (from "farm" to "rural area"), a 50 percent increase in preferences for rural areas was reported. Researchers using Dillman's community formulation and Fuguitt-Zuiches' dual set of size-location questions have found internally consistent results, but these questions were not comparable. No one has yet developed measures comparable to census categories for purposes of comparing redistribution expectations with actual patterns. Simply equating "rural" with "nonmetro" and "suburbs" with "the metro area outside a central city" is completely inadequate. If studies are going to link attitudes with place characteristics and migration to the place, we must be able to identify consistently the spatial and demographic attributes of the place in a manner understandable to survey respondents.

Research on the broader meaning of community preferences needs to be done in order to determine the subjective and objective attributes of the ideal community. A person's preferred place of residence is probably a composite of many factors: region of the country, distance from relatives, quality of the schools, recreational amenities, density of housing, racial or ethnic composition, etc. Each of these place attributes could contribute to the decision to stay or move. Therefore, each needs to be evaluated to determine the implications of the present satisfaction and willingness to accept tradeoffs for the growth or decline of specific communities. Stevens (1980), in an innovative survey of rural Oregon inmigrants, demonstrated the acceptable tradeoffs between income preferences and preferences for public goods (in this case, public safety, clean air and water, and low population densities). Additional studies should evaluate the tradeoffs in housing, schools, other amenities, and community services.

Individual and Household Characteristics

More research is needed on how individual and household characteristics influence preferences. Although social demographers have incorporated age, sex, race, community attachment, employment status, family size, home ownership, and duration of residence in models of migration, the linkage of these characteristics with preferences needs to be expanded. In order to understand the dimensions of locational choice, studies ought to focus on specific subgroups of the population (i.e., the aged and the young, primary and return migrants, the employed and the unemployed, whites and Blacks, and individuals and families).

Community and Place Attributes

Research ought to examine the possible influence of geographic place attributes on the directional flows of migration and a place's record of population change. In addition to the ideals people hold for community, geographic locales possess subjective and objective characteristics that contribute to their viability and potential for growth. Fredrickson (1980) has argued that two previously unconsidered community attributes should be tied to individual preference rankings: locational stereotypes, and the advantage of early discovery. Each of these features is hypothesized to affect a place's ability to attract differential numbers and types of people. MacRae and Carlson (1980) also used measures of collective preferences for states, which, even after controlling for economic differentials in wages, income, and labor force structure, played an important and significant part in predicting net in-migration.

Societal Characteristics

Research is needed on how changing societal conditions affect the development and realization of preferences. Changes in the structural aspects of the economy, income, and labor force and in the technology for transportation and communication seem to be associated with the increased achievement of preferences. Since changes in individual and aggregate preferences will have serious consequences for migration patterns, what are the future structural changes that might affect migration? Particularly, what is the effect of rising energy prices? Will this lead to a reconcentration in metro areas, or will it restore a central place hierarchy in rural areas regardless of locational preferences? Regional variations in preferences have not been previously considered. Yet, significant streams of migration flow from north to south. As energy prices escalate, regional variations in climate, population density, and energy availability will have a definite effect on the achievement of preferences. If one of the structural changes facilitating the living-out of preferences is the locational patterns of industry and public institutions, further research ought to examine the decision-making process for employers and correlate locational plans of firms with those of the labor force. The interaction between economic and noneconomic factors in population redistribution remains to be understood.

Policy Studies

Policy questions in need of research include (1) What do people really want from their communities, and (2) Who is responsible for satisfying these desires? Surveys of preferences, especially those that go beyond the minimum size-of-location attributes of a place, provide insight into the kinds of services and lifestyles desired by people and their commitment to obtaining them. We also need to determine the acceptable threshholds for satisfaction and the appropriate mix of services. Case studies of local issue resolution may be more beneficial than large-scale surveys to understand the mechanisms and processes by which policy decisions get made, and the local consequences of those decisions. The role of federal, state, and county governments needs to be considered because these larger political units are already involved in decisions about land use, sewage disposal, water supplies, and industrial plant locations. Such decisions often determine the growth or decline of a particular community with little input from it.

Organization of a migration and preferences research program that complements the migration studies of current population surveys and other census studies could provide the basis for integrating structural, social-psychological, and aggregate analysis. Complementing large-scale national and state surveys with in-depth small-area studies would provide a valuable counterpoint. National estimates of mobility trends would be complemented with the detailed insight of the others.

CONCLUSION

Fundamentally, residential preferences are expressions about two values of Americans: the geographic environment in which they would like to live, and how they would like their community to be organized–socially, politically, economically, and physically. The demographic interpretation of preferences has provided extensive underpinning for work in migration decision making, population distribution patterns, and policies; the sociological elements remain our challenge. The continued efforts of rural sociologists to study smaller, substate, state, or regional areas need to be encouraged and supported. As migration and population distribution increase in political and sociological importance, the gaps in theoretical understanding and empirical information need attention at both national and local levels.

REFERENCES

Blackwood, L. G., and Edwin H. Carpenter. 1978. "The importance of antiurbanism in determining residential preferences and migration patterns." *Rural Sociology* 43:31–47.

Carpenter, Edwin H. 1977. "The potential for population dispersal: A closer look at residential preferences." *Rural Sociology* 42(Fall):352–370.

Cosby, Arthur G., and William G. Howard. 1976. *Residential Preferences in America: The Growing Desire for Rural Life*. Washington, D.C. Economics, Statistics, and Cooperatives Service, U.S. Department of Agriculture, Rural Development Seminar Series.

DaVanzo, Julie. 1980. *Microeconomic Approaches to Studying Migration Decisions*. Santa Monica, California: Rand Corp., N-1201-NICHD.

DeJong, Gordon F., and Ralph R. Sell. 1977. "Population redistribution, migration, and residential preferences." *Annals* 429:13–144.

Dillman, Don A. 1973. "Population distribution policy and people's attitudes: Current knowledge and needed research." Paper prepared for the Urban Land Institute under a grant from the U.S. Department of Housing and Urban Development.

______ . 1979. "Residential preferences, quality of life, and the population turnaround." *American Journal of Agricultural Economics* 61:960–966.

Dillman, Don A., and Russell P. Dobash. 1972. *Preferences for Community Living and Their Implications for Population Redistribution*. Pullman, Washington: College of Agriculture Research Center, Washington State University, Bulletin 764.

Fredrickson, Carl. 1980. "Toward new theories of aggregate migration behavior." Paper presented at the annual meetings of the Midwest Sociological Association, Milwaukee, Wisconsin.

Fredrickson, Carl, Tim Heaton, Glenn V. Fuguitt, and James J. Zuiches. 1980. "Residential preferences in a model of migration intentions." *Population and Environment* 3(Fall/Winter):280–297.

Fuguitt, Glenn V., and James J. Zuiches. 1975. "Residential preferences and population distribution." *Demography* 12:491–504.

Heaton, Tim, Carl Fredrickson, Glenn V. Fuguitt, and James J. Zuiches. 1979. "Residential preferences, community satisfaction, and the intention to move." *Demography* 16:565–573.

MacRae, Duncan, Jr., and J. R. Carlson. 1980. "Collective preferences as predictors of interstate migration." *Social Indicators Research* 8:15–32.

Ritchey, P. Neal. 1976. "Explanations of migration." In Alex Inkeles (editor), *Annual Review of Sociology*. Palo Alto, California: Annual Reviews, Inc.

Sofranko, Andrew J., and James D. Williams (editors). 1980. *Rebirth of Rural America: Rural Migration in the Midwest*. Ames, Iowa: North Central Regional Center for Rural Development, Iowa State University.

Stevens, Joe B. 1980. "The demand for public goods as a factor in the nonmetropolitan migration turnaround." In David L. Brown and John M. Wardwell (editors), *New Directions in Urban-Rural Migration*. New York: Academic Press.

Wardwell, John M. 1977. "Equilibrium and change in nonmetropolitan growth." *Rural Sociology* 42:156–179.

Williams, James D., and David B. McMillan. 1980. "Migration decision-making among nonmetropolitan-bound migrants." In David L. Brown and John M. Wardwell (editors), *New Directions in Urban-Rural Migration*. New York: Academic Press.

Zelinsky, Wilbur. 1974. "Selfward bound? Personal preference patterns and the changing map of American society." *Economic Geography* 50:144–179.

Zuiches, James J. 1981. "Residential preferences in the United States." In Amos H. Hawley and Sara M. Mazie (editors), *Toward an Understanding of Nonmetropolitan America*. Chapel Hill, North Carolina: University of North Carolina Press.

Zuiches, James J., and Glenn V. Fuguitt. 1972. "Residential preferences: Implications for population redistribution in nonmetropolitan areas." In Sara Mills Mazie (editor of Volume 5), U.S. Commission on Population Growth and the American Future (editors), *Population, Distribution, and Policy*. Washington, D.C.: U.S. Government Printing Office.

Zuiches, James J., and Jon R. Rieger. 1978. "Size-of-place preferences and life cycle migration: A cohort comparison." *Rural Sociology* 43(Winter):618–633.

25
Changing Communities

WILLIS J. GOUDY
VERNON D. RYAN

Word of the demise of small-town America has been greatly exaggerated. Once thought to have lost significance in modern society, the small community has not only survived but, as Zuiches reports in Chapter 24, has become the preferred place to live for a majority of Americans. This has occurred because small communities have kept their residential and social functions despite losing many of their commercial functions (McGranahan, 1980). Yet, because most recent research has been conducted in urban rather than rural areas, we know little about the magnitude of change in small communities, its direction, and its effects. Indeed, whether the characteristics of a small community influence the attitudes, behaviors, and well-being of residents remains relatively untested, as does the assumption that resident characteristics somehow influence the community. We are without basic cumulative knowledge that would aid in making decisions about policies and programs affecting changing rural communities.

THE COMMUNITY STUDY LEGACY

There is a rich tradition of community studies in rural sociology, a history that provides a unique opportunity to learn from the past. This legacy began with the work of Galpin (1915) in the early 1900s. Emulated by numerous others, it still influences the work of rural

Willis J. Goudy is a professor in the Department of Sociology and Anthropology, Iowa State University, Ames, Iowa. Currently editor of *Rural Sociologist*, he has published numerous articles about community attributes, relationships between research and action in community development, and the transition from work to retirement. **Vernon D. Ryan**

sociologists. Case studies of specific locales were highlighted in many early agriculture experiment station bulletins and were reported in *Rural Sociology*. In these early studies, many different aspects of community life were described, often using the various local institutions (e.g., family, education, religion, commerce, recreation) as the framework for analysis.

In the late 1930s, the Bureau of Agricultural Economics of the USDA asked rural social scientists to conduct a series of community studies in various sections of the country using the same methodology (see, for example, Leonard and Loomis, 1941; or Moe and Taylor, 1942). These studies provided ample evidence of differences among rural American communities. Another comparative study of that time (Goldschmidt, 1947) examined the effects of corporate farming on small communities (see Chapter 33). Unfortunately, these reports signaled an end to comprehensive community studies and the start of a trend toward examination of specific attributes (e.g., power, participation in voluntary associations, principles of social action) of a single locale. The culmination of this trend was the proliferation of studies of community power structures.

This change in focus, which really became an exercise in studying specific events occurring within a community rather than examining the community itself, soon affected other areas of research (e.g., service delivery and satisfaction, industrialization, quality of life). Except for a few publications, fragmentation characterized most community research in the 1950s and 1960s. Indeed, the situation was such that Summers et al. (1970:218) called for the "renewal of community sociology" at the beginning of the 1970s. Unfortunately, this call for cumulative knowledge about communities was not heeded by most community researchers.

RESEARCH ISSUES

Small communities are being affected differentially by changes related to such factors as the population turnaround, rural industrialization, and the current energy crisis. These factors can be examined within the framework of four research needs that seem to be of paramount importance: community decision making, community attachment, community development, and comparative community studies.

---

is associate professor, Department of Sociology and Anthropology, Iowa State University, Ames. His research has focused on rural communities in the context of community development strategies.

Community Decision Making

Renewed research is needed on the forces that affect how community decisions take place. The communities of the 1980s bear little resemblance to those of the 1950s and early 1960s, from which our knowledge of who controls community decisions was derived. More decisions are made outside the community in line with Warren's (1978) description of the greater importance of ties with organizations located elsewhere. It seems likely that governmental employees are now more influential in these decisions because of their linkages with federal, state, and regional agencies. Also, it seems likely that women are playing a more significant role in small-town power structures (Bokemeier and Tait, 1980). If many small towns are no longer run by a "boss" or "triumvirate" (Vidich and Bensman, 1958), we need to determine the magnitude and consequences of this transition.

Two other forces influence local participation in decision making in rural communities. First, the population turnaround is adding to communities residents who may wish to participate in local affairs. This, in turn, may mobilize long-time residents to join the action. Thus, we have an opportunity to understand the persistence with which local elites attempt to maintain control in the face of recent migrants who presumably have different values and goals. Whether the power structure changes is itself an issue about which we have little data (Nix et al., 1977).

The second force influencing local decision making involves the decline in people's trust of local leadership. During the last decade, confidence in the entire American political system declined noticeably. With growing economic and energy concerns, trust in government and those who govern continues to fade. As part of this erosion, local governments find it increasingly difficult to withstand the pressures exerted by local constituents; this, in turn, steers qualified candidates away from elected and appointed public offices. Thus, we need to determine what changes, if any, have occurred in patterns of local participation and decision making as a result of these changes in attitudes toward governance. Shifts in decision making at the local level should influence relationships among groups and institutions within the community, but the magnitude of the effect is not known.

The influence of decisions about a community by units outside local boundaries continues to grow, resulting in less community autonomy. The attempt to treat all small communities the same often means that decisions are not appropriate for specific local communities. In addition, the external affiliations of many community organizations produce internal fragmentation, i.e., an absence of community cohesion and informal mechanisms for getting things done. Despite the difficulties associated with the determining influence of forces outside of local control, there is little prospect of returning to the past, although more local autonomy recently has been prescribed (Sundquist, 1969). The alternative, therefore, is to determine appropriate procedures for taking into account the influence of external forces in local decision making to assure outcomes that are in the community's best interest. Rural sociologists, with their long-standing tradition of community studies, should direct more research attention to developing and evaluating coordination strategies for enabling communities to balance local needs with external constraints.

Thus, the effect of decision making both within and outside the local community deserves increased attention. A fundamental issue is to identify the types of decisions that are more effectively made at the community level in comparison with those requiring a larger coordination base. The influence on community viability should be determined. It is also important to know how a community can assess the effect of external factors—what information is needed and how it should be obtained.

Community Attachment

Research is needed on how community attachment contributes to local quality of life, local decisions, local development efforts, and the maintenance of community groups and institutions. Community was once thought of as a place where people could and typically did satisfy most of their basic needs. More and more, residents make lifestyle choices that are independent of the local community. Transportation, media, and other factors have broadened residents' horizons so that they have options for work, play, and participation beyond those supplied by their own communities. Because of these alternatives, attachment to the local community may dwindle, leading to concern for a loss of the "sense of community."

But little is known about the consequences of different levels of community attachment on either residents or the community itself. The concept of attachment, whether measured as an attitudinal expression of local solidarity or in terms of participation in community activities, has only recently received the attention of community researchers (Buttel et al., 1979). Yet, programs continue to surface in the name of strengthening community identity and commitment.

Three areas deserve added research. First, there is a need to determine more conclusively the relationship between community attachment and human welfare. Little is known about the influence of attachment as a community characteristic on the incidence of crime, school drop-out rates, and other indexes commonly used as indicators of local quality of life. Unless attachment is shown to have positive effects on quality of life, there is little justification for programs directed at strengthening community attachment. Second, as community attachment expands or diminishes, changes may occur in who makes decisions at the local level and who benefits. If such a relationship exists, a stronger case can be made for greater emphasis on the community attachment component of community development. Finally, assuming relationships are found on the above two research issues, community attachment needs to be evaluated as either an outcome or a constraining factor of programs affecting rural communities. To achieve this, rural sociologists should examine the impact of specific intervention programs, which vary greatly in strategy and purpose, on community attachment.

To illustrate the potential importance of community attachment, Hirschman (1973) presents a model demonstrating that attachment (or loyalty, as he calls it) can serve a socially useful purpose of preventing organizational deterioration. Applying his model to a community setting, rural sociologists might explain why some communities manage to overcome major setbacks while others cannot. Thus, attachment may serve as a catalyst for solving problems at the community level as well as becoming an integral target of programs focusing on rural community development.

Community Development

Additional research is required to answer questions about relationships between community structure and community development efforts, variables leading to the success or failure of development programs, and differences between communities selecting various development strategies. (Additional community development research issues are developed in Chapter 26.) Effrat (1973:1) describes the attempt to define community as "like trying to scoop up jello with your fingers. You can get hold of some but there's always more slipping away from you." Adding the term *development* to community compounds the problem because it too is an illusive concept. One view of community development defines it as any purposive action attempting to improve the community so that a better environment is available to residents. Because "better" must be defined before improvement can be attempted, community development should be recognized as a normative concept. The "ideal" or "good" community, often used to establish a purpose for community development programs, has "effective structures and processes which make the community adaptive to its changing environment and the changing needs and desires of its citizens" (Nix, 1977:3). Any attempts to improve the effectiveness of these structures and processes are therefore thought of as community development.

At present, little is known about the effects of alternative development strategies on the working relationships that occur among community groups and organizations. Evaluation research that studies communities before and after development efforts is required. To conduct such research, a good understanding of the intended consequences of development programs on factors such as patterns of participation, communication, and organizational coordination is needed. However, this is more difficult than it would seem. Only a few authors, including Wilkinson (1972), Nix (1977), Warren (1978), and Kaufman (1979), have outlined community development from a theoretical perspective. Both the development of appropriate theories and before/after studies of the implementation of specific development strategies must therefore be completed if the community itself is to be recognized as an important target of community development programs.

Other issues should help guide research in this area. For example, the effectiveness of programs offering outside technical and/or financial assistance for doing local community development work should be examined. Research is needed to determine the type of information that is most pertinent to community development. Because both problems and decision-making capabilities vary from one community to another, sources of information and diffusion processes used on state and national levels may not be appropriate at the local level. Until more research is completed in these areas, the effectiveness of community development programs will be more a matter of speculation than of fact.

Comparative Community Studies

Comparative community studies are needed to determine the diversity of rural community situations and to test potential policies in these different environments through simulations and experimental implementation of action programs. Although case studies can yield useful information, especially for those in community development, they add little to the basic data needed to test propositions about communities themselves. This lack of cumulative data underlies all other research issues on the changing community (Summers et al., 1970) and leads to situations in which communities of a certain population size are frequently thought to be similar because of similarity on that one variable—population size.

Comparative community studies should include three dimensions: examination of numerous communities, longitudinal collection of information, and the use of a variety of research techniques. Rural sociologists typically employ both quantitative and qualitative research methods; multiple methods must be encouraged because results may vary somewhat depending on the technique used. But even using the same method in one community at various points in time would add to our knowledge about changing rural communities. There is much to be learned despite many prior contributions by rural sociologists (e.g.,

Smith, 1974; Richardson and Larson, 1976; Nix et al., 1977; Murdock and Schriner, 1978; McGranahan, 1980; Bokemeier and Tait, 1980). For example, changes produced by such important factors as rural industrialization or the population turnaround tend to be available from only a few community case studies.

Some information already exists from which comparative data sets could be constructed. For example, census and other secondary sources can be tapped to generate data for samples of rural communities at various time periods. With the 1980 U.S. Census data, social and economic information of interest to rural sociologists will be readily available on far more small communities, making it easier to conduct comparative community research similar to that reported by urban sociologists for standard metropolitan statistical areas. But additional data on attitudinal and behavioral aspects of people and organizations will still need to be gathered and aggregated. This information will complement that available from secondary sources and make possible comparisons among types of communities such as those gaining, remaining the same, or losing population.

This final research issue—the creation and analysis of comparative rural community data files—is the key to increasing contributions to policy decisions regarding changing communities. Meeting this challenge will allow joining some elements of previous studies, such as the comparative focus exemplified by the 1941–1943 series of rural life studies and the comprehensive examinations of entire small communities completed by early rural sociologists, with recent advances in research techniques. Such data sets will provide researchers sufficient opportunities to answer questions related to policy, to predict more accurately the form and extent of future change within and across rural communities, and to design meaningful experiments for intervention programs.

REFERENCES

Bokemeier, Janet L., and John L. Tait. 1980. "Women as power actors: A new trend in rural communities." *Rural Sociology* 45:238–255.

Buttel, Frederick H., Oscar B. Martinson, and E. A. Wilkening. 1979. "Size of place and community attachment: A reconsideration." *Social Indicators Research* 6:475–485.

Effrat, Marcia Pelly. 1973. "Approaches to community: Conflicts and complementarities." *Sociological Inquiry* 43:1–32.

Galpin, C. J. 1915. *The Social Anatomy of an Agricultural Community*. Madison, Wisconsin: Agricultural Experiment Station, University of Wisconsin, Research Bulletin 34.

Goldschmidt, Walter. 1947. *As You Sow*. Glencoe, Illinois: Free Press. Reprinted in 1973 with Part III added. Montclair, New Jersey: Allanheld, Osmun, and Co.

Hirschman, Albert O. 1973. *Exit, Voice, and Loyalty: Further Reflections and a Survey of Recent Contributions.* Cambridge: Harvard Institute of Economic Research, Harvard University, Discussion Paper 281.

Kaufman, Harold F. 1979. "The activity field – A perspective for community development." In Dan A. Chekki (editor), *Community Development: Theory and Method of Planned Change.* New Delhi, India: Vikas Press.

Leonard, Olen, and C. P. Loomis. 1941. *Culture of a Contemporary Rural Community: El Cerrito, New Mexico.* Washington, D.C.: Bureau of Agricultural Economics, U.S. Department of Agriculture, Rural Life Studies 1.

McGranahan, David A. 1980. "Changing central place activities in northwestern Wisconsin." *Rural Sociology* 45:91–109.

Moe, Edward O., and Carl C. Taylor. 1942. *Culture of a Contemporary Rural Community: Irwin, Iowa.* Washington, D.C.: Bureau of Agricultural Economics, U.S. Department of Agriculture, Rural Life Studies 5.

Murdock, Steven H., and Eldon C. Schriner. 1978. "Structural and distributional factors in community development: A comparative analysis of evidence from four western states." *Rural Sociology* 43:426–449.

Nix, Harold L. 1977. *The Community and Its Involvement in the Study Planning Action Process.* Washington, D.C.: Public Health Service, U.S. Department of Health, Education, and Welfare, Publication 78-8355.

Nix, Harold L., Paula L. Dressel, and Frederick L. Bates. 1977. "Changing leaders and leadership structure: A longitudinal study." *Rural Sociology* 42:22–41.

Richardson, Joseph L., and Olaf F. Larson. 1976. "Small community trends: A fifty-year perspective on social-economic change in thirteen New York communities." *Rural Sociology* 41:45–49.

Smith, T. Lynn. 1974. "Socio-cultural changes in twelve midwestern communities, 1930–1970." *Social Science* 49:195–207.

Summers, Gene F., John P. Clark, and Lauren H. Seiler. 1970. "The renewal of community sociology." *Rural Sociology* 35:218–231.

Sundquist, James L. 1969. *Making Federalism Work.* Washington, D.C.: Brookings Institute.

Vidich, Arthur J., and Joseph Bensman. 1958. *Small Town in Mass Society.* Princeton, New Jersey: Princeton University Press.

Warren, Roland. 1978. *The Community in America.* Chicago: Rand McNally and Co.

Wilkinson, Kenneth P. 1972. "A field-theory perspective for community development research." *Rural Sociology* 37:43–52.

26
Community Development

JAMES A. CHRISTENSON

Community development (CD) has been and will continue to be a major means of problem solving in America. Community development is defined here as the purposive efforts of a group of people in a community to improve their social, economic, or cultural situation (Christenson and Robinson, 1980:26). Such improvements should contribute to the overall public good. However, there are usually costs or hardships imposed on some segments of the community as a result of any type of change (e.g., displacement, relocation, additional taxes, loss of farm land–see Summers, 1977; and Robinson, 1980). Rural sociologists have been particularly concerned about the consequences of change and who benefits from it. Rural sociologists, either directly through research or indirectly through the efforts of trained community development specialists, play a prominent role in addressing the critical community development issues that confront rural America (Phifer et al., 1980).

The forces that shaped rural America and community development strategies to alleviate rural problems are undergoing a substantial change. Issues such as poverty, inadequacy of many public services, declining number of farms, and geographical isolation continue to predominate in rural areas, and new forces have emerged. They include industrial relocation to rural areas, migration from urban areas, increased competition for development monies, and an increase in social pathologies such as rural crime. These trends demand that community

---

James A. Christenson, a professor in the Department of Sociology and director of the Survey Research Center, University of Kentucky, Lexington, is the editor-elect of *Rural Sociology*. He has published extensively on community and community services and is coeditor of the book *Community Development in America*.

Work on this chapter was partially supported by the Kentucky Agriculture Experiment

development practices and philosophies be reassessed and changed, if necessary, to meet the challenges of the 1980s.

Community development becomes even more important in this decade because it can stimulate local initiative by involving people in the process of social and economic change; build channels of communication that promote solidarity; and improve the social, economic, and cultural well-being of community residents. Community development can provide government with a rationale for working in partnership with community leaders to solve various social and economic problems. It takes the burden off government to "do for people." As stated in the 1979 *Small Community and Rural Development Policy*: "The role of the federal government should be to encourage and support the resources and resourcefulness of rural America and to be the partner of its local leaders. Nowhere is the sense of partnership, neighborliness, and shared responsibility more evidenced than in the communities across rural America" (Carter Administration, 1979).

Federal administrators were directed to "make special efforts to provide local citizens and their leaders with the assistance needed for effective community decision making and development efforts" (Carter Administration, 1979:7). President Reagan, in his five-year economic program, called for a cutback in government intervention at the local level, a curtailment of spending increases on many social programs, and a return to people doing for themselves rather than government doing for people. Local initiative and self-reliance in rural development is likely to assume a stronger stature in national policy as a response to citizen support for those values, as reflected in the 1980 election and anticipated cutbacks in many federal subsidy and income transfer programs.

Rural development cannot be equated with community development. The meaning of the two concepts can be debated, but in this chapter we place rural development in the same category as economic development (e.g., rural industrialization). Community development is more concerned with the process of change, particularly how people effect and are affected by planned change. Wilkinson (1979) argues that community development encompasses the humanistic concept of self-actualization. He points out that economic development as a national policy to help people meet primary needs overlooks the overall goal of social well-being. Industry and business can be stimulated to locate in rural areas, but this is more rural economic development than community develop-

---

Station. The critical comments of Vern Ryan, Paul Warner, Louis Swanson, Richard Maurer, Milton Coughenour, and Donald Voth on earlier versions of this chapter are appreciated.

ment. "Economic development without community development can increase the gap between social classes and reduce the expression of natural human tendencies toward interpersonal warmth, cooperativeness, tolerance, and respect. Community development as a purposive activity is needed to realize the potential social well-being benefits of economic development" (Wilkinson, 1979:14).

The humanistic aspects of community development are difficult to document and its outcomes are not easy to measure. Therein lies the challenge! How do we measure the training of a leader and the value of having done so? How do we measure the effect of providing information so that people can choose among alternatives? How do we measure building channels of communication? Community development is extremely important in the 1980s precisely because it works with changes in people and not just with changes in programs and projects. Community development is the process of people improving themselves with a little help from their friends. This is not an excuse to avoid doing research on community development or justification for continued funding. We need to understand, evaluate, and document this humanistic aspect of development.

This chapter discusses critical research needs that involve the ability of people and appropriate tactics to plan, implement, and sustain change in the 1980s. Our focus is on changing conditions in rural America and how these conditions will affect the likelihood of people becoming involved in community development and engaging in efforts to improve humanistic aspects of community life.

Citizen Involvement in Decision-Making

Hans Spiegel (1980) predicts a bifurcation of citizen participation during the 1980s. On the one hand, government, concerned with public support, increasingly mandates citizen participation as an element in all their assistance programs (Voth, 1977). Because these citizen task forces, hearings, and forums exemplify only a ritualistic involvement of citizens, the public is beginning to see this type of citizen participation as futile (see Gittell et al., 1980). On the other hand, some citizens have been forming more autonomous advocacy groups that approach local government more from a confrontation than a partnership perspective. Such advocacy groups manifest a "new localism" to counter public agencies perceived as nonresponsive. Most advocacy groups are comprised of moderate-income people from middle-class residential areas whose financial and psychological situations are in need of enhancement and defense (Spiegel, 1980). Citizen advocacy groups tend to focus on single issues and are often heatedly involved in a community's decision making concerning the provision of goods and services. Such groups tend to represent only a very small segment of the public. But, with financial backing and good organization, advocacy groups are very effective in getting their demands heard and acted upon. Will representation through advocacy groups become the only effective model of action to affect decision making in the years to come?

A new type of public participation in local decision making may be provided through the use of polls, surveys, and other types of solicited feedback. Rural sociologists have experimented with different types of surveys to solicit public input for making local and state decisions. Their pioneering work in developing new efficient and inexpensive methodologies to assess public needs, concerns, goals, and priorities for funding allocation suggests new avenues for public involvement (cf. Chapter 27; see also Dillman, 1972, 1977, 1978; Christenson, 1973, 1975; Goudy, 1975; Burdge and Warner, 1975; Burdge et al., 1978; and Christenson et al., 1979). The technique may vary from mail or telephone surveys to television interactive systems; the point is that modern technology can be used to stimulate public involvement. For example, the Iowa State DIAL system allows communities to get help in conducting small-scale surveys from rural sociologists at a land grant university.

Citizen participation is not synonymous with community development, but it is a means toward realizing the humanistic aspects of community development, for community development can only be sustained effectively through public involvement. Types of citizen participation are part of the larger issue of participation in decision making. Put in a social exchange perspective, the cost of participation today seems to be outweighing the benefits of participation. Costs include the feeling by individuals that their participation has little influence on the decision-making process and the lack of free time (the dramatic increase of women in the labor force and dual-career families tend to restrict discretionary time). Benefits include a sense of fulfillment of a public duty, right of free expression, and a sense of achieving a desired goal. Surveys, polls, and other formalized means of obtaining feedback have their negative side in that they may make public participation illusory, involving the public only indirectly, and may remove a person from deriving a sense of active participation in decision making. But surveys and other involvement enhanced by technological means do diminish the time cost and provide other avenues of participation to offset the growing influence of advocacy groups. *Research is needed to evaluate the social costs and benefits of employing different survey methods or technologies as vehicles of public participation in local decision making and to determine the relationship between the use of public surveys and pressure from advocacy groups in affecting local decision making.*

Renaissance of Self-Help Efforts

Phifer and his associates (1980), in tracing the history of community development, comment on the self-help efforts which have been generated by rural sociologists in the United States. The self-help approach is generally defined as a process of people coming together, examining their situation, designing strategies to deal with problems, and implementing plans to achieve some goals. External assistance, while usually present, is nondirective. Self-help in the United States often has been used interchangeably with community development. However, self-help is only one of three main approaches to community development, the others being the technical assistance, "top-down" approach often used by government, and the confrontation approach often used by those outside traditional lines of power (Christenson, 1980). In the 1960s and 1970s, the federal and state governments assumed a much greater role in "doing for people" through various types of technical and economic assistance. The 1980s are already seeing a decrease in citizen expectation of government to deal effectively with local problems. This is due partly to government complexity, citizens' reactions against rising taxes, and decreasing service manpower. This trend would be heightened if and when the federal government cuts back on programs such as revenue sharing, CETA, CD block grants, and urban renewal programs. The increasing recognition of the limitations of government to "do for people" appears to be stimulating the renaissance of self-help efforts among all segments of the population.

There is an increased demand from people to initiate group efforts such as food cooperatives, community gardens, and the rebirth of volunteerism (e.g., return to volunteer fire departments). Likewise, there needs to be greater involvement of citizens in the provision of local services. The likely result is that the unorganized or politically inactive segments of the population may be excluded from self-help efforts. The renaissance of self-help efforts will probably occur primarily in small towns and urban neighborhood settings. Farmers and the rural nonfarm segment of nonmetropolitan United States may participate to a lesser extent in these self-help efforts because of geographical dispersion, transportation costs, and decline in importance of farm organizations. However, the development of a critical need for specific services could lead to the renaissance of self-help efforts among these groups.

Littrell (1980:69) suggests that today's community development self-help efforts demand a greater concentration on helping people learn new skills of participation (e.g., litigation, grantsmanship, advocacy). "Effective participation is necessary for self-help to occur since it is the participation of people learning to do for themselves that distinguishes the self-help approach from others that assume people must be directed" (Littrell, 1980:69). Public agencies such as the Cooperative Extension Service can and should play a major role in training people to help themselves. Although extension CD specialists have a long tradition of self-help training for community leaders and organizations, the kinds of information provided need to be reassessed in light of the changing economic structure and population characteristics of rural America. *Research is needed to evaluate the relevance of the content of community development training efforts that public agencies provide when working with citizens' groups to implement different self-help efforts.*

Fiscal Crises and Reactive Decision Making

Skill for handling conflict may be the most sought-after ability in local leaders, administrators, planners, and citizen advocates during the 1980s. The declining support to small towns (e.g., revenue-sharing, CETA, CD block grants, eroding tax base, mandated ceilings on tax increases, such as Proposition 13) is changing public agencies from Santa Claus to Uncle Scrooge. Increased pressure is being felt to balance budgets by curtailing services and improving efficiency in most units of government. For example, loss of funds from programs such as CETA would likely cut the number of employees in some government units by as much as one-third. In addition, large-scale resource development projects (e.g., coal gasification plants, nuclear reactors) proposed to generate rural industrial development and energy self-sufficiency will stimulate considerable conflict both from those impacted and from nonlocal advocacy groups. The inability of local government and public agencies to deal with the complexities of intergovernmental programs and regulations, along with the multiplicity of pressure groups, overloads decision-making capacity. Increasingly, local governments are pressured to react to strikes of public employees and specific issues contested by advocacy groups so that management of their fiscally planned programs begins to take a back seat to reactive decision making.

Rural sociologists have conducted some research on crisis management. For example, Robinson and Clifford (1972) have systematized an educational program in process skills, and Robinson (1980) has developed an operational framework on conflict management. In the 1980s, conflict management may be essential for effective local decision making in rural areas. Reactive governmental systems invite conflict as the only avenue to stimulate change. Some of the consequences may be detrimental, while others are beneficial. Conflict will be detrimental if it eliminates the goal attainment possibilities (equality of opportunity, desired quality of life, security, and freedom) of varous groups in society. It can be beneficial if it reduces stagnation, rigidity, or artificial barriers (see Robinson, 1980, for other social and economic costs/benefits of conflict). Warren (1977) has argued that no meaningful change occurs without conflict. Conflict management facilitates increased rationality in discussion, stimulates nonjudgmental communication about feelings and conflict issues, explores alternative group adjustments, helps in securing additional resources to mitigate adversary roles, and seeks to develop incentives for accommodation.

Increasingly, CD agents are getting pulled into conflict situations. In fact, Robinson (1980:90) comments that "management of conflict is probably the most appropriate role for the CD professional." However, most professional CD agents work for organizations that encourage consensus and cooperation. What happens to professionals in their relationships with their employer and other people when they function as conflict managers? Does the person serving as a conflict manager become the scapegoat for both sides? Would extension agents or regional planners working to resolve conflict jeopardize their future efforts with the people involved in community development work? *Two research issues need to be studied: (1) the effect on organizational support, client relationships, and CD professionals when they become involved in conflict management; and (2) the situational and personal factors that contribute to conflict resolution.*

Regional Help for Small Towns

Substate (regional) development organizations (councils of governments, economic development districts, regional planning organizations) are increasingly being used as mechanisms through which the federal government funnels assistance for the development of small cities and towns. The substate development concept was partly conceived to increase participation by leaders of small government units in decisions that affect their localities (Doeksen et al., 1975). For example, small towns generally have no city planners or writers to seek money from federal agencies. Substate organizations were designed in part to help small towns take advantage of federal and state grant opportunities. While the substate concept was not intended to generate another level of government or infringe upon the autonomy of local officials, many officials see them as contributing to a loss of community autonomy.

A recent evaluation of such agencies by rural sociologists (Christenson et al., 1980) reveals that small towns and cities are not taking advantage of substate services because of the structure of the substate organization. Small towns are often excluded from formal membership because of their size. In addition, inadequate record keeping and lack of data about their towns that are required for loan and grant applications inhibit working with substate agency staffs. Fears of losing autonomy are also a concern. The resulting noninvolvement means that many small towns are not getting federal and state assistance for community development efforts. *Research is needed on the developmental implications (including capacity building and autonomy) of participation, or the lack of it, in substate organizations, and to learn how these organizations might be restructured to encourage greater participation.*

CONCLUSION

Change is a pervasive condition of our times, and it will continue. Rural people have the opportunity to effect change or be affected by it. The growing complexity of American society makes it almost impossible for an individual, working alone, to initiate change. But a group of people working together can initiate purposive efforts to improve their social and economic well-being.

The goal of community development is to help "community people to become subjects instead of objects, acting on their stituation instead of simply reacting" (Voth, 1979:75). Community development is concerned with rural improvement and with economic development, but it is primarily concerned with people involvement and humanistic elements of social well-being. To accomplish these goals, *a major research need of the 1980s is to evaluate the broad range of community development efforts in the United States to see which ones are producing tangible results and to evaluate whether the results are meeting expectations.*

REFERENCES

Burdge, Rabel J., Ruth M. Kelly, and Harvey J. Schweitzer. 1978. *Illinois: Today and Tomorrow.* Urbana, Illinois: Cooperative Extension Service, University of Illinois, Special Series 1.

Burdge, Rabel J., and Paul D. Warner. 1975. *Issues Facing Kentucky.* Lexington, Kentucky: Cooperative Extension Service, University of Kentucky.

Carter Administration. 1979. *Small Community and Rural Development Policy.* Washington, D.C.: The White House.

Christenson, James A. 1973. *Through Our Eyes: People's Goals and Needs in North Carolina.* Raleigh, North Carolina: Agricultural Extension Service, North Carolina State University, Publication 106.

———. 1975. *North Carolina: Today and Tomorrow: Quality of Public Services.* Raleigh, North Carolina: Agicultural Extension Service, North Carolina State University.

———. 1980. "Three themes of community development." In James A. Christenson and Jerry W. Robinson, Jr. (editors), *Community Development in America.* Ames, Iowa: Iowa State University Press.

Christenson, James A., and Jerry W. Robinson, Jr. (editors). 1980. *Community Development in America.* Ames, Iowa: Iowa State University Press.

Christenson, James A., Paul D. Warner, McGuire Colliver, and Ron Crouch. 1980. "Are substate R.D. units serving small towns?" *Rural Development Perspectives* 2(March):29–32.

Christenson, James A., Paul D. Warner, and Sue Greer. 1979. "Quality of life in Kentucky counties." *Community Development Issues* 1(1):1–8.

Dillman, Don A. 1972. "Increasing mail questionnaire response in large samples of the general public." *Public Opinion Quarterly* 36(Summer):254–257.

______. 1977. "Preference surveys and policy decisions: Our new tools need not be used in the same old way." *Journal of the Community Development Society* 8(1):30–43.

______. 1978. *Mail and Telephone Surveys: The Total Design Method.* New York: Wiley-Interscience Publications.

Doeksen, Gerald, O. W. Holmes, John Kuehn, Leon Perkinson, and Stan Voelker. 1975. *The Role of Multi-County Development Districts in Rural Areas.* Washington, D.C.: Economics, Statistics, and Cooperatives Service, U.S. Department of Agriculture, ERS-307.

Gittell, Marily, Bruce Hoffacker, Elinor Rollins, Samuel Foster, and Mark Hoffecker. 1980. *Limits to Citizen Participation: The Decline of Community Organizations.* Beverly Hills, California: Sage Publications.

Goudy, Willis. 1975. *Studying Your Community: Community Summaries.* Ames, Iowa: Department of Sociology, Iowa State University, Sociology Report 128B.

Littrell, Donald W. 1980. "The self-help approach." In James A. Christenson and Jerry W. Robinson, Jr. (editors), *Community Development in America.* Ames, Iowa: Iowa State University Press.

Phifer, Byron, E. Frederick List, and Boyd Faulkner. 1980. "History of community development in America." In James A. Christenson and Jerry W. Robinson, Jr. (editors), *Community Development in America.* Ames, Iowa: Iowa State University Press.

Robinson, Jerry W., Jr. 1980. "The conflict approach to community development." In James A. Christenson and Jerry W. Robinson, Jr. (editors), *Community Development in America.* Ames, Iowa: Iowa State University Press.

Robinson, Jerry W., Jr., and Ray Clifford. 1972. *Process Skills in Community Organizations.* Urbana, Illinois: Cooperative Extension Service, University of Illinois.

Spiegel, Hans B. C. 1980. "New directions." In James A. Christenson and Jerry W. Robinson, Jr. (editors), *Community Development in America.* Ames, Iowa: Iowa State University Press.

Summers, Gene. 1977. "Industrial development of rural America." *Journal of the Community Development Society* 8(1):6–18.

Voth, Donald E. 1977. *Citizen Participation in Rural Development.* State College, Mississippi: Southern Rural Development Center, Mississippi State University, SRDC Series 6.

______. 1979. "Social action research in community development." In Edward Blakely (editor), *Community Development Research.* New York: Human Sciences Press.

Warren, Roland. 1977. *Social Change and Human Purpose.* Chicago: Rand McNally Co.

Wilkinson, Kenneth P. 1979. "Social well-being and community." *Journal of the Community Development Society* 10(1):5–16.

27 Needs Assessment Surveys for Decision Makers

RABEL J. BURDGE

The first county agents, school superintendents, and community nurses asked their client groups what major problems they faced. Based on these assessments, programs were designed and implemented to address the clients' preferences, concerns, and needs. Historically, needs assessment was as casual as a "windshield survey" or as systematic as careful consultation with identified community leaders (Beal and Hobbs, 1964), and was generally satisfactory. However, beginning in the 1960s, many legislative and regulatory statutes in transportation, health, and land use planning, as well as in extension programs, required that the needs of the client or community be determined. The requirement for systematic public input provided the impetus for social scientists and managers of public programs to modify and adapt the methods of survey research to needs assessment surveys.

Surveys were initiated when it was found that representativeness and thoroughness were important for making sure that the true needs of the client population were identified. Armed with information on public perception of problems and secondary needs assessment data on stan-

---

Rabel J. Burdge is professor of Environmental Science, Rural Sociology, and Leisure Studies at the Institute for Environmental Studies, University of Illinois, Urbana, Illinois. He has published numerous articles on public input into decision making, environmental impact assessment, and outdoor leisure behavior.

Thanks are expressed to James Christenson, Herbert Lionberger, Robert Howell, Paul Warner, Lionel Beaulieu, Daryl Hobbs, Don Johnson, Dan Moore, and Vern Ryan for

dards and indicators, policy makers and program planners ideally could design programs or modify existing ones in line with expressed public need.

Planning standards, such as acres of park land or number of hospital beds per thousand population, is a traditional form of needs assessment. Needs may also be inferred through secondary indicators, such as number of students per classroom teacher, incidents of violent crime, or persons admitted to mental institutions (see Chapter 28). More police or teachers may be added or subtracted depending upon the direction of the needs assessment indicators. This chapter deals only with surveys as a method of needs assessment.

FIVE TYPES OF SURVEYS

Needs assessment research usually operates on the assumption that people can verbalize their problems or preferences on a given issue, that they can respond to a questionnaire, and that programs based on citizen input will be better received by the public. Many of the techniques used in needs assessment are applicable in obtaining public participation and citizen input into governmental decision making (Koneya, 1978).

For analytical purposes, we identify the following five approaches to needs assessment surveys: (1) citizen-developed community surveys; (2) standardized community surveys; (3) community leader surveys; (4) regional/statewide independent surveys; and (5) synchronized policy surveys.

The bases for differentiating five approaches to needs assessment surveys are the following seven dimensions:

1. *Focus of the survey* (Cohen et al., 1977): Will the questionnaire deal with limited issues, such as mental health or education, or will it be "omnibus" in nature, including all community problems?
2. *Use of the information* (Blake, et al., 1977): Will the information be used for decision making, to identify priorities for action, to identify the preferences of key organizations or categories of people, to

---

detailed input to this chapter. Some research issues suggested in this chapter are from interviews with sixty decision makers in Illinois on the degree to which the needs or problem areas identified by the *Illinois: Today and Tomorrow* study was used in the programs of their organizations (Safman and Burdge, 1980). A summary of the purposes of community surveys prepared by Blake et al. (1977), a review of data-gathering techniques assembled by Butler and Howell (1979), and a summary of needs assessment research prepared by Garkovich and Stam (1980) were also quite useful.

identify support for a particular program, or to enhance a sense of community?

3. *Who decides what goes into the questionnaire* (Goudy, 1975; Goudy and Wepprecht, 1977): Will the questions be developed by local citizens, a collection of local leaders, a community development professional, or an outside consultant such as a rural sociologist?
4. *The geographical boundaries*: Will the needs assessment effort be limited to one neighborhood, an area of a community, an entire city, a county, a substate region, or an entire state?
5. *Who is to be interviewed*: Will the sample frame be restricted to persons who have received a service, such as former mental patients? Will it be limited to formal community leaders or will a sample be drawn from the general population?
6. *The survey technique* (Dillman, 1978): Will personal interviews, telephone interviews, mail questionnaires, or some combination of these techniques be used?
7. *Extent of involvement by professionals*: Will the rural sociologist or community development specialist assume total responsibility for all phases of the needs assessment survey or, at the other extreme, only act as an occasional consultant?

Citizen-Developed Community Surveys

Surveys initiated by the local community members are used to identify individual and organizational support for projects such as schools, health delivery, and sanitation, or to improve a sense of community (Wells et al., 1980). The boundaries of the study are the local community, and full participation of community members is an essential objective. Therefore, contacting all community members with a questionnaire may be as important or even more important than obtaining a representative sample. Face-to-face interviews are often preferred because they increase contact among community members.

In some settings, a rural sociologist or other professional may be available to work with the community on the survey research process (Horton, 1980). In the case of the citizen-developed survey, the process is almost as important as the results, for proposed solutions may flow from a heightened sense of community awareness and involvement (Blake et al., 1977).

However, preparing a questionnaire, interviewing, and recording the results is a time consuming and difficult task that may discourage many communities. Further, the local community survey may be criticized on methodological grounds unless expert help is available. Finally, unless the action alternatives are well specified in advance, nothing may come from the study.

Standardized Community Surveys

The first step in this type of community survey is for the community development specialist, rural sociologist, or other consultant to meet with community leaders to help identify problems to be studied. The rural sociologist may provide technical assistance in many ways (e.g., standardized questionnaires, sampling techniques, interviewer training, data analysis and write-up) (Hobbs, 1977; Ryan, 1980). Local people generally do the interviewing, either using a personal interview or dropping off a questionnaire with an explanation of the need for it. Representativeness is crucial because results will be used to determine needs, evaluate programs, or develop an agenda for community action. This approach may be a part of the synchronized policy issue surveys described later (Garkovich, 1979).

Local community surveys using standardized formats have the appearance of being locally initiated because the community decides what questions are to be used and community volunteers collect the data. The rural sociologist can use the latest technology in data collection, thereby improving turnaround time and minimizing the possibility of breakdown in the survey process. The results of community needs assessment apply only to the local situation, and may suffer from the criticism of being "just another study" unless some connection is established between needs identification and action programs.

Community Leader Surveys

Community leader surveys focus on elected, appointed, professional, and/or volunteer informal leaders of political, social, business, and professional organizations. Leader surveys are often based on the hope that those who are surveyed will take action on problems they identify (Basson, 1970).

The community development specialist, regional planner, or extension agent may initiate the study with outside technical assistance. The telephone or mail technique is generally used because the numbers and geographical limits of the sample are known. Interviews with leaders could be a first step in developing either the statewide independent survey or the synchronized policy issue survey.

Needs assessment surveys of leaders may be used to identify opposition and support for proposed community development programs. In addition, leaders may be better informed about community issues and therefore in a better position to respond to a complex policy issue on a questionnaire. However, needs assessments that survey only leaders may be open to the charge that the real needs of the population are not being identified. Substantial research by rural sociologists has demonstrated that leaders differ from the general population in their perception of community needs (Miller, 1953).

Regional and Statewide Independent Surveys

Needs assessment information from independent regional and statewide surveys generally includes many issues of concern to state and local governments. Results are used for identifying, prioritizing, and comparing problem areas. Items selected for regional/statewide surveys come from consultation with state agencies, legislators, planning groups, and research and extension professionals. However, the final decision on questionnaire content is usually made by the research organization. Because of the expense incurred in contacting large numbers of people, data gathering is often limited to some combination of the telephone and mailed questionnaire approach (Dillman et al., 1974). Advances in survey technology have produced response rates between 68 and 75 percent for mail questionnaires and up to 85 percent for telephone interviews. Except for checking with local and state leaders on question selection, the entire research process is usually administered by the university rural sociologist. Successful statewide/regional surveys have recently been completed by rural sociologists in Arizona, Colorado, Florida, Indiana, Illinois, Michigan, Kentucky, North Carolina, Pennsylvania, and Washington (see Burdge et al., 1978; Burdge and Warner, 1975; Beaulieu and Korsching, 1979; Moore and Ishler, 1980; and Dillman et al., 1974).

The statewide/regional survey has the advantage of providing reliable information on needs assessment in a short time. Because samples are large, comparisons are possible among counties and communities (Christenson, 1976). If funds are available, the surveys can be repeated at frequent intervals to identify shifts in priorities and preferences.

At the community level, the independent survey is useful only in comparing preferences and problems among communities. It provides no indication of citizen acceptance of specific policies or goals (Blake et al., 1977). A major complaint about independent surveys is that citizens do not have enough information about the variety of problems facing a community to make intelligent responses (Dillman, 1977). Furthermore, they sometimes fail to provide information specific to the needs of individual communities.

Synchronized Policy Issue Surveys

Elements of the independent and leader surveys have been combined into an approach called "synchronized policy issue surveys" in an attempt to make needs assessment surveys an integral part of the policy process (Dillman, 1977; Wardwell and Dillman, 1975). The approach involves obtaining information on problem areas, goals, or preferences from an audience of leaders or community representatives similar to the leader survey described earlier (Garkovich, 1979; Cohen et al., 1977; Goudy and Wepprecht, 1977). Information obtained from leaders is then used as the basis for developing an independent survey for a general population. The community leaders (task force members, extension committee, planning board, etc.) then modify and finalize policy recommendations based on their evaluation of the citizen answers to the independent survey. If time allows, reformulated policies and goals could again be put before the citizen population through another survey.

The procedure could be applied to one community, as reported by Garkovich (1979) in the case of Jessamine County, Kentucky, or used for a state, as in the case of *Alternatives for Washington*, as outlined by Wardwell and Dillman (1975). Improvements in the telephone and mail questionnaire techniques allow rural sociologists to provide decision makers with quality evaluation of policy alternatives within a short time.

Synchronized policy issue surveys require both a financial commitment on the part of the sponsoring organization and willingness on the part of the rural sociologist to become involved in the policy process. However, this approach combines the strengths of the community leader surveys with the representativeness of regional/statewide independent surveys.

RESEARCH ISSUES

Uses of Needs Assessment Surveys

Research is needed to identify the appropriate problem areas and decision settings for which needs assessment surveys can be most effectively used. Few decisions should be made solely on the basis of public surveys, but better decisions could be made if more information were available on preferences of the general population. Research needs to identify the best timing, setting, and content of surveys. Decision makers in Illinois reported the following uses of information from a statewide independent needs assessment survey: a topic of discussion with other people, legitimization for development of new programs and discontinuance of old programs, the expansion or constriction of current programs, support for agency positions and legislative proposals, general background reading about the state of Illinois, justification for political lobbying efforts, programming materials for community affairs activity, and, finally, to refute or support other public opinion surveys (Safman and Burdge, 1980).

Legislated Programs

Research is needed to identify state and federal legislated programs that require needs assessments as a form of citizen input. Programs in social services, health care delivery, and environmental impact assessment, among others, require that the congruity between needs of the clients and proposed or ongoing programs be specified. However, the methods for obtaining public "needs" are seldom specified. For example, in the case of environmental impact assessment, the laws simply say that the impacted human population be consulted about possible consequences. Nothing is said about the approach or content of the assessment or who is to be consulted. Previews of federal and state legislation with an eye to providing the most appropriate form of needs assessment input is needed.

Appropriate Types of Surveys

Research needs to identify the appropriate policy use for each of the five types of needs assessment surveys outlined above. The statewide independent survey is excellent for providing information on problem area priorities in subgroups of the population. However, this approach does not provide an evaluation of policy alternatives. Community leader surveys adequately describe the perceived needs of the persons that are most likely to implement a program, but leader views may not be those of the general population. Standardized community surveys identify possible directions for social action, but only within geographic-specific areas. The synchronized policy issue survey approach may be useful for combining the strengths of the community leader survey and the regional independent surveys when specific issues or goals are decided. By case study, the benefits of each survey approach must be linked to the appropriate needs assessment setting.

Differences between Leader and Citizen

Research is needed on the similarities and differences between leader and citizen perceptions of needs. Except for citizen-initiated surveys, leaders either partially or totally decide what needs assessment items are to be included in the questionnaire. Research needs to document the assumption that community and state leaders are more likely to use the results of needs assessment surveys as a basis for policy formulation if they have been a part of the needs assessment process. A second research question is: Do state and local leaders, whether elected or appointed, perceive needs the same as the general population?

Standardized Procedures

Research is needed on developing components of a "needs assessment" survey package for use in a variety of policy and geographic settings. The successful implementation of needs assessment surveys during the 1970s suggests that decision makers, program planners, and "average" citizens find the results of the studies useful (Safman and Burdge, 1980). However, consolidation is needed to bring together a consistent and comparable list of questions, formats, sampling plans, and other procedures that, with appropriate alterations, could be used in a variety of settings. Hobbs (1977) and Ryan (1980) have developed materials on survey procedures that can be implemented by local communities. However, recent advances in mail and telephone techniques (Dillman, 1978) and methods of formatting and tabulating the regional/statewide independent and community leader surveys are not widely available. With validated survey technology at hand, the researcher would be better able to make needs assessment surveys an integral part of the policy process.

Results from Different Procedures

Research is needed on which type of questionnaire and sampling framework works best for the five approaches to needs assessment surveys and the degree to which each survey technique yields the same quality of response. The basic research question is to what degree the mail, telephone, or personal interview yields similar quality responses (Dillman and Mason, 1979). If responses are the same regardless of the type of questionnaire, then research may address the issue of what combination of techniques works best for each of the five approaches to needs assessment.

Sources of names for sample selection include telephone books, city directories, professional listing services, voter registration lists, motor vehicle registration lists, and lists of licensed drivers (Warner et al., 1977). Each source has different characteristics in terms of cost, availability, accessibility, representativeness, and provision of background information on sample respondents. Research should specify which sample source works best for each of the five types of needs assessment surveys.

Relationship to Secondary Information Sources

Research is needed on the relationship between responses to needs assessment surveys and available census counts and other secondary statistics. The approaches to needs assessment surveys outlined in this chapter represent a primary input to needs assessment. However, survey data would be more valuable if it could build upon available information in the form of data on standards, census counts, and regularly accumulated evaluation statistics. An independent survey showing that health care is a major community problem might be supported by county health statistics showing unmet standards (e.g., too few doctors and inadequate hospital space).

WHO WILL CONDUCT NEEDS ASSESSMENT SURVEYS IN THE 1980s?

Two developments in the 1970s elevated needs assessment surveys to widespread importance for citizens and public officials. The first was advances in the mail and telephone techniques. The other was recognition by policy makers that citizen input to government programs was necessary. Impetus for this turn of events came from three sources: the availability of funds under the Rural Development Act of 1972 to land grant colleges for the study of rural communities, the increased costs of personal interviews, and the availability of state and federal funds for planning in such areas as social services, health delivery, and community and regional planning. Social scientists, particularly rural sociologists, at land grant universities are in a position to continue advances in needs assessment surveys if the research program outlined in this chapter is followed.

As society becomes more complex, citizen involvement becomes more important, both for maintaining a sense of community and to ensure that government programs remain in tune with the needs of the citizens. The research program outlined here could help meet this crucial need and, at the same time, strengthen the tie between the university researcher and decision makers at the community, state, and federal levels.

REFERENCES

Basson, Priscilla. 1970. "Planning and perception of needs in five upstate New York counties." *Journal of the Community Development Society* 1(2):23–29.

Beal, George M., and Daryl J. Hobbs. 1964. *The Process of Social Action in Community and Area Development*. Ames, Iowa: Cooperative Extension Service, Iowa State University Publication 16.

Beaulieu, Lionel J., and Peter F. Korsching (editors). 1979. *Focus on Florida: The Citizens' Viewpoint*. Gainesville, Florida: Center for Community and Rural Development–IFAS, University of Florida, Special Series 1.

Blake, Brian F., Ned Kalb, and Vernon Ryan. 1977. "Citizen opinion surveys and effective CD efforts." *Journal of the Community Development Society* 8(2):92–104.

Burdge, Rabel J., Ruth M. Kelly, and Harvey J. Schweitzer. 1978. *Illinois: Today and Tomorrow*. Urbana, Illinois: Cooperative Extension Service, University of Illinois, Special Series 1.

Burdge, Rabel J., and Paul D. Warner. 1975. *Issues Facing Kentucky*. Lexington, Kentucky:

Cooperative Extension Service, University of Kentucky.

Butler, Lorna Michael, and Robert E. Howell. 1979. "Community needs assessment techniques: An essential part of coping with the impacts of rapid community growth." Pullman, Washington: Department of Rural Sociology, Washington State University. Unpublished paper.

Christenson, James A. 1976. "Public input for program planning and policy formation." *Journal of the Community Development Society* 7(Spring):33–39.

Cohen, Mark W., Grayce M. Sills, and Andrew I. Schwebel. 1977. "A two-stage process for surveying community needs." *Journal of the Community Development Society* 8(1):54–61.

Dillman, Don A. 1977. "Preference surveys and policy decisions: Our new tools need not be used in the same old way." *Journal of the Community Development Society* 8(1):30–43.

______ . 1978. *Mail and Telephone Surveys: The Total Design Method.* New York: Wiley-Interscience Publications.

Dillman, Don A., James A. Christenson, Edwin H. Carpenter, and Ralph M. Brooks. 1974. "Increasing mail questionnaire response: A four-state comparison." *American Sociological Review* 29:744–756.

Dillman, Don A., and Robert Mason. 1979. "The use of face-to-face, telephone, and mail surveys in state, substate, and community needs assessment efforts." Proposal submitted to the Western Rural Development Center, Oregon State University, Corvallis, Oregon.

Garkovich, Lorraine. 1979. "What comes after the survey? A practical application of the synchronized survey model in community development." *Journal of the Community Development Society* 10(1):29–38.

Garkovich, Lorraine, and Jerome M. Stam. 1980. "Research on selected issues in community development." In James A. Christenson and Jerry W. Robinson, Jr. (editors), *Community Development in America.* Ames, Iowa: Iowa State University Press.

Goudy, Willis. 1975. *Studying Your Community: Community Summaries.* Ames, Iowa: Department of Sociology, Iowa State University, Sociology Report 128B.

Goudy, Willis J., and Frederick E. Wepprecht. 1977. "Local/regional programs developed from residents' evaluations." *Journal of the Community Development Society* 8(1):44–52.

Hobbs, Daryl. 1977. *Surveying Community Attitudes: A Technical and Procedural Manual for Communities.* Columbia, Missouri: Missouri Division of Community Development, Manual 108.

Horton, Billy D. 1980. "Personal correspondence on the role of the rural sociologist in local community development efforts." Unpublished paper.

Koneya, Mele. 1978. "Citizen participation is not community development." *Journal of the Community Development Society* 9(2):23–29.

Miller, Paul A. 1953. *Community Health Action.* East Lansing, Michigan: Michigan State University Press.

Moore, Dan E., and Anne S. Ishler. 1980. *Pennsylvania: The Citizens' Viewpoint.* University Park, Pennsylvania: Agricultural Experiment Station, Pennsylvania State University.

Ryan, Vernon. 1980. *CD-DIAL.* Ames, Iowa: Department of Sociology and Cooperative Extension Service, Iowa State University.

Safman, Phyllis, and Rabel J. Burdge. 1980. "Taking the last step: Reporting the influence of community problem studies on government policy making and program development." Paper presented at the annual meetings of the Rural Sociological Society, Ithaca, New York.

Wardwell, John A., and Don A. Dillman. 1975. *Alternatives for Washington: The Final Report, Volume 6.* Olympia, Washington: Office of Program Planning and Fiscal Management, State of Washington.

Warner, Paul D., Susan D. Hoffman, and Rabel J. Burdge. 1977. "Drivers license list as a sampling frame." *Public Data Use* 5(September):3–10.

Wells, Betty, Arthur H. Johnson, and John L. Tait. 1980. "Citizen involvement in local action: Much work for little – but sufficient – gain." *Newsline* (Rural Sociological Society) 9(November):40–44.

28
Social Indicators of Well-Being

PAUL R. EBERTS

"If we could first know where we are and whither we are tending," President Abraham Lincoln once said, "then we could better judge what to do and how to do it." Although Lincoln's principle was not rigorously applied to policy analysis of social trends for over a century, its outline of the four basic steps in producing and implementing policy is much used in the modern social indicator movement (Land and Spilerman, 1975).

PREVIOUS RESEARCH

The social indicator movement received important impetus during the 1960s when social scientists and government officials produced *Toward a Social Report* (U.S. Department of Health, Education, and Welfare, 1969), the first comprehensive federal report on social indicators. The report intended to supplement the monthly federal reports on economic indicators and to stimulate work on indicators of well-being such as health, poverty, housing, and unemployment (Bauer, 1966; U.S. Department of Health, Education, and Welfare, 1969:xi ff.; Land and Spilerman, 1975:Chapter 1). The interest it generated stimulated the executive branch of the government to begin publishing social reports on a regular basis. Two such reports, *Social Indicators, 1973* and *Social Indicators, 1976*, have been

---

Paul R. Eberts is associate professor, Department of Rural Sociology, Cornell University, Ithaca, New York. He is the author of numerous articles on social indicators and quality-of-life issues.

Great appreciation is extended to Frank Young, Sharon Contanche, and Helene Vigorita for their helpful comments on an earlier draft of this chapter.

published; a third will appear in 1981. Most researchers are critical of these volumes because they lack interpretations (Taeuber, 1978) and direct policy relevance (De Neufville, 1975). Indeed, only 22 percent of upper-level federal officials are even aware of their existence, although over one-third use social indicator data in their work (Caplan and Barton, 1978).

The 1960s' social indicator movement was optimistic that social research would contribute to "the Nation's ability to chart its social progress . . . and plan for the way ahead" (U.S. Department of Health, Education, and Welfare, 1969:iii). As the movement developed, a number of issues arose, including the definition of a social indicator. The 1969 HEW report makes the appealing suggestion that a social indicator should have a normative quality: "It is in all cases a direct measure of welfare and is subject to the interpretation that, if it changes in the 'right' direction, while other things remain equal, things have gotten better or people are 'better off' " (U.S. Department of Health, Education and Welfare, 1969:97).

This definition does not account for the difficulties in analyzing the extensive interrelations of many social indicator trends (there are 555 tables in *Social Indicators, 1976*) and their interacting causes and effects (Parke and Sheldon, 1975). To handle the data adequately requires complex statistical methodologies (Land and Spilerman, 1975; Stokey and Zeckhauser, 1978). Many researchers maintain that we can only really know where we are and whither we are tending when we also specify the theoretical and empirical causes of the trends (Land and Spilerman, 1975, passim). Certainly, if we do not know why certain social phenomena behave as they do, then it is impossible to create effective policies to alter undesirable trends. For example, De Neufville (1975:Chapter 6) maintains that crime rates are "unsuccessful social indicators" because their causes are not well enough known and the causes that are known do not relate directly enough to specific public policies for coherent alterations to be made.

Research during the 1970s made at least two major contributions to these general problems. First, although the causes and effects of many social indicator trends are yet to be specified, progress on the statistical methodology for determining them is being made (Land and Spilerman, 1975). Second, a consensus is emerging on a general model that categorizes social phenomena into meaningful components for policy development (see, among others, De Greene, 1973:Chapter 1; Fox, 1974:Chapter 7; Land and Spilerman, 1975:Chapters 1, 15; and Eberts and Sismondo, 1978).

Figure 28.1 presents a version of this general model. This model assumes the possibility of measurable social indicators – whether "objective" as obtained through the census or "subjective" as obtained through

FIGURE 28.1 A General Model of Public Policy, Implementing Agencies, Social Structures, Social Indicators, and Social Research.

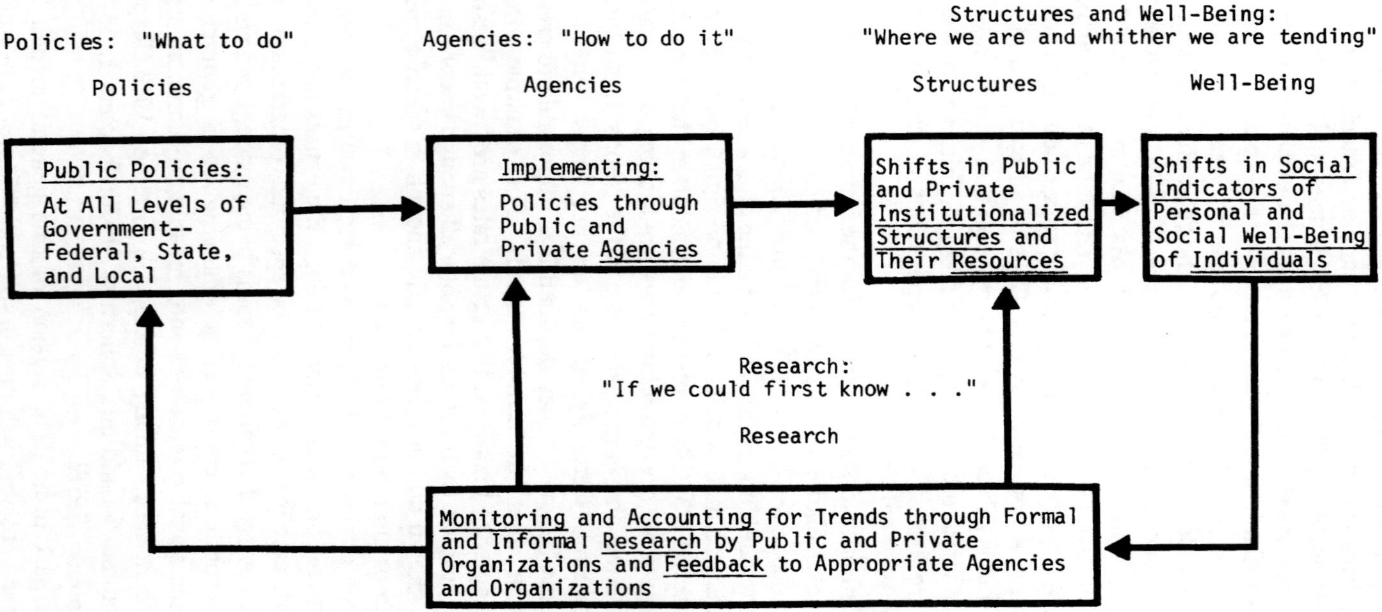

opinion surveys. It also assumes that social indicators of well-being are not directly dependent upon policy initiatives by governments. As in Lincoln's analysis, implementation of policy is separate from policy making–legislatures are separate from executive branches. Implementation occurs through agencies that in turn affect other private and public institutions and resources, from which the actual level of well-being of people is generated. Policy-oriented social research monitors indicators of the four components, builds models to account for trends in each component, and feeds these analyses back to appropriate bodies (De Neufville, 1975).

Apparently the most successful social indicator programs are those where indicators for each component in the model are explicit, well known, and effective in influencing indicators in adjacent components. De Neufville (1975:Chapter 6) maintains that unemployment rates meet these criteria and can therefore be considered a successful social indicator, whereas, as noted above, crime rates do not. A major need for the future is to produce a greater number of successful social indicators. Current data from the 1980 census, combined with opinion surveys from many sources, provide the technical information bases from which to reexamine models of social indicator trends. Social crises due to inflation, unemployment, energy costs, environmental degradation, center city deterioration, government fiscal constraints, inequality, discrimination, and alienation provide the moral stimuli for taking advantage of the opportunities.

The comprehensive model presented as Figure 28.1 informs us that future research on social indicators goes beyond improvement in the quality and reliability of the indicators. Research is also needed on the policy formation process, which establishes goals and either uses or fails to use the indicators to produce policy. Consequently, the research needs identified in this chapter are concerned with both improving the indicators and assessing the process by which they are used or ignored.

RESEARCH ISSUES

Rural localities and urban ghettos have one thing in common: they frequently show the worst readings on most social indicators (Smith, 1973; Holland, 1976). As industries and populations continue to shift away from central cities toward suburbs and rural areas, policy makers are becoming more impressed with the importance of social indicators. Locally initiated lawsuits about the 1980 census counts represent one measure of this awareness. Moreover, the new federalism, whereby state and federal assistance to localities is based on indicators of population size and local need (Sundquist, 1969), gives additional stimulus for local policy makers to understand and use social indicators (Carter et al., 1977). Localities have nearly the same policy-making process as other levels of jurisdiction (see Figure 28.1). The major difference is that local staff research is much more informal in collecting information. Many rural localities have no staff for this role and find themselves at a disadvantage in competing for facilities and programs (Foley, 1976). The following research suggestions are intended to alleviate such inequities.

Toward Finding Out Where We Are and Whither We Are Tending

With all the available data, it seems simple to find out where we are and where we are going. But effective policy depends on understanding the causes and interrelations among the original trends. Such a task is especially difficult for local policy makers because data have been extremely limited at the village, town, and township levels.

Research is needed on how important well-being indicators vary for people on different local jurisdictional levels. The policy process of Figure 28.1 is impossible to implement if there are no data on which to base judgments. For instance, county policy makers need data for minor civil divisions (villages, towns, and townships) within their counties in order to assess the adequacy of their efforts to affect social indicators in the more rural parts of their localities (Schmidt, 1978). Likewise, state policy makers need data on cities and counties. Only meager amounts of minor civil division data have been available in the past, and even fewer trend data have been compiled. Analyses based on such data are minimal (Rosen et al., 1979) and therefore provide little guidance to those responsible for resolving important local issues. Much data of this nature exist, but they must be organized and disseminated. The census will build tapes on selected indicators for 1970 and 1980, making trend data on minor civil divisions generally available for the first time. Additional research is needed on these local data under a framework like that of Figure 28.1 in order to discover where the population segments within them are and where they are tending.

Research is needed that compares trends on issues relating to basic values in our society. The United States was founded on the idea that there should be liberty, equality, mutuality, democracy, and justice for all, that its citizens might have a good life and pursue happiness. These are the great value premises built into our institutions (Winter et al., 1968; Hoult, 1974). Opinion surveys consistently show that some people do not participate in or feel committed to all the institutions structured to ensure these basic values (Hoult, 1974:240ff.). On most issues, those in rural (and ghetto) areas and/or lowest in social status are most disaffected (Hamilton, 1972; Christenson and Yang, 1976; Holland, 1976; Buttel et al., 1976; Moxley and Wimberley, 1979). More research is necessary to discover the extent of disaffection among various population segments and to learn which structures and social conditions lead to reducing the disaffection (Christenson, 1976b; Clark 1973a, 1973b). Such information is necessary so that policies can be modified to align people's stated value preferences with society's value premises.

Research is needed to disaggregate locality data by differences in sex, age, minority status, and class position. The U.S. Commission on Civil Rights felt so strongly that analyses of key elements in equality among population subgroupings were missing from *Social Indicators, 1976* and other government reports that it commissioned a study, *Social Indicators of Equality for Minorities and Women* (1978:2). This report compares twenty-four indicators of inequality–including income, education, and employment–for sixteen population segments. Equality, a fundamental value premise of society, underlies other values. For example, justice implies equality in access to legal institutions (Rawls, 1971), and is a major determinant of other well-being indicators (Foley, 1977; Falkin, 1979). Data and research on equality among major local subgroupings are needed so that local policy makers can become aware of local conditions on these major value issues (Carter et al., 1977).

Research is needed on how social indicator trends cluster. Data glut is enormous in social indicator analysis. Too many indicators already exist, and the above suggestions for further disaggregations would create even more. Clustering techniques, such as factor analysis and Guttman scaling, are the most informative ways of tackling the problem. Factor analyses of objective indicators were used by Smith (1973) and by Ross et al. (1979), while Andrews and Withey (1976) applied factor analysis to subjective life satisfaction indicators of well-being. Christenson (1976b) used Guttman scaling on subjective indicators, while Eberts and Young (1971) and Perry and Bauder (1980) used Guttman scales as inputs into their factor analyses. Such analyses should also be applied specifically to rural localities and low-status populations. Identifying clusters accurately is often the first step in clarifying each component in Figure 28.1. Such clarity is essential for further causal and policy analysis (Eberts, 1979, 1980).

More research is needed on building statistical causal models for individual well-being indicators. Although many models were built on 1970 and earlier data and were intended to be universal and stable through time, in fact, they have proven to be neither (Henry and Short, 1954; Duncan, 1975). Accurate new models to account for developments such as energy shortages and inflation are essential (Land and Spilerman, 1975; Stokey and Zeckhauser, 1978). Furthermore the structures of institutions and policies should be included as variables in the models (see Figure 28.1

and below). Moreover, data sets should separate rural from other localities since models for rural, urban, and suburban places often differ (Foley, 1979). Such differences in models suggest that policies for increasing well-being in each level of jurisdiction will probably differ. Given the vast number of indicators, the task of building current models is enormous yet essential.

More research is needed on using community structure variables in models as causal determinants of community resources and social well-being. Many government policies aimed at expanding community resources and services also affect localities by forcing shifts in relationships among established local groups and individuals. For example, improvements in transportation, utilities, housing, schools, plants, and shopping centers shift spatial locations and usually enhance local socioeconomic capabilities and structures. With a lag, these changes produce related changes such as increased income and educational levels, shifts in socioeconomic resource distribution, differentiation in numbers and types of local public and private services, and shifts in local political competitiveness, participation, and power structures (Young and Young, 1973; Clark, 1973a, 1973b; Perry and Bauder, 1980; Christenson, 1980; Eberts, 1980). Access to such facilities and resources are primary variables for determining well-being in both subjective and objective indicators (Duncan, 1975; Foley, 1977; Wilkening and McGranahan, 1978; Eberts, 1979; Christenson, 1976b; Young, 1980; Wasserman and Chua, 1980). These findings demonstrate how policy outcomes affect structural variables and resources and, in turn, indicators of well-being (see Figure 28.1). More detailed specification should be useful to policy makers at all governmental levels (Campbell, 1976).

Research is needed to discover how individual causal factors affect a range of well-being indicators. Causal models generally use one indicator of well-being at a time as the "effect" or dependent indicator (Land and Spilerman, 1975). A consequence is that each causal element is not examined for its range of effects. Comprehensive assessment of key influencing factors requires both an extensive search through previous studies and large data sets to separate the effects of multiple causal influences. Causal variables themselves are often interrelated and must also be sorted out through clustering techniques (Eberts and Young, 1971; Perry and Bauder, 1980). Identifying a smaller but more comprehensive set of causal relations enables the probable effect of policy shifts to be more easily foreseen and, in the long run, produces more accurate and concise theory (Blalock, 1969; Kuhn, 1970). There is nothing as practical as a good theory that adequately summarizes disparate studies – it keeps people from shooting at everything that moves and provides direction for producing more effective policy alternatives (De Neufville, 1975).

Toward Figuring Out What to Do and How to Do It

In general, social researchers have worked more on problems of well-being and their causes than on policy implementation. Indeed, policy makers are often frustrated with researchers because they spend too much time on analysis and too little on producing strategies. Although in reality policy development is most often separated from program implementation at the theoretical level, they closely interrelate and will therefore be considered together here.

Research is needed on the conceptual nature of policy and the appropriateness of different types of policy in producing desired outcomes. The "old liberalism" of identifying an important need and then creating another bureaucracy to meet it is no longer the only or main policy tool (Lowi, 1979). The "new federalism" of closer cooperation between local, state, and federal agencies and the "new economics" of creating conditions for competitive markets to work are increasingly important alternatives (Dahl and Lindblom, 1953; Sundquist, 1969). New policies are not easy to hammer out, and social indicator researchers must be aware of how their research feeds into the several levels of the policy process (see Figure 28.1; De Neufville, 1975; and Caplan and Barton, 1978).

Policy debates between Republicans and Democrats reflect different approaches to policy instruments. Representatives of both parties see themselves as standing in the noble traditions of Western civilization and its great values of liberty, equality, justice, democracy, and mutuality with the less advantaged. Differences arise over the rank ordering and weighting given to these values. Democrats give more weight to equality and mutuality, Republicans stress freedom for individuals to use their private property as they see fit (Hamilton, 1972). That the outcomes of the debates are often doubtful underscores the necessity of using several different policy orientations in research. Policy analysts must produce programs that demonstrate commitment to certain of these values over others but that do not submerge the others.

More research is needed on how policies interrelate among multilevels of government and how local government staffs affect local development. The new federalism assumes coordination among local, state, and federal agencies. Nevertheless, considerable variation is found from one locality to another (Stam and Reid, 1980). Richer places have more staff and planning capacity, more resources in the private sector, and usually fewer needs than poorer (often rural) localities (Moxley and Wimberley, 1979; Foley, 1979; Christenson, 1976a). Poor rural places are especially caught in a "Catch-22" condition (Holland, 1976). Regional planning boards and commissions, community action programs, "circuit riders," and research and extension under Title V of the Rural Development Act are the usual federal and state policy instruments used to alleviate the inequities. These too show differential success – among states and between rural and urban places – in developing proposals for and receiving funding from state and federal agencies (Sundquist, 1969). Sources, costs, results, and tradeoffs of these alternative strategies ought to be better documented, as should their effects on various local institutional structures and well-being indicators.

"If We Could First Know . . ."

Research is needed on how research fits into the policy process. To act on the above research suggestions will require considerable commitment from both researchers and policy makers to work together in the others' unfamiliar territory. As Caplan and Barton (1978) assert in their study, research use by upper-level federal officials depends less on social scientists' technical expertise in monitoring social trends (see Figure 28.1) than on commitment by government officials to set quality-of-life goals and establish specific indicators of progress toward achieving the goals. More research is needed on how policy makers routinely obtain and use social indicators and on how their routines might be changed so that they obtain and use them more effectively.

CONCLUSION

The 1980 census, along with increasing availability of subjective indicators through national research organizations, will give considerable impetus to new social indicator research. Computerization of these data provides more access to more data, including time series, for smaller units of analysis (townships, villages, counties) than ever before. In addition, federal, state, and even local policy makers are now more aware of the importance of social statistics. Current federal emphasis on revenue sharing and categoric grants forces the use of social statistics.

Social indicator research can make significant impacts on both social scientists' and policy makers' understanding of how social changes affect well-being in rural America. Despite recent advances on some indicators, inequalities in the distribution of things people value in America life remain, and inflation and energy costs signal that even this distribution is in danger of slipping backward. Such conditions are potentially disastrous for several population segments on well-being indicators (Dillman and Tremblay, 1977; Eberts, 1979; Buttel, 1980). The opportunities are present for social researchers to be imaginative in their research and active in the policy process. The model presented in Figure 28.1 is viable for dealing with these problems. The payoffs of applying the model in these times of crises in American life are clearly worth the considerable efforts required.

REFERENCES

Andrews, Frank M., and Stephen B. Withey. 1976. *Social Indicators of Well-Being: Americans' Perceptions of Their Life Quality*. New York: Plenum Press.

Bauer, Raymond A. (editor). 1966. *Social Indicators*. Cambridge: Massachusetts Institute of Technology Press.

Blalock, Hubert M., Jr. 1969. *Theory Construction: From Verbal to Mathematical Formulations*. Englewood Cliffs, New Jersey: Prentice-Hall.

Buttel, Frederick H. 1980. "Agricultural structure and rural ecology: Toward a political economy of rural development." *Sociologica Ruralis* 20:44–61.

Buttel, Frederick H., Eugene A. Wilkening, and Oscar B. Martinson. 1976. "Ideology and social indicators of the quality of life." *Social Indicators Research* 4:353–369.

Campbell, Donald T. 1976. "Focal local indicators for social program evaluation." *Social Indicators Research* 4:237–256.

Caplan, Nathan, and Eugenia Barton. 1978. "The potential of social indicators: Minimum conditions for impact at the national level as suggested by a study of the use of *Social Indicators, 1973*." *Social Indicators Research* 5:427–456.

Carter, Keith A., Gerald E. Klonglan, Frank A. Fear, Richard D. Warren, Christopher E. Marshall, Rodney F. Ganey, and Erik R. Andersen. 1977. *Social Indicators for Rural Development: Descriptive Social Reporting*. Ames, Iowa: Department of Sociology, Iowa State University, Sociology Report 141.

Christenson, James A. 1976a. *North Carolina: Today and Tomorrow: People's Views on Community Services*. Raleigh, North Carolina: Agricultural Extension Service, North Carolina State University.

______. 1976b. "Quality of community services: A macro-unidimensional approach with experimental data." *Rural Sociology* 41(4):509–525.

______. 1980. "The impact of size of government and number of administrative units on the quality of community services." *Administrative Science Quarterly* 25:89–101.

Christenson, James A., and Choon Yang. 1976. "Dominant values in American society: An exploratory analysis." *Sociology and Social Research* 60:461–472.

Clark, Terry N. 1973a. *Community Power and Policy Outputs*. Beverly Hills, California: Sage Publications.

______. 1973b. "Community social indicators: From analytic models to policy applications." *Urban Affairs Quarterly* 9:3–36.

Dahl, Robert A., and Charles E. Lindblom. 1953. *Politics, Economics and Welfare: Planning and Politico-Economic Systems Resolved into Basic Social Processes*. New York: Harper and Row.

De Greene, Kenyon B. 1973. *Socio-Technical Systems: Factors in Analysis, Design, and Management*. Englewood Cliffs, New Jersey: Prentice-Hall.

De Neufville, Judith Innes. 1975. *Social Indicators and Public Policy: Interaction Processes of Design and Application*. New York: Elsevier Scientific Publishing.

Dillman, Don A., and Kenneth R. Tremblay, Jr. 1977. "The quality of life in rural America." *The Annals of the American Academy of Political and Social Science* 429:115–129.

Duncan, Otis Dudley. 1975. "Measuring social change via replication of surveys." In

Kenneth C. Land and Seymour Spilerman (editors), *Social Indicator Models*. New York: Russell Sage Foundation.

Eberts, Paul R. 1979. "Growth and the quality of life: Some logical and methodological issues." In Gene F. Summers and Arne Selvik (editors), *Nonmetropolitan Industrial Growth and Community Change*. Lexington, Massachusetts: D. C. Heath and Co.

______. 1980. "Socio-economic models in renewable natural resource utilization." In Enrique Campos-Lopez (editor), *Renewable Resources: A Systematic Approach*. New York: Academic Press.

Eberts, Paul R., and Sergio Sismondo. 1978. "Principles in design and management of policy research for public planning agencies." In David L. Rogers and Larry R. Whiting (editors), *Rural Policy Research Alternatives*. Ames, Iowa: Iowa State University Press.

Eberts, Paul R., and Frank W. Young. 1971. "Sociological variables in development: Their range and characteristics." In George Beal, Ronald Powers, and E. Walter Coward (editors), *Sociological Perspectives of Domestic Development*. Ames, Iowa: Iowa State University Press.

Falkin, Gregory P. 1979. *Reducing Delinquency: A Strategic Planning Approach*. Lexington, Massachusetts: D. C. Heath and Co.

Foley, John W. 1976. "National linkages, political competition, and local public planning: A multivariate analysis of 300 communities." *Social Science Quarterly* 57:660–669.

______. 1977. "Trends, determinants, and policy implications of income inequality in U.S. counties." *Sociology and Social Research* 61:441–461.

______. 1979. "Community structure and public policy outputs in 300 eastern American communities: Toward a sociology of the public sector." *Ethnicity* 6:222–234.

Fox, Karl A. 1974. *Social Indicators and Social Theory: Elements of an Operational System*. New York: John Wiley and Sons.

Hamilton, Richard F. 1972. *Class and Politics in the United States*. New York: John Wiley and Sons.

Henry, Andrew F., and James F. Short. 1954. *Suicide and Homicide: Some Economic, Sociological, and Psychological Aspects of Aggression*. Glencoe, Illinois: Free Press.

Holland, Stuart. 1976. *The Regional Problem*. New York: St. Martin's Press.

Hoult, Thomas Ford. 1974. *Sociology for a New Day*. New York: Random House.

Kuhn, Thomas S. 1970. *The Structure of Scientific Revolutions*. Chicago: University of Chicago Press.

Land, Kenneth C., and Seymour Spilerman (editors). 1975. *Social Indicator Models*. New York: Russell Sage Foundation.

Lowi, Theodore J. 1979. *The End of Liberalism*. New York: W. W. Norton and Co.

Moxley, Robert L., and Ronald C. Wimberley. 1979. *Changing Social Structure and Quality of Life in North Carolina*. Raleigh, North Carolina: Agricultural Extension Service, North Carolina State University, Publication 69.

Parke, Robert, and Eleanor B. Sheldon. 1975. "Social indicators." *Science* 188:693–699.

Perry, Charles S., and Ward W. Bauder. 1980. "Equality, economic resources, and structural differentiation: Dimensions of development in the northeast United States." *Social Indicators Research* 8:327–340.

Rawls, John, 1971. *A Theory of Justice*. Cambridge: Harvard University Press.

Rosen, Beatrice M., Harold F. Goldsmith, and Richard W. Redick. 1979. "Demographic and social indicators: Uses in mental health planning in small areas." *World Health Statistics* 32:101–102.

Ross, Peggy J., Herman Bluestone, and Fred K. Hines. 1979. *Indicators of Social Well-Being for U.S. Counties*. Washington, D.C.: Economics, Statistics, and Cooperatives Service, U.S. Department of Agriculture, Rural Development Research Report 10.

Schmidt, Frederick E. 1978. "Taking computers to the community: Who is our audience?

For what? And, why bother?" In Carol A. Chapman, Craig L. Infanger, Lynn W. Robbins, and David L. Debertin (editors), *Taking Computers to the Community: Prospects and Perspectives*. Lexington, Kentucky: College of Agriculture and Cooperative Extension Service, University of Kentucky.

Smith, David M. 1973. *The Geography of Social Well-Being in the United States*. New York: McGraw-Hill Book Co.

Stam, Jerome M., and J. Norman Reid. 1980. *Federal Programs Supporting Multi-County Substate Regional Activities: An Overview*. Washington, D.C.: Economics, Statistics, and Cooperatives Service, U.S. Department of Agriculture, Rural Development Research Report 23.

Stokey, Edith, and Richard Zeckhauser. 1978. *A Primer for Policy Analysis*. New York: W. W. Norton and Co.

Sundquist, James L. 1969. *Making Federalism Work*. Washington, D.C.: Brookings Institute.

Taeuber, Conrad (editor). 1978. *America in the Seventies: Some Social Indicators*. Philadelphia: The Annals of the American Academy of Political and Social Science, Volume 435.

U.S. Commission on Civil Rights (editors). 1978. *Social Indicators of Equality for Minorities and Women*. Washington, D.C.: U.S. Government Printing Office.

U.S. Department of Commerce (Bureau of the Census). 1977. *Social Indicators, 1976*. Washington, D.C.: U.S. Government Printing Office.

U.S. Department of Health, Education, and Welfare. 1969. *Toward a Social Report*. Washington, D.C.: U.S. Government Printing Office.

U.S. Office of Management and Budget. 1973. *Social Indicators, 1973*. Washington, D.C.: U.S. Government Printing Office.

Wasserman, Ira M., and Lily Aurora Chua. 1980. "Objective and subjective social indicators of the quality of life in American Standard Metropolitan Statistical Areas: A reanalysis." *Social Indicators Research* 8:365–381.

Wilkening, Eugene A., and David McGranahan. 1978. "Correlates of subjective well-being in northern Wisconsin." *Social Indicators Research* 5:211–234.

Winter, J. Alan, Jerome Rabow, and Mark Chesler. 1968. *Vital Problems for American Society: Meanings and Means*. New York: Random House.

Young, Frank W., and Ruth C. Young. 1973. *Comparative Studies of Community Growth*. Morgantown, West Virginia: West Virginia University Press.

Young, Ruth C. 1980. "Poverty and inequality in the U. S.: A nonMarxist explanation." *Social Indicators Research* 8:103–114.

29
Social Impact Assessment

WILLIAM R. FREUDENBURG

Unlike most of the topics in this book, social impact assessment (SIA) is not an "area" that has been defined by researchers and their shared substantive interests. It is a field shaped largely by legal requirements, and expressed through research that cuts across a variety of preexisting research areas.

Rural sociologists have performed social impact assessments of one variety or another for as long as the profession has existed, but social impact assessment did not exist as a self-conscious field before the 1970s. The first presidential act of that decade was the signing of the National Environmental Policy Act (NEPA) of 1969, which Congress had passed just a few days earlier. The act was designed to improve federal decision making on environmental issues, and its best known provision was the requirement that environmental impact statements (EISs) be prepared for major Federal actions "significantly affecting the quality of the human environment." The act also stipulated that to the fullest extent possible, federal agencies should make "integrated use of the natural and social sciences . . . in decisionmaking which may have an impact on man's environment" (P. L. 91-190, Section 102).

Although NEPA is only five pages long, its impacts have been enormous. Between January 1, 1970, and December 31, 1978, seventy federal agencies prepared over 11,000 environmental impact statements. Over the same time period, individuals and organizations filed well over a

---

William R. Freudenburg is assistant professor, Department of Sociology, and assistant rural sociologist, Department of Rural Sociology, Washington State University, Pullman, Washington. He is the author of numerous publications in the area of energy and social impact assessment.

This chapter is from Scientific Paper Number 5890, Project 0478, Agricultural Research

thousand NEPA-related lawsuits (U.S. Council on Environmental Quality, 1979: 589-590). Relatively few of the lawsuits to date have focused explicitly on social assessments.[1] Social impacts are not intended by themselves to require preparation of an environmental impact statement, but if an environmental impact statement needs to be prepared for environmental reasons, and if "social and natural or physical environmental effects are interrelated, then the environmental impact statement will discuss all of these effects on the human environment" (U.S. Council on Environmental Quality, 1978:29).

It is likely that social impacts will receive increasing legal attention in the 1980s. As agencies respond to lawsuits by improving their assessments of environmental impacts, opponents of new developments will be forced increasingly to turn their attention to areas of the environmental impact statements that have greater inadequacies. For the present, their best possible targets may be the social impact assessments the documents contain.

Even without the threat of lawsuits, however, SIAs have the potential to play an increasingly important role in policy making. Social impact assessments are meant to provide a means for anticipating potentially adverse impacts of decisions. When they are properly performed, impact assessments are not targets for lawsuits; rather, they are a source of rational and technically competent information. Some policy makers have already begun to demand that social impact assessments fulfill the information-providing role more fully, and it seems likely that the coming decade will see a major increase in the weight placed on the SIAs' full scientific sufficiency.

During the first decade under NEPA, the scientific progress of social impact assessment has been only moderate. Part of the difficulty was the newness of the field. The difficulties were increased by the fact that SIAs extend across such a broad range of more traditional research areas.

Researchers have assessed the impacts of highways and high voltage lines, mines and military bases, dams and dumps, nuclear facilities, national parks, and a broad range of other developments. Studies have analyzed the developments' impacts on population and politics, institutions and individuals, families, friendships, farming practices, and other social variables at local, regional, and national levels. Such a broad range of tasks clearly makes it difficult to establish any single body of theories and methods for social impact assessment. Another limiting factor is the simple fact that the field is a hybrid of scientific and political forces:

Center, Washington State University. The author wishes to thank Linda Bacigalupi, Ronald Little, and an anonymous reviewer for their helpful suggestions on an earlier draft.

social impact assessment is a servant as well as a product of the political process, and political forces have placed important constraints on the improvement of science in social impact assessment. The newness of the field, its breadth, and the presence of political pressures are all likely to continue limiting scientific progress during the 1980s. As the scientific quality of SIAs comes under increasing scrutiny in the 1980s, political distortions of their scientific performance are likely to set the context for virtually all other issues.

The remainder of this chapter considers those other issues. It is divided into two sections: The first section considers issues of data and methods; the second section considers broader issues of the researcher's proper role, i.e., special issues created in part by social impact assessment's hybrid heritage.

RESEARCH ISSUES

Data and Methods

Data from Impact Areas. / In the 1970s, social impact assessments showed a tendency to use existing, census-type data. If this practice continues into the 1980s, it is likely to become a concern, particularly in rural areas. Census data are an important and highly useful source of information in urban areas, where they are often available in considerable richness even at the city-block level. However, in rural areas, data other than head counts may not be available for any geographic units smaller than counties. Some rural western counties are larger than our smaller eastern states, with truly significant impacts taking place fifty to one hundred miles away from the larger population concentrations of the county. Even if more census data were to become available for rural areas, however, they might not help us answer the most important SIA questions. "The use of available data tends to direct attention away from questions that *need* to be answered and redirects attention toward questions that *can* be answered" (Little, 1977:33). Selectivity based on simple data availability is as unacceptable scientifically as selectivity based on sheer political expediency. It is probably not possible to assess all the social impacts of a given project, but a reliance on available data may preclude a researcher from analyzing other changes identified by relevant theories as having significant consequences for human well-being. *In order to improve the scientific adequacy of social impact assessments during the 1980s, it is important that researchers develop and use data that are both adequate and appropriate to the SIA questions that need to be asked.*

Data on Prior Impacts. / Social impact assessments can be accurate only if they are based on information and made understandable through clear and logical statements of cause and effect. The most rational course of action for the long run would be to do assessments of individual facilities based on "categorical" knowledge – information about "other impacts like this one" – which is then tailored to the uniqueness of any particular situation (Freudenburg, 1980). For this to occur, however, the more general data base must first exist, and, in many cases, it must first be developed. *Therefore, research is needed that will determine the extent to which categorical data can be developed and used for filling gaps in existing knowledge, for testing existing propositions, and for other applications to specific impact situations.*

SIAs in rural areas often involve population growth because the facilities being considered require a work force much larger than that which can be supplied by the local area. Probably the most sophisticated SIA areas are those that analyze the economic and demographic consequences of facilities. Despite the technological sophistication of economic and demographic projection models, few of them have been tested in empirical situations, and relatively little is known about their accuracy. *Research is required to assess the accuracy of alternative economic and demographic project models and to identify the factors that affect their usefulness.*

Available SIA models have rather limited usefulness for a number of important questions about the social and cultural consequences of growth (Murdock and Leistritz, 1979:306). Aside from economic and demographic consequences, little is known about the effects of growth (or decline or displacement) on specific subgroups of individuals in communities. How are these effects mitigated or altered by individual personalities, social supports, public services, or other intervening factors? In the case of rapidly growing communities, how real are the frequently mentioned "boomtown pathologies," e.g., drunkenness, depression, and delinquency? Under what conditions are local residents better off and worse off? How are the answers to these questions altered if developments lead to increased contact between different cultural groups? Although significant research on sociocultural impacts is under way, it is not possible now to address adequately many questions about the impacts of growth upon human and social well-being. *Greater research emphasis needs to be placed on assessing the sociocultural impacts of population growth.*

More is currently known about the sociocultural consequences of rapid growth, however, than is known about many of the significant impacts that occur in the absence of growth. Researchers and policy makers need to pay increasing attention to the consequences of decline or displacement, and to facilities that maintain stable demographic conditions but still create significant social or cultural changes. Also needed is increased attention to the social impacts of environmental changes per se and of changes in resource and land use policies. Many of the changes in this area, while not as visible as Wyoming strip mines, may still have significant long-range consequences. *Researchers need to address the subtle yet important "nongrowth" impacts of developments.*

The Researcher's Role

Relationships between Agencies and SIA Practitioners. / Perhaps no characteristic distinguishes social impact assessment from "academic" social science as clearly as the fact that SIA practitioners are often employed by agencies that have authority over the content of the assessment. Agency personnel and social scientists often have different backgrounds, interests, expectations, and criteria for adequacy. Researchers sometimes complain that agencies prefer that assessments be performed quickly, using available data, according to standard agency procedures, and with little emphasis on follow-up research. The researchers prefer methodologies that are more widely accepted in the social science community. Often these methods cannot be compressed in time because much of the research that the researcher believes to be important requires the collection of longitudinal data. Agency personnel, on the other hand, complain that researchers are often more interested in abstract theoretical concepts than in the relatively specific questions that need to be addressed, and are more interested in maintaining "academic" ritual purity than in meeting firm deadlines. In short, the complaint is that SIA researchers often have little understanding of the constraints within which the assessments must take place. In addition, they often fail to realize that the SIA is intended to be only one of many sources of information taken into account in decision making.

The differences in perspective are real and significant. Both the agencies and researchers have legitimate and sincere points of view. Yet, for social impact assessment to be successful, researchers and agencies must negotiate mutually agreeable settlements whenever possible. Despite the importance of reaching mutually satisfactory arrangements, however, the negotiations are likely to become extremely delicate at times, for the differences in viewpoints often grow out of two areas of deep and basic significance for a professional's functioning: the extent to which any SIA can be routinized, and the proper level of autonomy for an SIA researcher. These two issues are clearly interrelated: the greater the extent to which an activity can be routinized, the less the importance of a researcher's autonomy. However, the only way that social impact assessments can be routinized is if the needed data base, both categorical and site-specific, already exists.

One of the most significant problems that emerged during SIA's first decade was "premature routinization." Agencies' practical desires to perform SIAs efficiently led to a proliferation of "how-to" manuals, despite weaknesses and massive gaps in existing knowledge. It also led to the performance of supposedly "social" impact assessments by persons who had little or no social science expertise, such as engineers. An ironic consequence is that, as SIA enters its second decade, the agencies' case for genuine routinization is not as strong as it could be. Because of the "premature routinization" of the 1970s, there is an extremely strong need for nonroutine research in order to build a strong knowledge base during the 1980s. *The delicate and interrelated issues of researcher autonomy and research task routinization are likely to be increasingly important research issues for social impact assessment in the 1980s.*

Relationships between Research and "Action." / Social impact assessment adds delicacy to the issue of a researcher's personal involvement with an issue. Under many definitions, SIA includes not only "assessment" but also making recommendations for mitigating or avoiding adverse impacts, setting up public participation programs to gather public input, and conducting education programs to explain an agency's actions and rationale to the public. Critics have charged that the education programs sometimes become attempts to co-opt potential opposition; even in suggesting alternatives to policy makers, however, the SIA practitioner is stepping out of the role of the value-free researcher. Ironically, the risk of an "action role" introducing distortion to the assessments may be most serious for programs designed to gather public input. The most vocal persons in a population are not necessarily those who will be most affected by a proposed development. Indeed, there is a serious risk that public participation may lead to the internalization of standard political pressures rather than to more thorough or better balanced assessments. Unpopular facilities (e.g., nuclear plants) are often located in poor or sparsely settled rural areas because such areas are not as effective in protecting their interests in the political arena as others are. An SIA that is largely a means for allowing interest group input into the policy-making process is likely to encourage quite different decisions than would a full, balanced, and professional assessment that also includes explicit attention to the impacts likely to fall upon groups that are *not* effectively organized. *As the scientific performance of social impact assessment comes under increasing scrutiny, the relationships between value-free research and "action" need to be carefully examined.*

Equity and Societal Rationality. / The most basic of all SIA issues are those of equity and diseconomies. A developer is unlikely to pursue a project that will lose money. The problems that led to environmental and social impact assessments are matters of a broader societal balance sheet, i.e., the fact that a developer's profit can sometimes be made at the expense of other persons or groups.[2] The equity issue is particularly relevant in rural areas in that many of the most noxious types of facilities (power plants, waste dumps, and so on) are often placed in rural areas, even though most of their beneficiaries are urban residents. In some ways, the arrangement is entirely logical. If an installation may be genuinely dangerous, it is preferable to locate it away from large concentrations of people. However, if an installation is too dangerous to have near the human beings living in an urban area, then is it also too dangerous to have near people living in rural areas?

The question of equity also goes much deeper; indeed, it is in some ways the core of the SIA process. This chapter has repeatedly referred to social impact assessment as a process designed to provide rational input to decisionmaking. In the long run, however, an equitable treatment of all members of society may be the procedure that has the greatest rationality of all. In a sense then, this chapter has come full circle. Although the political components of SIAs may tend to distort the scientific performance of assessments, it may be that a more positive kind of complementarity is also inherent in the process. Scientifically sound SIA research can help to *reduce* the inequities and other distortions inherent in political processes. This should lead to a more equitable and hence a more fully rational functioning of the political system. *Thus, the scientific competence of social impact assessment research may be the central research issue of the 1980s, and SIA practitioners' ability to contribute to a better reasoned decision-making process may be the largest research issue of all, for this or for any other decade.*

NOTES

1. Until the number of lawsuits increased, environmental impact statements often ignored social impacts altogether. In a review of eighty randomly selected environmental impact statements that had been prepared between 1970 and 1974, Wilke and Cain found that absolutely "no social research method or technique could be determined in 86.5 percent of the cases" (Wilke and Cain, 1977:107). In recent years, agencies appear to have paid increasing attention to truly social impacts, perhaps in part through an increase in the number of rural sociologists and other social scientists hired.

2. An example of "diseconomies" occurs when a factory cuts costs by dumping dangerous wastes into a stream – or into a Love Canal – rather than investing in expensive clean-up equipment. The factory has thus externalized part of the true cost of production, leaving part of that cost not to itself or its customers but to persons who live downstream or come to the area in future generations.

REFERENCES

Freudenburg, William R. 1980. "The effects of rapid population growth on the social and personal well-being of boomtown residents." Paper presented at the Western Rural Development Center Conference on "Coping with the Impacts of Rapid Growth," Scottsdale, Arizona.

Little, Ronald L. 1977. *Some Social Consequences of Boomtowns.* Los Angeles: Lake Powell Research Project, Bulletin 57.

Murdock, Steve H., and F. Larry Leistritz. 1979. *Energy Development in the Western United States: Impact on Rural Areas.* New York: Praeger Publishers.

U.S. Council on Environmental Quality. 1978. *Regulations for Implementing the Procedural Provisions of the National Environmental Policy Act.* Washington, D.C.: U.S. Government Printing Office.

U.S. Council on Environmental Quality. 1979. *Environmental Quality, 1979: The Tenth Annual Report of the Council on Environmental Quality.* Washington, D.C.: U.S. Government Printing Office.

Wilke, Arthur S., and Harvey R. Cain. 1977. "Social impact assessment under NEPA: The state of the field." *Western Sociological Review* 8:105–108.

REFERENCES

Part 6
AGRICULTURE

In some areas of the United States, it is difficult to drive along a familiar rural road without the impression that "it's not what it used to be." In the Midwest, these roads once exhibited a familiar unanimity: similarly constructed white houses, similar outbuildings dominated by a red barn, similar livestock, and a similar array of farm implements. These farmsteads confirmed a homogeneity with respect to what constituted the farm. It was typically diversified and usually the sole source of the family's livelihood. The only disruptions to the nearly monotonous repetition of similar farmsteads was an occasional one-room country school, church, or crossroads elevator or general store.

The 1980 scene portrays the changes that have come to agriculture and rural life. The country schools have disappeared and only an occasional church remains. Many of the farmsteads have disappeared entirely, replaced by uninterrupted fields of corn, soybeans, or wheat. Others have a ghostly half-there, half-gone appearance; on these farmsteads, a well-kept lawn and house are shadowed from behind by weed filled barn lots and decaying outbuildings. They confirm the division of the farm that was once here. The land was incorporated into another farm; the buildings were rented or sold as a place to live to someone whose livelihood comes from a nearby town. On still other farmsteads, the outbuildings give a half-used appearance—automatic feeders and waterers for a few hogs or cattle that need only occasional attention. This enterprise is well suited to the lifestyles of mostly retired farmers, part-time farmers, or urban transplants for whom a few chores are therapeutic and may provide a little income. Still other farmsteads are simply abandoned and in the advanced stages of deterioration.

Another change along the roadside—and a startling one—is the number of new homes where there used to be none. The homes are tied to the road rather than to the land. They have no outbuildings or, if they do, they were likely made from a kit. A few are hand constructed, giving the appearance of being miniature replicas of the functional hay and livestock barns that once dominated the roadway. Even more striking is the diversity of homes that no suburb would tolerate: expensive brick ranchstyle homes next to mobile homes with attachments, the result of construction methods that no city code would approve. The occupants are as diverse as the homes they occupy, except for their common dependence on nonfarm jobs and the pick-up trucks that confirm their "rural" status. The signs in front of many homes advertising registered beagles, hairstyling, light automobile repair, etc., give ample evidence that tillage of the land is not the only or even the main source of income being generated by rural residents.

However, the biggest change of all has occurred on the farms that remain. The unanimity of appearance and function has disappeared. On some farms, there is no longer any livestock. The outbuildings have been converted to machinery sheds for the large and specialized equipment required to farm several hundred or thousand acres. On other farms, huge silos and hundreds of feed bunks confirm the existence of feeding operations that fatten cattle, most of which were purchased in another state when they were already a year old. Another farm has ultramodern, air conditioned buildings where newborn pigs are born, to be sold a few weeks later as feeder pigs. A nearby farm may have a large, remodeled barn with new concrete floors where purchased feeder pigs (though not necessarily from a nearby farm) are fattened to market weight. There are now far fewer farms in rural America, and those that remain are often quite specialized and different from others in the same community.

Finally, there are a number of farms that are no less deceptive than a desert mirage. Machinery, buildings, and activity give the appearance of a full-time farming operation. Yet the "farmer" has a full-time city job. Judicious planning of vacations, occasional hired help, and dependence upon nearby farmers to do custom tillage and harvesting make it possible for these moonlight farmers to produce more food and fiber than some current full-time farmers, and more than virtually all farmers of past decades.

The heterogeneity of the farms that now occupy rural America and the forces that have brought about these changes is the topic of the chapters that follow. This section's introductory chapter by Havens (Chapter 30) contends that the structure of contemporary U.S. agriculture is a product of state (government) intervention. He points out that rural sociologists have not made research on government policy a focus of their attention, and he outlines a series of questions to which the answers should enhance our understanding of how changes in agriculture are connected to changes in the broader political economy.

Chapter 31, by Stockdale, describes the replacement of an agricultural production policy with a food policy that is influenced significantly by a concern over balance of payments, consumer costs, and the environment. This competition to control agriculture raises a host of research issues. Perhaps the overriding issue is to understand the consequences of different interests dominating U.S. agriculture in the 1980s.

The dramatic rise in food production per farm that has occurred throughout most of this century has been accompanied by an equally dramatic drop in the number of farmers. A decline in so-called family farms and the rise in corporate agriculture is a result. In Chapter 32, Rodefeld identifies research issues that surround the continuing debate of who will operate America's farms.

The number and types of farms that comprise American agriculture also has consequences for rural communities. However, relatively little is known about how the change in structure of agriculture, which includes changes in marketing, processing, distributing, and farm production, influences the quality of community life. Heffernan, in Chapter 33, considers these issues, developing a series of research questions that need to be addressed.

Not all U.S. farms are commercial and capital-intensive. Six percent of American farmers produce over 50 percent of the total output; the other 94 percent have often been overlooked. Some of these are farmers struggling to hang on by maintaining full-time jobs off the farm and doing the farm work by moonlight and on weekends. Others have made a lifestyle choice and, by doing something they enjoy on a part-time basis, produce significant amounts of food and fiber for the market place. The small and part-time farmer, whose numbers are increasing in most regions of the country, is the focus of Chapter 34 by Coughenour and Wimberley.

30
The Changing Structure of U.S. Agriculture

A. EUGENE HAVENS

Recent interest in analyzing the changing structure of U.S. agriculture is a product of general economic crisis and changing worldwide alliances that affect access to nonrenewable natural resources. Long-term growth in our agricultural productivity is largely a result of state intervention in the agricultural production process, i.e., technological development, subsidies and price controls, guaranteed access to international markets, and provision of cheap energy for farm production and food processing (Hopkins and Puchala, 1978). Economic crisis has affected the fiscal capacity of the state, limiting its ability to pursue certain types of interventions; the realignment of international control over petroleum has brought an end to the cheap energy policies of the state. These factors will seriously affect the future structure of American agriculture. The chapters that follow address major changes that are likely to occur and what future research should be undertaken to document these changes. This chapter provides an overall framework within which to cast analysis of these changes.

The significance of government policy within agriculture is difficult to overestimate if by agriculture we mean the production of food and not simply farming. Today, farming is only one link in the food production chain, which remains a highly significant part of modern economic activity. In the United States, the entire chain of food production activities

A. Eugene Havens is a professor in the Department of Rural Sociology, University of Wisconsin, Madison, Wisconsin. He has written ten books and more than fifty articles concerning class relations and rural development.

accounts for about 30 percent of the labor force, second only to government bureaucracy. This "food sector" has been shaped and molded by government intervention in agriculture throughout the twentieth century. The kind of agriculture and, to a large extent, the kind of rural society that now exists can be attributed to the nature and form of this intervention.

Surprisingly, rural sociologists have not included an analysis of the state as an integral part of their research on changing agrarian structure. Thus, research on changing structure has remained largely descriptive. Part of the explanation for this lack of analysis of the state can be attributed to pluralist conceptions of power and the assumption that state policy is merely an output of the conflict management process.

Pluralists define society as an aggregate of dissimilar but equally influential special interest groups with diverse and conflicting interests (Bentley, 1967; Truman, 1951; Dahl, 1961; Rose, 1967; Easton, 1971). These special interest groups range from corporations to sporting clubs; with supposed relatively equal power they attempt to influence government policy, which is seen as the product of the countervailing pressure of all the groups, with no single group or alliance of them being dominant. The balance of conflicting demands on the state is represented by state policy. The various interest groups negotiate and bargain to reach a mutual enhancement of effort. In the political process, this tends to maximize the interests and concerns of all participants.

There are two principal problems with the pluralist view of power. First, the assumption that society is composed of a wide diversity of equally powerful groups organized around conflicting interests is not empirically defensible. For example, only about half of the U.S. population belongs to a voluntary association. It is precisely for this reason that membership in organizations is frequently measured as a dimension of a person's relative status. Moreover, it is likely that the fifteen million members of the AFL-CIO do not have as much effect on state policy as does the thirteen-hundred-member Council on Foreign Relations. Finally, most voluntary associations make decisions without consulting their members (Szymanski, 1978).

Second, the assumption that output of the state is an accurate and direct result of the relative strength of the various interest groups implies that any state policy is a real possibility. That is, the determination of state "output" is a function of the "input" of the various pressure groups. In reality, there are only a limited number of effective policies that the state can follow in any area without causing general socioeconomic disruption. Although various interest groups may want a given policy, it may not be feasible vis-à-vis the very structure that the state is charged with preserving.

These underlying assumptions–pluralism, volunteerism, and conflict regulation governed by mutual restraint–have guided research on the structure of agriculture away from the *political* component of political economy. It has been assumed that any category of farmers (family farms, commodity groups, farm workers) have rather equal capacities to protect their interests. However, power is not like air–indeed, the state is a major component of the concentration of power that allows for the perpetuation of unequal access to resources.

THE RURAL SECTOR

Access to production resources as a dimension of the class structure of rural communities has been a neglected area of research. The neglect stems from a dominant view that the major role of rural communities is to provide a source of "primitive accumulation." That is, rural communities provide a pool of labor that can be displaced from agriculture without any consequent drop in food production because of the application of labor-saving production technology. This displacement process is generally suggested to be harmonious because adequate jobs at a reasonable wage can be found by these displaced people in an expanding urban sector. In fact, this is not the case, as amply documented by Coles (1977).

Nevertheless, most institutions in rural communities are concerned with facilitating this displacement rather than servicing local need. Consequently, measuring the stratification pattern in rural communities by such variables as education, membership in voluntary associations, and available services is probably an adequate measure of urbanism but not of *rural structure.*

If the term *rural* means anything other than a nonmetropolitan residence, its definition must include the labor process as well as geographical or community boundary definitions. The tendency to treat any town of less than twenty-five hundred residents as rural, for example, and to consider them as similar regardless of how production is organized in these rural areas, is very prevalent. The number of communities with less than twenty-five hundred members has declined, and many rural sociologists have felt that the field of study for rural sociology is diminishing (Newby, 1980). In reality, the field of study is expanding and becoming more complex from the point of view of relations of production. Capitalist development brings about not only urban growth and industrialization but also complex and contradictory changes in relations of production in agriculture. Surprisingly, very little attempt to document these changes in relations of production can be encountered in the sociological and economic literature on agriculture in the United States. Consequently, there is no basis for determining class structure and class relations in agriculture. Little information exists on how agricultural producers are simultaneously transformed into an industrial proletariat, an agricultural proletariat, owners of land and equipment who lost control over what to produce and how to produce it, tenants, contract farmers, and a class of surplus appropriators both in and out of agriculture. In brief, class analyses have not been part of the historical record of America's agricultural social scientists.

RESEARCH ISSUES

Historically, one of the most dynamic sectors of the U.S. political economy has been agriculture. Broad transformations in the production relations in agriculture have seriously impacted the class structure of the United States, producing imbalances in power relations and shifting class alliances as different sectors of the U.S. population have attempted to maintain or enhance their levels of living and life chances. These transformations have included a move from slavery to plantation agriculture based on share-cropping to "machinofacture" of cotton in the South; family farms to agribusiness, particularly in California and the Southwest; subsistence farms to the capitalization of family farms through new technologies based on a cheap energy policy in the Midwest and the Grain Belt; and industrialization to the struggle to reestablish a labor-intensive agriculture in the Northeast. One observable consequence of these historical transformations was the dramatic expulsion of agricultural producers in rural United States and their conversion to urban residents and workers. However, very little research has been conducted to develop an understanding of the consequences of these changes for the class structure of the United States. Most studies have been descriptive at best, and they have failed to forge the analytical link between town and country. Once again, sweeping change is affecting American agriculture. *It is imperative to analyze these changes and develop this link between changes in agriculture and the broader political economy.*

In the 1970s, agriculture in the United States underwent far-reaching changes. These changes not only produced national concern about production but also internationalized issues that affect the survival capacity of hundreds of thousands of American farmers. For example, before 1970, the United States was not a major exporter of food and fiber. Today, the United States is the world's leading food exporter, accounting for half of the world's trade in grain alone. Agricultural exports have become critical to the U.S. balance of trade as industrial productivity has declined vis-à-vis western Europe and Japan. However, export demand is subject to wide price fluctuations and market uncertainty largely determined by political and natural phenomena (e.g., drought, floods), making planning of production difficult. A political shift, like the recent embargo of grain exports to the Soviet Union, can plunge many farmers into bankruptcy.

Moreover, the rate of increase in agricultural productivity has slowed considerably in the past decade due in part to the forced departure from a subsidized energy policy that has caused cutbacks in use of fertilizers, pesticides, irrigation, and machinery. If the United States loses its worldwide productivity advantage, the results could range from reduced exports and thus severe food shortages in some countries, to rising food prices that will affect the real income of urban workers and rural unemployment in the United States.

In addition, the disregard by some farm production processes for natural resource preservation and conservation is beginning to affect productivity and the future resource base (see Chapter 35). Indiscriminate use of water is causing alarm as aquifers are not being replenished and conflicts over use of the declining supply of water in some areas of the country are increasing (see Chapter 37). Pesticides and fertilizer use have, in some cases, irreversibly affected the water supply, vegetal cover, and soil chemistry.

Another factor affecting American agriculture has been the reversal (at least in the short run) of the long-term migration from country to city (see Chapter 3). Since 1970, about half of all population growth has occurred in nonmetro areas, particularly in the Sun Belt. Industries faced with rising labor costs and increased concern for environmental impact have begun to locate in rural areas where zoning, labor unions, and environmental control are weaker. The new jobs may have benefited long-time residents, but evidence suggests that many others have been squeezed out by the newcomers and rural poverty has increased.

All of these changes have seriously affected the survival capacity of certain types of farm units. As the families residing on these units have been buffeted by wide price fluctuations for their products, increased energy costs, changing international trade restrictions, and decreased natural resource productivity through soil and water depletion (and thus declining incomes), they have had to change their own labor distribution schemes. Women's roles have become increasingly differentiated on the family farm (see Chapter 12) and children are frequently sent down a mobility path that moves them into the urban labor markets or increasingly segmented rural labor markets (see Chapter 10).

Changes in rural politics include newly emerged alliances between farm and labor groups in the U.S. Congress. Consumer and environmental groups are making their voices heard in the Department of Agriculture. As these new political processes unfold, the state is forced to play an ever-increasing role in directing, or attempting to direct, the nature of changes in the relations of production in agriculture. *We must analyze how these political processes present rural families with changing conditions for survival and how families attempt to respond by presenting the state with contradictory demands for subsidies, cheap credit, restricted land use, new markets, more water, and new technology, or, at times, for the state to adopt a nonintervention policy.*

As farm production changes, urban life chances and earning capacity may vary. The result will be a mobilization of urban peple to protect their interests. Therefore, research must be directed toward understanding how state policy is formulated and the consequences of the resultant policy for the changing survival strategies of rural families.

The major research foci outlined above should be set within an analytical framework that will capture the relevant national and international dimensions that influence rural change and produce changes in class structures and alliances. One of the critical concerns that this research must attempt to determine is the causes of changing structure of agricultural production. We contend that the causes of structural change in U.S. agriculture reverse the roles of the market economy and state in attempting to mediate conflicting interests and developing a definition of how agricultural production (its organization and its output) relates to changing notions of the public interest. How agriculture should be organized, what it should produce at what prices, and what is in the public interest are partly determined by general economic conditions; international relations; class structure and interest, expressed through organizational capacity to pressure the state and organize the market; and through agents of the state's own definition of the public interest (Buttel and Newby, 1980).

These considerations produce the first set of basic research questions, which are:

1. What have been the changing socioeconomic conditions that have affected the organization of agricultural production?
2. How have the different sectors of agricultural producers organized to protect their own interests vis-à-vis these changing conditions?
3. What types of alliances have occurred (or not occurred) between sectors of agricultural producers and other classes in the American society in their attempts to determine how agricultural production should be organized and what should be produced?

FIGURE 30.1 Model for Analysis of Changing Structure of U.S. Agriculture.

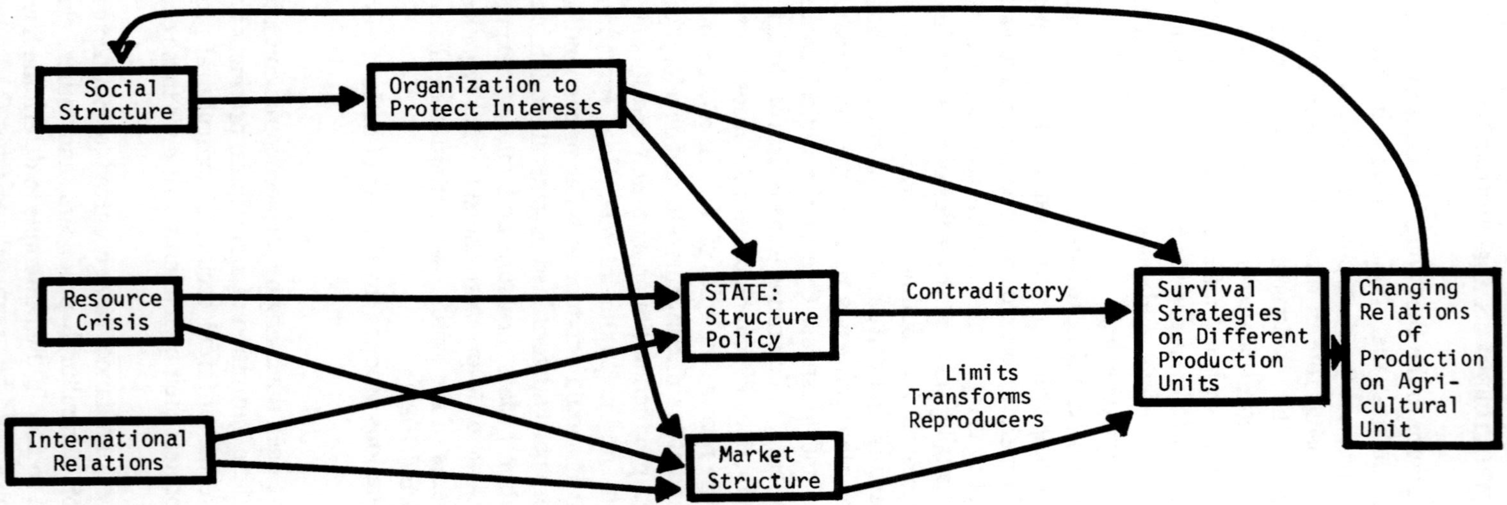

Focus on Structure: --How current structure developed: historical analysis; class analysis.

--How it is changing: survey; interview; project evaluation; policy research.

4. How have the conflicts of interest between and within these sectors been reflected in the construction of government agricultural policy?
5. How does the structure and policy of the American state affecting agriculture compare with state intervention in other advanced capitalist societies?

Developing answers to this set of questions is necessary for analyzing the changing survival strategies of different agricultural production units. These strategies in turn explain the changing relations of production on different agricultural production units. The concern with survival strategies forms the analytical link between causes of changing structures, the nature of state intervention in organizing agricultural production, and the changing class structure of the rural sector of the United States. This concern produces the second set of basic research questions (expressed graphically in Figure 30.1). These questions are:

1. What are the different labor processes encountered in the U.S. food production chain?
2. How have the direct producers involved in these distinct labor processes attempted to reproduce themselves?
3. How has state intervention affected this reproduction process?
4. What are the current structural limitations on these different survival strategies?
5. How do these structural limitations affect the potential for establishing and/or reproducing different forms of agricultural production?

This research program assumes that the state is a reflection of power *and* a source of power that reproduces the various forms of domination that exist in a society. It also assumes that the changing structure of rural society is best studied by mapping the relations of production that determine people's capacities to affect the governmental policy that impinges on their everyday lives.

REFERENCES

Bentley, Arthur. 1967. *The Process of Government.* Cambridge, Massachusetts: Belknap Press.

Buttel, Frederick, and Howard Newby (editors). 1980. *The Rural Sociology of the Advanced Societies: Critical Perspectives.* Montclair, New Jersey: Allanheld, Osmun, and Co.

Coles, Robert. 1977. *Children of Crisis.* Boston: Little, Brown, and Co.

Dahl, Robert. 1961. *Who Governs?* New Haven, Connecticut: Yale University Press.
Easton, David. 1971. *The Political System.* New York: Alfred A. Knopf, Inc.
Hopkins, R. F., and D. J. Puchala (editors). 1978. *The Global Political Economy of Food.* Madison, Wisconsin: University of Wisconsin Press.
Newby, Howard. 1980. "Rural sociology: A trend report." *Current Sociology* 28(1):1–141.
Rose, Arnold. 1967. *The Power Structure.* New York: Oxford University Press.
Szymanski, Albert. 1978. *The Capitalist State and the Politics of Class.* Cambridge, Massachusetts: Winthrop Publishers.
Truman, David. 1951. *The Governmental Process.* New York: Alfred A. Knopf, Inc.

31 Who Will Speak for Agriculture?

JERRY D. STOCKDALE

The agricultural policy process in the United States has never been simple. It has long been characterized by competing interests, and no farm organization, commodity group, protest movement, or political candidate has ever been able to speak for all farmers, let alone for all of agriculture. In the last two decades, however, an already complex situation has become even more complicated. World food needs, consumerism, environmentalism, international conflicts, and balance of payments have intruded into the agricultural policy arena. From the perspective of many in the old agricultural establishment, "all hell has broken loose." Not only are new issues and new power bases competing with the old; new definitions are competing as well.

This chapter is concerned with research on this new reality. It is concerned with changes in agriculture and food policy and with the forces responsible for these changes. It is concerned with the need for research on who will "speak" for agriculture and the contexts within which they speak, what interests they represent, how they speak, and their likely impacts.

EVOLUTION OF AGRICULTURAL POLICY

A review of how control over U.S. agricultural policy has changed during the last century is necessary for understanding the importance of cur-

---

Jerry D. Stockdale is a professor in the Department of Sociology, Anthropology, and Social Work at the University of Northern Iowa, Cedar Falls, Iowa. His writings include

rent research issues. According to Paarlberg (1978, 1980), agricultural policy is now in its third stage of evolution.

Agricultural Development Agenda

The first stage of evolution was an "agricultural development" agenda; emphasis was on research and education to increase farm productivity. It was assumed that agricultural development would contribute to both rural development and overall societal development. The appropriate role for government involvement was support of research and education, and it was generally felt that agriculture should develop with a minimum of government regulation.

Establishment of the USDA and the land grant colleges in 1862, the agricultural experiment stations in 1887, and the Cooperative Extension Service in 1914, were highlights of the first agenda. Many of the research and education initiatives of this period and their impact on agricultural structure continued into the second agenda period and will probably continue well into the future.

Commodity Programs Agenda

The late 1920s and the 1930s were times of considerable stress for agriculture, and a new orientation toward the role of government in agriculture emerged. This second policy period was characterized by commodity programs (Paarlberg, 1980). The primary objective was to reduce deprivation and control discontent by stabilizing farm income (Talbot and Hadwiger, 1968). Most of the big budget programs were directly concerned with the increasing tendency of American agriculture to "overproduce," resulting in low commodity prices and serious economic problems for farmers and rural communities. The remedies included supply controls, import limits, export stimulation, price supports, and food purchase and diversion.

The government influenced commodity supplies and prices in order to achieve an acceptable balance of farm income, food costs, and government expenditures. Although these commodity programs had widespread support, the issues contained tremendous potential for conflict.

Issue definition and policy setting during this and the first policy period were dominated by the "production coalition" (Hadwiger, 1981). It included a close alliance of industry groups, the American Farm Bureau Federation and the National Farmers' Union (which often disagreed with

---

a book in the Rural Sociological Monograph series, *Area Development through Agricultural Innovation: The New York Sugar Beet Fiasco.*

one another), commodity groups, large farmers, some members of Congress, personnel in USDA agencies, and representatives of the land grant colleges. In general, they supported agricultural research, education, and commodity programs and shared a desire to maintain a stable and productive agricultural system.

During the second policy period there was general support for limiting the farm policy agenda. Policy was not to go too far in treating the individual problems of rural people and the social problems of rural places. Evidence of this is provided by the demise within the USDA of the Farm Security Administration (FSA) and the Bureau of Agricultural Economics (BAE).

The FSA, which had been established in the 1930s to provide assistance to low-income farmers, came to be seen by "the Farm Bureau, especially in the South, . . . as socialistic, racially integrationist, and a threat to the Farm Bureau power position." By 1946, the FSA had been stripped of many of its programs and "submerged into a new and weaker organization, the Farmers' Home Administration" (Talbot and Hadwiger, 1968:12).

The problem of the BAE may have been that it collected too much of the "wrong kinds" of information. By exploring issues of structural change in agriculture and their social implications, the BAE went well beyond what the production coalition considered appropriate. An important example, and possibly a pivotal one for the future of the BAE, was Walter Goldschmidt's (1946) classic study of two California communities, Arvin and Dinuba. That study, which suggested possible social costs associated with the trend toward large-scale agriculture, was partially suppressed by large farm and corporate interests (Goldschmidt, 1978). The BAE was deprived of its planning function in 1945 and "was scattered asunder by Secretary Benson in 1953" (Talbot and Hadwiger, 1968:29).

For a variety of reasons, perhaps including the ferociousness of the attacks on the Goldschmidt study and the BAE, research on social impacts of technological and structural change in agriculture received little support within the USDA and agricultural experiment stations. The problems were quite visible but were kept off the research and policy agendas.

Food and Agriculture Issues Agenda

During the 1960s and the 1970s, important changes developed in the agricultural policy agenda. They resulted from a greatly increased ability to measure pollution and health impacts, urban unrest, problems of declining rural communities, and concerns for equity issues. In addition, important beliefs and values (e.g., belief in progress, technology, efficiency, materialism) were being questioned. The old production coalition was forced to make room for a new "externalities coalition" (Hadwiger, 1981). Paarlberg's third policy stage, the period of "new agenda" *food* and agricultural policy, had begun (1978, 1980).

Food and agricultural policy was being influenced increasingly by events off the farms, outside agriculture, and even outside the United States. Although the old establishment, especially agribusiness interests and commodity groups, can be expected to continue or even increase their efforts to shape policy, there is little doubt that the issues that dominate the 1980s' policy agenda will be influenced by concerns for:

- worldwide food production, consumption, and needs
- foreign policy
- stabilizing the American economy, including employment, inflation, and balance of payments
- structure of the total domestic food production system, including concentration of ownership and control
- the problems of marginal farmers
- the well-being of farm workers
- population location and residential preferences
- rural development
- food needs of domestic low-income populations
- food quality, safety, and price
- resource availability and cost, including competition for land, water, and energy
- environmental quality, including agricultural chemicals and wastes and soil erosion
- public health
- the costs of financing programs at the local, state, and federal levels

RESEARCH ISSUES

Competing Goals in U.S. Food and Agriculture Policy

Research is needed to delineate the full range of goals that various interested groups and individuals would like to have met through food and agriculture policy. It is important that the goals underlying policy choices be made explicit. Who wants what from food and agriculture policy? To what extent are various goals complementary and to what extent competing? What changes in goals are occurring? Why are the goals changing? Goals most likely to have major impacts on food and agriculture policy in the

1980s include productivity goals, structure of agriculture goals, environmental goals, and rural development goals.

Productivity Goals and Impacts

Food has become a major instrument in economic and foreign policy. There are now strong pressures to produce huge quantities of food for domestic consumption and export. On the domestic scene, food represents a major expenditure for low-income families. Food costs are also very important in the fight against inflation.

Agricultural exports are crucial to the economic well-being of the United States. In 1970, the United States had positive agricultural and nonagricultural trade balances. By 1976, however, partly as a result of increased petroleum prices, the United States was experiencing a $15.5 billion deficit for nonagricultural products. The impact of this was softened greatly by a tenfold increase in the net trade balance for agriculture, an increase from $1.3 billion in 1970 to $12.2 billion in 1976 (Carter and Johnston, 1978:472). Agricultural trade policy is therefore crucial to the value of the U.S. dollar and to the stability of the U.S. economy. This can be expected to influence heavily future food and agriculture policy.

Food is also an important foreign policy tool. After much talk about the possibility of using food as a weapon, this has come to pass. The most obvious example was when President Carter restricted grain shipments to the Soviet Union following Soviet intervention in Afghanistan.

These considerations seem to strengthen the position of those who regard efficiency and productivity as the key concerns for food and agriculture policy. At the extreme, such considerations could be used to stifle policy emphasis on environmental issues, on the structure of agriculture, and on rural communities. Therefore, *research is needed on how policies aimed at increasing agricultural productivity affect the structure of agriculture, rural communities, patterns of resource consumption, and environmental pollution.*

Structure of Agriculture

Agricultural production is increasingly concentrated on a relatively small number of highly productive farms. In 1977, 162,000 farms with sales of $100,000 or more (6 percent of all farms) produced slightly more than half of all cash receipts from farming; the 18.9 percent of farmers with sales of $40,000 or more produced nearly four-fifths (78.2 percent) of all cash receipts. Approximately four-hundred cattle feedlots, averaging over 30,000 head, now feed over half of the cattle fed in the United States. In 1974, "slightly more than 5,000 farms, each with 20,000 birds or more, accounted for nearly 70 percent of U.S. egg production" (Schertz, 1979:4).

Much of the agricultural production is concentrated in the hands of relatively few producers, and most of the farm population is characterized by relatively low levels of agricultural product sales. In 1977, approximately 1.9 million farms, or 69 percent of the total, received only 11 percent of the cash receipts to farming. Although many of the relatively low-volume producers worked full-time on their farms, most of them also worked off the farm. In fact, 1.3 million farm families, with farm product sales of less than $2,500 each, received 91 percent of their 1977 income from nonfarm sources (Paarlberg, 1980:196).

It has been suggested that we are moving toward a bifurcated or dualistic farm system. One part of it is composed of a large number of small part-time, subsistence, retirement, and hobby farms that provide a pool of surplus labor in rural places. The other is a smaller number of large, highly capitalized, commercial farms that generate profits for agribusiness firms and financial interests by purchasing large volumes of production inputs and producing relatively inexpensive agricultural commodities (Carter and Johnston, 1978; Davis, 1980; Goss et al., 1980; Wunderlich, 1976).

A related concern is that farmers are losing control of their farms through credit, land tenure, and various contract schemes (Goss et al., 1980). Some sectors are already highly integrated. All sugar cane and sugar beets are now grown under contract, as are 95 percent of vegetables for processing and 85 percent of citrus fruits. The percentages for livestock products range from 98 percent for milk for drinking and 97 percent for broiler chickens to 2 percent for hogs. Forty percent of all eggs in the United States are produced under contract, as are 22 percent of fed cattle (Paarlberg, 1980:192). The contracts vary considerably in the extent to which they restrict farmers' management prerogatives and the extent to which contracting provides opportunities for monopolistic exploitation of prices.

The American system of agricultural production is extremely diverse. Even the situations and interests of part-time farmers vary greatly depending on whether they are planning to remain in part-time farming, are attempting to become full-time farmers, or are phasing out of farming. The amount and sources of income of part-time farmers also vary tremendously. Greater attention to this diversity is needed. *Research is needed to specify the variety of roles, situations, and interests of the various populations involved in production of agricultural commodities. Research is also needed on likely impacts on the structure of agriculture of alternative food and agriculture policies.*

The desirability of protecting family-type farms is likely to be a key structure-of-agriculture issue during the next decade. The family farm is often seen as one of the last vestiges of independence and family entrepreneurship in America. In this view, family farming involves a variety of noneconomic values having to do with freedom, independence, and a way of life. Family-type farmers have been willing to accept below-average returns on investment in order to maintain these values. At one extreme, family-type farming is seen as an important bulwark of democracy. At the other extreme, it is viewed as false consciousness: family farmers are seen as a propertied semiproletariat who are forced by the exigencies of the larger economic system to exploit themselves and their families by working long hours for low returns (Davis, 1980). In this view, the family farm is little more than a myth used to legitimize programs that actually serve the interests of the largest commercial farms and agribusiness firms (Bonanno, 1980). *Research is needed to clarify the meaning of "family farming" and on the motivations and sources of satisfaction of family farmers. Research is also needed on the extent to which family farmers are losing control over their own farming operations.*

Agricultural policy has been concerned primarily with on-the-farm production of agricultural commodities, but this is only a small part of agriculture. Suppliers of farm inputs and the processors and handlers of farm outputs loom ever larger on the food and agriculture scene. In general, this agribusiness sector is much more concentrated and highly capitalized than the farm sector. Consumer groups and others are likely to give critical attention to this agribusiness sector in the future. If such firms appear to threaten the independence of farmers and the long-term availability of relatively inexpensive food, policy efforts may be made to curb their power. A related issue is the potential effectiveness of cooperatives in restricting the economic power of such firms (Martinson and Campbell, 1980). *Research is needed on the impacts of agribusiness and financial interests on the structure of agricultural production and on their ability to restrict the policy agenda. Research is also needed on the potential of cooperatives to reduce the economic dominance of agribusiness firms.*

Policy is very important in shaping the structure of agriculture, but that structure is also shaped by many other forces. One of the most important is the nature of the overall economy with its tendencies toward specialization and concentration. As Buttel suggests, "American agriculture is part of a larger crisis of resource scarcity and redundancy of labor that afflicts the whole of society" (1980:455). Future energy costs and the kinds of technology available are also likely to become very important. So will the effective demand for agricultural products on world markets. *Research is needed on the kinds of forces, other than policy, that are likely to have an impact on the structure of agriculture and on the availability and cost of food.*

Environmental Impacts

Concern for soil conservation has influenced agricultural policy since the 1930s. Recently, these concerns have been joined by a variety of other environmental issues. A major turning point was the publication in 1962 of Rachel Carson's *Silent Spring.* The book raised very important issues. With a holistic perspective it questioned methods of technology and raised concern for environmental impacts and quality-of-life issues, thus challenging prevailing policy biases. Environmental groups and coalitions quickly formed and flexed their muscles. Considerable environmental legislation has since been passed, including laws creating the Environmental Protection Agency. Numerous agricultural chemicals have been banned or restricted, and a variety of other environmental regulations have been created and enforced.

Environmental and public health concerns will definitely be part of the food and agriculture agenda throughout the 1980s. *Research is needed on the way and extent to which environmental concerns are incorporated into food and agriculture policy. Research is also needed on likely environmental impacts of alternative food and agriculture policies.*

Rural Development Goals

Policies that affect the structure of agriculture have important rural development impacts because they affect the economic base of rural communities. This effect was most pronounced in the 1940s, 1950s, and 1960s, when changes in agriculture had devastating effects on thousands of rural communities. To the extent that food and agriculture policies influence employment or the flow of funds into rural places, they will continue to have important impacts on rural communities. Indeed, one of the important arguments in favor of maintaining family farms is that they aid rural development. Much can be learned from experiences in European countries where concerns for the spatial distribution of population and for the overall employment situation have long influenced agricultural policy (Sinclair, 1980). *Research is needed on the likely rural development impacts of alternative food and agriculture policies.*

Power Structure and the Policy Process

The structure of power in food and agriculture policy is expanding. It is more open than in the past and is represented by a greater variety of interests. It is far from clear, however, precisely who is likely to be involved in the policy process in the 1980s. It is even less clear how much power the various interested parties will have. Some assert that industrial and financial interests have long dominated food and agricultural policy and will continue to do so (see Davis, 1980; Mann and Dickinson, 1980). Others feel that farmers and their representatives have dominated policy but are now losing power to consumer groups, environmentalists, representatives of the poor, farm workers, and others. The roles of the USDA and the land grant colleges are increasingly ambiguous and their influence on policy seems to be declining. Other agencies, such as the Department of State, the Department of Labor, the Environmental Protection Agency, and the Food and Drug Administration, impinge more and more on the old production coalition.

The power of farmers seems especially unclear. How effective are the traditional farm organizations? Which segments of the farm population do they represent? How satisfied are various farmers with them? To what extent are they being displaced by commodity groups?

Research is needed on who is involved in what ways in shaping food and agriculture policy, their interests and goals, their access to policy makers, their efforts to influence policy, and their impacts on policy. Research is also needed on the changes in the ability of various individuals and interest groups to influence food and agriculture policy.

Besides knowing *who* is involved in the policy process, it is important to know *how* policy is formed. The current emphases on food, environmental issues, the overall economic situation, and foreign policy, mean that the locus of policy making is changing. Critical decisions are being made outside the USDA and the House and Senate agricultural committees. Expert testimony on food and agricultural issues increasingly comes from outside the USDA/land grant college orbit. Lobbying on structure-of-agriculture issues is complicated by the entrance of new contestants and the increase in the number of decision centers to which attention must be given. Coalition formation, long an important feature of the policy process, is likely to become much more important in the future. *Research is needed on changes in the process of making food and agriculture policy, i.e., the changing loci of decisions and control and the patterns of interaction among the public and various interest groups.*

Our final concern is with the outputs of the policy process. How effectively does the policy process generate policies that deal meaningfully with the food and agriculture issues facing the nation and the world? Is the process characterized by action or stalemate? Why? Whose interests are reflected in the policy outputs? Whose interests are neglected or subverted? *Research is needed on the effectiveness of the policy process in generating policies and on how the nature of the policy process influences the kinds of policies that are produced.*

REFERENCES

Bonanno, Alessandro. 1980. "The logic of capitalist accumulation behind the myth of the family farm." Paper presented at the annual meetings of the Rural Sociological Society, Ithaca, New York.

Buttel, Frederick. 1980. "Agriculture, environment, and social change, some emergent issues." In Frederick Buttel and Howard Newby (editors), *The Rural Sociology of the Advanced Societies: Critical Perspectives.* Montclair, New Jersey: Allanheld, Osmun, and Co.

Carson, Rachel. 1962. *Silent Spring.* Boston: Houghton Mifflin Co.

Carter, Harold O., and Warren E. Johnston. 1978. "Some forces affecting the changing structure, organization, and control of American agriculture." *American Journal of Agricultural Economics* 60(December):738–748.

Davis, John E. 1980. "Capitalist agricultural development and the exploitation of the propertied laborer." In Frederick Buttel and Howard Newby (editors), *The Rural Sociology of the Advanced Societies: Critical Perspectives.* Montclair, New Jersey: Allanheld, Osmun, and Co.

Goldschmidt, Walter. 1946. *Small Business and the Community: A Study in the Central Valley of California on the Effects of Scale of Farm Operation.* Report of the Special Committee to Study Problems of American Small Business, U.S. Senate. Washington, D.C.: U.S. Government Printing Office.

_____. 1978. *As You Sow: Three Studies in the Social Consequences of Agribusiness.* Montclair, New Jersey: Allanheld, Osmun, and Co.

Goss, Kevin, Richard Rodefeld, and Frederick Buttel. 1980. "The political economy of class structure in U.S. agriculture." In Frederick Buttel and Howard Newby (editors), *The Rural Sociology of the Advanced Societies: Critical Perspectives.* Montclair, New Jersey: Allanheld, Osmun, and Co.

Hadwiger, Don F. 1981. *The Politics of Agricultural Research.* Lincoln, Nebraska: University of Nebraska Press.

Mann, Susan A., and James A. Dickinson. 1980. "State and agriculture in two eras of American capitalism." In Frederick Buttel and Howard Newby (editors), *The Rural Sociology of the Advanced Societies: Critical Perspectives.* Montclair, New Jersey: Allanheld, Osmun, and Co.

Martinson, Oscar B., and Gerald R. Campbell. 1980. "Betwixt and between: Farmers and the marketing of agricultural inputs and outputs." In Frederick Buttel and Howard Newby (editors), *The Rural Sociology of the Advanced Societies: Critical Perspectives.* Montclair, New Jersey: Allanheld, Osmun, and Co.

Paarlberg, Don. 1978. "A new agenda for agriculture." In Don F. Hadwiger and William P. Browne (editors), *The New Politics of Food.* Lexington, Massachusetts: D. C. Heath and Co.

_____. 1980. *Farm and Food Policy Issues of the 1980s.* Lincoln, Nebraska: University of Nebraska Press.

Schertz, Lyle P. 1979. *Another Revolution in U. S. Farming.* Washington, D.C.: U.S. Department of Agriculture.

Sinclair, Peter. 1980. "Agricultural policy and the decline of commercial family farming: Comparative analysis of the U.S., Sweden, and the Netherlands." In Frederick Buttel and Howard Newby (editors), *The Rural Sociology of the Advanced Societies: Critical*

Perspectives. Montclair, New Jersey: Allanheld, Osmun, and Co.

Talbot, Ross B., and Don F. Hadwiger. 1968. *The Policy Process in American Agriculture.* San Francisco: Chandler Publishing Co.

Wunderlich, Gene. 1976. "Property and the future of agriculture." *American Journal of Agricultural Economics* 58(November/December):946–952.

32 Who Will Own and Operate America's Farms?

RICHARD D. RODEFELD

Throughout much of U.S. history, farm businesses have been controlled by individuals and families who owned most of the land and capital, made most of the decisions, and provided most of the physical labor. These owner-operated or "family" farms were generally of small and medium size, and have dominated U.S. agriculture except in the South, where tenancy rates are high, and in the West, where employment of hired farm workers has been extensive. Larger farms with separate ownership, management, and labor have been relatively few, but often they are quite important; some of the labels applied to these farms are "nonowner operated," "hired manager operated," "hired worker," "factory," "corporate," and "industrial type."

The last four decades have produced extensive changes in farm ownership, management, and labor, which may continue into the future. Since the mid 1930s, many new mechanical, biological, chemical, and cultural practices have been adopted by farmers. Yields of many crops and production efficiency of many types of livestock have doubled and, in some cases, tripled. In forty years, total farm production doubled, while the total hours of farm work were reduced by three-quarters. Simultaneously, the number of farms and farmers fell by more than two-thirds. Average acres per farm more than tripled. Large increases were

---

Richard D. Rodefeld is assistant professor, Department of Agricultural Economics and Rural Sociology, Pennsylvania State University, University Park, Pennsylvania. He is senior editor of the book *Change in Rural America,* and has written numerous other publications on social changes taking place in U.S. agriculture.

registered in the quantities and values of acreage, nonland resources, production, sales, debt, income, and wealth per farm operator and per farm.

These changes have not affected all types of farms and regions equally. The most dramatic decreases were registered for the following types of farms: small and medium-sized; full-time; dryland; diversified; producers of livestock, dairy, poultry, and cotton; those located in the South; and those with Black operators. Other types expanded in number and importance. For instance, the number of farms with less than one thousand acres declined by 39 percent from 1959 to 1974; larger farms increased by 11 percent. In addition, farm resources, production, debt, sales, and income became more concentrated in the largest farms. The share of total farm sales by the nation's fifty thousand largest farms rose from 23 percent in 1960 to 36 percent in 1977. The causes of these changes are numerous and interrelated, and have produced consequences for both rural and urban United States. However, our knowledge of these changes is quite incomplete (Rodefeld et al., 1978; Tweeten and Huffman, 1980; Rodefeld, 1981).

IMPORTANCE OF THE TOPIC

There are several reasons for the imminent concern in the 1980s with current changes in who owns, manages, and works on America's farms. These changes also provide reasons for the continued and improved monitoring of related trends in the 1980s.

Many of the conditions responsible for the past predominance of individual and family farm owners have been altered. There are reasons to expect that future farm owner-operators will have a reduced share of land and capital ownership and will provide less management and labor, resulting in a decline in family farms (Emerson, 1978; Rodefeld, 1974; Rodefeld et al., 1978; Schaefer et al., 1978; Bergland, 1981).

The public, the Congress, and other branches of government have expressed preferences on these questions (Goss and Rodefeld, 1978; Emerson, 1978; Schaefer et al., 1978; Bergland, 1981). In a recent nationwide Harris poll, more than 80 percent expressed a preference for the farm sector to be dominated by small and medium-sized family farms (U.S. Department of Agriculture, 1980). Numerous government programs and policies have been implemented to strengthen and maintain family farms and farmers. Current trends show that public preferences and government intentions for farm sizes and types are not being met.

Changes in farm ownership, management, and labor may have consequences for farm workers, farm characteristics, and the communities where they are located. The question of who runs America's farms affects nonfarm as well as farm people.

Finally, knowledge about present changes in who controls America's farms is important for allocating scarce public, policy, and research resources in the 1980s. If resources in the 1980s are inadequate for relevant farm sector issues, choices will be necessary.

CURRENT KNOWLEDGE

Information about the types and rates of recent changes in who owns, manages, and works on U.S. farms is valuable for predicting changes in the 1980s.

Land ownership by individuals managing farms on a daily basis and by farm business owners declined from 58.2 percent in 1954 to 54.3 percent in 1964 (the last year assessed). The remainder was owned by landlords and the employers of hired managers. The former include investors, active and retired farmers, nonfarm heirs, and farm residents with nonfarm jobs. In 1910, operators who owned all their land had 53 percent of the farm land in the United States. This proportion dropped to 37 percent in 1935 and to 29 percent in 1964. Increasing percentages were recorded by part owner-operators, hired managers, and cash renters. In 1974, 27 percent of all farm businesses (including nonfamily corporations and hired manager-employers) both owned and rented land. They held 53 percent of the total acres operated.

The decline of land ownership by farm business owners is also reflected in land purchase data. Farmers' share of farmland acquisitions fell from 67 percent of the total between 1959 and 1967 to about 61 percent between 1970 and 1977. Purchases by family farmers may be overstated because nonfamily corporations and the employers of hired managers and/or workers were also classified as farmers. A USDA study estimated that those who reported farming as their major occupation constituted 26 percent of all farmland owners in 1978. They owned 57 percent of the private and noncorporate farm and ranch land. Remainders were accounted for by those with blue- and white-collar occupations, retirees, and others. Regional variability was considerable and nonfarmers owned more than 50 percent of the farmland in only twenty-seven states (Gustafson, 1981).

There are no definitive data on past, present, or changed levels of ownership or management of farm capital (i.e., nonland resources). Perhaps ownership and management by farm operators have been so prevalent, and evidence of change so limited, that more detailed assessments were considered unnecessary. Nonetheless, current evidence, though often incomplete and indirect, suggests reduced control by farm operators.

Expenditures for machine rental and custom and contract work tripled from 1949 to 1974. Rental and leasing of dairy cows and the equipment for milking, feeding, and manure handling seem to be growing rapidly. The extent of custom growing and feeding is unknown, but in 1969–1970, nine-tenths of Texas feedlot cattle were custom-fed (Meisner and Rhodes, 1974). In all of these cases, capital is owned by individuals other than the farm operator.

The numbers of agricultural service firms and their employees increased greatly from 1969 to 1978. In 1978, there were 93,120 such firms with 994,000 employees. From 1960 to 1974, the value of farm production involved in production and/or marketing contracts grew from 19 to 25 percent. Some agricultural service firms and integrators own capital used or located in farms.

In the past, large portions of both organizational and operational management were undoubtedly provided by farm operators, and they probably still are. However, ownership of land and capital by farmers seems to have declined. Because decisions about the use of these resources rest ultimately with their owners, managerial involvement by nonfarm owners may have increased. Levels and types of farmer and nonfarmer involvement vary depending on the arrangement (i.e., rental, leasing, integrator provision, custom or contract hiring, and custom and contract feeding and/or growing). As levels of farm debt have grown, creditors may have become more involved in farm unit decision making. Decision-making power may also be delegated to hired employees.

Acreage on farms operated by hired managers increased from 1954 to 1964. One secondary analysis of agriculture census data indicated that the number of business owners employing hired managers grew from 18,000 in 1964 to about 141,000 in 1969. Also, governmental rules and regulations have been implemented to deal with farm irrigation, drainage, land use, herbicides, pesticides, safety standards, and other issues. As a result, involvement of farm business owners in these decisions has been reduced.

Provision of labor by farm business owners and operation managers has also dropped. The number of hired full-time and seasonal workers increased from 21 percent of the total farm work force in the mid-1940s to 31 percent in the mid-1970s. The absolute number of hired farm workers, particularly those employed full-time, increased throughout the 1970s. These data exclude the growing number of workers employed on a custom or contract basis and those employed by agricultural service firms. The number of farm business owners reporting expenditures of

$10,000 or more for hired labor, machine hire, and custom and contract work grew substantially between 1964 and 1974.

The number of farms with substantial unity between ownership, management, and labor has declined relative to others. In addition, family farms declined relative to larger farms from 1959 to 1969. The latter (employing 1.5 or more man-years of hired labor) increased their portion of total U.S. farm production from 30 percent in 1959 to an estimated 38 percent in 1969. Their increase was observed in all regions and production areas.

Accepted at face value, present knowledge indicates reduced levels of farmland and capital ownership, of management decision making, and of labor by the individuals and families operating farms, and increased levels by other farm types. If a family farm is defined as a farm business where a majority of ownership, management, and labor is supplied by one family, then it is clear that this farm type has declined relative to the nonfamily types.

RESEARCH ISSUES

A considerable lack of knowledge has been noted concerning the ownership and operation of farms in the United States. Research is needed to improve monitoring of farm characteristics and their changes in the 1980s. We cannot specify the exact past, present, and changed levels and types of capital ownership, or organizational and operational decision making by farm business owners. We do not know the past or present characteristics of farm business owners, nor do we know much about individuals other than farm business owners who are involved in farm decision making.

Adequate data for the nation will probably have to be collected and reported by either the census of agriculture or the USDA. Much of the data needed to assess land ownership and labor sources is already collected by the census. The types, quantities, and/or values of capital are determined; ownership is not. The extent of farm owners' involvement in all organizational and operational decisions could be determined in a general context; determining who makes specific decisions is more of a problem (Rodefeld, 1976; U.S. Senate, 1978).

The census and the USDA may not be able to collect all the needed data, and other special surveys may be necessary in regular series. Farm business owners and other work force members need to be enumerated and surveyed. The ownership, rental, management, and labor data obtained by such surveys would provide baselines for future investigations and would enable determination of types and rates of changes. Intensive case studies of fewer work force members may be necessary to determine different types of farm capital and decisions, who owns capital or is otherwise involved in decision making, and the relative contributions of different individuals to particular decisions.

The characteristics and changes of commercial farms and farmers participating in some state university farm record-keeping and analysis programs might be analyzed (Walton, 1977). In addition, documents related to land and capital renting and leasing, production and marketing contracts, loans, custom growing and feeding, and relevant governmental rules and regulations could be analyzed. Plat books, deed registrations, and transfers can be analyzed to determine farm land ownership and its changes (U.S. Senate, 1979).

Assuming that current farm trends continue at similar rates in the 1980s, research is needed on the consequences of change for the structure of agriculture and for nonfarm sectors of both rural and urban United States. This information is essential for policy deliberations about attempts that would encourage or discourage current trends.

There is strong support for the proposition that changes in farm characteristics have wide-ranging consequences, such as the dramatic decline in the number of farms, operators, farm workers, and farm families (Rodefeld et al., 1978; Rodefeld, 1981). Research has shown that changes in the types and proportions of owners, managers, and workers have also been associated with changes in work force characteristics such as age, race, educational level, income, and community participation. Such changes have also been associated with changes in the characteristics of farms, e.g., acres operated, amount of capital, and size of work force (Rodefeld, 1974, 1979).

The difficulty with present knowledge is the inability to predict the consequences of changes in farms and farm work force examined here. Much of the relevant research was carried out twenty or more years ago. More importantly, there has been little or no research on many recent farm work force and unit changes.

Many types of research can illuminate the consequences of these changes. The types of work force individuals, families, and farm types about which we know so little could be identified and surveyed. A "snowballing" technique might be used to identify all the business, land and capital owners, the organizational and operational decision makers, and the workers associated with their units. Information would be obtained about aspects of background and family structure and their compositional, participation, attitude, and value characteristics. Information could also be obtained about the type of farm units containing these work force members. Using this information, simulations could show how farms and farm work force traits would likely be altered with increasing numbers and proportions of each of the different owner, manager, worker, and unit types. These projections could then be compared to present farm work force and unit traits to estimate the types and magnitudes of likely changes (Rodefeld, 1974).

Similarly, rural areas and communities that presently contain a preponderance of any of the new types of farms could be identified and their major characteristics determined. These would then be compared to the characteristics of communities containing other types of farms and farm work forces. The differences observed would provide a basis for estimating the consequences of future farm changes (LeVeen, 1979).

Samples or panels could be used to study farm units, their work forces, and rural communities across time. In general, longitudinal analysis would yield more definitive data about consequences. Another approach should concentrate on rural areas or communities that have experienced major recent changes in their farm work force and associated farm types. Historical data could be collected from public and private documents. With these data, determinations could be made about the dynamics of change of farm types and the processes by which they occur (Tetreau, 1940).

Research is also needed on the causes of changes in farm ownership, management, and labor. If policy makers decide that there is no need to alter current trends, they will need accurate knowledge about the factors causing ownership, management, and labor changes. Such analysis will provide another means of assessing the likelihood, types, rates, and extent of future changes.

We already have considerable knowledge about the causes of change in land and capital ownership, management, and the provision of labor by farm business owners and managers (Rodefeld, 1974, 1979; Emerson, 1978; Rodefeld et al., 1978; Schaefer et al., 1978; U.S. Senate, 1979; Bergland, 1981). However, our present knowledge is incomplete.

Many of the changes examined here are so recent that the reasons for them have been given little attention. Also, many efforts have been directed toward the causes of rather broad and encompassing changes, such as the decline of the family farm. When the causes of shifts in family and nonfamily farms have been addressed, they usually have not been linked to specific ownership, management, and labor changes.

Perhaps the greatest deficiency is that few of the logical explanations for the changes dealt with here have been subjected to systematic investigation or empirical testing. As a result, we do not know the levels of relevancy or completeness associated with the causes identified so far. Expanded surveys and interviews will be necessary to improve our knowledge about the causes of changes occurring in farm business, land and capital ownership, organizational and operational decision making, and labor.

CONCLUSION

The family farm and its associated work force are major parts of the social and economic heritage of American society. They are credited with major contributions to the values of the society and with being among the most economically efficient and productive sectors of the economy. However, a plethora of recent changes have contributed to an uncertain future for this socially desired institution. The changes have been so many, varied, and complex, that understanding lags far behind the pace of change. The survival and viability of the family farm depend tremendously on a more definitive understanding of the causes and consequences associated with its decline and change.

REFERENCES

Bergland, Robert. 1981. *A Time to Choose: Summary Report on the Structure of Agriculture.* Washington, D.C.: U.S. Department of Agriculture.

Emerson, P. M. 1978. *Public Policy and the Changing Structure of American Agriculture.* Washington, D.C.: U.S. Congress.

Goss, K., and Richard D. Rodefeld. 1978. *Corporate Farming in the United States: A Guide to Current Literature, 1967–1977.* University Park, Pennsylvania: Pennsylvania State University, AE & RS 136.

Gustafson, Greg C. 1981. *Who Owns the Land? A State and Regional Summary of Landownership in the United States, 1978.* Washington, D.C.: Economics, Statistics, and Cooperatives Service, U.S. Department of Agriculture.

LeVeen, E. Phillip. 1979. "Enforcing the Reclamation Act and rural development in California." *Rural Sociology* 44(Winter):667–690.

Meisner, J. C., and V. J. Rhodes. 1974. *The Changing Structure of U.S. Cattle Feeding.* Columbia, Missouri: University of Missouri, Special Report 167.

Rodefeld, Richard D. 1974. "The changing organizational and occupational structure of farming and the implications for farm work force individuals, families, and communities." Madison, Wisconsin: University of Wisconsin. Doctoral dissertation.

———. 1976. "The assessment of farm (operating unit) and farm operator characteristics by the U.S. Census of Agriculture: Shortcomings and procedures for their alleviation." In Committee on Post Office and Civil Service, U.S. Senate (editors), *Agricultural Census.* Washington, D.C.: U.S. Government Printing Office, Serial 94-97.

———. 1979. *The Family-Type Farm and Structural Differentiation: Trends, Causes, and Consequences of Change, Research Needs.* University Park, Pennsylvania: Department of Agricultural Economics and Rural Sociology, Pennsylvania State University, Staff Paper 24.

———. 1981. *The Direct and Indirect Effects of Mechanizing U.S. Agriculture.* Montclair, New Jersey: Allanheld, Osmun, and Co.

Rodefeld, Richard D., Jan Flora, Donald Voth, Isao Fujimoto, and Jim Converse (editors). 1978. *Change in Rural America: Causes, Consequences, and Alternatives.* St. Louis, Missouri: C. V. Mosby Co.

Schaefer, E., et al. 1978. *Changing Character and Structure of American Agriculture: An Over-*

view. Washington, D.C.: U.S. General Accounting Office, CED-78-178.

Tetreau, E. D. 1940. "Social organization in Arizona's irrigated areas." *Rural Sociology* 5 (June):192–205.

Tweeten, Luther, and W. Huffman. 1980. "Structural change: An overview." In Luther Tweeten et al. (editors), *Structure of Agriculture and Information Needs Regarding Small Farms*. Washington, D.C.: National Rural Center.

U.S. Department of Agriculture. 1980. "Public attitudes toward the structure of American agriculture." In (title and publication status unknown). Washington, D.C.: Office of the Secretary, U.S. Department of Agriculture.

U.S. Senate (Committee on the Judiciary). 1978. *Priorities in the Agricultural Research of the U.S. Department of Agriculture*. Washington, D.C.: U.S. Government Printing Office.

U.S. Senate (Committee on Small Businesses). 1979. *The Preservation and Control of Farm Land*. Washington, D.C.: U.S. Government Printing Office.

Walton, Francis K. 1977. "A preliminary technology assessment of large-farm tractors and combines." East Lansing, Michigan: Michigan State University. Doctoral dissertation.

33 Structure of Agriculture and Quality of Life in Rural Communities

WILLIAM D. HEFFERNAN

The term *structure of agriculture* is used to describe the organizational characteristics and complex relationships in the food and fiber production and distribution system. Much of the research interest in the structure of agriculture has focused on the family farm, which is only one portion of our system of agricultural production. This system also includes input, marketing, processing, and distribution sectors.

Under subsistence agriculture, production does not require an elaborate infrastructure because farms depend little on outside organizations for supplies or markets. However, as agricultural production becomes increasingly commercialized, farms become much more dependent on a marketing sector. In a similar way, the development of a "scientific agriculture" based on sophisticated machinery, seeds, fertilizer, and pesticides creates dependency on an off-the-farm supply sector. For many years, the structure of agriculture in the United States was virtually synonymous with the structure of the production sector; however, today there is an extremely complicated agricultural structure, which includes the intricate dependency and power relationships described by Stockdale (see Chapter 31).

William D. Heffernan is associate professor in the Department of Rural Sociology, University of Missouri, Columbia, Missouri. He is the author of many publications on the sociological dimensions of agriculture, including the relationship between agriculture and the rural community.

Historically, the family farm has dominated American agriculture. Despite a lack of agreement about the essential attributes of a family farm, most researchers agree that family farms are characterized by dispersed ownership of land and capital. In addition, most agree that the day-to-day managerial decisions are made by the farm family, who also provide the capital; less agreement exists concerning the proportion of the labor that must be provided by the farm family. On the other hand, there is general agreement that a corporate agricultural structure is characterized by a separation of capital, management, and labor.

Many analysts of U.S. agriculture have felt that the family farm and the infrastructure supporting it were positively related to a higher quality of life for people in rural communities and, indeed, that both were consistent with the democratic political system of the country (Bailey, 1905). This argument contends that a farm family that owns its own land, works the land with its labor, and makes most of the managerial decisions will be characterized by freedom, independence, and ability to resist oppression. It is felt that family farmers have the power to control their own destinies and avoid domination by others. The belief that individuals have control over their own destiny implies opportunity for advancement in society, which in turn supports the societal value placed on equal opportunity. Because power concentrated in the hands of a few persons often leads to inequality and concentration of wealth, a dispersed power base provides the opportunity for more equality in the community. Granting that "quality of life" tends to be a very subjective perception of well-being, the argument is made that certain factors must surely provide some indication of the quality of life in a community. These factors include a sense of belonging, a sense of having the opportunity to control one's own destiny, a feeling of self-respect and involvement in the affairs of the community, and a general feeling that one has the opportunity to effectively pursue one's own needs and wants.

The issue addressed in this chapter is the relationship between agricultural structure and quality of life in rural communities. Although a larger issue concerns the social impact that changes in the structure of agriculture will have for society in general, the questions that have received most research attention by rural sociologists have focused on the impact of agricultural structure on rural communities.

Nonfamily farm operations, which represent 5 percent of all farms in the country, now produce 35 percent of all farm products. This and related changes have led Loomis and Beegle (1975:147) to conclude that "the family farm, once proclaimed as the backbone of the nation, is weakening." If the structure of agriculture bears no relationship to the quality of life in rural communities, then policy makers need not be concerned. However, if, in fact, the shifting structure of agriculture is reducing the quality of rural life, then current policies that tend to undermine the family farm should be reexamined.

PREVIOUS RESEARCH

In 1944, Walter Goldschmidt (1978a) conducted what has become a classic study on the social effects of different types of agricultural structures. His anthropological study of Arvin, California, a community characterized by large farms with a hired labor force, and Dinuba, California, a community surrounded predominantly by family farms, indicated that the type of agriculture influenced the quality and quantity of community services. Dinuba ranked higher than Arvin on a number of measures, including family income, level of living, social and physical amenities, social and religious institutions, and the degree of local control over the political process.

Arvin and Dinuba were restudied by La Rose (1973) in 1970 and by the Community Services Task Force of the Small Farm Viability Project (1977) in the mid-1970s. Although neither study was as comprehensive as the original Goldschmidt study, the results indicated that differences in the levels of services provided by the two communities were as great or greater than in the 1940s.

Another study in the Goldschmidt tradition compared 130 towns in the San Joaquin Valley of California. The researchers concluded that "the smaller-scale farming areas tend to offer more to local communities than their larger counterparts" (Small Farm Viability Project, 1977:242).

In the late 1950s, Ploch (1960, 1965a, 1965b) studied the relationship between various attributes of communities where the production of eggs and broilers occurred under contract compared with those serving independent egg and broiler producers. He concluded that there was little evidence that the two groups of poultry producers represented different community status levels.

In 1968, Heffernan (1972) interviewed integrated broiler growers, family famers, and owners (or managers) and hired workers of corporate-type farms in Louisiana. He concluded that there was little difference between growers and family farmers with regard to community involvement. In corporate-type structures, however, owners (and managers) were more involved in community and political activities, while the workers participated little in such activities.

While Heffernan was working on the Louisiana study, other researchers were examining the community activities of those working on incorporated family, larger-than-family, and industrial farms in Wisconsin. They also found that individuals on family farms were more involved in local voluntary associations and political or social activities than were the workers on other farm types (Rodefeld, 1974; Martinson et al., 1976). A similar study of grape producers in Missouri in 1976 (Heffernan and Lasley, 1978) again showed a relationship between the type of farm ownership and operation and involvement in the social activities of the local community.

Meanwhile, Flora and Conby (1977) used secondary data from Kansas to test hypotheses derived from Goldschmidt's earlier research. They predicted that, as multinational corporations became more involved in agriculture, a decline would occur in "mean community well-being." In his most recent analysis, Goldschmidt (1978b) used secondary data to show that large-scale farm operations were associated with a larger proportion of the community population being found in the lower class. He concluded that family farms are positively related to democratic rural communities. A replication of Goldschmidt's recent study supports his findings and offers numerous questions for future lines of inquiry (Harris and Gilbert, 1979).

Each of the studies summarized here has followed one of three major methodological approaches in examining the relationship between type of agriculture and the quality of life in rural communities. Goldschmidt's original study (and most of the California studies) focused on services and facilities, such as number of parks, newspapers, and retail sales outlets available to members of the agricultural community. Goldschmidt argued that the greater the choice available to residents, the higher the quality of life. The second methodological approach, followed by Ploch, Heffernan, Rodefeld, and others, made use of personal interviews to determine the farmers' involvement in the formal and informal activities of the community, with special emphasis on the level of alienation from and/or the level of integration into the community. The third methodological approach, characterizing Goldschmidt's second analysis as well as studies by Flora and Conby and Gilbert and Harris, used secondary data sources, such as census data, to focus on measures of equality and economic well-being.

Although there are few studies focusing on vertical integration, the research that has been done finds little alteration in the quality of life in rural communities that can be attributed to a trend toward vertical integration. On the other hand, all relevant research to date suggests that a corporate type of agriculture results in a reduction in the quality of life for at least some people, especially the hired workers in rural communities. No single study or set of studies can answer all of the research questions, but it seems significant that a dozen studies, spanning four decades and all regions of the nation and performed by different researchers using different methodologies, have rather consistently shown that a change toward corporate agriculture produces social consequences that reduce the quality of life in rural communities. Despite this consistency of results, however, researchable questions remain.

RESEARCH ISSUES

Research is needed to identify key variables in the agricultural system that, if altered, lead to a change in the quality of community life. Past studies indicate a relationship between agricultural structure and measures of quality of life, but they provide limited insight into the ways that certain features of the structure lead to deterioration in quality of life. A better understanding of the social factors involved might enhance anticipation of the consequences as structural changes occur. For example, if a key variable is loss of worker control and power in a corporate structure, could a corporate structure characterized by a democratic management style lead to retaining the quality of life associated with a family farm structure?

More research must be focused on the input, marketing, processing, and distribution sectors of the agricultural system. In an effort to develop a manageable research problem, most sociologists have usually limited their analysis to the production sector. Confining analysis to the production sector results in ignoring the centralization of power in the overall agricultural system. The key variables for explaining changes in the interdependency among the various sectors of agriculture do not necessarily lead directly to the concentration of power in the hands of nonproduction sectors. Instead, much of the control over other sectors results from individuals and organizations trying to reduce their risks and uncertainties. Because the production sector is relatively unorganized, it is less able to resist domination by the supply and marketing sectors.

Many questions exist concerning organization of the nonproduction sectors. Who owns and controls agribusiness corporations? What relationships exist among agribusiness firms? To what extent do agribusiness firms cooperate and share information and to what extent do they compete with one another? How do agribusiness firms acquire control over other sectors of the agricultural system with or without ownership? What is the impact of increased domination of the local farm supply and marketing sector as national and multinational corporations exert more control over local businesses, especially when various sectors of the agricultural system are combined under a single organization? Who assumes the relatively high risk associated with agricultural production and what mechanisms exist to shift the risk from one sector to another? Finally, how does the organization of nonproduction sectors impact rural communities?

Research needs to determine whether groups and collective-bargaining associations representing producer interests are effective means for producers to maintain or increase power in the agricultural system, and research must study the consequences for the farm family and rural community. The production sector is represented by many associations that seek to develop some farmer control in the agriculture system. General farm organizations, commodity groups, and cooperatives represent different approaches to providing collective effort on behalf of farmers. But the relatively low level of participation and commitment of farmers to many of these organizations raise additional research questions. Does any organization or coalition of the organizations represent a viable alternative through which farmers can regain some control of the production sector? If so, who controls these farmer organizations? Is the farmer's relationship to such an organization different from his or her relationship to a corporate agribusiness firm? If not, how could these farm organizations be structured to better serve their members?

Research is needed on the relationships that exist among agricultural structure, ecology, and quality of life in the rural community. The vertically integrated poultry industry is most dominant in the eastern and southeastern United States, especially in counties characterized by marginal agricultural land. Most of the large confinement cattle feed lots are in the southwestern United States. Large corporate farms are prevalent in arid regions and family farms dominate the Midwest and Northeast. Because the dominant agribusiness corporations (equipment manufacturers, grain companies, and so forth) are national or international in scope, and because of regional differences in agriculture, ecological factors tend to have an independent effect on the structure of agriculture. One of the trends in industrial society is convergence; agricultural convergence implies an increased similarity in all segments of the agricultural system and in all areas of the country. Does ecology mediate against convergence in U.S. agriculture? The opposite question is what consequences the structure of agriculture has for the ecology of an area. Studies have shown that lands owned and operated by the farmer receive better soil conservation than do rented lands (also see Chapter 35). Much speculation exists concerning whether family farms or corporate farms practice better soil conservation practices; little empirical evidence is available. The long-range question is whether organizational structure is related to future productivity of the land. The future productivity of farmland has an obvious impact on the local community, but it also has consequences for the quality of life for the total society.

Comparative research needs to examine structural arrangements that are experimental, less common, or even nonexistent in this country. Studies have focused primarily on comparing the family farm with the corporate farmhand and corporate integrated structure, but other structural arrangements exist in this and other countries. For example, research should focus on the relationship between quality of life and various forms of cooperatives found in this country. The family farm structure has developed a collective-bargaining component through the formation of cooperatives that vertically integrate the market sector with the production sector (e.g., the dairy industry). On the other hand, less traditional cooperative structures, such as the Moshav style of cooperative being established in some southwestern states, have different arrangements. A closer examination of communal societies and cooperatives in this and other societies may be necessary. Research should be directed to forms of agricultural structure not found in this country but which represent more direct government involvement in the agricultural system, ranging from the Saskatchewan plan of Canada (in which the government buys farm land and leases it to beginning farmers) to the collective state farms of eastern Europe.

Research needs to determine whether or not future changes in the structure of agriculture are likely to have any significant impact on the social life of rural communities. In many rural communities, the proportion of the populace actually living on farms is very small, often less than 10 percent. Perhaps there are so few farmers that future changes will make no difference. However, emphasizing only the farm population may neglect those in the agricultural infrastructure who also reside in rural communities. Even where the number of people in the rural communities who directly serve agricultural production is twice that of the farm population, those involved in agriculture may represent a minority in many rural communities. Do farm families and people in agribusiness hold key leadership positions or have a disproportionate influence on the social vitality of rural communities?

To understand the process involved in the changing structure of agriculture and the process involved in rural community dynamics, longitudinal studies are needed. With the exception of Arvin and Dinuba, research on the structure of agriculture and rural communities has consisted of cross-sectional studies that take a "snapshot" of the community at one point in time. Rural communities and changes in agriculture need to be studied over time.

More research is needed on the relationship between the quality of life in the larger society and structural changes occurring in the agricultural system.

What, if any, difference does it make to members of the society if changes occur in the agriculture structure? What are the consequences for the consumer in terms of the quantity, quality, and price of food? Because the agricultural system involves over one-fourth of the total work force of the United States, do changes in structure of the agriculture system produce social impacts that go beyond the rural community and the cost of food? What effect does the concentration of power within the agricultural system have for the larger society?

The definition, measurement, and interpretation of efficiency in agriculture has been considered only an economic issue, but the concept also involves sociological dimensions that should be researched. The conventional view is that changes in the structure of agriculture leading toward larger and larger units have brought increased efficiency and that this efficiency should not be sacrificed for other social concerns. Accumulation of economic evidence suggests, however, that most economies of scale are reached by relatively small organizations (Madden, 1976; Hall and LaVeen, 1978). More importantly, the definition and measurement of efficiency is being challenged. Is measurement of efficiency using firm level analysis expressed only in monetary units the most appropriate basis on which to make societal decisions? Should key input variables such as units of labor and capital inputs, units of energy, or inputs of other nonrenewable resources be emphasized? Advantages related to economies of size are often benefits accruing to the organization, but not necessarily to society, because of economic power. A better understanding of the ways in which economic power is developed and maintained is critical to understanding how size is related to what has been called "efficiency." Researchers in this area should also understand what "efficiency" contributes to the quality of life in rural communities and the larger society.

We must develop a better understanding of the impact of changes in the larger society, including government rules and regulations, on the structure of agriculture and rural communities. Can direct markets provide an alternative to the highly concentrated markets now predominant? What impact does the urban-to-rural migration pattern have on agriculture structure and rural communities? How do various issues of land use and ownership in the United States relate to agricultural structure and rural communities? What is the social impact of government restrictions on various chemical compounds used in agriculture? Would special tax considerations for family farms increase or decrease equality in this country? Many of the current and future rules and regulations directed toward the food and fiber system have a direct influence on rural communities, but more often the consequence of such legislation is indirect, stemming from the effects that such rules and regulations will have on the structure of agriculture. For example, many income tax regulations represent forces that undermine the family farm, while certain Environmental Protection Agency guidelines on point pollution sources and proposed legislation restricting the use of antibiotics as feed additives may support the family farm. Often, the structure of agriculture and the quality of life in rural communities is an unintended consequence of government policy addressing other societal issues.

REFERENCES

Bailey, Liberty Hyde. 1905. *The Outlook to Nature.* New York: Macmillan Co.

Flora, Jan L., and Judith Lee Conby. 1977. "Impact of type of agriculture on class structure, social well-being, and inequalities." Paper presented at the annual meetings of the Rural Sociological Society, Madison, Wisconsin.

Goldschmidt, Walter. 1978a. *As You Sow: Three Studies in the Social Consequences of Agribusiness.* Montclair, New Jersey: Allanheld, Osmun, and Co.

______. 1978b. "Large-scale farming and the rural social structure." *Rural Sociology* 43(3): 362–366.

Hall, Bruce F., and E. Phillip LaVeen. 1978. "Farm size and economic efficiency: The case of California." *American Journal of Agricultural Economics* 60(4).

Harris, Craig K., and Jess C. Gilbert. 1979. "Large-scale farming, rural social welfare, and the agrarian thesis: A re-examination." Paper presented at the annual meetings of the Rural Sociological Society, Burlington, Vermont.

Heffernan, William D. 1972. "Sociological dimensions of agriculture structures in the United States." *Sociologia Ruralis* 12:481–499.

Heffernan, William D., and Paul Lasley. 1978. "Agricultural structure and interaction in the local community: A case study." *Rural Sociology* 43(3):348–361.

La Rose, Bruce L. 1973. "Arvin and Dinuba revisited." In Select Committee on Small Business, U.S. Senate (editors), *Role of Giant Corporations: Corporate Secrecy and Agribusiness.* Hearing before Subcommittee on Monopoly, Select Committee on Small Business, U.S. Senate. Washington, D.C.: U.S. Government Printing Office.

Loomis, Charles P., and J. Allan Beegle. 1975. *A Strategy for Rural Change.* New York: John Wiley and Sons, Inc.

Madden, J. Patrick. 1976. *Economics of Size in Farming: Theory, Analytic Procedures, and a Review of Selected Studies.* Washington, D.C.: Economics, Cooperatives, and Statistics Services, U.S. Department of Agriculture, Agricultural Economic Report 107.

Martinson, O. B., E. A. Wilkening, and R. D. Rodefeld. 1976. "Validity and reliability of indicators of alienation and integration applied to a selected rural sample." Madison, Wisconsin: Department of Rural Sociology, University of Wisconsin. Unpublished manuscript.

Ploch, Louis A. 1960. *Social and Family Characteristics of Maine Contract Broiler Growers.* Orono, Maine: Agricultural Experiment Station, University of Maine, Bulletin 569.

______. 1965a. *Maine's Contract Broiler Growers—A Restudy.* Orono, Maine: Agricultural Experiment Station, University of Maine, Bulletin 669.

______. 1965b. *A Comparison of the Social Characteristics of Maine's Contract and Independent Table Egg Producers.* Orono, Maine: Agricultural Experiment Station, University of Maine, Bulletin 670.

Rodefeld, Richard D. 1974. "The changing organizational and occupational structure of farming and the implications for farm work force individuals, families, and communities." Madison, Wisconsin: University of Wisconsin. Doctoral dissertation.

Small Farm Viability Project (editors). 1977. *The Family Farm in California.* Sacramento, California: Small Farm Viability Project.

34
Small and Part-Time Farmers

C. MILTON COUGHENOUR
RONALD C. WIMBERLEY

The loss of farms, the growth of large-scale farming, the decline of small farms as producers of food and fiber products, and periodic food "crises" have alarmed many citizens and policy makers. However, this is only one side of the picture.

Another side is highlighted by the 1964–1974 increase in the number of farms with less than fifty acres in all regions except the South (Nichols et al., 1979). Although the overall number of farms has declined, the proportion having less than $20,000 in sales did not change between 1966 and 1978 in constant 1978 dollars (Schertz, 1979). There also has been an increase in various specialty farms such as "organic" farming.

These contrasting trends indicate the complexity of issues concerning small and part-time farms. Because both the causes and consequences of those changes involve sociological forces, increased knowledge of these forces is necessary if policy initiatives are to affect the direction of trends as desired.

One of the major problems facing policy makers and researchers is the lack of consensus on the appropriate policy unit. Although the family farm has been the principal target of farm policy, there is a lack of con-

---

C. Milton Coughenour is professor and associate chairperson of the Department of Sociology, University of Kentucky, Lexington, Kentucky. He has written extensively on the organization of farming operations, decision making and work roles, and the commitment to farm enterprises. **Ronald C. Wimberley** is an associate professor in the Department of Sociology and Anthropology at North Carolina State University, Raleigh. He has published

sensus on an appropriate definition for statistical purposes. The situation is similar regarding small and part-time farms.

Of course, many part-time farms are also small farms. But what is a small farm? The Food and Agricultural Act of 1977 simply defines a small farm as having annual sales of farm products greater than $1,000 but less than $20,000. This definition may be useful in dealing with issues of "concentration in agricultural production and marketing, dependence on capital-intensive technology, use of harmful production practices, and land reform" (Carlin and Crecink, 1979). However, the $20,000 sales limit leaves several social ambiguities. First, it fails to distinguish the small-scale "retirement" and "hobby" farmers and other nonfamily types of farms where income may be a secondary goal. Second, this classification obscures the relationship of the farm to other business operations that the farm operator, family, or business organization may have. In view of policy objectives for reducing poverty and encouraging rural development, a third serious weakness of this definition is its insensitivity to differences in individual or family economic well-being and to the role of farm families in rural communities (Brewster, 1979).

To better identify farm operator families "having a low level of economic well-being," USDA researchers have recently offered an alternative definition: "All farm families (a) whose family net income from all sources (farm and nonfarm) is below the median nonmetropolitan income of the state, (b) who depend on farming for a significant though not necessarily a majority of their income, and (c) whose family members provide most of the labor and management" (Carlin and Crecink, 1979).

This definition has several attractive features. It focuses on the family rather than the farm and recognizes that the social standard by which relative deprivation or smallness should be judged is not uniform across the nation. Moreover, it sets forth the general criteria for distinguishing small family from larger-than-family, part-time, or other types of family farms.

What this definition does not do, perhaps wisely in this initial formulation, is specifically indicate what a significant portion of family income is (clause b) or what constitutes "most" of the labor and management (clause c). The relationship between these variables and characteristics of

---

numerous articles on political and religious behavior.

This chapter is a contribution of S-148, "The Changing Structure of Agriculture: Causes, Consequences, and Policy Implications" (number 80-14-211). It is published with the permission of the director, Kentucky Agricultural Experiment Station.

families and farms need to be researched prior to setting any boundaries on smallness of scale or part-time operation.

There are other more important sociological and economic variables that need to be studied in establishing criteria for identifying relevant policy units. For example, a definition might include the value of products grown for household consumption by small farm households in addition to value of farm products sold. Also, although it is important to separate small family from part-time family farms, the latter cannot be ignored. As a group, they are far more numerous than small family farms as defined, they are quite heterogeneous, and they have their own special production and input problems. It will not do to write them off as outside the concern of agricultural policy makers simply because they have external sources of income. The effort to identify types of part-time family farms has languished since the 1960s (Bertrand, 1967). Resolving issues connected with establishing suitable definitions of small and part-time family farms is a major research problem.

IMPORTANCE OF SOCIOLOGICAL RESEARCH

Most American farm families live on small and part-time farms, and their needs are great. As recently as 1978, 70 percent (1.9 million) of the nation's farms sold less than $20,000 each of farm products. Thirty-nine percent of farm operators reporting in 1974 listed their principal occupation as other than farming. Many have low family incomes. Carlin and Crecink (1979) estimate that 1.4 million farm families (52 percent) in 1975 had "total family incomes below the median nonmetropolitan income for their region." Consequently, improvement in rural family and community well-being involves small and part-time farm families (Brewster, 1979; Rodefeld et al., 1978; Gasson, 1977).

Also, small and part-time farm families produce an important share of many commodities, and their share could be increased. The very existence of small and part-time farm families strengthens the resilience of U.S. agriculture in economic resource and market crises to which large-scale farms are more vulnerable.

A third reason for strengthening small and part-time farm families is that they supply many consumption needs in their own households, and they can further supply many local markets while using less transportation and energy. Ironically, many can produce more than they can effectively market.

Fourth, small farms offer supplementary employment. For older persons, the opportunity to run a small farm offers a desirable way of life that can serve to reduce dependency on welfare or limited pensions.

Fifth, small and part-time farm families represent an important segment of many rural–and urban–communities. Therefore, strengthening the socioeconomic position of these farm families enhances community well-being and development.

Sixth, a farm lifestyle is cherished by many citizens. For some, it is their work. For others, it is their recreation or a means of hedging inflationary pressures. And it is an American heritage.

During the 1960s, environmentalists, minority groups, and advocates of rural development joined critics of "establishment" policies in educational institutions and the USDA to place the small, family-type farm issue on the policy agenda (Hadwiger and Browne, 1978). Such heightened interest has led to efforts to describe families on small farms (Marshall and Thompson, 1976; U.S. Congress, 1978; U.S. General Accounting Office, 1978; Carlin and Crecink, 1979; Larson and Lewis, 1979). The profiles vary with the particular sources of data. Despite limitations, such studies of small farms help identify research and policy issues.

Various research agendas have been developed to fill knowledge gaps and provide a basis for policy (U.S. Department of Agriculture and Community Services Administration, 1978; Madden and Tischbein, 1979; U.S. Department of Agriculture, 1979; Saupe, 1980). Interested analysts should examine these agendas in conjunction with the one here, which emphasizes areas of needed sociological research.

RESEARCH ISSUES

Descriptive Data on Small and Part-Time Farm Families

Existing government data sources and methods on data collection do not provide adequate information for research or policy purposes. The U.S. Census and related surveys offer data on farm people, but little on farming. The census of agriculture provides considerable information about farming, but little on small and/or part-time farmers or members of their households.

There is a growing agreement that policy issues can best be handled as a people problem rather than a farm problem. For problems of small and part-time farms, the household or family is the most appropriate unit of analysis. In addition to data that is used to establish meaningful classifications of small and part-time farm families, sociological research on the composition, structure, resources, aspirations, developmental patterns, linkages with farm and nonfarm structures, and needs of such families is largely uncharted territory.

To make matters worse, no data are available from the census of agriculture to analyze farm or family units. The public data only contains statistics aggregated for entire counties. County-level data are neither appropriate nor sensitive to many research questions. An anonymous listing of farm units in a public use sample, as provided by the census of population, is urgently needed so that other government and research agencies will not have to use their limited budgets to collect information already gathered at public expense.

What are the survival and turnover rates of farms? How do these differ by type of farm, in scale or in commitment to farming? How do farming operations expand or contract and nonfarm activities change over time? There are no national data bases for researching the processes of getting into, staying in, or getting out of farming or for researching farm development and decline. *The national information sources that determine important farm and farm family characteristics are too limited for adequate analysis, and their improvement represents a high priority research need. Legislative authorization will be required.*

Enhancement of Opportunity Structures

Currently, government, economic, and social constraints seem to place smaller farmers at a disadvantage in marketing farm products and in acquiring land, capital, credit, information, and supplies. Provision of resources and services for modern farming is not exclusively an economic process. The patterns and processes of resource acquisition and marketing are imbedded in complexes of social relationships among farmers, agribusinesses, and public agency representatives. In relationships among people, social factors such as race and ethnic background, prestige, and power, as well as ecological conditions of physical location and concentration, come into play. These factors affect the relationships through which needed information and resources are acquired or products are marketed. They often constitute subtle forms of socioeconomic discrimination.

The social networks sustaining part-time farmers comprise an even more complex structure because of their relationships with nonfarm industries and services. Farm family members differ in their personal abilities to compete for nonfarm jobs and to embark on nonfarm careers. Local areas differ in the types of industries and services providing job and career opportunities. Areas close to urban centers are richly endowed with a range of career opportunities, but these are often lacking in more remote areas, which often have truncated structures and where opportunities may be limited to the lower ranges of white-collar and blue-collar occupations. Social factors also affect job acquisition and career advancement and consequently nonfarm opportunities for men and women.

What social and cultural conditions constrain the opportunities for small and part-time farmers? What changes in opportunity structures are occurring? How do market and nonmarket forms of agribusiness organization affect opportunity? How do government policies and regulations affect opportunities? What is the impact of policies in different communities and regions? *Sociological research is needed to identify localities and regions where opportunities are limited, and to identify the factors that restrict access to the opportunities that are available.*

Farm and Nonfarm Careers: Opportunity and Constraint

The growth of off-the-farm employment of farm family members has contributed to family income, levels of living, and slowing the decline of small farms. Patterns of multiple job holding and careers vary widely among families and during life spans. How do these patterns relate to off-the-farm employment? What are the personal and family disadvantages in maintaining multiple careers or jobs? Does part-time farming diminish participation in the organizational life in the community? What are the social costs to communities and institutions of the time commitment of families with multiple careers?

Because of the integration of farm and nonfarm labor markets, farm enterprises compete with nonfarm enterprises for labor. Although this has been recognized in the case of hired farm labor, it also applies to farm operators with nonfarm careers. Research suggests that off-the-farm employment affects both enterprise selection and specialization of the farming operation, but little is known about the social factors affecting operator decisions.

A more fundamental problem is the extent to which full-time off-the-farm employment constrains development of the farm. How much farm income, income security, and personal gratification from enlarging farming operations must a farmer receive in order to forego an off-the-farm job? How does this vary by type of off-the-farm work? The issue also has implications for market development. In areas with high concentrations of part-time farms, competition from nonfarm jobs may be an important constraint to development of markets for specialty crops that part-time farmers often produce.

Although alternative theories of intersectoral labor mobility address the problems of low returns for labor in farming and the assumed surplus of labor resources in agriculture, the movement of nonfarmers into farming as an occupation has not been addressed explicitly. Understanding the choice of career patterns requires information about motives, goals, and social and psychological rewards. Advances in understanding patterns of individual and family mobility may be more amenable to sociological perspectives and methods than those typically employed by economists. *Off-the-farm employment may contribute to in-*

dividual, family, and community quality of life, but this issue needs to be systematically investigated.

Technology and Changing Farm Structure

"Innovative" farmers using the products of science and technology have transformed the structure of American agriculture. They have been supported by governmental programs, social and economic organizations, communication networks, and transportation systems. *If survival of small farm families is becoming a more important social goal, research to help plan more favorable social institution and organization arrangements will be needed.*

Development of more "appropriate" types of technology will require a more "appropriate" system of research and development–one that is committed to promoting the survival of small family farms and that acknowledges the importance of changing research goals (Friedland and Kappel, 1979). What is the institutional and organizational nature of our present system of agricultural science and technology? How did the relationship among modern agricultural science, agricultural extension, and large-scale agriculture develop? What social norms and supporting organization structures, such as research, technology development, and information dissemination, need to be changed? What strategies of change can be employed effectively?

An important research issue is whether appropriate technology for small farmers differs in degree or in kind from that for large-scale commercial farmers (see Chapter 5). Some old technologies (e.g., organic inputs) and some new ones (e.g., minimum tillage and integrated pest management) are possibilities. Each new item of technology must be seen as part of a system of technology for the production of commodities by small and part-time farmers. *Research to identify the social linkages of new technology with the well-being of farm families will be required.*

New Forms of Political and Economic Organization

Although small and part-time farmers are the majority of all farmers, they have had little success organizing in their own interest. They are poorly represented in farm organizations and commodity groups. Differing situations and interests, spatial separation, low education, and reluctance to participate in organized activities seem to hamper identification of mutual interests and enduring commitments to mutual benefit groups. Consequently, they are easily co-opted by representatives and organizations of larger farmers and agribusinesses.

Also important is the extent to which small farmers have resisted or failed to develop effective economic organizations (Marshall and Thompson, 1976; Dorner, 1977). New forms of marketing, including cooperatives, are needed to increase the competitive position of small farmers. Policies that provide greater support for such small farm organizations are needed, but what kinds of support are required and how much? Even with appropriate support, Dorner concludes that the "primary problems of group farming will be those of effective internal organization and of member commitment and morale" (1977:8).

There are diverse signs of a social reform movement in agriculture. However, it has not yet focused on collective issues or captured the interest of many farmers. What are the barriers to the movement becoming more widespread? What institution and organization models would enable farmers to effectively negotiate the bases for a commitment to group action? What elements of group consciousness and rules of cooperation are necessary for the development of effective organizations? What strategies of change and development can be effectively employed? *Research is needed on the extent and nature of organizational participation of small and part-time farm families, their political socialization and interests, and the barriers to association and commitment that inhibit political mobilization.*

The Crucible of Historic Forces

Changes in the structure of agriculture are recognized increasingly as largely a consequence of sociological and economic developments external to farm families (U.S. Congress, 1978; Rodefeld et al., 1978; Buttel and Newby, 1980). These external forces include government agricultural and economic policies, population growth and relocation, growth of international markets, changes in transportation and communication, increased size and concentration of agribusiness on both the input and output side, increased costs of key resources, development of center and peripheral industries, new labor market structures, spatial diversification, and changes in lifestyles and consumer tastes. At present, the economic bases and processes associated with these developments are much better understood than the related social and political factors.

Answers to many questions require sociological research. What is the impact of rising energy costs on population redistribution and creation of local market demand for farm land and food products? How do changes in the population of rural communities, including women who work, affect nonfarm and farm labor supply? How do improvements in rural community services and institutions on the one hand, and revitalization programs for central cities on the other, affect trends in industrial relocation and preferences of families for rural living? What is the future of social movements involving use of renewable energy resources, "organic" agriculture and food, and environmental conservation, and what will be their impact on consumer tastes, the interests of those entering farming, and the encouraging of new modes of agricultural production? How will the national effort to attain energy self-sufficiency affect these social movements and those rural communities and farming areas where energy resources are located?

Finally, the development of policy to provide a more secure place in American society for small and part-time farm families will require research to better understand the factors and processes of large-scale social and cultural change.

REFERENCES

Bertrand, Alvin L. 1967. "Research on part-time farming in the United States." *Sociologia Ruralis* 7:295–304.

Brewster, David. 1979. "Perspectives on the small farm." In Economics, Statistics, and Cooperatives Service, U.S. Department of Agriculture (editor), *Small Farm Issues: Proceedings of the ESCS Small Farm Workshop.* Washington, D.C.: Economics, Statistics, and Cooperatives Service, U.S. Department of Agriculture, ERS-60.

Buttel, Frederick, and Howard Newby (editors). 1980. *The Rural Sociology of the Advanced Societies: Critical Perspectives.* Montclair, New Jersey: Allanheld, Osmun, and Co.

Carlin, Thomas F., and John Crecink. 1979. "Small farm definition and public policy." *American Journal of Agricultural Economics* 61(December):933–939.

Dorner, Peter (editor). 1977. *Cooperative and Commune: Group Farming in the Development of Agriculture.* Madison, Wisconsin: Wisconsin University Press.

Friedland, William H., and Tim Kappel. 1979. *Production or Perish: Changing the Inequities of Agricultural Research Priorities.* Santa Cruz, California: University of California (Santa Cruz) Press.

Gasson, Ruth (editor). 1977. *The Place of Part-time Farming in Rural and Regional Development.* Ashford, Great Britain: Centre for European Agricultural Studies, Wye College Press.

Hadwiger, Don F., and William P. Browne. 1978. *The New Politics of Food.* Lexington, Massachusetts: D. C. Heath and Co.

Larson, Donald K., and James A. Lewis. 1979. "Small farm profile." In Economics, Statistics, and Cooperatives Service, U.S. Department of Agriculture (editor), *Small Farm Issues: Proceedings of the ESCS Small Farm Workshop.* Washington, D.C.: Economics, Statistics, and Cooperatives Service, U.S. Department of Agriculture, ERS-60.

Madden, J. Patrick, and Heather Tischbein. 1979. "Toward an agenda for small farm research." *American Journal of Agricultural Economics* 61:940–946.

Marshall, Ray, and Allen Thompson. 1976. *Status and Prospects of Small Farmers in the South.* Atlanta, Georgia: Southern Regional Council.

Nichols, E. H., F. C. Fliegel, and J. C. Van Es. 1979. *Growing Numbers of Small Farms in the Northcentral Region.* Urbana-Champaign, Illinois: Department of Rural Sociology, University of Illinois.

Rodefeld, Richard D., Jan Flora, Donald Voth, Isao Fujimoto, and Jim Converse (editors). 1978. *Change in Rural America: Causes, Consequences, and Alternatives.* St. Louis, Missouri: C. V. Mosby Co.

Saupe, William E. 1980. *Information Needs Relating to Small Farm Programs and Policies.*

Washington, D.C.: Economics, Statistics, and Cooperatives Service, U.S. Department of Agriculture.

Schertz, Lyle P. 1979. *Another Revolution in U.S. Farming?* Washington, D.C.: Economics, Statistics, and Cooperatives Service, U.S. Department of Agriculture, ERS-441.

U.S. Congress. 1978. *Public Policy and the Changing Structure of American Agriculture.* Washington, D.C.: U.S. Government Printing Office.

U.S. Department of Agriculture (Economics, Statistics, and Cooperatives Service). 1979. *Small Farm Issues: Proceedings of the ESCS Small Farm Workshop.* Washington, D.C.: Economics, Statistics, and Cooperatives Service, U.S. Department of Agriculture, ERS-60.

U.S. Department of Agriculture (Science and Education Administration) and Community Services Administration. 1978. *Regional Small Farms Conferences: National Summary.* Washington, D.C.: Science and Education Administration, U.S. Department of Agriculture.

U.S. General Accounting Office. 1978. *Changing Character and Structure of American Agriculture: An Overview.* Washington, D.C.: U.S. General Accounting Office, CED-78-178.

Part 7
NATURAL RESOURCES

Natural resources epitomize what is distinctive about rural America. People's relationship to natural resources and the methods of extracting them has been responsible for the development of diverse rural lifestyles. Miners, cowboys, lumberjacks, migrant workers, fishermen, and the various types of farmers derive distinctive subcultures and popular images from how they associate with natural resources.

Natural resources are also the foundation of civilization and economic growth. It has been observed that the last thing a fish might notice is water. A scant twenty years ago, only a few alarmists seemed concerned about environmental deterioration and depletion of nonrenewable resources. Natural resources were taken for granted, occupying a back seat to economic growth through technological development and enhanced labor productivity. However, concern tends to be directed toward the scarcest production input. Public perception of natural resources has shifted dramatically from one of inexhaustibility to one of scarcity.

However, public concern with natural resources stops considerably short of a consensus. The conflict between developers and environmentalists arises in new locations and new issues almost daily. Present and future energy sources head the list of concern and conflict, but, as noted in this section, water and land use may not be far behind.

The nation's natural resources are located almost entirely in its rural areas. Only two decades ago, the major sources of rural employment were farming and extracting natural resources. However, the rural economy has diversified through industrialization and a newly perceived natural resource: open space. The result has been a population turnaround and greatly increased recreational use of rural areas. Thus, the ground has been laid for conflict not only between rural suppliers and urban consumers of natural resources, but also between residents within the same rural communities or regions. New rural residents, vacationers, and industries compete with farmers and other interests for land, water, timber, and space.

The conflicting expectations placed on rural America have led some to characterize it as an underdeveloped country that exists to meet the needs of an urbanized society–needs and whims that are subject to frequent change. In reality, there is a mutual dependence, for rural people are no less dependent on the products of industry than are urban people. But the fact remains that we face difficult dilemmas and the nature of the conflicts and prospects for resolution are not well known. This dilemma is the focus of this section's introductory chapter by Buttel (Chapter 35). Appropriately titled "Rural Resource Use and the Environment," research issues that concern the use of resources are identified, as are issues concerned with protection of the environment. Each of the remaining chapters deals with a specific resource.

Few natural resources illustrate the conflict between preservation and exploitation as extensively as land use, the topic of Chapter 36, by Brown. One of the most important issues in this chapter is the competition in the larger society for residential, industrial, and food production uses.

Water is characterized by Francis in Chapter 37 as the ultimate natural resource; it has no substitutes. Water quality issues are raised in this chapter, as are concerns about distribution. The lack of sufficient quantities of water in places where our society insists on creating greater needs for it characterizes a crucial emerging issue. Will water become our next societal resource crisis?

O'Leary and Lee's chapter on forestry (Chapter 38) and Yetley's chapter on fishing (Chapter 39) identify issues of relatively recent concern to social scientists. Although both are perceived as renewable resources, conflicts over their use are beginning to emerge. Both chapters call attention to the possible need to change practices in timbering and fishing, thus suggesting the value of a traditional area of rural sociological research–diffusion of innovations–not previously applied to these two areas.

35
Rural Resource Use and the Environment

FREDERICK H. BUTTEL

The rural environment, once viewed as having pristine and limitless natural resources, is now exhibiting its limits and fragility. The heritage of resource abundance throughout American development makes this recognition painful and frequently conflict ridden.

The principal issue concerning rural resources and the environment is escalated social demand in the face of limited resources and fragile rural ecosystems. However, the ultimate concern is not only the preservation of rural resources: The challenge for research and policy is to provide insights into how rural resources can yield higher levels of socioeconomic well-being at the same time that they are used in ecologically prudent ways.

The range of problems associated with rural resource use is vast, but their scope is captured by the two-dimensional typology of Table 35.1. The first dimension distinguishes between environmental problems of the renewable resource extraction sectors (agriculture, forestry, and fisheries) on one hand, and the secondary, tertiary, and consumption[1] sectors on the other. The latter includes extraction of nonrenewable resources such as coal and other minerals.

The second distinction is between resource depletion and environmental pollution. Depletion refers to the degradation of renewable natural

Frederick H. Buttel is associate professor in the Department of Rural Sociology at Cornell University, Ithaca, New York. He has written numerous articles on the sociology of natural resources and the environment and is coeditor of *The Rural Sociology of the Advanced Societies: Critical Perspectives* and coauthor of *Environment, Energy, and Society*.

Table 35.1 A Typology of Rural Resource Use and Environmental Problems, with Examples

Forms of Environmental Problems	Sector	
	Renewable Natural Resource Production	Secondary, Tertiary, and Consumption
Depletion	Soil erosion; destruction of forest lands through imprudent harvesting techniques; exhaustion of fishery resources; overgrazing.	Loss of agricultural land through development of dispersed rural housing; national or local exhaustion of nonrenewable resources such as tin.
Pollution	Soil contamination from improper pesticide use; human pesticide poisonings; nitrate runoff caused by excessive or improper fertilization.	Air and water pollution from rural industries and power plants; acid seepage from coal mines; improper solid or toxic waste disposal; reduction of ecological diversity caused by water impoundments.

resources (e.g., soil erosion) and to declining levels of availability of nonrenewable resources (e.g., exhaustion of coal deposits). Pollution refers to contamination of ecosystems, which alters their dynamics in ways that are unfavorable to human and other biological survival.

I distinguish between environmental problems of the renewable-extractive sector[2] and the secondary, tertiary, and consumption sector because the environmental problems of these two sectors have different causes and origins. Resource depletion and degradation in agriculture, forestry, and fisheries have relatively specific origins in the industries themselves, as the subsequent chapters by O'Leary and Yetley demonstrate. For example, many of the ecological problems of agriculture can be traced to structural changes in agriculture such as increasing farm size, overproduction, economic insecurity, and the adoption of capital-intensive technology by farmers (Buttel and Larson, 1979; Buttel, 1981). Problems of the secondary, tertiary, and consumption sectors, however, generally have a more diffuse set of causes, many of which derive from the structure of the larger urban economy and society. For example, air and water pollution from industrial branch plants in nonmetropolitan areas is less related to the structure of rural communities than it is to economic and political forces (e.g., expensive labor and stringent environmental regulations of metropolitan regions in the

Midwest and Northeast) that have increasingly led to rural industrialization (Lonsdale, 1979).

The typology offered in Table 35.1 does not reflect ironclad distinctions. There are connections and interactions between the problems of the renewable-extractive and the secondary, tertiary, and consumption sectors. For example, increasingly dispersed nonmetro housing results in substantial loss of agricultural land (Brown, 1979); acid rain, augmented by rural industrial and power plant pollution, has increasingly been linked to deteriorating productivity of farm and forest land in the upper Midwest and New England. Depletion and pollution also have a common thread in ecological scarcity; rapid depletion of a renewable resource such as timber can lead to leeching of nutrients and water pollution, while salinization of an agro-ecosystem from irrigation will render it less productive. Nevertheless, the typology of Table 35.1 illustrates the range of rural resource problems and provides insight into their numerous causes.

Despite the varied origins of rural resource and environmental problems, two master trends, both of which were experienced initially in the 1970s and can be expected to continue through the 1980s, deserve special mention. These two trends are energy scarcity and the resurgence of population growth in rural America.

Energy scarcity will be pivotal in shaping rural resource use. Because agricultural production is relatively energy-intensive and has a low price elasticity of demand for consumption of energy (Buttel et al., 1980b), protracted energy scarcity may compel dramatic shifts in agricultural practices. Depletion of petroleum and natural gas will intensify the use of nonmetro-based energy resources such as coal, oil shale, timber, and biomass. Nonmetro communities are disproportionate recipients of nuclear and coal-powered electrical generation facilities as utilities expand generation capacity to compensate for declining availability of other fuels (Wilkening and Klessig, 1978). Also, rural households consume more energy, per household and per capita, than their urban counterparts, largely because of increasing levels of residential dispersion in nonmetro areas (Brazzel and Hunter, 1979). Therefore, a deteriorating energy situation, accompanied by escalating energy prices, will have disproportionately adverse effects on rural people, especially those who are poor. In sum, energy scarcity promises to expand the already high demands on rural resources, and threatens to marginalize rural people in the process.

The resurgence of rural population growth is less a single specific cause of rural environmental degradation than it is a symptom of a further set of escalating demands on rural natural resources. To be sure, the influx of metro-to-nonmetro migrants places greater stress on rural resources, partially because of the preference of many of these migrants to live on large lots outside of population centers. The result is loss of agricultural and forestry lands, water pollution from inadequate septic tanks, and so forth (Brown, 1979). Nevertheless, the population turnaround in many regions reflects more potent ecological forces, such as nonmetro industrialization in the Sun Belt and energy extraction projects in the West.

A final but extremely significant aspect of rural resource use is equity, both among rural people and between the metro and nonmetro segments of society. Equity has several interrelated components. Rural people often do not hold title to or control the bulk of the resources on or around which they live. The most obvious cases include private absentee ownership of forests in New England, coal fields in Appalachia, and farm land in the South. A related issue concerns use of public lands for private benefit and under private control (e.g., coal mining in the West). Rural people often are not the major beneficiaries of resource use in peripheral areas of the country. Yet they are frequently compelled to absorb the social and ecological costs of nonmetro resource development.

IMPORTANCE OF RURAL RESOURCE ISSUES

Environmental quality assumed a *prima facie* importance during the 1970s, albeit with a continuing debate over the ultimate biophysical limits to societal and economic growth. The rural environment is the location of the vast bulk of raw materials used by the larger society. Excessive degradation of those resources would undermine the economic fabric of the United States. Therefore, husbanding of the rural environment is important.

Several aspects of rural resource use make rural resource issues especially urgent. A distinctive aspect of many rural resource problems is the undermining of renewable resource production. Continued depletion of nonrenewable resources, such as petroleum, will cast renewable resources – especially various types of biomass – in a more central role for future restructuring of advanced industrial economies. Unnecessary destruction of renewable resources, such as agricultural and forest lands, may make the transition from a fossil fuel based economy to a less energy-intensive economy (if this transition is necessary) far more difficult than it otherwise would be (see Chapter 5).

A second reason for research and policy to enhance rural environmental quality was implied earlier: Although rural communities are becoming increasingly diversified industrially and occupationally, they are still dependent on the viability of their natural resource based industries–agriculture, forestry, fisheries, and mining. Although only about 11 percent of the labor force in nonmetro communities are employed in these four industries (Hines et al., 1975), these industries' importance to rural economies may extend far beyond their fractions of the labor force. This is particularly the case in the Great Plains and many small rural trade centers where the characteristically rural extractive industries remain predominant (Morrill and Wohlenberg, 1971).

One further rationale for assigning particular importance to rural resource problems is that demands on rural resources are certain to escalate in the next decade even if rural resources need not be called upon for a massive shift toward a "soft energy" economy. In some cases, these demands will reach ecological limits such as regional shortages of marketable timber or irrigation water. Just as frequently, however, the barriers will be ecological and socioeconomic. For example, expansion of energy development in western states will clearly not be limited to coal supplies. Instead, public concern about pollution and the dislocations of potential boomtown development, along with conflicts over the allocation of benefits and costs of coal development, will be of principal importance (Markusen, 1980; Murdock and Leistritz, 1979).

CURRENT KNOWLEDGE

Our knowledge of rural resource problems is limited because these problems have become a national and scholarly concern only recently. The literature has expanded greatly during the 1970s, but it would be misleading to suggest that rural sociological interest in natural resource questions was solely a product of the environmental movement during the late 1960s and 1970s. Rural sociologists were among the first social scientists to research natural resource issues, and the Natural Resources Research Group (a group of volunteer researchers in the Rural Sociological Society) existed long before the notions of "ecology" and "the environment" became faddish.

Rural sociological research on rural resource issues has proceeded primarily on two interrelated fronts: identifying causes of the origins of rural environmental problems, and investigating the efficacy of present or potential strategies to meliorate these problems.

Soil erosion can be regarded as the principal environmental problem of agriculture; considerable effort has been devoted to understanding the macro and micro influences that lead to excessive soil erosion. Much research on agricultural erosion has focused on values of farmers and how those values might be connected to farm practices that lead to erosion. Interesting historical and contemporary questions have been raised. Nowak et al. (1980) have presented evidence that land "stewardship"—the notion that family farmers are stewards of the soil and are best able to uphold the moral obligation to ensure the viability of land resources for future generations—has long been a major component of farmers' value systems. At the same time, Nowak et al. find that farmers have little awareness of the severity of agricultural erosion, and that farmers with higher levels of concern about erosion do not differ greatly in their farm practices from farmers with lower degrees of concern.

The modest association between farmers' erosion attitudes and their practices conceals some significant aspects of farmers' attitudes toward soil erosion that suggest hypotheses as to why these attitude/behavior correlations are so low. Perhaps the most interesting research finding is that farm size is inversely related to the degree to which farmers are concerned about soil erosion, as well as to the degree of concern over water pollution from fertilizers (Buttel et al., 1980a).[3] Even though smaller farmers, older farmers, and farmers having a largely noneconomic orientation toward agriculture are more concerned about soil erosion than operators of larger farms, farm size appears to have little relation to the use of erosion-related agricultural practices (see also Pampel and Van Es, 1977, who report a slight tendency for smaller operators to use more conservation practices than larger farmers). These anomalies suggest other hypotheses: First, many strategies to curb erosion (e.g., terracing, rotating crops, planting hedges) require substantial financial investments or sacrifice of income at least in the short run, and smaller operators are less able than large farmers to make these investments. Second, there may be little correspondence between erosion attitudes and behavior because of the competitive milieu of agriculture; the marginal economic returns of many farmers require them to maximize short-term economic returns and forego investments in erosion control in order to remain in business.[4]

Rural sociological research has focused on several other micro and macro factors that may be causally related to the extent of soil erosion, including absentee ownership, part-time farming status, and mechanization. Research results on these factors have often been inconclusive. Davis' (1979) research on ecological aspects of contractually integrated production of vegetables in Ontario County, New York, found that farmers tended to grow ecologically demanding and erosion-producing crops primarily on rented land while using their privately owned farm land less intensively (e.g., for dairy production). Dillman et al. (1978), however, found no tendency for absentee ownership of wheat land in the Palouse Country of eastern Washington and northern Idaho to lead to disproportionate soil erosion. There is stronger evidence that mechanization of U.S. agriculture has led to greater levels of soil erosion. Mechanization in the form of heavy equipment can increase erosion and reduce yields because of soil compaction (Rodefeld, 1980:33). The use of large machinery also makes use of contour farming, hedges, and terraces more difficult.

As noted previously, the causes of resource and environmental problems in the secondary, tertiary, and consumption sectors are more diffuse, and only a short synopsis of a number of diverse research efforts can be reported here. It has been noted repeatedly that ownership of major manufacturing or mineral extraction facilities in rural communities conveys a high degree of social power, and corporate owners are frequently willing to use their power to avoid the costs of environmental protection (Rickson and Simpkins, 1972). In a related sense, the economic insecurity of rural communities and rural people has tended to place them in a powerless position vis-à-vis resource extraction and manufacturing firms (Caudill, 1971).

A host of social forces—the search for cheap (nonunionized) labor, lower taxes, and less stringent environmental and business regulations—have fostered nonmetro industrialization (Summers et al., 1976). Likewise, they have led to increased demands on rural environmental resources. Another set of factors centering around economic, environmental, and aesthetic deterioration of metro areas has led metro residents to seek out rural places of residence (Lonsdale, 1979). Finally, rural communities typically have meager tax bases and high per capita costs because of their small size. As a result, they are unable to provide adequate pollution abatement, solid waste disposal, and other environmentally related services (Tweeten and Brinkman, 1976; Wilkening and Klessig, 1978).

Rural sociological and related social research on the feasibility and desirability of alternative policy strategies has been much less thorough. The intellectual heritage underlying conceptualization of alternative policy strategies has been the liberal critique of *laissez faire* and economic individualism. It is frequently presumed that the only way to make natural resource decision making more ecologically responsible is to consolidate centralized political control over these decisions. The opposite end of the continuum is generally conceived as one of local control, a total lack of public control, and a minimum regulation of economic growth. The research question thus is typically posed in narrow economic terms: What is the optimum level of centralized governmental regulation to maximize the benefits or minimize the costs of environmental quality regulation?

There are two major limitations to this formulation that are increasingly recognized by rural sociologists. First, the centralized government/economic individualism continuum may be a false dichotomy, and it conceals many feasible strategies for equitable resolution of rural resource problems. For example, the liberal critique of local control and economic individualism is premised, often quite rightly, on the tendency for parochial or "special" interests to be dominant in local community politics. However, centralized government control of natural resource decisions does not guarantee that these decisions will reflect dispassionate management criteria insulated from dominant economic interests (Geisler, 1980). Second, the traditional formulation of rural resource policies implicitly presumes a rather ironclad logic of economic growth versus the environment. In doing so, it is assumed that the economic well-being of rural communities and their residents is inversely related to environmental quality so that the role of resource management becomes one of developing the optimum tradeoffs between economic growth and welfare on one hand and environmental quality on the other. The development of alternative formulations of public policy approaches to rural resource questions will be a major focus of the following section.

RESEARCH ISSUES

Socioeconomic Factors Leading to Rural Environmental Degradation

The most basic research need is a comprehensive understanding of the socioeconomic factors that have led to degradation or excessive exploitation of rural resources. We need to know the characteristics and/or trends in the structure of the agricultural system (and kindred forestry and fishery production systems) that lead to environmental degradation or that present constraints on the long-term viability of renewable natural resource ecosystems. There is a broad need for research for understanding the major processes of social and economic change that have led to environmental degradation associated with the secondary, tertiary, and consumption sectors. Both questions demand a variety of methodological approaches, encompassing historical, longitudinal, and cross-sectional methods.

Suggestive results from relatively recent research on these two aspects of rural resource problems present promising foci for further inquiry. In the sphere of agriculture, much attention has focused on a cluster of factors (increasing farm size, inequality of land ownership, absentee ownership, mechanization, specialization, land inflation) related to the increasing scale of agricultural production in the United States (Small Farm Viability Project, 1977). In light of the high degree of attention paid to farm size and scale in recent USDA research on structure issues in agriculture, the historical and contemporary and micro and macro impacts of scale on quality of the agricultural environment are a high-priority research need.

In the area of resource problems related to the secondary, tertiary, and consumption sectors of the rural economy and society, a high-priority avenue of research concerns the extent to which inequalities of political and economic power among rural people and between the metro and nonmetro segments of society are a key causal force. Do power inequalities among nonmetro people enable the privileged to misallocate rural resources in pursuit of narrow economic benefits? Is the power of metro institutions (e.g., absentee owners of rural resources, metro industrialists and mining firms, and even the federal government) typically employed to play rural communities off against one another and to use the economic insecurity of rural people to justify excessive levels of environmental degradation? These two high-priority aspects of rural resources research should not be construed as the only possible foci for a research agenda. Nevertheless, these research questions are innovative, provocative, and closely related to the new agenda of rural policy debates inaugurated during the 1970s; they deserve continuing attention.

Role of Government Policy in the Use of Rural Resources

Much more study is needed to identify the historical and contemporary roles of government policy in rural environmental quality. Government, through its various organizations and programs, is alternatively a cause and a meliorating factor in rural resource degradation. For example, future research may reveal that government agricultural policies that have disproportionately benefited large farms may have contributed to a decline in the quality of the agricultural environment, yet the Soil Conservation Service has long had a cadre of committed, progressive professionals who have made valiant efforts to curb soil erosion and related problems. Nevertheless, general government policy (as well as the familiar contradictory character of government policy) is a key research issue for understanding both the causes of and the possible policy alternatives to rural environmental degradation.

Energy Scarcity and the Population Turnaround

There is need for sustained investigation of possible environmental impacts of two key trends affecting nonmetro United States: energy scarcity and the population turnaround. Several important questions were implicitly identified previously, especially how and to what degree energy scarcity and the rural turnaround may increase demands on rural resources. Another concern is the equity consequences of this escalating demand for rural resources. Will these additional demands on rural resources confer benefits on rural people generally, or will the economic advantages and ecological costs of intensifying rural resource use benefit only a small segment of rural and larger society in the United States?

Alternatives to the Environmental Degradation Caused by Economic Growth

If the rural environment is to be protected and the livelihood of rural people improved, research must be devoted to conceptualization and evaluation of alternative property institutions and organizational forms directed at resolving the economic growth versus the environment dilemma. These research issues have been inspired largely by the work of E. F. Schumacher (1973) and the efforts of persons in the appropriate technology and economic democracy movements (also see Chapter 5). Many researchers argue that economic well-being inherently conflicts with environmental quality when socioeconomic organization is highly centralized and based on nonrenewable resources, and when rural communities become specialized in "exporting" natural resources for national industrial growth. However, much recent thought has focused on the design and feasibility of qualitatively different strategies of rural resource development. These strategies have two major components, each of which may have major implications for rural welfare and environmental quality: decentralization of production and consumption systems, and community and/or employee ownership and control of commodity production and distribution organizations.

A key research issue in the next decade will be whether these two strategies, singly or in combination, can provide a lever for increasing rural economic welfare and enhancing rural environmental quality. Much of the impetus for decentralization comes from increasing energy prices, which make it more and more expensive to transport raw materials from the rural hinterland to the metropolis and to transport manufactured commodities from the metropolis to the hinterland. Basically, decentralization can be conceptualized as "import substitution"; the rural community's production system begins to produce commodities that were previously "imported" from external regions. Two examples are the substitution of local food marketing and processing for foods brought into the community from elsewhere, and the substitution of energy from wood for externally produced petroleum and natural gas.

The argument for community or employee ownership of enterprises initially derived from efforts of rural communities in Oregon to offset the problem of plywood manufacturing firms considering relocation outside Oregon. The employees of several plywood firms were able to purchase plants and equipment, and have been successful in maintaining employment and the viability of their enterprises. It is increasingly argued, however, that employee ownership of enterprises may have relevance beyond salvaging employment from departing corporations. Indeed, much attention has been paid to the feasibility of establishing cooperatively owned and controlled enterprises for import substitution activities. For example, several community development corporations have undertaken the coordination and food processing necessary to allow local farmers to supply a higher proportion of the community's food needs (Britt et al., 1978). Likewise, community development corporations have engaged in harvesting and marketing wood for home heating fuel.[5]

The tentative enthusiasm for these two alternative organizational strategies for rural communities is based on two hypotheses. First, these alternative property institutions and a reorientation of local production to meet local needs may allow rural people to capture a larger share of the benefits of rural resource use. Local ownership will ensure that profits from production operations and capital gains remain in the community rather than being diverted to external financial or industrial institutions. Second, these two cornerstones of an alternative rural development strategy may produce environmental quality and resource conservation benefits. Focusing more on local use of renewable resources may help insulate residents of a rural community from future dislocations due to energy scarcity. Also, because owners of the resource enterprise are residents of the community, there may be a structural incentive for the firm to avoid decisions that result in excessive exploitation of the community's natural resource base; because the community's viability is based on its natural resources, more attention may be given to ensuring the future sustainability of the community's resource base. Despite the apparent attractiveness of these options, they have not been systematically observed and evaluated; visible successes in a few communities may in fact be overshadowed by the failures in many areas. However, because of the overall promise of this alternative vision of rural economic and resource development (especially its possibilities for bridging economic growth and environmental dualism), it deserves very high research priority.

Centralized Versus Local Control

Further research is needed to specify what mix of local and centralized governmental control can best lead to equitable development of rural resources. The centralized/local continuum does not exhaust the range of strategies to protect rural environmental resources, and this debate will certainly remain important in the coming decade. It is important to recognize that rural sociologists have not been heavily involved in this set of issues, and considerably more attention should be directed toward them. Nevertheless, issues to be addressed in the debate over centralized or local control should be broadened to include socioeconomic equity concerns that are frequently glossed over in the traditional cost/benefit approaches to these problems.

NOTES

1. Following conventional terminology, the secondary sector refers to manufacturing (including construction) and the tertiary sector refers to the provision of services. The consumption sector pertains to nonindustrial or noncommercial activities, such as family consumption of housing, personal transportation, and water, that have potential environmental impacts.

2. I focus on the agricultural portion of the renewable-extractive sector in this chapter because parallel issues pertaining to forestry and fisheries are discussed in chapters that follow.

3. This research, indicating an inverse relation between farm size and concern with soil erosion, parallels other studies that provide tentative evidence of a connection between farm size and energy intensity of agricultural production at the macro level (Buttel and Larson, 1979).

4. There have been suggestions that government agricultural policy has contributed substantially to structural changes in agriculture (such as increasing farm size), which have, in turn, contributed to degradation of the agricultural environment. However, these arguments have not received rigorous research support.

5. Rural social scientists increasingly recognize the deleterious impacts that private property on agricultural land (especially resultant land inflation) has on family farmers and on the quality of the agricultural environment (see, for example, Raup, 1978). A strategy for dealing with these problems that is closely akin to import substitution and community ownership is that of community land trusts. The essential logic behind community land trusts is that farmers and forest landowners surrender the development and transfer rights of their land for use rights and a degree of insulation from the effects of land inflation. Structurally, community land trusts are nonprofit corporations with elected boards of trustees, usually with open public membership from the community. A trust acquires land through purchase or donation, retaining title to the land and removing the land from the speculative market. Appropriate uses of the land are decided by the board of trustees, and the land is leased to individuals, families, cooperatives, public agencies, or businesses, generally for lifetime (or in an inheritable ninety-nine-year lease). Leases may be terminated if the board feels that the land is being misused. In economic terms, the purpose of the community land trust is to capture the increasing value of landed property and use it for collective purposes, rather than having this value be appropriated by absentee landowners.

REFERENCES

Brazzel, John M., and Leon J. Hunter. 1979. *Distributional Patterns in Energy Expenditures Among Farm and Nonfarm Households.* Washington, D.C.: Science and Education Ad-

ministration, U.S. Department of Agriculture.
Britt, Carolyn, Tom Walker, and Michael Schaaf. 1978. *Jobs and Energy in New England: Food Production and Marketing.* Bath, Maine: Coastal Enterprises.
Brown, David L. 1979. "Agricultural land use: A population distribution perspective." In *Farmland, Food, and the Future.* Ankeny, Iowa: Soil Conservation Society of America.
Buttel, Frederick H. 1981. "Environmental quality and protection in rural America." In A. H. Hawley and V. Rock (editors), *Rural Renaissance and Urban Phenomena.* Chapel Hill, North Carolina: University of North Carolina Press.
Buttel, Frederick H., Gilbert W. Gillespie, Jr., Oscar W. Larson, III, and Craig K. Harris. 1980a. "The social bases of agrarian environmentalism: A comparative analysis of New York and Michigan farm operators." Paper presented at the Fifth World Congress for Rural Sociology, Mexico City.
Buttel, Frederick H., and Oscar W. Larson, III. 1979. "Farm size, structure, and energy intensity: An ecological analysis of U.S. agriculture." *Rural Sociology* 44(Fall):471–488.
Buttel, Frederick H., William Lockeretz, Martin Strange, and Elinor Terhune. 1980b. *Energy and Small Farms: A Review of Existing Literature and Suggestions Concerning Future Research.* Washington, D.C.: National Rural Center, Research Agenda for Small Farms Monograph 2.
Caudill, Harry M. 1971. *My Land is Dying.* New York: E. P. Dutton and Co.
Davis, John Emmeus. 1979. "Property without power: A study of the development of contract farming in the United States, with cases from New York and Tennessee." Ithaca, New York: Cornell University. Master's thesis.
Dillman, Don A., John E. Carlson, and William R. Lassey. 1978. *The Influence of Absentee Owners on Use of Erosion Control Practices by Palouse Farmers.* Pullman, Washington: College of Agriculture Research Center, Washington State University, Circular 607.
Geisler, Charles C. 1980. "The quiet revolution in land use control revisited." In Frederick Buttel and Howard Newby (editors), *The Rural Sociology of the Advanced Societies: Critical Perspectives.* Montclair, New Jersey: Allanheld, Osmun, and Co.
Hines, Fred K., David L. Brown, and John M. Zimmer. 1975. *Social and Economic Characteristics of the Population in Metro and Nonmetro Counties, 1970.* Washington, D.C.: Economics, Statistics, and Cooperatives Service, U.S. Department of Agriculture, ERS-272.
Lonsdale, Richard E. 1979. "Background and issues." In Richard E. Lonsdale and H. L. Seyler (editors), *Nonmetropolitan Industrialization.* New York: John Wiley and Sons.
Markusen, Ann R. 1980. "The political economy of rural development: The case of western United States boomtowns." In Frederick Buttel and Howard Newby (editors), *The Rural Sociology of the Advanced Societies: Critical Perspectives.* Montclair, New Jersey: Allanheld, Osmun, and Co.
Morrill, Richard L., and Ernest H. Wohlenberg. 1971. *The Geography of Poverty in the United States.* New York: McGraw-Hill Book Co.
Murdock, Steve H., and F. Larry Leistritz. 1979. *Energy Development in the Western United States: Impact on Rural Areas.* New York: Praeger Publishers.
Nowak, Peter J., Donald J. Wagener, Robert Thompson, and Roy E. Rickson. 1980. "Stewardship and environmental concern." Paper presented at the annual meetings of the Rural Sociological Society, Ithaca, New York.
Pampel, Fred, Jr., and J. C. Van Es. 1977. "Environmental quality and issues of adoption research." *Rural Sociology* 42:57–71.
Raup, Philip M. 1978. "Some questions of value and scale in agriculture." *American Journal of Agricultural Economics* 60:303–308.
Rickson, Roy E., and Charles E. Simpkins. 1972. "Industrial organizations and the ecological process: The case of water pollution." In M. B. Brinkerhoff and P. R. Kunz (editors),

Complex Organizations and Their Environments. Dubuque, Iowa: W. C. Brown Publishers.

Rodefeld, Richard D. 1980. *The Direct and Indirect Effects of Mechanizing U.S. Agriculture.* Montclair, New Jersey: Allanheld, Osmun, and Co.

Schumacher, E. F. 1973. *Small is Beautiful: Economics as if People Mattered.* New York: Perennial Library.

Small Farm Viability Project. 1977. "Natural resources task force final report." In Small Farm Viability Project (editors), *The Family Farm in California.* Sacramento, California: Small Farm Viability Project.

Summers, Gene F., Sharon D. Evans, Frank Clemente, E. M. Beck, and Jon Minkoff. 1976. *Industrial Invasion of Nonmetropolitan America.* New York: Praeger Publishers.

Tweeten, Luther, and George L. Brinkman. 1976. *Micropolitan Development.* Ames, Iowa: Iowa State University Press.

Wilkening, Eugene A., and Lowell Klessig. 1978. "The rural environment: Quality and conflicts in land use." In Thomas R. Ford (editor), *Rural U.S.A.: Persistence and Change.* Ames, Iowa: Iowa State University Press.

36
Land Use

DAVID L. BROWN

During the 1970s, land use became a focus of public attention. Farm land conversion, urban sprawl, reservoir construction, and strip mining have been subjects of intense coverage by the media; these issues are highly politicized at the state, local, and national levels. The bulldozer, the backhoe, the dragline, and the electric tower are all implicated in the rhetoric of groups concerned with environmental protection, farm land preservation, maintaining fish and wildlife habitats, and historic preservation. Social awareness and political action reflect a reexamination of attitudes and policies concerning land resources. Land is being viewed increasingly as a natural resource to be protected and managed–not merely a commercial commodity that owners should be able to use as they wish.

Sociological analysis can contribute to a more informed basis for this discussion. Our current knowledge of the role that natural resources play in shaping rural community structure is rudimentary at best. We do not even know how many acres of farmland are converted to urban and built-up uses per thousand immigrants to rural areas. A rigorous examination of the relationships between sociodemographic structure and change on the one hand, and the land use and land use change on the other, is essential for informing policy makers and the public and for furthering our scientific knowledge of the process of community change in rural America.

David L. Brown is principal sociologist for the Science and Education Administration, U.S. Department of Agriculture, Washington, D.C. He has written numerous articles and reports on migration, population distribution, and rural development policy, and is coeditor of the book *New Directions in Urban-Rural Migration*.

Few aspects of social and economic life are totally independent of the land. Land provides living space. It is a matrix from which raw materials are extracted and the physical base for providing food, fiber, and building materials. Land is also scenery, open space, and a setting for recreation. Hence, consideration of the relationships between land use and other aspects of social life is essential for a comprehensive understanding of community growth and development.

Impacts of public action on rural land are often unintended and not always consonant with program objectives. Understanding the sociodemographic and economic determinants of land use patterns and change will better enable policy makers to anticipate effects of public programs. Such information will be useful in developing effective methods for intervening in land use change, where such action is justified, and in monitoring and evaluating programs.

On a more practical political level, the research issues considered here will contribute to identifying the constellation of community interests concerned with land use. This information is important for understanding the political arena in which competition among vested interests takes place. It is also essential for building coalitions and directing political action in promotion of land use management and control.

Land use has become a highly political issue in recent years. The capstone of this issue is the perceived relationship between agricultural land loss, the declining competitive position of relatively small farms, and nonagricultural population and economic growth in rural areas. Social scientists find themselves in the difficult position of "knowing" that certain events are occurring (i.e., that rural development requires a land base for its accomplishment) but not having adequate research to document such relationships, let alone explain them. For example, we know that acceleration of the conversion of agricultural land to nonagricultural uses occurred simultaneously in rural America during the 1970s with decentralization of population and nonfarm economic activity. Unfortunately, little research has focused on the relationship between these two trends. Moreover, existing research is generally bivariate, and the implied relationship between sociodemographic change and land use change could thus be attributed to other factors, or could even be coincidental (Zeimetz et al., 1976). Consequently, "land preservation" rhetoric has increased faster than our knowledge of the structure and process of land use change in rural America.

The truth is that we do not have a good measure of the nature or magnitude of the "land use problem." And, of course, the definition of the problem depends on the perspective from which it is viewed. The interests of farmers, developers, miners, conservationists, wildlife preservationists, and those who merely want to preserve the aesthetics of open space and a natural environment come together in the rural land use arena. Whether land use is viewed as a problem is a normative question, to be determined by competing interests. Such competition generally takes place at the local level–not in the halls of Congress or the state capitol.

Survey researchers have noted a growing "land ethic" in our country. Land is now viewed as a natural resource, not merely a commodity to be bought and sold without reference to the public good (Harris, 1980). However, even in this regard there are complicated differences of opinion among the population. For example, most farmers would agree with the preservationist ethic, but would strongly disagree with any proposed regulation that would constrain their treatment of land as the "last crop," i.e., buying and selling as needed to ensure their economic security. Hence, the most important general issue for land use research is to gain a better understanding of the nature, magnitude, and significance of the land use problem in present-day America.

RESEARCH ISSUES

Process of Rural Land Use Change

Processes of sociodemographic change are inextricably tied to the pattern of settlement and land use. These relationships have long been recognized by sociologists. Robert Park and his associates (1925) pointed to the critical link between social and spatial structure in their early book on the city, and Otis Dudley Duncan (1959) identified the linkage between population and environment as a principal dimension of the human ecological complex. However, land use has not been a major focus of sociological research.

The most noteworthy sociological analysis of land use issues has been in metropolitan areas, and relatively little attention has been focused outside the urban fringe. This urban-oriented research derives mostly from the Chicago school of human ecologists and later from a more generalized urban sociology with its interest in the succession of land use and population groups among areas of the city (Schnore, 1959), the provision of community services and facilities (Elesh and Schollaert, 1972), housing (Pynoos, 1973), and the redevelopment of blighted areas (Greer, 1965).

Some social science research has focused on rural land use issues, especially in relation to the structure of farming (Rodefeld, 1980), diffusion of innovations (Rogers and Burdge, 1972), and outdoor recreation (Burch et al., 1972). However, little of their research has described or explained the relationship between social, economic, and demographic change in rural areas on the one hand and land use on the other.

Demographic, economic (local and national), agricultural, infrastructural, and public policy factors all bear potential relationships with rural land use. However, solid theory and conceptual development is lacking, as is empirical support for such relationships. Theory needs to focus at the macro level, explaining interarea differences in the development of settlement patterns and operation of the land market and, at the micro level, explaining the decisions of developers, speculators, and individual land owners. *Thus, a major research need for the 1980s is a set of propositions and hypotheses integrating social, economic, and agricultural factors on land use and land use change.*

The Land Markets. / The land market is one of many interrelated institutions comprising the rural community. The allocation of land among competing uses that takes place through such a market is influenced by a constellation of community forces. As Barlowe (1978) points out, institutions set limits on what individuals, groups, and governments can accomplish in their development, use, and conservation of land resources. Economic, educational, family, social class, religious, legal, and political/governmental institutions provide a system of constraints that influence "acceptable" land use behavior. Recent changes in rural areas have led to new demands for land and have brought new participants into the land market (Healy and Short, 1979). *Sociologists need to research the internal structure of the land market and its relationship to other institutions of the rural community.*

Land Use Decision Making. / Increasingly, communities are discussing management and control of land within their jurisdictions. Many states and local areas are developing programs to protect farmland and other uses of open space. For example, differential assessment, agricultural zoning, purchase (and/or transfer) of development rights, and exclusive agricultural zoning are being used in some communities to reduce the vulnerability of their farmland to conversion (Urban Land Institute, 1975). Some important research questions are: What attributes affect the probability of the community initiating public action to manage and control local land? Are differences in local governmental structure related to taking public action and/or to the type of action taken? What role do public attitudes play in forming initiatives? Has recent urban-to-rural migration altered the bases of support for land use programs? *Research is needed on the processes by which communities decide* *on avenues of policy, and on the implementation of programs once they are in place.*

The structure of political action in relation to land use also is an important focus for research. What interest groups are involved (agriculture, economic, residential, recreation, fish and wildlife, mining, etc.)? How do coalitions among interests develop? What is the nature of competition and conflict among these groups? Have changes in the distribution of land among individuals and/or groups in the community altered the bases of community power and of subsequent decisions on land use?

The nature of formal governmental action is another relevant aspect of the decision-making process. Studies of governmental action should focus on the great variety of programs developed and implemented by state and local governments to manage and control land use, the legal bases of such programs, the anticipated and unanticipated effects of such programs, and the relationships between levels of government in program development and implementation.

Multivariate Analysis of the Determinants of Natural Land Use. / Analyses of the determinants of changes in rural land use patterns have been limited usually to two variables at a time. Bivariate correlations must be transcended to understand land use as an element of rural community structure. Such analyses enable the evaluation of the relative effects of social, economic, demographic, and political factors on the settlement pattern of rural life.

Among the many possible explanations of the conversion of agricultural land to nonfarm uses are population and economic activity, both of which have deconcentrated since 1970. Other trends relevant to land conversion include: (1) a pronounced growth in number of households as the baby-boom cohort moves through the family-forming ages and as the general population redistributes itself into more and smaller families; (2) changes in the structure of agriculture, including a near abandonment of share-cropping and the growth of part-time farming among smaller operators; (3) economic trends, including rural industrialization, revitalization of coal strip mining, and land purchases as a hedge against inflation; (4) additions to infrastructure, including the near completion of the interstate highway system, the construction of numerous reservoirs and fully equipped industrial sites, the extension of centralized water and sewer systems, and rural electrification; (5) growing popularity of rural areas for outdoor recreation and second home development; and (6) federal policy and programs, such as the Rural Development Act of 1972, which seek to stimulate growth and development in rural areas.

Obviously, no single analysis can include all these variables, but the multiplicity of factors producing potential effects on rural land use give an indication of the complexity of the issue. Establishing relationships between social and economic trends and trends in land use may appear to be relatively straightforward, but it is, in fact, a complicated task. Direct effects are easily identified (acreage of farmland converted to subdivisions or industrial sites, etc.), but some effects are indirect and less obvious. For example, land must be converted to accommodate economic growth, yet the jobs created may supplement farm family income, helping farmers retain their land in production. Moreover, land use can either be a determinant or a consequence of social and economic change. *Therefore, a high-priority research need for the 1980s is the multivariate analysis of the determinants of land use for the nation as a whole in which the direction of causation is correctly specified.*

Local Area Case Studies. / Highly aggregated regional and national studies are not well suited for addressing some of the more local aspects of land use change. Case studies, combining survey and ethnographic methodologies, can be used to monitor actual changes in the distribution of land among various uses, among households and individuals, and among household members (Selznick, 1966; Salamon, 1980; Patel, 1980). Analyses of prior and present use of converted farmland can be made, and some notion of the trend of conversion as a consequence of sociodemographic change can be noted. For example, local studies can address such questions as: What are the housing characteristics of migrants to rural communities (lot size, type of waste disposal, type of dwelling unit, etc.)? Where do migrants locate their residences in the community? Has the location of roads, sewer lines, and flood control structures influenced the location of new housing and commercial development? What was the land used for previously? Local study information is a valuable supplement to more highly aggregated studies: It gives a local perspective and demonstrates the diversity of rural situations.

Anderson and Perri's (1978) analysis of urbanization of rural land along the Colorado Front Range is a good example of local area research. They used aerial photography to document actual land conversion. A wide range of information available in the local communities was collected to explain land use changes. They looked at rural subdivision activity, land use and zoning policy, building costs, interest rates, credit availability, and utility hook-up and service fees. These data were gleaned from local sources including state, county, and municipal records, newspaper accounts, minutes of local meetings, and conversations with informed persons. Census data were also used. The result is a comprehensive and systematic explanation of the determinants of land use change in a particular area of the country. Replication of such studies in other areas of the country would help to establish the generalizability of the social and economic processes described. *A high priority should be given to the conduct of local area case studies throughout the United States during the 1980s.*

Effects of Changes in Land Use and Ownership on Community Structure

Land is a determinant of community structure as well as a consequence of it. Changes in distribution of land among various areas, among individuals and households, and among household members, can contribute to transformations of community structure and function. Perhaps the most obvious examples concern agriculture. The distribution of land uses in a community affects the viability and structure of its agriculture. This multifaceted situation involves numerous questions for sociological inquiry. *For example, research is needed on how changes in the distribution of land among various uses affect the price of agricultural land and farmers' ability to compete for it in the land market.*

This question is relevant to understanding the structure of agricultural operations and for explaining the process by which new persons enter farming. Moreover, it is a contributing factor to rural poverty in some parts of the nation. This is particularly true for limited resource farmers, especially if they are Black, undereducated, and very old or very young (Lewis, 1976).

The conversion of agricultural land to nonagricultural uses has potential implications for farm practices, management, and decision making. For example, farmers have had to adjust to their fields being bisected by roads, powerlines, and pipelines; they have had to change their operations to comply with nuisance regulations in urbanizing fringe areas; and land stewardship is thought to be related to farmers' perceptions of the future of agriculture in rapidly urbanizing areas (Berry, 1978). *Hence, the association of agricultural land use patterns with urbanization is an important area for research.*

Almost one-third of U.S. land is publicly owned. As explained by Buttel (in Chapter 35), public land is frequently a source of critical natural resources–fiber, minerals, energy–and it is increasingly important as a setting for recreation. Public land is of extreme national importance and decisions about its use bear directly on rural economic structure and the nature of rural society. As resource scarcity issues become more prominent, how public land is used is certain to become a more active concern. *The interface between public land use and the nature, change, and viability of associated rural communities is an emerging focus for sociological research.*

Rural land and settlement patterns are important determinants of cost and availability of services in rural communities. Population deconcentration poses a great challenge to providers of services. *Sociological analysis can contribute by focusing on the relationships among population composition and settlement patterns and the need for community services.*

Land ownership is a determinant of class, status, and power in the community (Warren, 1978). Hence, changes in land ownership can contribute to altering the bases of community decision making and the pace and nature of socioeconomic change. Particularly important are questions of internal versus external control (if land ownership passes to outsiders) and farmers' influence in the community (if their share of land and other natural resources diminishes). *Research is also needed on the effect of nonresident land ownership on rural community decision making and autonomy.*

REFERENCES

Anderson, Raymond L., and Karla Perri. 1978. *Urbanization of Rural Land in the Northern Colorado Front Range–1978.* Washington, D.C.: Economics, Statistics, and Cooperatives Service, U.S. Department of Agriculture.

Barlowe, Raleigh. 1978. *Land Resource Economics: The Economics of Real Estate.* Englewood Cliffs, New Jersey: Prentice-Hall.

Berry, David. 1978. "Effects of urbanization on agricultural activities." *Growth and Change* 9(3):2–7.

Burch, William R., Neil Cheek, and Lee Taylor (editors). 1972. *Social Behavior, Natural Resources, and the Environment.* New York: Harper and Row.

Duncan, Otis Dudley. 1959. "Human ecology and population studies." In Philip Hauser and Otis Dudley Duncan (editors), *The Study of Population.* Chicago: University of Chicago Press.

Elesh, David B., and Paul T. Schollaert. 1972. "Race and urban medicine: Factors affecting the distribution of physicians in Chicago." *Journal of Health and Social Behavior* 3:236–250.

Greer, Scott. 1965. *Urban Renewal and American Cities.* New York: Bobbs-Merrill Co.

Harris, Louis. 1980. "Outline for a press briefing on a survey of the public's attitudes toward soil, water, and renewable resources conservation policy." Washington, D.C. Mimeograph.

Healy, Robert G., and James L. Short. 1979. "Rural land: Market trends and planning implications." *American Planning Association Journal* (July):305–317.

Lewis, James A. 1976. *White and Minority Small Farm Operators in the South.* Washington, D.C.: Economics, Statistics, and Cooperatives Service, U.S. Department of Agriculture, Agricultural Economics Report 353.

Park, Robert E., Ernest Burgess, and Roderick D. McKenzie. 1925. *The City.* Chicago: University of Chicago Press.

Patel, Dinker I. 1980. *Exurbs: Urban Residential Developments in the Countryside.* Washington, D.C.: University Press of America.

Pynoos, Jan, Robert Shafer, and Chester Hartman. 1973. *Housing Urban America.* Chicago: Aldine Publishing Co.

Rodefeld, Richard D. 1980. *The Direct and Indirect Effects of Mechanizing U.S. Agriculture.* Montclair, New Jersey: Allanheld, Osmun, and Co.

Rogers, Everett M., and Rabel Burdge. 1972. *Social Change in Rural Societies.* New York: Appleton-Century-Crofts.

Salamon, Sonya. 1980. "Ethnic differences in farm family land transfer." *Rural Sociology* 45(2):290–308.

Schnore, Leo F. 1959. *The Urban Scene.* New York: Free Press.

Selznick, Philip. 1966. *T.V.A. and the Grass Roots: A Study in the Sociology of Formal Organization.* New York: Harper and Row.

Urban Land Institute. 1975. *Management and Control of Growth: Volume II and III.* Washington, D.C.: Urban Land Institute.

Warren, Ronald L. 1978. *The Community in America.* Chicago: Rand McNally and Co.

Zeimetz, Kathryn A., Elizabeth Dillon, Ernest E. Hardy, and Robert C. Otte. 1976. *Dynamics of Land Use Change in Fast Growth Areas.* Washington, D.C.: Economics, Statistics, and Cooperatives Service, U.S. Department of Agriculture, Agricultural Economics Report 325.

37 Water

JOE D. FRANCIS

Water will become an urgent environmental issue in the 1980s and beyond. Although this resource is usually taken for granted, occasional shortages occur even in the more humid regions of the nation. Scientific and public attention is increasingly drawn to discoveries of undesirable organic and inorganic chemical compounds–bacteriological, viral, and other physical contaminants–in our drinking water. This continues despite the apparent reversal in water pollution trends following the Clean Waters Act of 1966, the Water Pollution Control Act Amendments of 1972, and the Safe Drinking Water Act of 1974. If water shortages increase and if we continue to degrade the crucial reserves of potable water, the consequence could be drastic for the natural environment and current patterns of social organization.

Water is fundamental to the survival of man. All human activities depend in some way on having an adequate water supply in the right form, in the right place, at the right time. Water is essential for direct ingestion. It is essential to the production of all foodstuffs and fiber. Further, it is used in virtually every process of resource extraction and manufacture. The location of water reserves has had a major influence on settlement patterns, transportation networks, economic development, and energy production.

A nationwide water crisis would be the ultimate resource crisis. Unlike the current petroleum crisis, for which alternatives can be developed (wind, solar, biomass conversion, hydro), there are no alter-

---

Joe D. Francis is an associate professor in the Department of Rural Sociology at Cornell University, Ithaca, New York. His writings include publications on survey methods and rural water quality.

natives to water. Effective stewardship is the only way to avoid the possibility of a water crisis before it starts, and effective stewardship depends on accurate information about the nature and extent of the resource and threats to it. *The overriding research concern for the 1980s is the development of a more accurate information base with which to assess (1) the nature and extent of existing and anticipated water shortages, and (2) the current and future quality of crucial reserves of potable water.*

EXTENT OF WATER SHORTAGES

No one really knows the extent to which we may be facing a problem of quantity because there are no accurate estimates of available water. Instead, we have "ballpark" estimates from various federal agencies about the general availability of water on an average yearly basis. In addition, there are journalistic accounts of large cities extending their tentacles into the countryside in order to satisfy their needs. We also have accounts of water conflicts over the use of limited supplies (e.g., irrigation versus the production of hydroelectric power).

Based on information available from various federal agencies (U.S. General Accounting Office, 1979; U.S. Department of the Interior, 1974; U.S. Environmental Protection Agency, 1976), it appears that Americans currently use about 60 percent of the available supply of fresh water. However, this estimate can lead to the false conclusion that it will be a decade or so before we exhaust our replenished supply of fresh water. Though the fresh water available to the nation as a whole through precipitation runoff and impoundment is relatively stable from year to year, usage has been increasing at a slightly accelerating rate. Moreover, national estimates do not recognize the extreme regional variations in available water or the crisis-level shortages already faced in many localities. Compounding problems of regional variation is the existence of water rights that limit accessibility to the newcomer, the small community, ethnic minorities, and other politically and economically disadvantaged groups. Even along major waterways and reservoirs in the Northwest and Southwest, unequal allocations resulting from tenaciously forged rights produce other local shortages.

Historically, water shortages have been associated with the arid West and semi-arid Plains States, but during the last decade many states in the Southeast faced problems as population growth outstripped available supplies. The Second National Water Assessment showed that there are major water problems in most of the twenty-one water resource regions and 106 subregions (U.S. Water Resources Council, 1978). If present trends continue, water shortages can become prevalent and recurring.

RESEARCH ISSUES

Present and anticipated problems matching water supply with needs make it important that the United States develop more accurate information, on a regional level, of the quantity of fresh water available, along with an assessment of aggregate demand within and across categories of usage (e.g., irrigation, transportation, industrial, municipal, and domestic). Also needed are models for predicting shortages so that localities, businesses, and individuals can adjust their consumption patterns.

Social scientists can make an important contribution to the development of these information systems and models. Patterns of population migration and settlement, the type and rate of economic and industrial growth in an area, shifting of priorities in allowable use of scarce water, and other factors affecting use are at least as important in developing such models as are supply factors such as precipitation rates, stream flow, and various hydrologic variables. *Research is needed to trace patterns of settlement and resettlement that result from the demise of supplies in some localities and the development of new supplies in other localities.*

If large cities continue to reach into their hinterlands for water to quench their thirst, major conflicts will occur among cities as well as between cities and the surrounding countryside. As an example of such a conflict, Philadelphia is in litigation with the city of New York over rights to water in the Delaware River. Knowing who wins and who loses such conflicts, and why, will inform us of future patterns of social organization and political influence. *Research is needed on the patterns of litigation accompanying the acquisition of new water rights or the protection of old rights.*

In the West, cities are extending their hydrophilic roots farther and farther into the countryside. Los Angeles has effectively drained Owens Lake and has designs on Mono Lake; the impact of this action on agriculturalists and others in the Owens Valley has been substantial (Brower, 1980). If we are to understand and anticipate the social and economic consequences of such activities, *research is needed on changes in agricultural production, growth or demise of small villages in the affected area, and possible movement of families from the affected rural areas.*

Development and Management of Water Resources

Faced with dwindling amounts of fresh water, various solutions have been proposed: increase the number of impoundments (reservoirs) to catch precipitation and runoff, institute interbasin transfers, allow greater access to unused water on government-owned lands, tap deeper aquifers, and desalinate. More esoteric schemes for weather modification, transporting icebergs, and long-distance piping have at least been discussed. Of these proposals, the most feasible short-run possibilities are increased impoundments, interbasin transfers, and deep aquifer supplies. Each proposal raises a series of issues in need of research.

Development of reservoirs involves a number of economic and social issues: conversion of present land use on which newly constructed or expanded reservoirs will sit, use of eminent domain, restrictions of design criteria and other constraints associated with federal funding, and equity. Do these projects mean a net loss of agricultural productivity, or will there be a net increase from greater irrigation? What are the effects of displaced homesteads and uprooting of small communities on the social and cultural fabric of a region? *More research is needed on the long-term changes in land use patterns accompanying the construction or expansion of impoundments.*

Knowing the actors, the political processes, and the patterns of decision making will help us understand the ways that localities and regions interact with state and federal agencies. Such research will also reveal the political and social structure of localities and ways in which inter-community cooperation or conflicts evolve. *Research is needed on the entire sociopolitical process involved in the construction and use of new or expanded reservoirs.*

Extraction from deep aquifers involves issues of water rights, lowering the water table, economic feasibility, and the moral issue of whether such a move, akin to the increasingly widespread practices of "mining the water," amounts to robbing future generations' water supplies. Research questions on this practice fall mainly in the category of economic and technological feasibility. *However, research on water rights conflicts and the moral dilemmas of water mining is needed.*

Allocating Available Fresh Water to Different Purposes

Allocation of existing quantities of fresh water to diverse and frequently competing demands raises a set of issues at least as important as those pertaining to new water. Despite the increasingly apparent limits of available fresh water, each sector of American society clamors for a larger proportion. Industrialization means that water is used not only for domestic consumption but also to extract natural resources, manufacture goods, create energy, transport people and products, and carry our garbage. In this milieu, the two biggest issues are the preservation of an adequate supply of potable water essential for maintaining public health, and abating the degradation of fresh water that results from multiple uses.

Irrigation remains the largest consumer of fresh water, yet it is generally acknowledged that current irrigation practices (flooding and central pivot sprinkling) are wasteful. Irrigation of food and fiber crops is the primary reason for water mining. Tile lining between crop rows, drip irrigation, and various direct watering techniques are some conserving technologies that should be implemented. *Research is needed on people's acceptance of more efficient irrigation technology. Companion research is needed to demonstrate the viability and improvements obtained by these new techniques.*

Other industries need significant quantities of fresh water, and competition for supplies will become more intense during the 1980s. This competition will put small communities and individual home owners, who are trying to supply their own requirements, in an increasingly precarious position. Their ability to compete is impaired by pricing methods that encourage greater usage by industrial plants and other bulk consumers by giving price breaks through "declining block rates." *Research should investigate current water pricing strategies and their effect on water use.*

Arizona is already contemplating reductions in the amount of water available for irrigation vis-à-vis domestic consumption. In Washington State, an issue has emerged around allocation of river water to the production of hydroelectricity with concomitant reductions in the quantity available for irrigation. *More research is needed on the nature and consequences of explicitly formed or implicitly evolved policies of fresh water allocation.*

As irrigation and industrial water supplies decline, entrepreneurs will likely turn to deeper aquifers and exacerbate the process of water mining. Observable effects will include lowered water tables, land subsidence, redistribution of wildlife, accelerated encroachment of pollutants from surface sources into aquifers, and increased cost of extraction. *Research is needed on the current extent of water mining and the prospects of expansion.*

Water Quality

Concern for the quality of fresh water in the nation's lakes, ponds, rivers, streams, and reservoirs has existed for some time. Difficulties in maintaining safe, clean, healthy, potable supplies reached governmental and public attention during the 1970s, culminating in the Safe Drinking Water Act of 1974 and its amendments. Because we know considerably more from research on the quality of water in lakes and rivers, attention will be restricted here to potable water.

We appear to be finding more and more pollutants in our drinking water, which is partly the result of stepped-up monitoring requirements of the Safe Drinking Water Act. Toxic chemicals, radionuclides, and various viruses have been added to conventional public health concerns about bacteria, turbidity, and color. Yet no one currently has an accurate systematic assessment of the extent of the problems. *One of the most pressing research problems in the water resource area is to assess the status of drinking water quality, particularly in the nation's rural areas.*

Probably the most efficient mechanism for regular monitoring of the quality of drinking water is to require water suppliers to continue testing for constituents considered injurious to health. However, the cost of quarterly detection of some of the more complex constituents (metals, herbicides, and pesticides) may be prohibitive for smaller water suppliers. Compounding the problem is the cost of corrective treatment required when constituents are at or above levels considered potentially injurious to health (above the Primary Maximum Contaminant Level). *Research is needed on the economic feasibility of extending this testing and treatment program to smaller water supply organizations (e.g., those systems serving less than one thousand connections).*

Social Organization and Economics of Water Supply

Water supply systems are crucial to the development and management of water for a large segment of society. Yet relatively little research has been done on these types of social organization.

Water supply companies behave unlike any other utility. Locally based, capital-intensive, heavily subsidized, and lacking financial reserves, they appear to be perpetually unprepared for the future. If a water crisis is coming, only a few managers of these organizations appear to recognize it. Few purveyors seem concerned with limiting demand; therefore they do little to encourage conservation. Many even seem to lack the means to anticipate future demand. *Studies of water supply managers' and operators' plans for dealing with the future are seriously needed.*

Municipal water supply departments are inextricably bound to local politics, budgeting, and planning processes. *Similarities and differences in private and public water supply organizations, particularly as these distinctions apply to the quality of service or pricing of water, should be investigated. The manner in which water supply is used to encourage or limit community growth should also be investigated.*

Little research exists on the nature and functioning of rural water districts. How are they serving rural development? Assuming that readily accessible supplies are dwindling, regional cooperation leading to the establishment of collective supplies through rural water districts may provide an alternative. *Studies of local initiatives that establish rural water districts, and investigation of the degree to which they fulfill local water ser-*

vice needs, would inform us of the viability of this means of promoting rural development in the future.

A Plea for Water Conservation

If shortages become more prevalent, conservation will probably be the only long-term solution. Increased impoundments, exploitation of deep aquifers, interbasin transfers, desalinization, and weather modification all represent short-term efforts to overcome present supply problems. They do not pretend to address the other side of the issue: limiting demand. Nor do such efforts face up to the difficult decisions of allocation.

Some areas of conservation, such as more efficient irrigation practices, have been mentioned. Much more can be done in the area of community and domestic water conservation. For example, there is urgent need to repair the leaks in older water main systems like the one in Boston, where it is claimed that 50 percent of the distributed water is lost. Building on the experience of military and apartment complexes, improved recycling technology or use of two water systems could be developed. However, it is quite a different story to get people to use these systems. *Research on ways to promote the acceptance and adoption of various methods of conserving water must be conducted during the 1980s.*

REFERENCES

Brower, Kenneth. 1980. "Sucking the land dry." *Country Journal VII* 8:40–51.

U.S. Department of the Interior (Geological Survey). 1974. *Rain—A Water Resource.* Washington, D.C.: U.S. Government Printing Office.

U.S. Environmental Protection Agency. 1976. "National safe drinking water strategy: One step at a time." Washington, D.C. Mimeograph.

U.S. General Accounting Office. 1979. *Water Resources and the Nation's Water Supply: Issues and Concerns.* Washington, D.C.: U.S. Government Printing Office.

U.S. Water Resources Council. 1978. *The Nation's Water Resources, 1975–2000. Volume I: Summary of the Second National Water Assessment.* Washington, D.C.: U.S. Government Printing Office.

38 Forestry

JOSEPH T. O'LEARY
ROBERT G. LEE

The natural resources in the 1.7 billion acres of forest and range land and water in the United States (71 percent of the total area) contribute significantly to the quality of life of our nation. More than 500 million acres of forest lands provide wood, water, forage, wildlife, recreation, scenery, and timber products. Nearly two-thirds of the forest land is privately owned, contrary to the perception of many people (U.S. Department of Agriculture, 1980). In addition to their traditional value in timber products and recreation, forest lands are now taking on additional significance as a supplementary source of energy.

The value of forests is enhanced because they represent a renewable resource. With proper management, they can continue to contribute importantly to the quality of life of present and future generations. Responsibility for the management of forests, however, is shared by a wide range of users and interests. In addition to the Forest Service and parallel state agencies, large and small producers of wood products, communities whose well-being depends on forests, private landowners, and consumer and environmental groups all have an active interest in what the forests can and will continue to supply. Attempts to understand the often conflicting interests of these groups, especially as they have changed over re-

Joseph T. O'Leary is associate professor, Department of Forestry and Natural Resources, Purdue University, West Lafayette, Indiana. He has published numerous articles on community impacts of recreation development and leisure behavior. **Robert G. Lee** is an associate professor in the College of Forest Resources, University of Washington, Seattle. He has written articles on the relationship between society and its wildland base.

cent years, have led forest managers to seek help from social scientists.

Sociologists have only recently begun working with foresters to address problems that have emerged as a result of new and intensified demands on our forests. Initially, sociological expertise was applied to wildland fire problems and the extremely rapid growth in recreational use of forest lands. However, assistance to the forester in the management of conflicting demands and interests is now emerging as a more important focus. This relationship between sociologists and foresters remains tentative as sociologists discover the management questions that they should address—questions often different from those addressed by economists, psychologists, and other social scientists. Sociologists are learning how alternative solutions to problems might be incorporated into the foresters' perspective. Critical forestry issues to be faced in the 1980s include forestry's impact on community, conflict management, complex organizations and administrative behavior, technology transfer, and energy needs. In each of these areas, the sociologists could help foresters deal with planning, policy, and decision making.

CURRENT KNOWLEDGE

The vast amount of forest land in the United States suggests that forestry would have previously attracted the interest of rural sociologists. Forestry is primarily a rural-based activity, but sociological studies of forestry activities other than leisure and recreation are quite rare. For example, *Rural Sociology* has not contained an article addressing forestry issues since 1965. Most of the material published on forest resources is not in the mainstream of sociology journals, even those dealing with rural issues. There are, however, a few articles written by social scientists for foresters that have appeared in the *Journal of Forestry* and have dealt with issues such as technology transfer (Muth and Hendee, 1980) and the wood products labor force (Stevens, 1979). Similarly, research reports published by resource management agencies, including the Forest Service, National Park Service, and land grant university experiment stations, have described the results of research by agency personnel and cooperative research done by university personnel. There are a few classic studies of forestry and forestry problems (Kaufman, 1964; Schiff, 1962; Burch, 1972), as well as several contemporary unpublished doctoral dissertations (see, for example, Culhane, 1977; and Stumbo, 1974).

RESEARCH ISSUES

Several key forestry issues should be investigated from a sociological perspective in order to improve the manner in which forestry planning and management is conducted, and to understand the impacts of these activities on communities and other social groups.

Community Dependency and Impacts

Research is needed to determine the nature and extent of rural community dependence on the extraction and/or use of forest resources. Sociological studies of rural communities have provided an extensive literature applicable to forest-based towns and regions, but few of the studied communities were dependent on the extraction of wood products from adjacent forest lands. Only three empirical studies of forest-based communities are available (O'Leary, 1974; Kaufman and Kaufman, 1946; Hayner, 1945).

Foresters have long been concerned about the impact of resource outputs on community stability. However, their lack of knowledge about communities is a problem for planning and policy analysts; it is unclear what linkages exist between extractive activities and community stability and welfare. Profiles of community residents' opinions toward forest lands, management activities, and organizations would also be useful to community planners for monitoring changing values and beliefs. Such investigations should provide a better basis for understanding *occupational* change in the wood products labor force, the structure of that labor force, and how changes in forestry activities affect people living in the areas adjacent to managed forests. These studies are appropriate for forestry activities worldwide, for multinational corporations are actively extracting wood from moist tropical forests in South America and Southwest Asia.

Conflict Management

Research is needed to provide forest planners and managers with an understanding of the character of social conflicts over land uses and management, as well as with techniques for managing such conflicts. Forest land use conflicts date back two centuries to the beginnings of forestry. However, foresters have only recently discovered the relevance of sociological expertise to social conflict. Intensifying concern by an expanding number of interest groups, in combination with the emergence of requirements for involving the public in forestry decision making, have led foresters to search for techniques to productively channel conflict. Extension of social conflict approaches to forest planning issues is found in the work of Freeman (1972), Alston and Freeman (1975), and Twight and Patterson (1978). Involvement of the public in decision making requires further investigation as a potential device for channeling social conflict. Relationships between political, administrative, and citizen action also need to be studied in order to find more appropriate means for responding to competing interests.

Administrative Behavior

Research is needed to provide forest planners and managers with a better understanding of the administrative behavior of public and private organizations charged with forest management responsibilities. Kaufman's *The Forest Ranger* and Schiff's *Fire and Water: Scientific Heresy in the Forest Service* are classic studies of a complex forest land management organization and its decision-making process. These kinds of studies must be elaborated in order to understand organizational adaptation and to provide guidance for future administrative practices. The study of human behavior as it relates to wildfire has been identified as a major research need by the National Wildfire Prevention Task Force.

Other administrative functions need to be investigated in order to make resource management more effective. For example, multi-resource planning decisions within organizations are increasingly made by interdisciplinary teams, with individual members often selected to assure a balanced distribution of viewpoints and knowledge. Knowledge about how these teams should be structured and identification of team member responsibilities on various issues would be useful. Public involvement techniques are also an important area for examination.

Technology Transfer

Research is needed on the social processes by which knowledge and techniques are transferred to forest decision makers. The successful transfer of new technology is becoming an important concern in forestry, yet there has been no sociological research on innovation, diffusion, and adoption pertaining to forest management technologies. Rural sociologists have conducted a large number of studies on the adoption/diffusion process in agriculture (Rogers and Shoemaker, 1971; Taylor and Miller, 1978). The need for extending such studies to forestry is heavily influenced by efforts to improve productivity through substituting more efficient technologies for labor–computerized sawmills are an example. Widespread concern with "inefficient" forest management by small private nonindustrial landowners is also an important impetus for additional technology transfer research. Concern with productivity and small landowners resembles similar historic concerns in agriculture that gave rise to sociological research on adoption of farm practices. Sociological studies of technology transfer and adoption/diffusion would also apply to numerous other forest management functions and would provide a basis for determining how particular technologies can be fitted to field situations.

Energy Resources

Research is needed to determine organizational means by which wood resources and forest lands can be used to help meet domestic energy requirements. Throughout history, as well as throughout the lesser-developed world today, the primary use of wood has been fuel for cooking, heating, transportation, and industrial production. Increasingly high costs of imported petroleum have forced our domestic industries and home owners to seriously consider wood as a fuel. Wood, unused in the manufacture of consumer products, is increasingly used as a fuel. Conversion of wood to a liquid fuel also has potential for meeting energy needs. Sociological research is needed to design institutions that will be responsive to these new industrial uses for wood.

Home owner demand for fuel wood is increasing dramatically with the purchase and installation of wood stoves; in some rural counties, more than 50 percent of the residents have installed them. Serious local and regional imbalances between limited fuel wood supply and uncontrolled demand has already become a problem in some areas of the United States. Relationships between landowners and local residents need to be studied to determine more effective means for organizing the production and distribution of fuel wood without the social chaos and forest exploitation that typifies regions with fuel wood shortages in other parts of the world. Citizen attitudes, shifts in wood use, and landowner responses to excess demand are examples of research issues that sociologists should investigate.

Large-scale energy production on forest lands may also be more important in the 1980s. Biomass potential, geothermal hydroenergy, kinetic energy potential, and air motion over forest areas are of prospective interest. How decisions on these sources of energy are made, the legislative mandates given to organizations for their management, the producer organizations that emerge, and the impact of these activities on other resource objectives will require the expertise of sociologists working cooperatively with planners, managers, and policy makers.

CONCLUSION

The emerging relationship between the sociologist and the forester is important to both of them. Only a few foresters have been exposed to and have thought about the application of sociological concepts to resource management activities. The sociologist that works with the forester must understand the perspective of forestry professionals in order to provide relevant knowledge and techniques. Substantial information exists in sociology that can be synthesized to provide additional insight regarding some of the critical problems that forestry will face in the 1980s.

REFERENCES

Alston, R. M., and D. M. Freeman. 1975. "The natural resources decision maker as political and economic man: Toward a synthesis." *Journal of Environmental Management* 3:167–183.

Burch, W. R., Jr. 1972. "The American forester: History and mythology." In *Proceedings: Society of American Foresters' National Convention.* Hot Springs, Arkansas.

Culhane, Paul. 1977. "Politics and the public lands: Local policy processes of the United States Forest Service and the Bureau of Land Management." Evanston, Illinois: Northwestern University. Doctoral dissertation.

Freeman, D. M. 1972. "Politics of planning and the problem of public confidence: A sociology of conflict approach." In *Proceedings: Society of American Foresters' National Convention.* Hot Springs, Arkansas.

Hayner, N. S. 1945. "Taming the lumberjack." *American Sociological Review* 35:217–225.

Kaufman, H. S. 1964. *The Forest Ranger: A Study in Administrative Behavior.* Baltimore, Maryland: Johns Hopkins University Press.

Kaufman, H. S., and C. L. Kaufman. 1946. "Toward the stabilization and enrichment of a forest community." Missoula, Montana: University of Montana. Unpublished paper.

Muth, Robert M., and John Hendee. 1980. "Technology transfer and human behavior." *Journal of Forestry* 78:141–144.

O'Leary, Joseph T. 1974. "Community conflict and adaptation: An examination of community response to change in natural resource policies and strategies." Seattle, Washington: University of Washington. Doctoral dissertation.

Rogers, E. M., and F. F. Shoemaker. 1971. *Communication of Innovations.* New York: Free Press.

Schiff, Ashley L. 1962. *Fire and Water: Scientific Heresy in the Forest Service.* Cambridge: Harvard University Press.

Stevens, J. B. 1979. "Six views of wood products' labor force." *Journal of Forestry* 77:717–720.

Stumbo, Donald. 1974. "An exploration of a quantitative approach to community development planning for the forest products' industry." Minneapolis, Minnesota: University of Minnesota. Doctoral dissertation.

Taylor, D. L., and W. L. Miller. 1978. "The adoption process and environmental innovations: A case study of a government project." *Rural Sociology* 43:643–648.

Twight, B. W., and J. J. Patterson. 1978. "Public participation effects on a natural resource conflict." Paper presented at the annual meetings of the Rural Sociological Society, San Francisco.

U.S. Department of Agriculture (Forest Service). 1980. *An Assessment of the Forest and Range Land Situation in the United States.* Washington, D.C.: U.S. Government Printing Office.

39
Fisheries

MERVIN J. YETLEY

In 1976, the Ninety-Fourth U.S. Congress passed the Fishery Conservation and Management Act. Known as the "200-Mile Bill," it protects the fishing rights of American fishermen within two hundred miles of U.S. shores from encroachment by foreign fishermen. This was done to enhance the economic viability of and employment opportunities within the U.S. fishing industry. It was also intended to conserve these fisheries as a source of food and for their aesthetic value.

To conserve fisheries, the act established regional fishery management councils with regulatory powers to control fishing within the federal conservation zones. These councils are charged with managing national (salt water) fishery resources to achieve "optimal yield," with due consideration given to social, economic, and environmental factors in the development of policy.

The rationale for the act is that fisheries, if left unregulated, would be destroyed through overfishing by a combination of foreign and domestic fishermen. The result would be economic hardship or ruin for several thousands of American fishermen and the loss of an invaluable natural resource to the public. Hence, the act directs that a management plan be prepared for virtually every species having commercial or recreational value.

The central problem faced by the fishery management councils is to balance the traditional right of fishermen to harvest fish with the public's need for an assured food supply and right of access to a natural resource.

Mervin J. Yetley is a sociologist in the International Economics Division of the Agricultural Development Branch, U.S. Department of Agriculture, Washington, D.C. He was formerly rural sociologist on the Scientific and Statistical Committee of the Gulf of Mexico Fishery Management Council.

That difficulties have been encountered in reaching this balance should come as no surprise. First, there has been a lack of reliable information upon which to base decisions in all aspects of fishery management. Second, fishermen, like farmers, are fiercely independent. Many have not taken kindly to the imposition of government regulations on what, for generations, had been a private domain characterized by traditional rules and regulations enforced by the fishermen themselves.

Authors of the act foresaw the scope and complexity of the impending problem and directed that management plans be formulated with consideration for a broad spectrum of issues associated with social, economic, and environmental impacts. The law further stated that regulations were to be "based upon the best scientific information available." The concern of this chapter is the paucity of sociological knowledge about salt water fishermen, and the opportunity it represents for sociological research.

RESEARCH ISSUES

The best strategy for sociologists to gain credibility in fishery research is interdisciplinary studies. This is because social science research is unknown and therefore not considered relevant by the majority of biologists currently involved in fisheries research. This is especially true of sociological research. Economics, in contrast, has recently made considerable progress toward respectability in fisheries research. For this reason, the thrust of much of the research suggested in this chapter is interdisciplinary.

One important issue for research is to determine "fishing effort," i.e., the actual amount of time spent fishing. A study on this topic that incorporates sociology, economics, and biology is diagrammed in Figure 39.1. This model was developed for the express purpose of illustrating how the three disciplines might successfully be combined in an interdisciplinary study of a fishery. As shown, each discipline has analytical variables that relate to fishing effort.

Research areas of mutual interest to sociology and economics are "tastes and preferences," "marketing activity," and "payment incentives" as related to fisheries (see Figure 39.1). Payment incentives may be especially fruitful for joint research because of the many strong, socially defined traditions that dictate who (boat owners, captains, crew) shares what percentage of profits and expenses. If traditional patterns are not economically optimal, sociological information could be used to encourage change.

The research area common to sociology and biology is that of the

FIGURE 39.1 Interdisciplinary Model of the Fish Industry.

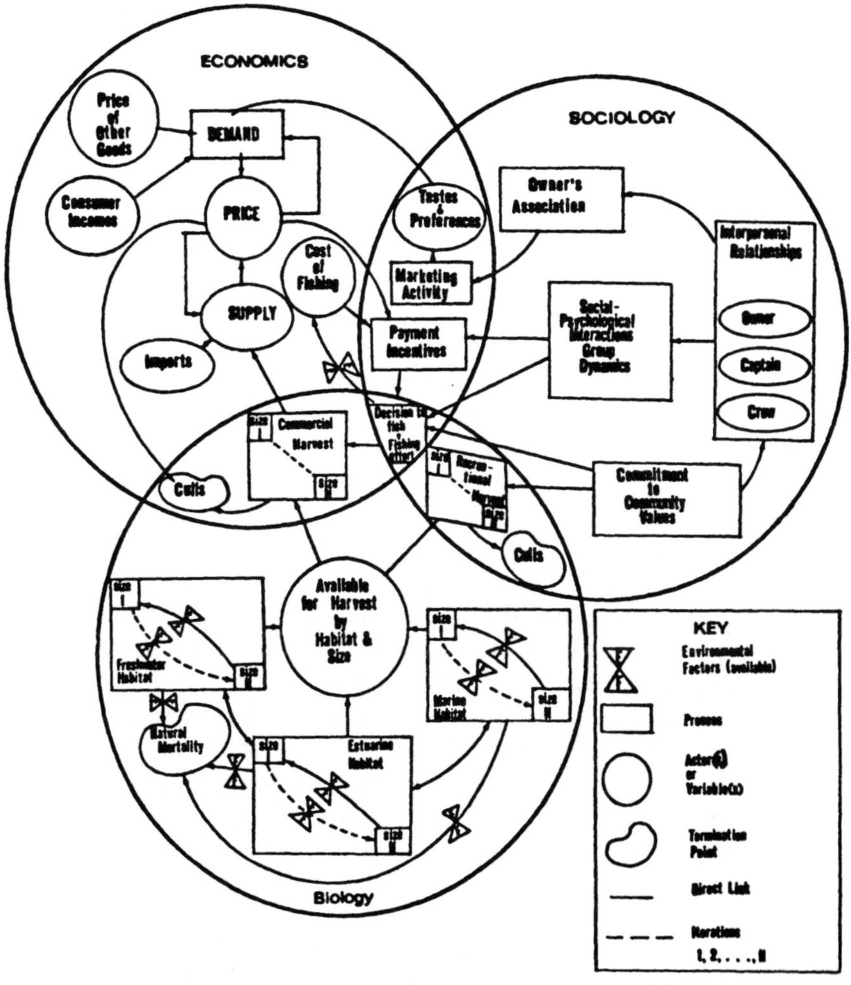

Source: The author, a biologist, and an economist developed this model for the express purpose of illustrating how the three disciplines might successfully be combined into an interdisciplinary study of a fishery.

recreational catch (see Figure 39.1). Information on characteristics and behavioral patterns of salt water recreational fishermen is scarce. Knowledge of their motivations and perceived benefits derived from fishing is fragmentary, as is information on the size of the recreational catch. The competitive and potentially conflicting nature of the recreational versus commercial catch is another area where systematic information is lacking. But it is also an area where sociologists can make an important contribution by describing and quantifying the underlying motivations and benefits provided by recreational salt water fishing.

Research is also needed on socioeconomic characteristics of fishermen, such as fishing income, fishery-related (but nonfishing) income, income from other sources, and total family income. Because fishermen are not a homogeneous group, this information should be made available separately for boat owners and crew, with the latter further subdivided into captains and regular crew. Where possible, this information is needed for individual fisheries.

There is currently a need for information on fishermen's commitment to fishing as an occupation. These data are needed because prevailing economic conditions in several major fisheries have caused the loss of fishermen to other occupations. The essence of commitment to fishing is similar to the idea of "farming as a way of life as opposed to commercial farming," although the setting is different.

A frequently used measure of commitment is fishing income as a percent of total individual or family income. Several other indicators of commitment could be used. Total time spent on activities directly related to fishing or actual fishing time (fishing effort) could be used. Knowing the level of financial investment may help measure the commitment of boat owners. From a sociological perspective, various sociopsychological commitment and aspiration scales could be used to gain insight into the commitment of fishermen and their sons and daughters to fishing. To be maximally useful, this information should be made available separately for boat owners and crew members. Further breakdown by geographic region, community, or fishery would also be useful.

In fishery management plans, there is often a need for restricting fishing seasons or fishing areas, or even entry into a fishery. In such cases, there is an obvious need to know who will be impacted, the magnitude of economic impact, alternative employment opportunities, and the probability that a fisherman will decide to leave the occupation. Thus, the above types of information relate not only to fishery management but to community planning as well. This information could be used by planning agencies at the community and state levels to estimate tax revenues, population and demographic shifts, and future public service needs. Much of this information is currently in "best guesstimate" form.

Research is also needed on the use of new fishing technology. Changes in technology and equipment used in the fishing industry parallel in magnitude and scope the technological changes that have occurred in agriculture. But little is known about who uses the technology and equipment, or at what levels of efficiency and effectiveness. Is it used primarily by younger, better educated fishermen, or is use of advanced technology strictly a function of the boat owner's wealth? Adoption/diffusion studies of a fishery would provide insight into these issues.

If this information could be integrated with economic cost/benefit analysis, both types of studies would be more useful. Such a study could determine the characteristics of those using specific pieces of equipment most efficiently in a given fishery. Information of this nature would be welcomed by fishery management councils, financial institutions, and the fishing industry itself. Certainly fishery extension agents could use this information in working with individual fishermen and fleet and boat owners.

Research is needed on how fishing technology has impacted social relationships. New equipment and boats have increased time at sea. The result may be changes in intrafamily power structure and decision-making patterns and in fishermen's participation in community activities. It is of interest to know not only what has occurred but what will likely happen as time at sea and away from the home port increases. Do nonfishermen become the real community decision makers in fishing villages? The answer to this question probably varies by fishery and by boat owners and crew members. Community development agents could find this information very useful in program planning and development.

Research is also needed on how the new technology has impacted social relationships among fishermen. It is important to understand how technology may have changed the social standing, decision-making authority, and incidence of conflict among crew members and the influence of these changes on productivity. That these changes may have occurred is understandable when one considers differences in tasks performed and knowledge required as equipment becomes more technical and automated. Sociologists are capable of providing information needed to more adequately address problems associated with these changes.

During the 1980s, problems associated with the lack of data, access to existing data, and primary data generation must be squarely faced by sociologists. Those contemplating research on salt water fishermen, either recreational or commercial, will find that no organized sampling frames exist. In many states, information contained on fishing licenses is difficult to work with because it is not computerized. Even if it were, information essential to construction of a sampling frame is often missing. For example, a commercial license may cover all or several fisheries, and is therefore of limited value for constructing a sampling frame for a specific fishery. The seriousness of this problem is shown by the fact that information by fishery, and by region or community, is critical to many fishery management decisions, fishing community planning efforts, and fishery extension activities.

Research using data collected for or by federal agencies is hampered by federal regulations regarding "confidentiality of information." The National Marine Fisheries Service has gathered, or will soon gather, large sample sizes of survey data from fishermen. However, under existing confidentiality guidelines, the raw data cannot be released for analysis, even for bonafide research purposes. It is interesting that this ruling holds even though the Fishery Conservation and Management Act requires that regulatory decisions be made on the basis of the "best scientific information available."

Because of the way census data are aggregated, it is only possible to determine gross characteristics of commercial (salt and fresh water) fishermen. Thus, despite the obvious need, sociodemographic information on fishermen is sparse and fugitive in nature. Such basic information as age and educational attainment, length of time as a fisherman, family size and composition, and ethnic background or nationality is available only in highly aggregated form or from individual studies.

REFERENCES

Acheson, James M. 1975. "The lobster fiefs: Economic and ecological effects of territoriality in the Maine lobster industry." *Human Ecology* 3(3):183–207.

______. 1977. "The role of the social sciences in fisheries management under extended jurisdiction." In Office of Technology Assessment, U.S. Congress (editors), *Working Papers: Establishing a Two-Hundred Mile Fisheries Zone*. Washington, D.C.: Office of Technology Assessment, U.S. Congress.

Alexander, Paul. 1975. "Innovation in a cultural vacuum: The mechanization of Sri Lanka's fisheries." *Human Organization* 34(4):333–344.

Cook, W. R., and C. King. 1971. *Annotated Bibliography of Socio-Economic Information: Sea Grant Program*. Ann Arbor, Michigan: Bureau of Business Research, University of Michigan.

Fricke, Peter H. (editor). 1971. *Index of Current Maritime Research*. Cardiff, Wales, Great Britain: Institute of Science and Technology, University of Wales.

Gibson, Gordon D. 1960. "A bibliography of anthropological bibliographies: The Americas." *Current Anthropology* 1(1):61–75.

Griffin, Wade L., Newton J. Wardlaw, and John P. Nichols. 1976. *Cost and Return Analysis of Selected Vessel Characteristics: Gulf of Mexico Shrimp Fishery, 1971–1975*. College Station, Texas: Agricultural Experiment Station, Texas A & M University, TAMU-SG-77-210.

Hippler, Arthur E. 1970. *Eskimo Acculturation: A Selected Annotated Bibliography of Alaskan and Other Eskimo*. Fairbanks, Alaska: Institute of Social, Economic, and Government Research, University of Alaska, Acculturation Studies 28.

Hippler, Arthur E., and John R. Wood. 1977. *The Alaska Eskimos: A Selected Annotated Bibliography*. Fairbanks, Alaska: Institute of Social, Economic and Government Research, University of Alaska, Report Series 45.

Jones, Dorothy, and John R. Wood. No date. *An Aleut Bibliography*. Fairbanks, Alaska: Institute of Social, Economic, and Government Research, University of Alaska, Report Series 44.

LaMonte, Edward. No date. *A Preliminary Annotated Bibliography of Socio-Cultural Research on Fishermen, Fishing Communities, and Fisheries' Social Systems*. Seattle, Washington: Institute for Marine Studies, University of Washington.

Landberg, Leif C. W. No date. *A Bibliography for the Anthropological Study of Fishing Industries and Maritime Communities*. Kingston, Rhode Island: International Center for Marine Resources, University of Rhode Island.

Okraku, Ishmael O. 1975. "Fishing and fertility: A study of a Nova Scotia fishing village." *Social Biology* 22(4):326–337.

Pollnac, Richard B., Carl Gersuny, and John J. Poggie, Jr. 1975. "Economic gratification patterns of fishermen and mill workers in New England." *Human Organization* 34(1):1–7.

Smith, Courtland. 1976. "Intracultural variation: Decline and diversity in North Pacific fisheries." *Human Organization* 35(1).

Wadel, Cato. 1973. *Now, Whose Fault is That? The Struggle for Self-Esteem in the Face of Chronic Unemployment*. St. John's, Newfoundland, Canada: Institute of Social and Economic Research, Memorial University of Newfoundland, Newfoundland Social and Economic Studies 11.

White, David R. M. 1977. "Environment, technology, and time/use patterns in the Gulf Coast shrimp fishery." In M. Estellie Smith (editor), *Those Who Live from the Sea*. New York: West Publishing Co.

Wilson, W. Alan. 1971. *The Socio-Economic Background of Commercial Fishing in British Columbia*. Vancouver, British Columbia, Canada: Fisheries Service–Pacific Region, Department of the Environment, Provincial Government of British Columbia, Canada. Detail Report 1.

Part 8

THE CAPACITY TO RESPOND

It is one thing to list several hundred research issues and questions; it is quite another to actually conduct the research. In this final section, we consider factors that will influence rural sociological research in the 1980s.

In Chapter 40, Lacy and Busch outline some of the constraints under which rural sociological research is implemented. They note how employing institutions, professional expectations, and the values and career aspirations of rural sociologists interact to determine what research gets done and what does not get done. The authors take these issues one step further by recommending that each be the subject of research. The hoped-for result is an enhanced capability for doing policy-relevant research.

Chapter 41, by the editors, summarizes some of the research issues identified in the preceding chapters and identifies additional factors that will influence whether the research challenge will be met.

40 Institutional and Professional Context for Rural Sociology: Constraints and Opportunities

WILLIAM B. LACY
LAWRENCE M. BUSCH

The agenda for rural sociological research in the 1980s is indeed impressive! A neophyte entering the discipline should have no trouble locating significant, challenging, and worthwhile areas for research. However, each researcher is confronted, individually and as a member of the discipline, with a number of social, political, and economic contexts that guide the directions of research (Busch, 1980; Busch and Lacy, 1979). This chapter addresses some of the constraints and opportunities for rural sociological research, particularly within the land grant system where most of this research is conducted.

William B. Lacy is associate professor of sociology at the University of Kentucky, Lexington, Kentucky. He has published several articles on the sociological aspects of conducting agricultural research. **Lawrence M. Busch** is also an associate professor of sociology at the University of Kentucky, Lexington. He has published several articles on sociological aspects of agricultural research. Lacy and Busch are coauthors of a forthcoming book, *Science, Agriculture, and the Politics of Research*.

THREE OVERLAPPING CONTEXTS

The Institutional Context

American rural sociology emerged as part of the agricultural sciences, particularly at the land grant universities. Therefore, it is important to understand how the history of the agricultural sciences and the agricultural experiment stations have influenced our discipline. The agricultural sciences arose at the end of the nineteenth century as local markets were giving way, with help from the steamship and railroad, to a single global market for food and fiber. In a world market, relatively small differences in production efficiency could spell the difference between farm profit and loss. During this period, the institutional bases of the agricultural sciences developed in response to the needs and pressures of various interest groups (Rosenberg, 1976).

In 1886, Representative William H. Hatch created the congressional act that provided funds for state agricultural experiment stations. His most important objective was to ensure U.S. supremacy in agricultural exports to the rest of the world (Hatch, 1886:2). However, no specific research policy was described, perhaps because of the prevailing view, as outlined by Hatch, that "a scientific experiment is made not for the purpose of seeking or sustaining a theory but of learning a fact" (1886:4). Agricultural research, it was felt, proceeded best within a *laissez faire* research environment.

During the first two decades of the twentieth century, agricultural scientists, like their colleagues in education (Spring, 1972), engineering (Noble, 1977), and other fields began to reshape the social environment that had led to the initial development of their disciplines. This movement was caused in part by increasing skepticism about the ability of the *laissez faire* economy to produce the good society (e.g., Kumlein, 1927); concern for the rapid depletion of resources occasioned in part by the closing of the frontier (e.g., Frome, 1971); realization that the United States was now part of a complex international economic order in which it needed to compete effectively (e.g., Snyder, 1908); and desire on the part of institutional and disciplinary scientific leaders to avoid conflict–particularly class conflict (e.g., Duniway, 1915). As a result of

The investigation reported in this chapter (Number 80-14-236) was conducted in part in connection with a project of the Kentucky Agricultural Experiment Station and published with approval of the director. The authors wish to thank the anonymous reviewers for their insightful comments on a previous draft.

these concerns, scientists as different as Liberty Hyde Bailey and Gifford Pinchot joined in a broad-based movement to transform American society. Leaders of the agricultural sciences, of course, were primarily concerned with farmers and rural society.

Organization was necessary. The *laissez faire* economy of the nineteenth century was to be replaced by a corporate system in which large-scale organizations would plan for the production and distribution of goods and services. In their zeal, scientific leaders sought to apply science not just to technical matters but to the resolution of all conflict. There was no malice in this enthusiastic embracing of science. Indeed, at the time, it seemed to everyone that science and organization would make a better world for all. To quote Dean Butterfield, "The new farmer has his largest conquests yet to make. But he has put his faith in the strong arm of science; he has at his hand the commercial mechanism of a world of business. He believes he will win because he is in league with the on-going forces of our civilization" (1907:54).

Like their contemporaries in other sciences and the general public, agricultural scientists also saw the products of science as undiluted good. While society might be guided by science, it seemed that science itself was autonomous – a type of knowing that, through the use of certain special methods, ensured the emergence of truth and social progress (e.g., Jordon, 1907). Thus, the leaders of the agricultural colleges embarked on a program for remaking rural society through the application of scientific knowledge.

Simultaneously, the increasingly specialized, commodity-specific nature of scientific inquiry encouraged the development of a commodity orientation among clients (Rossiter, 1979). As an unanticipated consequence of these orientations, research programs not directly related to commodities were often underfunded or abandoned. Gradually, over the course of a century, this relationship began to appear to many as "natural" (McCalla, 1977).

Expression of this faith in the sciences and the commodity orientation of research was paralleled by the development of farm bureaus, a program initially encouraged by agricultural college deans as a quick and effective way of disseminating new knowledge among farmers. When, within a decade of its foundation, the Farm Bureau became a national federation with overt political objectives, station scientists and administrators were shocked. The Farm Bureau was formally separated from the Cooperative Extension Service by congressional action, but its development marked the beginning of institutionalized support for certain kinds of agricultural research.

Because Farm Bureau and commodity association members tended to represent a wealthier strata of the American farm population, they supported research that would improve farm productivity and management. They were less interested in questions of a broader social nature and even hostile to research they deemed not in their interest. The farm bloc, until its demise within the last decade, possessed sufficient power to eliminate research projects and action programs and to discourage other scientists from engaging in similar activities. However, even with the decline of the farm bloc, the impact of this long association between researcher and particular interest groups continued to flourish. Indeed, as McCalla suggests, "Many people in the agricultural research establishment have grown up with this association so that to a considerable extent those inside the system share the same values as clientele groups. Therefore, they implicitly identify with their objectives. It is by this access more than any other that commercial agriculture has had, and continues to have, pervasive influence on the scope of agricultural research" (1977:21).

The belief in the autonomy of science and the organization of influential clientele along commodity lines made it possible for productivity and efficiency to be treated as ends and for scientific work to be gauged more and more by the degree to which it contributed to these "ends." From the mid-1930s through the 1950s, only a rare voice questioned the primacy of the quest for increased productivity. It was occasionally suggested that the products of science were encouraging migration from the farm and that too great a decline in farm population might be undesirable. Others, however, saw this as the inevitable course of scientific advance (see, for example, Stewart, 1979). In the last decade, however, new questions have been asked: At what point does the decline in farm population stop? Is extreme regional specialization in agricultural production desirable? What is the structure of commodity production, of farm labor needs, and of the social organization of agribusiness? Can we afford such an energy-intensive agriculture? Can we continue to apply large quantities of chemicals without causing various kinds of environmental problems? Are there viable alternatives for agricultural production? These and other issues will not be resolved easily, but they focus attention on ends rather than on means and suggest the need for an examination of the research process itself.

Research is needed (1) to explore in greater depth the influence of the land grant system upon research in rural sociology and the other agricultural sciences; (2) to examine the institutional processes of research decision making; and (3) to analyze policy alternatives for research institutions. We need to know more about how these institutions operate and what influence these institutional settings have on research processes and products. For example, how is research policy determined? What are the research implications of a declining farm population and farm bloc as well as the rise of conflicting demands from consumers, environmentalists, and proponents of alternative forms of agricultural production? What is the impact on rural sociological research of changes in the goals, clientele, and funding in land grant institutions?

The Disciplinary Context

Within the context of land grant institutions, rural sociology began its development at the turn of the century. During the first two decades of this century, well-known agricultural scientists such as Liberty Hyde Bailey, Kenyon Butterfield, and Eugene Davenport, saw experiment station research limited by a lack of social and economic knowledge. They were concerned with the apparent deterioration in the conditions of rural life. Like their European contemporaries, they were concerned with the so-called "agrarian question." Convinced that there was insufficient knowledge about social conditions in rural areas, they encouraged rural surveys to uncover the facts. These surveys were not to be steeped in theoretical significance. Instead, as expressed by C. W. Thompson, a rural organizational specialist for the USDA, "the rural survey may be compared to the inventory taken periodically by the modern merchant" (1917:129). In that age of unswerving faith in the power of science, it appeared to all that, if the facts were known, the solutions to the problems of the day would be self-evident.

The first rural sociologists were frequently drawn from backgrounds in the natural sciences, but rural sociology was not integrated into the other agricultural sciences and was established as a separate, though peripheral, field. Indeed, given the strong reductionist tendencies in the sciences, the idea that rural sociology might be incorporated into the other sciences would have been anathema at that time.

Agricultural scientists who entered rural sociology soon abandoned their interests in the natural sciences; those who remained in the natural sciences had little interest in rural sociology. Similarly, rural sociology was not fully integrated into the broader discipline of sociology and strong differences of opinion arose over research directions and emphases for sociology. When the formal break between the two fields occurred in 1935, it was not without ill will. Thus, over the years, rural sociology emerged as a separate discipline within the agricultural sciences as well as within the broader discipline of sociology. It was and still is marked by its own interests and concerns and a lack of ties to the other agricultural sciences (Nelson, 1969).

Importantly, rural sociology also has lacked clearly definable client groups. The formation of client interest groups supportive of research in other agricultural disciplines, and a lack of such groups supporting rural sociological research, have left sociological research underfunded. In addition, the power exercised by these client groups tended to restrict research on certain controversial topics of social significance (Friedland, 1979; Hardin, 1955). Of course, all the sciences have been and remain subject to the influence of powerful vested interests (Schiff, 1962; Feyerabend, 1975). Of concern here is the particular ways in which the research agenda of rural sociology has been affected by its disciplinary context, four of which are discussed below.

First, rural sociology, like the other agricultural sciences but unlike most other disciplines, has been essentially relegated to a single institutional form: the agricultural colleges. Today, it is rare for an institution outside the land grant universities to support rural sociological research. This academic segregation is suggested in the employment status among active U.S. members of the Rural Sociological Society, approximately 60 percent of whom are currently employed at land grant institutions. Most of the remaining members are employed in nonresearch positions. Further, the research is concentrated at a small number of institutions, with fifteen land grant universities employing approximately 40 percent of the active U.S. members of the society. The training of rural sociologists may be even more homogeneous. Two-thirds of the active members report receiving their graduate degrees from land grant institutions. Two universities, Cornell and the University of Wisconsin, have educated over 20 percent of the active members; another nine land grant institutions have provided professional education for over 25 percent of the active members. The concentration of U.S. rural sociological research in land grant institutions is also suggested by the institutional affiliations of authors publishing in *Rural Sociology*, two-thirds of whom are currently at land grant universities. Ironically, this segregation is partially perpetuated by the erroneous assumption that the relevant social and sociological issues are adequately addressed by well-funded rural sociological research. Thus, rural sociological research that is not part of the land grant university research agenda is often not done at all.

Second, while other agricultural sciences have been supported by special interest groups, there are no pressure groups to support rural sociological research. On the one hand, this has given greater latitude to rural sociologists in developing research programs. On the other hand, rural sociologists often lack defenders and advocates for their particular research. Therefore, politically sensitive issues of central concern to rural sociology may be relegated to a secondary role or confined to international studies (e.g., rural class structure and stratification, agricultural sociology, rural community organization, farm labor studies, studies of the scientific development and impact of agricultural innovations).

Third, many of the land grant institutions and other agriculturally related research institutions employ only a few rural sociologists. For example, twenty-five land grant institutions employ three or fewer active members of the Rural Sociological Society. As a consequence, it is unlikely that these institutions have viable graduate programs, sufficient graduate research assistants, or active research programs. Opportunities for collaborative work are undoubtedly limited. Outside demands further reduce the number of rural sociologists available for research at a single institution. For example, rural sociologists often find themselves drawn from their research by international project responsibilities, teaching requirements, and field research.

Finally, there is a limited number of professional publishing outlets for the research of rural sociologists. Generally, rural sociologists are limited to *Rural Sociology*, and tangentially to two or three other professional journals, when seeking to publish research results. In contrast, most of the agricultural sciences and the mainstream of sociology have numerous professional journals from which to choose. In addition, the journals in rural sociology have the highest rejection rates of any agricultural field, including other agricultural social sciences. As a consequence, the major paradigms and established research agendas may unduly influence publication criteria and limit publishing opportunities to researchers whose ideas are in the mainstream. This, in turn, may reduce the willingness or ability of rural sociologists to pursue many of the research needs identified in this volume.

Research is needed to explore further the impact of the disciplinary context on the nature of rural sociological research. What are the constraints and opportunities generated by the separation of rural sociology from mainstream sociology as well as other agricultural sciences? Do disciplinary associations act as barriers to effective research on certain topics by defining them as marginal? What is the nature of the professional socialization of rural sociologists? Is it as homogeneous as suggested by the concentration of that training in land grant institutions? How should that socialization and education be changed to meet the demands of an expanding research agenda? What effects do size of rural sociology programs and institutional status have on the nature and direction of research? What are the implications of the journal publication system for research problem choice?

The Values and Aspirations Context

A third source of opportunities and constraints for research are the values and career motivations of rural sociologists. Scientists bring an array of values and motivations to the research setting that affect their responses to the institutional and disciplinary contexts. They may be open and responsive to the emerging research opportunities. On the other hand, as Newby and Buttel remark, "intellectual timidity and self-censorship are equally part of the problem" (1980:14). In short, many may be unwilling to address controversial topics and to accept the potential negative consequences. Moreover, others may see the higher pay, lower teaching loads, twelve-month appointments, and funded research in colleges of agriculture as means for rapid career advancement. While these individuals might pay lip service to rural issues by occasionally examining rural/urban differences or issuing an experiment station bulletin, they would prefer to focus on sociological rather than pressing rural social issues.

Research is needed to delineate the degree to which the values and career aspirations of rural sociologists act as constraints and/or opportunities for more effective rural research. We need to know what rural sociologists value, how they can better deal with controversial topics, and how career advancement can be made more compatible with relevant research.

A POLICY ROLE FOR RURAL SOCIOLOGISTS

The three contexts for rural sociological research oulined above promote certain research agendas and constrain others. While rural sociologists may bring their special perspective to bear on issues of research organization and policy, they cannot and should not become the final arbiters on such issues. The linguistic distinction between *politics* and *policy* in English tends to obscure the inexorable fact that policy issues are always political issues. They are questions of differing values even when (or if) the nature of the facts is agreed upon. Thus, the role for rural sociologists in formulating research policy may be to reveal the inextricable link between technical issues and value issues. This requires and assumes a far better acquaintance with the disciplines shared by our colleagues in other agricultural sciences than we currently possess. To provide this link, we need to inquire into the details of technical decisions and become more active in interdisciplinary research. We need to become better sociologists of our own discipline as well as sociologists of agriculture. Finally, this policy role necessitates a clear understanding of the methods and processes by which research policy is shaped and determined (Busch et al., 1980; Lacy et al., 1980).

Policy decisions are always of concern to special interests. Consequently, research of the kind advocated here will require commitment by both researchers and administrators. At both the state and federal level, support for multiple views and for administrative opposition to interference by special interests in the research process is essential. Until recently, it was extremely difficult for administrators to support academic freedom when research funding was provided largely through the efforts of a relatively narrow set of special interests. The newly broadened range of constituents should ease the burden on administrators and researchers and make possible the development of a more broad-based agricultural research program.

The kind of research advocated here is not without its hazards. It is risky to challenge the status quo, especially if those who are disturbed represent powerful interests. Nevertheless, if we are to contribute constructively to the debate and help the research establishment respond to a changing social and natural environment, this risk must be taken by individuals, disciplines, and institutions.

The time is right to address the broad range of topics suggested in this book and to develop a new critical role for rural sociology (Picou et al., 1978). The broadening of the support base for agricultural research should make it possible to address these research issues as well as issues of agricultural science policy and of agricultural and rural development policy. The scientists, the research administrators, the libraries with official documents relating to agriculture, and even the interest groups, are readily accessible. With the majority of rural sociologists located in land grant universities yet unattached to special interests, they may be ideally situated to respond to these new challenges and opportunities.

REFERENCES

Busch, Lawrence. 1980. "Structure and negotiation in the agricultural sciences." *Rural Sociology* 45(Spring):26–48.

Busch, Lawrence, and William B. Lacy. 1979. "Sources of influence on problem choice in the agricultural sciences: The 'New Atlantis' revisited." Paper presented at the annual meetings of the Rural Sociological Society, Burlington, Vermont.

Busch, Lawrence, William B. Lacy, and Carolyn Sachs. 1980. *Research Policy and Process in the Agricultural Sciences: Some Results from a National Study*. Lexington, Kentucky: Department of Sociology, University of Kentucky, RS-66.

Butterfield, Kenyon. 1907. *Chapters in Rural Progress*. Chicago: University of Chicago Press.

Duniway, C. A. 1915. "Economic science in agricultural and mechanical colleges." In *Proceedings: Twenty-ninth Annual Convention of the Association of American Agricultural Colleges and Experiment Stations*. Berkeley, California.

Feyerabend, Paul. 1975. *Against Method*. Atlantic Highlands, New Jersey: Humanities Press.

Friedland, William H. 1979. "Who killed rural sociology? A case study in the political economy of knowledge production." Paper presented at the annual meetings of the American Sociological Association, Boston.

Frome, Michael. 1971. *The Forest Service*. New York: Praeger Publications.

Hardin, Charles M. 1955. *Freedom in Agricultural Education*. Chicago: University of Chicago Press.

Hatch, William Henry. 1886. "Agricultural experiment stations." *Report of the Committee on Agriculture, United States House of Representatives*. Washington, D.C.: U.S. Government Printing Office.

Jordon, W. H. 1907. "The authority of science." In *Proceedings: Twenty-first Annual Convention of the Association of American Agricultural Colleges and Experiment Stations*. Lansing, Michigan.

Kumlein, W. F. 1927. "Responsibilities of the land grant colleges in teaching agriculture as a way of life." In *Proceedings: Forty-first Annual Convention of the Association of Land Grant Colleges and Universities*. Chicago.

Lacy, William B., Lawrence Busch, and Carolyn Sachs. 1980. "Perceived criteria for research problem choice in the agricultural sciences." Paper presented at the Fifth World Congress for Rural Sociology, Mexico City, Mexico.

McCalla, Alex. 1977. "Politics of the U.S. agricultural research establishment." Paper prepared for the Agricultural Policy Symposium, Washington, D.C.

Nelson, Lowry. 1969. *Rural Sociology: Its Origins and Growth in the United States*. Minneapolis, Minnesota: University of Minnesota Press.

Newby, Howard, and Frederick H. Buttel. 1980. "Toward a critical rural sociology." In Frederick H. Buttel and Howard Newby (editors), *The Rural Sociology of the Advanced Societies: Critical Perspectives*. Montclair, New Jersey: Allanheld, Osmun, and Company.

Noble, David F. 1977. *America by Design: Science, Technology, and the Rise of Corporate Capitalism*. New York: Alfred A. Knopf, Inc.

Picou, J. Steven, Richard H. Wells, and Kenneth L. Nyberg. 1978. "Paradigms, theories, and methods in contemporary rural sociology." *Rural Sociology* 43(Winter):559–583.

Rosenberg, Charles E. 1976. *No Other Gods: On Science and American Thought*. Baltimore, Maryland: Johns Hopkins University Press.

Rossiter, Margaret W. 1979. "The organization of the agricultural sciences." In Alessandra Oleson and John Voss (editors), *The Organization of Knowledge in Modern America*. Baltimore, Maryland: Johns Hopkins University Press.

Schiff, Ashley L. 1962. *Fire and Water: Scientific Heresy in the Forest Service*. Cambridge: Harvard University Press.

Snyder, J. L. 1908. "Agriculture and democracy." *Agricultural College Bulletin* (Michigan), 3(4, October):3–28.

Spring, Joel H. 1972. *Education and the Rise of the Corporate State*. Boston: Beacon Press.

Stewart, Robert E. 1979. *Seven Decades that Changed America*. St. Joseph, Michigan: American Society of Agricultural Engineers.

Thompson, C. W. 1917. "Rural surveys." In *Proceedings: Eleventh Annual Meeting of the American Sociological Society*. Columbus, Ohio.

41
Issues for the 1980s

DON A. DILLMAN
DARYL J. HOBBS

Rural America, long accustomed to supplying food and trained workers for urban-based economic growth, is now being asked to satisfy even more needs of the larger society. More energy, more clean water, more recreational space, more places to live, and more of many other resources are simultaneously being demanded of it. It is not clear how, or even if, most of these demands can be satisfied.

What happens in rural America is of concern to all Americans. In our highly interdependent society, rural problems quickly become urban problems and vice versa. Neither the urban nor rural portions of our society can flourish for long while the other languishes behind. Satisfying the needs of all Americans will require that many rural-based problems be solved during the remainder of this century.

This book has identified important issues for rural sociological research. This research will contribute to the resolution of rural problems that our society faces now, or will encounter soon.

THE ISSUES

In many ways, rural sociologists have become as diverse as the issues now facing rural America. The authors presented in this book have produced hundreds of research ideas on a wide array of topics. Some

---

Portions of this chapter are based on a presentation by Don A. Dillman at the Fiftieth Anniversary Symposium of the Department of Rural Sociology, University of Wisconsin, Madison, Wisconsin, May 9, 1981.

authors have called for the study of individual behavior, others have called for studying the structure of organizations and American society. Some researchers have cited the need for surveys and others for ethnographic studies. The need for conceptual clarification is frequently mentioned, as is the need for better statistical analysis. The need to know the percent of people having a certain characteristic is cited as often as the need for sophisticated multiple-variable analyses. The research needed in some regions of the country is very different from that called for in other regions. Some areas of research are as new to rural sociology as others are old. There is a richness of diversity that was not apparent to us when we began editing this book.

Certain issues would not have been included if this book had been written ten years ago. Most notable in this regard are the reversal of rural migration loss (Chapter 3), energy (Chapter 4), and appropriate technology (Chapter 5). The migration and energy issues penetrate most of the book's other chapters. Among the issues raised in the preceding chapters are the following:

- Rural crime has grown dramatically, raising many perplexing issues, one of which stems from the fact that farm buildings usually have been built to keep out the weather rather than people (Chapter 23).
- Retired people contributed heavily to the population turnaround in some regions of the country, producing unanticipated economic benefits as well as service needs that are not yet well understood (Chapter 9).
- At the beginning of the 1970s, residential preferences were viewed as a novelty – interesting but not very relevant; at the close of the decade, serious efforts were being made to integrate preferences into models of migration behavior (Chapter 24).
- The rural countryside has become the most preferred place to live and the place where strongly held housing norms could most readily be satisfied (Chapter 19).
- The wholesale application of urban models of education to rural places was brought into question as lower birth rates resulted in renewed discussion of another round of rural school consolidation (Chapter 18).
- Rural women are no longer viewed as just another "factor" in farm production; they have become an important object of study as farmers or farm partners (Chapter 12).
- Rural minorities, including American Indians, Blacks, Mexican-Americans, Mormons, and Amish, were found to face distinctly

different issues from one another as well as from their urban counterparts (Chapter 11).

- Transportation, taken for granted and mostly ignored by rural sociologists, has gained visibility, but it remains to be seen whether it has emerged as a significant topic for research (Chapter 15).
- The markedly successful line of sociological research on individual aspirations and achievement of rural youth continues, but recognition of rural job market limitations has led to research on what determines the opportunities available to them (Chapter 10).
- Government has created a new area of research, social impact assessment, giving rise to much needed studies of dramatic community change, particularly in the western United States (Chapter 29).
- "All hell broke loose" in trying to determine who should control American agriculture; this, and changes in who is doing the farming, have resurfaced as important issues (Chapter 31; Chapter 32).
- Five models for doing needs assessment surveys have emerged, most of them developed by rural sociologists. The new models provide a battery of alternatives for community development professionals (Chapter 27).
- Water, which may be the ultimate resource, emerged as a candidate for the next resource crisis in the United States (Chapter 37).
- Appropriate technology received attention from many sectors of society, and the specter of massive changes in how work gets done appeared on the horizon, perhaps to become a dominant issue of the next decade (Chapter 5).

The authors of the forty chapters have articulated many concerns that need to be addressed by rural sociologists. Only a few of them have been enumerated above. The result is a rich listing of ideas for research, but that list should not be considered *the* agenda for research in the 1980s. No matter how imaginative the authors might have been, it would be impossible to state all of the important research issues that will emerge in the 1980s. To do so would require a clairvoyance that rural sociologists and other mortals lack.

We view this book as an important reference for identifying needed research in the 1980s. However, it is not a substitute for the hunch, imagination, and creativity, which are the essential tools for sorting today's trend from tomorrow's countertrend. Just as a structured scientific survey can never be a substitute for the problem-finding informal walk or drive through a local community, a listing of research ideas cannot substitute for a researcher's creative thought.

THE DISCIPLINE

The issues identified in this book do not represent the unanimous view of the discipline of rural sociology. Despite our attempts to broaden the issues identified in this book through an extensive review process, the ideas expressed are ultimately those of the authors and editors. Had other authors been asked to write the chapters, the book would have been a different one, although the overlap of research issues would most likely be substantial. Rural sociology, like other sciences, is a field in which unanimity does not, and should not, prevail. The strength of a discipline stems from the development and testing of competing perspectives. For those rural sociologists and others who view the issues identified in this book differently from those expressed here, we hope this book provides a challenge, the ultimate result of which might be a new synthesis of ideas that contribute to our understanding of rural people and places.

The diversity among today's rural sociologists seems substantial when viewed within the discipline. When viewed by outsiders, these differences seem much smaller, and for good reason. Most rural sociologists share many common viewpoints and use similar concepts and methods. This combination of attributes and tools sets us apart from other scientific disciplines and makes it appropriate to speak of a rural sociological perspective.

Most of the problems specified in this book are not only sociological problems, just as soil conservation is not only an agronomic problem. Rural sociology does not offer exclusive or definitive answers to rural problems, just as other disciplines do not.

What rural sociology does offer, and the reason it exists as a discipline, is a particular scientific perspective on human behavior not held by any other discipline. The combining of concepts, theoretical approaches, and methods into that perspective facilitates the revealing of underlying relationships among rural phenomena that other disciplines usually fail to identify. Herein lies the paradox of rural sociology's (or any other discipline's) greatest strength for addressing rural problems also being its Achilles' heel: by focusing on only certain parts of a problem in a certain way, other significant aspects typically get missed. The solution to this paradox is for extensive interaction and joint efforts with researchers from other disciplines. We hope that by portraying a rural sociological perspective on many of society's pressing issues this book has taken a modest step in that direction.

In responding to the many issues developed in this book, we may find greater accomplishments if "problems" rather than "disciplines" more frequently become the basis for organizing and conducting research. It is difficult to identify any problem in rural areas to which the perspectives and skills of rural sociologists are not potentially pertinent. At the same time, we find it difficult to identify any problem for which a rural sociological perspective is self-sufficient.

THE CHALLENGE

Rural sociology can respond to far more problems than was once the case. Our numbers are greater and our interests are wider. However, the problems of rural America are far greater than the number of available rural sociologists. Because of being one of the few, and sometimes the only, noneconomic social scientists in the land grant agricultural universities, rural sociologists are frequently called upon to respond to problems that exceed our skills. For rural sociology to make its maximum contribution to solving problems, the temptation to be all things to all people must be resisted. A discipline cannot progress by studying everything, particularly if it tries to do it all at once. The department that tries to do research on most of the topics included in this book is likely to do a lot of research, but little of major significance.

Priorities must be determined. In doing so, it would be a serious mistake to ignore areas of established strength. Recently, we reviewed the research done on the resurgence of population growth in rural areas. We were intrigued to note how quickly and extensively rural sociologists responded to an issue on which there was no general awareness until about 1974. The two recent books on the topic, Sofranko and Williams (1980) and Brown and Wardwell (1980), are by rural sociologists and include the works of other rural sociologists. The research response of rural sociologists to this issue was rapid and significant because many rural sociology departments already had existing programs in population research. Demography is one of our traditional areas of strength, and commencing meaningful research on the population turnaround meant adjusting priorities, not establishing them and starting from scratch.

The preceding chapters reveal many other areas of research in which rural sociology has developed an impressive track record – for example, community change, natural resource use, and rural youth. We would be surprised if rural sociologists do not respond well to the research issues outlined in areas of this nature. The inclination and interests are clearly there. It is equally apparent that rural sociologists have done less in certain other areas of research—for example, rural crime, transportation, fisheries, food and nutrition, water, and energy. Yet these are areas of extremely significant change in rural America. Efforts to respond in areas such as these will likely require deliberate discussion with careful consideration given to the costs and consequences of developing sustainable research programs.

Responding to some of the research needs listed in this book may be difficult. The majority of active rural sociology research programs are located in the north-central and northeastern states. These regions, once the location of the country's most dramatic rural changes, are remote from the areas where some of the greatest rural changes are now occurring. As a result, some of the issues identified in this book may end up being ignored by rural sociologists. A disturbing example is the water issue identified in Chapter 37. Very few rural sociologists now have active research programs in the area, despite a crisis that seems imminent. It is not yet clear what water issues will surface first and most forcibly, but we are concerned about the incredible migration of our population to rural areas of the South and all areas of the West. Water resources are simply not available to support the demands now being projected for these regions. Sink holes in Florida, rationing of the Colorado River, mining of the Ogallala aquifer, competition between hydroelectric and irrigation needs along the Columbia River, and the potentially enormous need for water to exploit oil shale and coal represent difficult issues, resolution of which may dramatically affect the lives of the rural as well as urban people. The mismatch between our research resources and the location of issues seems likely also to affect the amount of research done on minority concerns, rural poverty, social impact assessments in boomtown areas, forestry, and certain aspects of corporate agriculture. As a discipline, we must be sensitive to this mismatch and find ways of addressing these important issues. Collaboration that stretches across state borders and traditionally regional boundaries needs to become a normal way of doing research. In the past, regional research supported through the cooperative state research service of the U.S. Department of Agriculture has always been important; in the future, it may become imperative.

When we began working on this book, it was with considerable encouragement of many supporters, from government agencies to private foundations. It was to be a call for policy-oriented research that would address rural issues that if not attenuated might produce real rather than rhetorical crises.

The scene before us is dramatically different from the one we faced when we started this project some eighteen months ago. As this is being written, during the early months of President Reagan's administration, massive changes are being made in what government does and how its work gets done.

We are reminded that one cannot usually predict the outcome of a movie during the first few scenes nor the outcome of a football game from the first series of downs. We feel a similar reluctance to discuss the prospects for rural America and the conduct of needed rural sociological research during these early months of the Reagan Administration. Yet, from this early and insecure vantage point, it appears that past trend lines are being broken. The new ways of doing things in the 1960s and 1970s are now being defined as old. New concepts of the federal, state, and local government relationships are being discussed. Perhaps we have reached a new watershed in American politics, the ramifications of which we can only guess at just now. We may be on the verge of an entirely new set of policy issues that will soon start working their way through the fabric of rural America.

Perhaps, then, the ultimate research challenge facing rural sociologists is to respond to the new as well as the enduring concerns of rural people; many of those concerns are identified in this book and will play a part in shaping the policy efforts of the current and future administrations. In addition, we must be sensitive to the new issues being formed by the political process that is now unfolding. The success of rural sociologists in meeting this challenge will influence the well-being of all Americans in the 1980s, the 1990s, and beyond.

REFERENCES

Brown, David L., and John M. Wardwell (editors). 1980. *New Directions in Urban-Rural Migration.* New York: Academic Press.

Sofranko, Andrew J., and James D. Williams (editors). 1980. *Rebirth of Rural America: Rural Migration in the Midwest.* Ames, Iowa: North Central Regional Center for Rural Development, Iowa State University.

The Reviewers for Rural Society in the U.S.: Issues for the 1980s

Stan Albrecht
Sandra J. Ball-Rokeach
James Barron
Calvin Beale
Alvin Bertrand
Ed Blakely
Donald Bogue
Joe Bohlen
Stephan Bollman
Gladys Bowles
Harold Breimeyer
Emory Brown
Minnie Brown
Frederick H. Buttel
Rex Campbell
Edwin H. Carpenter
Timothy Carter
K. Chavis
Neil Cheek
James Christenson
William Clifford
James Copp
Arthur G. Cosby
Raymond T. Coward
Charles Crawford
Thomas Dietz
Riley E. Dunlap
Everett Edington
Douglas Ensminger
Ronald C. Faas
Frederick Fliegel
William Flinn
William S. Folkman
Frank Fratoe
Willis Goudy
Bernal Green
Gary Green
Archibald Haller
Craig Harris
Edward W. Hassinger
Judith Heffernan
William Heffernan
Kenneth Hornback
Stan R. Ingman
Quentin Jenkins
Darryl Johnson
Harold Kaufman
William Kimball
Gary King
Gerald E. Klonglan
William Kuvlesky
Olaf Larson
Paul Lasley
William R. Lassey
Gary R. Lee
Suzanne Lindamood
Ronald L. Little
Albert Luloff

Pat Madden
Robert G. Mason
Alex McIntosh
Robert Meier
James Mikesell
Francena Miller
Edward Moe
James Montgomery
Dan E. Moore
Denton Morrison
Peter Morrison
Steven Murdock
James L. Murphy
Paul Nachtigal
Ted Napier
Howard Newby
Harold Nix
F. Ivan Nye
Marvin Olsen
Luther Otto
Ron Powers
Virginia Purtle
Betty Rios
Richard Rodefeld
David Rogers
Robert Rubel
Vernon D. Ryan
Robert Schafer
Harvey Schweitzer
William Sewell
Doris Slesinger
Pat Smith
Alvin Sokolow
Ray Sollie
Irving Spaulding
Richard Stuby
Marilyn Ihinger-Tallman
Evan Vlachos
Don Voth
John M. Wardwell
Rex Warland
Jerry Wheelock
Eugene Wilkening
Anne Williams
James Williams
Charles P. Wolf
Dean Yoesting
James Zuiches

Index